DATE DUE			
NOV 26 1970			
DUE JUL 1 1 1987			
JUN 2 2 1987			

PSYCHOLOGICAL
ECONOMICS

PSYCHOLOGICAL ECONOMICS
GEORGE KATONA

ELSEVIER
New York / Oxford / Amsterdam

ELSEVIER SCIENTIFIC PUBLISHING COMPANY, INC.
52 Vanderbilt Avenue, New York, N.Y. 10017

ELSEVIER SCIENTIFIC PUBLISHING COMPANY
335 Jan Van Galenstraat, P.O. Box 211
Amsterdam, The Netherlands

Library of Congress Cataloging in Publication Data

Katona, George, 1901-
  Psychological economics.

  Bibliography: p.
  Includes index.
  1. Economics—Psychological aspects.   I. Title.
√ HB74.P8K33   330'.01'9   75-8272
  ISBN 0-444-99003-8

Manufactured in the United States of America

64732

CONTENTS

v

PREFACE

This book is the result of studies carried out over the past thirty years on the psychological analysis of economic behavior, based on the collection of data about people's expectations and attitudes toward economic matters. The book is intended to answer three questions: What is psychological economics? Why is it needed? What has it accomplished?

In the course of these thirty years the author has published numerous research reports and articles as well as three books devoted in substance to these same ends. The first book, theoretical and programmatic to a large extent, *Psychological Analysis of Economic Behavior* (1951), is out of print both in its hard cover and its paperback editions. The second, *The Powerful Consumer* (1960), is still available, while the third, *The Mass Consumption Society* (1964), is out of print. Instead of revising and modernizing the out-of-print books separately, the author decided to integrate the discussions contained in all three books. Following his retirement from academic life in 1972, when he set himself to this task, he found himself overwhelmed by the quantity and significance of findings not presented in the earlier books, as well as by the pressure to air new ideas and theoretical notions. The result was this new book containing three types of material:

1. Unchanged passages from the 1951 and 1964 books, reproduced with the permission of the McGraw-Hill Publishing Company, publisher of the three books.
2. Discussion of issues set forth in the earlier books, supplemented with additional material and presented in a new manner.
3. Discussion of issues not presented in the earlier books, especially relating to developments or findings made after 1964.

Material of the first type consists of less than 20 percent of the present book, while that of the third type is close to 50 percent. It is especially the discussion of the relation of economics to psychology and of macroprocesses to microprocesses as well as material concerning profit maximization which are reprinted in unchanged form from the 1951 book.

While many empirical studies that provide support for the propositions presented in this book have been conducted in prosperous times, the book is being published at a time of a deep recession. The study of psychological factors contributing to economic behavior is equally necessary in bad and in good times. Moreover, the psychological methods introduced served to predict the recession of 1974-75 as early as December 1973 (see page 124); the analysis of earlier recessions in Chapters 8 and 11 and of the impact of the tax cut of 1964 in Chapter 21 yield useful conclusions for 1975; and the role of confidence, a major psychological factor analyzed in the book, as a prerequisite of recovery has been more widely acknowledged this year than ever before.

The author's concern with the interrelation between the two disciplines, economics and psychology, began much earlier than his systematic studies of psychological economics. As a young Ph.D. in experimental psychology, he lived through the hyperinflation of 1923 in Germany and rashly published a widely quoted (but mistaken) article about inflation being nothing but the result of mass hysteria. The success of this article led him to study economics. In the following several years there were some in which he functioned exclusively as a psychologist and others in which he worked as an economic journalist. From 1926 to 1933 as an associate editor of the leading German weekly, *Der Deutsche Volkswirt (The German Economist)*, he chronicled the origin and development of the Great Depression. In 1933, shortly after Hitler came to power, he made what he considers the most important prediction of his life: He expected life in Europe to become unbearable, and left for America.

The first few years in New York were filled with business activities as well as studies on the psychology of learning (resulting in the book, *Organizing and Memorizing,* in 1940). From 1940 to 1942 the author presented a series of courses at the New School for Social Research on psychological issues arising in a war economy. These lectures formed the basis of the book,

War without Inflation, published in 1942 and mentioned later in this volume (p. 346). Then followed two years in Chicago with the Cowles Commission for Research in Economics, where the author conducted his first sample interview surveys (described in the book, *Price Control and Business*, 1945), and two years in Washington with the Division of Program Surveys of the U.S. Department of Agriculture, devoted to survey research on economic topics.

Two mentors from the pre-World War II period must be mentioned as having been most responsible for the author's intellectual development. He had the good fortune to spend a few years in close personal association with Max Wertheimer, the founder of Gestalt psychology. In the psychology of thinking developed by Wertheimer he found the key to understanding economic behavior (see Chapter 4). Gustav Stolper, publisher of *The German Economist*, introduced the author to economic studies of the real world.

To a certain extent the foregoing personal remarks are out of place here because this book must be viewed as the product of group activities in an institution, the Survey Research Center of the Institute for Social Research at The University of Michigan. This organization was founded in 1946 by the leading personnel of the Division of Program Surveys. From 1946 up to the present time it has provided a unique atmosphere and favorable opportunities for large-scale, continuous interdisciplinary research and the exchange of ideas among scholars of different training and orientation. The substantial growth of the Institute over little more than a quarter of a century may serve as one indication of the acceptance on the American scene of systematic, quantitative social science research. Rensis Likert and Angus Campbell, the two individuals primarily responsible for the progress of the Institute, are those to whom the author is most indebted for having made it possible for him to carry out research as he desired.

The author's leading collaborators in the Economic Behavior Program of the Survey Research Center, which he directed from 1946 to 1972, were the late John B. Lansing, James N. Morgan, and, above all, Eva Mueller. Daily contact with them proved so productive that it is hardly possible to assign the origin of an idea to the one or the other.

In the last ten years the work of the Economic Behavior Program and thereby the author's thinking benefited greatly from collaboration with Jay Schmiedeskamp and Burkhard Strumpel. After the retirement of the author, Schmiedeskamp took over the direction of the quarterly attitude surveys with great skill and success. Strumpel has led the field of psychological economics into new fruitful directions and greatly influenced the author's thinking. He and Ernest Zahn (University of Amsterdam, Netherlands) were good enough to read the draft of this book. Zahn, the first to integrate sociological concepts with the analysis of economic behavior, helped substantially to broaden the author's views.

In addition to his primary responsibilities at the Survey Research Center, the author served for twenty-seven years as professor of economics and professor of psychology at The University of Michigan. In practically every one of these years his lecture course entitled Psychological Foundations of Economics was presented to students in both departments, many of whose questions and criticisms helped to develop the ideas in this book.

Because sample interview surveys provided most of the data used in the author's studies, his indebtedness and gratitude extend to those at the Survey Research Center who have been in charge of the survey work—to Charles Cannell, Leslie Kish, and several other experts in sampling and interviewing, as well as to a large number of interviewers and, of course, to masses of anonymous respondents.

The author wishes to express his thanks here for a grant from The Ford Foundation, which he received at the time of his retirement, covering expenses of his most recent studies and writings. This grant was of direct help in preparing this book.

Among the collaborators on the project, Sylvia Kafka deserves foremost mention. Mrs. Kafka skillfully edited the entire manuscript. Her suggestions induced the author to rethink and rewrite many passages of the book. Sincere thanks are also due to Nancy McAllister for her efficient secretarial assistance.

Ann Arbor, Michigan   GEORGE KATONA

PART I

ECONOMICS AS A BEHAVIORAL SCIENCE

1

THE HUMAN FACTOR IN ECONOMIC AFFAIRS

The psychological approach to economic analysis cuts through the time-honored boundaries of the two disciplines, economics and psychology. It considers economic processes as manifestations of human behavior and analyzes them from the point of view of modern psychology. Economics as a behavioral science studies the behavior of consumers, businessmen, and government policy makers in spending, saving, investing, price-setting, and other economic activities.

Although economic behavior is elicited by the environment and its changes, human beings do not react to stimuli as automatons. Their motives and attitudes, even their tastes, hopes, and fears, represent intervening variables that influence both their perception of the environment and their behavior. In order to understand economic processes, psychological considerations and subjective variables must be incorporated in the analysis.

Two critical reactions are sometimes aroused when such a program of study is formulated. In the first instance, there are those who shrug their shoulders and say there is nothing new in the program. Economists, they feel, have always considered human behavior. Even pure economic theory—the logical analysis of interrelationships among different economic processes in an ideal or imaginary system—has made use of psychological assumptions, albeit unrealistic ones. Such pure theory, however, according to this first line of thought, paved the way for the study of economic processes as they actually occur.

A second group of critics maintain that there is nothing to be gained by linking economics to psychology. Economics is the most advanced of all social sciences, they maintain, just because at an early stage of its development it gave up the con-

3

fused and muddled thinking that results from considering the immense variety of human behavior. It proceeded by using the scientific method of abstraction. It made progress by separating the basic variables and studying the relationship between them—for example, between income and consumption, or between money supply and price movements—instead of losing its bearings among the innumerable deviations and aberrations that occur because of human frailty.

In opposition to such arguments, this book purports to show that it makes a difference in our understanding of economic processes if we focus our attention on the human actors and on the psychological analysis of their decision formation and action, for economic processes are the result of people's behavior and are influenced by different patterns of behavior. More specifically, it will be shown that the motives, attitudes, and expectations of consumers and businessmen play a significant role in determining spending, saving, and investing and that modern psychology provides conceptual as well as methodological tools for the investigation of economic behavior. The results of psychological-economic studies may supplement, and sometimes even radically alter, the traditional analysis of supply, demand, income, and consumption.

In sharp contrast to the psychological approach to economics is the trditional approach, which may be described as stating that economics is concerned with the behavior of markets rather than with the behavior of men.[1] Extreme as this formulation may seem, it is warranted by the manner in which economic models are commonly used. Interrelations among objective variables are expressed in laws and principles of the behavior of prices, of interest rates, of unemployment —not of the behavior of the people who set the prices or whose actions bring about the higher or lower interest rates or unemployment. Economic affairs are seen as impersonal phenomena of the environment.

Traditional economics strives for laws that are generally valid by relying on alleged principles of human nature. It starts out with general models, which it then applies to the multitude

---

[1] "It is the behavior of commodities not the behavior of men which is the prime focus of interest in economic studies," wrote Kenneth Boulding (1956, p. 82), stressing that the economist "is not really interested in the behavior of men."

4

of actual phenomena. This approach differs greatly from the procedure of behavioral or psychological economics. The proximate goal of the latter is to understand and predict economic processes as they are found to occur in a given situation at a given time. Instead of establishing universally valid relations between changes in variables, the basic paradigm of behavioral science takes the following form: Under circumstances A_1, B_1, C_1 a stimulus constellation brings forth response X, under circumstances A_2, B_2, C_2, response Y.

Economics without Psychology

Although economic analysis in the main continues to disregard psychological studies, it is not devoid of psychological assumptions. Most commonly it proceeds on the premise that human beings behave mechanistically. If it were true that human beings could be counted on to show invariably the same reactions to the same developments in the economic environment, the human factor could rightfully be excluded from economic studies. If human beings were automatons, so that the response to the same stimulus would invariably be the same, psychology could, indeed, be thrown overboard. It is this "mechanistic psychology"—the assumption that human reactions are entirely determined by given external conditions—which has led economic analysis to what may be called the reification of economic data. Supply, demand, income, and capital become the things themselves with which economics is concerned.

Let us consider briefly a few examples of economic principles reflecting the assumption that human behavior is mechanistic. As our first example, we may cite the statement that "consumer expenditures are a function of income." This is usually understood to mean that, given the income (or the disposable income, and perhaps its distribution as well as the income in preceding periods), the amount of consumer expenditures can be determined and predicted. For under the same income conditions, human beings will spend the same proportion of their incomes. No need to analyze the behavior of the people involved; their motives or the attitudes underlying their actions become irrelevant.

"The rate of business investment is a function of profits" is a

5

further illustration of the same assumption. There is no need to study how businessmen perceive their profits or their economic situation, what they want to achieve, or what they hope or fear; the rate of investment is related to one single factor: the rate of past profits, which can be easily measured. To make the principle more realistic, the concept of profit expectations is sometimes introduced as the factor determining the rate of investment. It is then often assumed that profit expectations are based on, and determined by, past profits—and again the human actors can be shoved off the stage.

The so-called law of supply and demand, expressed, for instance, as "the amount demanded increases with a fall in price, and diminishes with a rise in price," may serve as another example of the reification of economic concepts. That human beings create the supply of goods, form the demand for goods, and determine their prices becomes unimportant if a one-to-one correspondence prevails between the stimuli (price changes) and the responses (changes in amounts demanded).

Finally, we may quote the most common explanations of inflation. We learn that "inflation is the result of an increase in money supply" or, that "inflation is the result of purchasing power exceeding available supplies." General and considerable price increases are seen as necessary consequences of the stated external conditions. It is assumed that the behavior of the human beings who charge and pay the increased prices is determined by those conditions. The statement that "more money competes for fewer goods" ceases to be an innocent metaphor or a shorthand expression. It becomes a scientific statement explaining the sequence of events and making it unnecessary to raise the questions of why, when, and under what conditions human beings use their increased supply of money to compete for the available quantity of goods.

It is clearly true that economic principles based on a mechanistic view of psychology are sometimes correct. The point is that they are not necessarily and not always correct. It is the consideration of psychological variables that enables us to determine some of the circumstances under which those principles are invalid.

Traditional economics might be more accurately described as "economics with mechanistic psychology" rather than as "economics without psychology." But the latter is equally appropriate if by "psychology" is meant the scientific discipline

6

as we know it today and not a priori psychological assumptions. Psychology is an empirical discipline. It acknowledges one source of evidence only, namely, controlled observation. It aims at the establishment of relationships between specific conditions and specific forms of behavior, rather than general laws of human nature. Because of the pliability and modifiability of behavior, psychology is skeptical about broad generalizations that posit invariable interrelationships. Human beings are capable of utilizing past experience and have great latitude within the limitations set by external forces.

Psychological Economics

A few behavioral scientists have, in recent years, attempted to do justice to these solidly established tenets of modern psychology in dealing with economic behavior. They have thus brought into being the beginnings of an "economics with psychology," which tries to find out what actually takes place when people—as consumers, businessmen, or policy makers—make economic decisions and act with respect to material goods. The prevailing complex conditions of economic life are taken as the starting point. The method of first setting up ideal conditions and then approaching realistic conditions step by step is abandoned. Study is shifted from the atomistic consideration of individual economic choices to group action. The main questions posed are: What kinds of behavior occur and what kinds of decisions are made under different conditions by different groups of people? Analysis is concentrated on the decisions they make about producing, buying, selling, price setting, investing, and saving.[2]

The conditions of decision formation encompass both external events and psychological states or, more correctly, the psychological field of the persons or groups making the decision. The psychological field includes people's perception of events—those events of which they are aware—as well as their motives, attitudes, and expectations.

[2] It should be noted that students of these problems have not been restricted to the United States. Among the European pioneers of psychological economics, Günter Schmölders (1966) in Germany must be mentioned first of all; P.L. Reynaud (1964) in France and Ernest Zahn (1960) in Holland have likewise been important contributors to the new discipline.

7

The psychological study of economic processes is possible because human decisions, and human behavior in general, are governed by laws, that is, are not arbitrary, unpredictable, or indeterminate. Human beings are not marionettes pushed around by external forces and yet the latitude of their choice is subject to scientific analysis. Differences in perceptions, motives, and behavior are measurable and can be related to causal factors.

Psychology is usually defined as the science of behavior. It is not just the study of mental behavior—of perceiving, learning, thinking. Nor is it merely the study of motives, or of emotions, or of the development of behavior from childhood to old age, or of "normal" and "abnormal" states of mind, or of individual differences in behavior. Psychology encompasses all these and many other aspects of behavior. It studies the factors that bring forth and determine the different forms of behavior.

Does it follow, then, that economics, and all social sciences, are parts of psychology? If it were true that the general principles of behavior, once established, would exactly determine human actions under all specific circumstances, it might be so argued. But human behavior is so rich and has so many different manifestations that it must always be studied under specific conditions. There is a wide gap between the laws and conditions, for example, of learning, thinking, or goal seeking, and the conditions determining behavior relating to the production, distribution, and consumption of goods. To bridge that gap, it is important to establish general principles of human behavior, but it is not enough. Nor is it enough to know the economic facts. What is necessary is to study specifically the behavior of people while they are producing, distributing, and consuming.

Is economic psychology therefore applied psychology? If the term "applied psychology" has any meaning, it is that psychology is first developed and the finished product is then taken and transferred to another specific field. Few people would say that child psychology, for example, is applied psychology in this sense. On the contrary, child psychology is developed by studying children's behavior. Just so, economic psychology can only be developed by studying economic behavior. To be sure, principles established by analyzing child behavior or economic behavior cannot contradict principles derived from the analysis of other forms of behavior, but they can and do supplement and

8

enrich those principles. Economic psychology, then, both borrows from and contributes to the study of other forms of behavior.

Such economic psychology is, however, a young discipline. While many economists have at least recognized the problem, and some have included psychological principles in their studies of economic behavior, there have until recently been but few psychological investigations into such common forms of everyday behavior as buying, selling, investing, going into business, increasing production, and the like. Still more unfortunately for the development of the young discipline, psychological investigations of motivation, habit formation, incentives and aspirations, or group belonging, which have used diverse fields of human activity to test hypotheses, have usually disregarded economic behavior. Businessmen's and consumers' motives in acquiring assets, their adopting or abandoning habits of spending or saving, or their forming and acting upon expectations—to mention only a few of the major problems of psychological economics—require special studies that have been neglected by psychologists.

The psychological analysis of economic behavior can, nevertheless, make use of conceptual as well as methodological principles of modern psychology. It must not consist merely of broadening economic analysis by adding to the traditional variables a few new variables, such as habits or attitudes. Psychology aims to do more than describe what people do under certain conditions. It attempts to discover why they act as they do under those conditions. It is "dynamic" insofar as it studies the motives and forces that bring about and explain behavior. Psychology must serve to make economic analysis, likewise, truly dynamic by shedding light on the question of why as well as what. Indeed, the basic need for psychology in economic research resides in the need to discover and analyze the forces behind economic processes, the forces responsible for economic actions, decisions, and choices.

"Economics without psychology" has not succeeded in explaining important economic processes and "psychology without economics" has no chance of explaining some of the most common aspects of human behavior. Has so little work been done making use of both disciplines because interdisciplinary research is inherently more difficult than any other research?

To be sure, psychological economics must use knowledge

from both economics and psychology. Given the vastness and complexity of each of the two disciplines, it could hardly be expected of anyone to master all the forms and branches of either one, let alone both of them. The usual boundaries of the various traditional disciplines are, however, quite arbitrary. Why should not some aspects of economics and some aspects of psychology be studied together, rather than different aspects of either field alone? It is clearly possible for one person to be both an "economist" and a "psychologist" in the sense of having a background of knowledge in both disciplines, and it is also possible to specialize in psychological economics. Such specialization involves not only some information on both economics and psychology but, above all, a specific point of view, namely, an empirical attitude: concern with actual developments and belief in the possibility of finding out what has happened and why.

The behavioral sciences study the actions of man and groups of men by applying the scientific method—observation, measurement, testing—to man himself. Economics as a behavioral science is both narrower and broader than traditional economics. It excludes, for instance, much of what is called institutional economics. Pure economic theory, describing the results of the behavior of the rational economic man, who is fully aware of all relevant considerations and seeks the best possible outcome, is likewise not part of behavioral economics. But propositions of economic theory do provide hypotheses to be used in the analysis of economic behavior. So likewise do propositions derived from psychology or sociology, which aid in incorporating the study of motives, attitudes, and expectations into the mainstream of economics.

Rather than elaborating further on the conceptual and methodological differences between the psychological and the traditional approach to economics, our purpose would perhaps be best served by attempting to answer the crucial question: What difference does it make whether or not psychological considerations are introduced into economic analysis? In the following sections the outcome of the two approaches will be illustrated by presenting six significant economic problems, to be discussed in detail in later chapters. In this way we shall indicate, albeit superficially, the nature and extent of the difference between psychological and traditional economics.

1. CYCLICAL FLUCTUATIONS IN CONSUMER DURABLE GOODS

In order to predict economic trends the traditional approach takes as its starting point aggregate data that reflect recent past activities. Personal income, business profits, consumer expenditures, and business investments are examples of the major statistical data that are extrapolated to the future. The aggregates are interrelated according to assumptions about their functional relations (e.g., consumer expenditures as a function of income) and several equations expressing these relations are solved simultaneously.

Behavioral economics makes use of additional information of a different kind. Data are collected on people's attitudes and expectations and their changes because behavioral theory assumes that they are predispositions to later action. It is further assumed that changes in discretionary expenditures, either of consumers or of businesses, do not necessarily correspond to changes in incomes or profits, being a function not only of ability to buy but also of willingness to buy. Changes in consumers' willingness to buy houses, automobiles, and other durable goods have been determined by repeated surveys conducted with representative samples and have been summarized in the Survey Research Center's *Index of Consumer Sentiment.*

Research carried out over the past twenty-five years, to be discussed later in this book, has led to the following major conclusions about the American economy in the post-World War II period:

1. Consumers contribute to economic fluctuations far in excess of the impact of changes in their income resulting from variations in the amounts disbursed by the business and government sectors of the economy.
2. Measures of consumer sentiment, expectations, and aspirations provide advance indications of changes in consumers' spending-saving behavior, and especially of major changes (turning points) in their expenditures on durable goods.

At this juncture, instead of presenting evidence for these propositions, we may refer to just one major development. The recession of 1970 was preceded by a considerable worsening of consumer attitudes as early as the spring of 1969 (while aggre-

11

gate personal income did not decline in 1969). Subsequently, in 1970, a sharp deterioration in consumer demand for automobiles, appliances, and other durable goods contributed greatly to increased unemployment.

Psychological studies not only help to improve predictions of change in certain important forms of economic activity, but also contribute to an understanding of these changes. In consumer surveys the crucial question of "why" may be asked directly. Respondents may be asked to explain, for instance, why they are optimistic or pessimistic, or why they increased or decreased their expenditures. Alternatively, answers to the question may be derived from the presence or absence of correlations between certain attitudes and certain forms of spending or saving. In this manner it has been possible, for instance, to clarify the role of inflation as it has contributed to a change in economic activity.

2. INFLATION

Traditional theory attributes inflation, a general and sustained increase in the price level, primarily to demand exceeding supply, with excess demand resulting from monetary expansion and government deficits. In addition to such a demand-pull inflation, the cost-push variety has also been accepted as originating in a secular trend of rising wages and salaries. Furthermore, the traditional view of inflation has given some recognition to a psychological factor: the expectation of price increases was thought to increase demand. When businessmen and consumers believed that prices would go up, it was thought to be rational for them to buy in excess and in advance of their needs, to beat inflation by stocking up and hoarding.

Psychological studies of inflation began with the observation that in the postwar years in the United States inflation was seen by most people as a bad thing. They felt that it created uncertainty and detracted from the well-deserved enjoyment of the fruits of their labor, namely, the income they had earned. The usual response to uncertainty, disappointment, or even anxiety is not that people are energized to action but rather that they adopt a wait-and-see attitude and postpone action. In periods of creeping inflation, when prices had advanced and were expected to advance year after year but to a moderate

12

extent only, consumers in general responded by doing the opposite of what was postulated in most economic treatises. Rather than spending more, they spent less and saved more.

Between 1951 and 1972 exceptions to this generalization were observed only occasionally with respect to buying a few specific products. However, in 1950 and again in 1973 buying in advance of needs was fairly widespread, both times under the impact of news and experiences of a dramatic nature (military defeat in Korea in 1950, rapid increase in food prices in 1973), which created fear of shortages and stimulated action.

Psychological economics does not postulate that people will always respond to inflation in the same manner. It asks: Under what circumstances do experiences with inflation and inflationary expectations induce consumers to increase and under what circumstances to decrease their rate of spending? In the course of answering this question behavioral theory and subsequent empirical studies lead to generalizations about the relationship between attitudes and behavior.

3. SAVING IN GOOD OR IN BAD TIMES

The question of whether the rate of personal saving would be larger or smaller in times of prosperity or of recession presented no problem to traditional economists. Giving consideration only to the ability to save, they naturally assumed that saving would be much greater in good times than in bad times. In times of prosperity and generally advancing incomes, families would obviously be in a much better position to save for the future, while under unfavorable conditions they would have to concentrate on satisfying immediate needs and would often not even be able to do that to the extent desired. Empirical data collected during the Great Depression of the 1930s confirmed these assumptions.

Behavioral studies break down saving behavior into several components, which differ from one another in the purpose they are meant to accomplish. The first of these is the incurrence and the repayment of debt—the former representing negative and the latter positive saving. Repaying a debt seldom calls for a new decision and is therefore hardly influenced by cyclical developments. Incurring debt is so influenced, with the decision involved being concerned with spending rather than with saving. When the number of people who decide to buy a car increases, borrowing likewise increases, because in the United States the accepted way of buying a car is to arrange to pay for it while using it. Thus, in times of prosperity, car purchases and the concomitant borrowing increase, while in periods of depression they both decrease to a substantial extent. It follows that the rate of saving runs contrary to the traditional assumption: Due to changes in the rate of borrowing—other things being equal—saving declines in prosperous times and increases in periods of recession.

Discretionary expenditures out of income or savings accounts have a similar effect on the rate of saving. Down payments on cars, purchases of small durable goods, or expenditures on vacation and travel as well as on hobbies are larger in good than in bad times. Thus, withdrawals of money from bank accounts to pay for these purchases in cash produce the same result as borrowing and installment buying, namely, a decrease in savings in times of prosperity—with no specific saving decision having been made.

Of course, quite frequently people do make specific decisions about saving. They accumulate reserve funds, primarily in banks and securities, for "rainy days" or to provide for their old age and retirement. Because rainy days appear more immediate and threatening prior to and during a recession than during an upswing, motives to save may be assumed to be stronger in bad than in good times. This assumption was confirmed between 1969 and 1972. The record rate of personal saving observed during the recession of 1970 did not come as a surprise to psychological economists.

4. SATURATION VERSUS
RISING LEVELS OF ASPIRATION

"The more goods and services people acquire the more likely they are to reach a point of saturation." This proposition, based as it is on a mechanistic view of behavior, has long been accepted by many as obvious. The same is true of the conclusion derived from the proposition: After long periods of prosperity, when large segments of the population have gratified many of their needs and desires, saturation, and consequently reduced

14

buying, can be expected to follow and prosperity to come to an end. Although many economists have taken exception to these simplistic assumptions about consumer saturation, few have taken the next step and developed appropriate principles on which to base valid conclusions. This was, however, done by the psychologist Kurt Lewin who postulated and confirmed by experiments in noneconomic areas that levels of aspiration are not given and fixed for all time, but are raised by a sense of accomplishment and success and lowered by a sense of frustration and failure. Accomplishments and progress serve as incentives and influence future behavior. They are subjective concepts, because what matters is how people feel about the progress they have or have not made.

It is possible, therefore, and has been seen to happen on a number of occasions, that wants and felt needs have continued to rise and broaden even after a number of prosperous years and widespread gratification of needs. By the same token, a feeling of saturation has been noted to occur following upon times when few people had been very active in acquiring large quantities of goods and services. Aspirations and saturation are clearly not a function of possessions alone.

5. RESPONSE TO FISCAL POLICY

It has been frequently assumed that a tax increase (or a tax cut) by X billion dollars decreases (increases) purchasing power by the same amount and therefore results in a decrease (increase) in effective demand to the same or a similar extent. Actually, such a notion expresses neither the average nor the usual situation. A tax increase may even result in consumers' increasing their rate of spending by reducing the amounts they save, and a tax cut may likewise have such perverse consequences, depending upon people's understanding of the situation and the expectations elicited by the new fiscal policy. Extensive studies were undertaken in 1963–65 and in 1967–68 to test and develop psychological assumptions about people's behavior in response to major changes in fiscal policy. Noneconomic considerations, such as the extent of trust and confidence in the government, were then found to have as important an influence on economic behavior as the fiscal measures themselves.

15

In this area the insights gained by psychological economics have not gone unrecognized. For instance, the *Economic Report of the President* to Congress of February 2, 1970, states that

> We have learned that there is a human element in economic affairs—habit, confidence, fear—and that the economy cannot be managed mechanistically (p.3).

6. GNP AND THE QUALITY OF LIFE

The development of national accounts in the 1920s inaugurated great progress not only in economic statistics, but also in the understanding and predicting of economic processes. But a good thing can be overdone, and this is true of the significance attached to the concept of Gross National Product (GNP). Today it is known that for the purpose of providing economic information, data on GNP and its components need to be supplemented by some objective indicators (about prices, number of unemployed, etc.) as well as by subjective indicators (changes in economic attitudes and expectations, plans and intentions). Furthermore, growth of GNP—the acclaimed goal of past decades—has become problematic rather than obviously desirable because an increase in the quantity of goods produced and consumed contributes to pollution and the exhaustion of available resources.

Social indicators have now come to be contrasted with economic indicators. Growth in GNP may or may not correspond to an improvement in the quality of life. With respect to social indicators, again objective data—number of physicians or hospital beds per capita, the rate of educational achievement, etc.—need to be supplemented by subjective indicators representing people's satisfaction with various aspects of life. Changes in satisfaction with housing, schools, or safety on the streets are related to but hardly identical with changes in objective conditions. Behavior is influenced not only by what actually is but also by what people believe to be.

It would be counterproductive to differentiate sharply between economic and social indicators. The subjective data of the two kinds are interrelated, although in a rather complex manner: Abject poverty does make for unhappiness, while riches may not contribute to happiness. Societal malaise, a

16

general feeling of dissatisfaction in the face of such social problems as poverty, violence, urban decay and pollution, differs from a pessimistic evaluation of one's personal financial situation and prospects. But the two are related and both play a role in influencing demand.

2
THE AFFLUENT CONSUMER

The American economy in the years following World War II differs in many significant respects from the economy before the war. Some of the major differences are closely related to the need for the study of psychological factors. These new features of the economy may be summarized as follows:

AFFLUENCE: Not a few individuals, nor a thin upper class, but the majority of families count on improving their standard of living and enlarging their stock of consumer goods year after year.

CONSUMER DISCRETION: Millions of consumers have latitude in deciding whether to spend or to save, on what to spend and how to save. Consumer discretion resulted from income developments as well as from the durability of many goods.

CONSUMER POWER: Cyclical fluctuations, inflation and deflation, and the rate of growth of the economy, all now depend to a large extent on the consumer.

Affluence, defined as more for the many rather than much for a few, is a new development. Throughout the course of human history, poverty has been the rule, riches the exception. In the past, societies were called rich when their ruling classes lived in abundance and luxury. But even in the rich countries of the past, the great majority of people struggled for mere subsistence. Today in the United States and in several other countries as well, minimum standards of nutrition, housing, and clothing are assured for the majority. Beyond these minimum needs, such former luxuries as home ownership, automobiles, appliances, travel, recreation, and entertainment are no longer restricted to a small select group. The broad masses participate in enjoying all these things and generate most of the demand for them.

What is known all over the world as the American standard of living does not consist of luxurious living by the wealthy. The prosperity of a small upper class would be neither new nor envied by millions abroad. What is new is the common man's sharing in the ways of living that in the past were reserved for the few. The common man's ability to use some of his money for what he wants rather than for what he needs represents the revolutionary change.

Another significant change in the economy over the past fifty years is the increasing importance attached by consumers to durable goods. The automobile is, of course, the most important single item, nonexistent in the nineteenth century and now an inevitably necessary possession and expenditure for most families. Television sets, refrigerators, and some other household appliances fall into the same category.

When a society spends all its income on perishable goods, such as food, on semidurables, such as clothing, and on services covering short periods, such as rent, its discretion in postponing purchases or in buying in advance of immediate needs is severly limited. This is not true of the purchases of durable goods, nor of many other discretionary expenditures. Some of what we spend on services and many of our expenditures on recreation, vacations, and luxuries are postponable. Alternatively, these expenses may be increased substantially depending both on our resources and our frame of mind.

The ability of consumers to exercise discretion in spending resulted in the development of consumer power. While at earlier times economists were justified in attributing economic changes exclusively to entrepreneurs or the government, today the consumer plays a large role in influencing or even determining the course of the economy. The individual consumer has little influence, and he is not aware of having any power. But similar decisions made by millions of consumers at about the same time may result in bringing about either prosperity or recession.

The methods of scientific inquiry used in studies of mass behavior are fairly new. It was only in the 1930s that sampling theory, a branch of mathematical statistics, was developed and made it possible to obtain data from small samples that are representative of a broad universe (for instance, all people or all families in the country). Scientific developments often occur when they are needed. This was the case with sample

20

interview surveys which were needed to provide information on consumer decision making only after World War II. The survey method which provides most of the data presented in this book will be described in the Appendix.

We shall consider here the two major developments that have contributed to the need for psychological economics: first, the substantial increase and spread of discretionary income among families in affluent societies, and second, a change in the composition of consumer expenditures resulting from the invention and acceptance of automobiles, household appliances, and other durable goods.

Discretionary Income

How did the American mass consumption economy come about? It derives from the interaction of a variety of forces. Changes in the composition of the population, in education, as well as in customs, attitudes, and aspirations have all contributed to the emergence of discretionary purchasing power among masses of people. But the sine qua non of a mass consumption economy is a substantial increase in the average family's income together with a great change in the distribution of income. We shall devote much of this book to a study of the new psychological forces brought into being by the "income revolution." We must first, however, take note of the change that has taken place in the distribution of purchasing power among the American people.

Surveys covering the distribution of income provide answers to two important questions. First, what proportion of families have an income of, say, less than $3,000 or more than $20,000; in other words, how large is the proportion of those with a fairly small, medium, or large income? Second, what share of aggregate income is in the hands of each income group, that is, to what extent is the total income controlled by those with large or medium or small incomes?

Traditionally, data on the distribution of income have been used to study the concentration of income. When, for instance, the share of the top 1 or 5 or 10 percent of families was found to be getting larger over time or to be higher in one society than in another, it was apparent that income inequality was increasing or was more pronounced in one place than in the other.

21

Similarly, information about the size of the lowest income groups was used to determine the extent of poverty and of the progress being made in reducing it.

Psychological economics interests itself in the size distribution of income primarily for a different purpose, the study of consumer discretion. The largest change in the American income distribution over the past several decades occurred neither at the top nor at the very bottom but rather in the upper-middle income groups, which have grown in size, and in their share of aggregate income. This conclusion was reached by dividing the American income population into four sectors, namely,

the wealthy,
the discretionary income group,
the lower-middle income group, and
the poor.

The definition of each group, that is, the limit of income set as the boundary dividing one group from the next, is somewhat arbitrary and must vary from year to year because of the erosion of purchasing power through inflation. But however within reasonable limits the boundaries are set, the conclusions drawn here remain unaffected.

The *wealthy* may be defined as the top 5 percent when all families are ranked by income. According to that definition, in the early 1970s about $25,000 annual pretax income would constitute the lowest income for those that would be called wealthy. In the early 1960s the limit would have been somewhat over $15,000, and in the early 1950s over $10,000.[1]

Only fragmentary and incomplete prewar data are available for purposes of comparison. There is good reason to believe that the share of aggregate income in the hands of the top income group was higher in 1929 than in 1945. In other words, the Great Depression of the 1930s and the war brought about some reduction in the concentration of income. Still, shortly after

---

[1] These are data for family units from the Surveys of Consumer Finances, conducted by the Survey Research Center of The University of Michigan. A family unit, the basic unit of the surveys, includes all related persons living in the same dwelling unit and is therefore not restricted to complete families but may also consist of widows or widowers with children or even of single persons. The income data obtained through sample surveys by the U.S. Bureau of the Census are published separately for families and unattached individuals.

World War II, the top 5 percent received over 20 percent of aggregate income. During two or three decades after the war there was apparently little change in this respect.

While our concern at the moment is with the distribution of income, it is obvious that the definition of the wealthy should also take into consideration their assets or wealth. We shall have an opportunity to note later that the concentration of wealth is much greater than that of income. The two rates of concentration are related, but far from identical.

The *discretionary income group* is defined to include those families who are not "wealthy" and yet are in possession of income they may use for discretionary expenditures. Their income exceeds what is needed for minimum necessities so that they can, to a smaller or larger extent, engage in spending not only on what they need but also on what they want. The wealthy, of course, likewise have discretionary income but differ from the second group in the much greater degree to which they may indulge in discretionary expenditures.

Where should the lower limit of the discretionary income group be set? Perhaps around $7,500 in the early 1970s and $6,000 in the early 1960s. When this is done, close to one-half of all family units are found to fall in this group. If a somewhat more stringent definition of discretionary income is used and the lower limit is set several hundred dollars higher, the size of the group may drop to 45 or even 42 percent of all families. The major conclusion remains unaffected: In the early 1970s about one-half of all families (including the wealthy) were in a position to make discretionary expenditures, while right after World War II only about 25 percent and, in the decade before World War II, only about 15 percent were in this position.

The share of total income controlled by the discretionary income group has likewise grown rapidly. In the early 1970s, the 5 percent called wealthy controlled over 20 percent of aggregate income and the almost 50 percent of families falling in the discretionary income group about 60 percent. The bulk of income received was in the hands of these two income groups. In earlier years the share of the discretionary income group was much lower, approximately 50 percent in the early 1960s and only 33 percent shortly after the end of World War II.

In the past few decades growth has taken place (1) in the total population, (2) in national income in constant dollars, and (3) in the number of families in the discretionary income

23

group. The crucial facts to be kept in mind are that, in relative terms, (2) has increased at a greater rate than (1), and (3) at a greater rate than (2); that is, the increase in real national income has been greater than the increase in population, and the growth of the discretionary income group has run far ahead even of that. Thus, from 1929 to 1961 the number of family units increased by approximately 55 percent; national income, in constant dollars, by almost 160 percent; and the number of families with discretionary income, when the limits of the group are adjusted for price increases, by 400 percent.

Since World War II the growth in these three areas, both in absolute and in relative terms, has also been remarkable. From 1947 to 1961 the number of family units increased by 28 percent. National income, in constant dollars, advanced by more than 60 percent. The size of the discretionary income group, measured in real income, doubled. Throughout the 1960s the growth of the discretionary income group remained substantial.

The third of the four groups, the *lower-middle income group,* is defined as having no discretionary income but not falling into the poverty group. It contains a variety of different people but includes a large part of one segment of the population, the young people: families the head of which is no more than 35 years of age. In a society such as existed in the United States as recently as 60 years ago, in which farmers and unskilled workers predominated, the earning power of young family heads was not much lower than that of middle-aged family heads. One of the radical ways in which today's American society differs from that earlier one is that skilled workers and white-collar workers, and generally better-educated people, represent the great majority rather than a small minority. We shall discuss in Chapter 12 the increase in the age at which different population groups obtain their top income as well as the impact of prevailing expectations of steadily rising income. At this point, it suffices to state that among the families with less than $7,500 annual income, there is a sizable group of younger people who have every reason to expect their income to rise substantially in the future.

The fourth group, the *poor,* have been the subject of many extensive studies. The poor are usually defined by considering the family income and the number of people dependent on that income, as well as by estimating the minimum budgetary re-

24

quirements of the family. In 1973 the upper limit of the poverty sector was set by means of such calculations at slightly over $4,500 family income for a nonfarm family of four, and lower for the average poor.

Using these limits, about 25 to 32 percent of all family units fell in the lower-middle income group and over 15 percent in the poverty group in the early 1970s. These are the data in Table 2-1, which presents rough approximations of the size of each of the four groups. In the case of the poverty sector, the number of persons provide a better indication of its size than the number of family units because this group includes many families with several children. In 1971 government statistics indicated that approximately 25 million persons were dependent on a family income below minimum budgetary requirements. Thus the poverty sector contained 12 percent of all persons, which is a substantial improvement over the 22 percent in that category as recently as 1959.[2]

Who are the poor? A great variety of people may fall in the poverty sector—for instance, even businessmen in certain years when they operate at a loss. Whether or not many farmers are included in the group depends primarily on the consideration given to nonmoney income. But irrespective of such considerations, the great majority of the poor are described by at least one, often several, of the following statements:

They are old.
They are nonwhite.
They have no male earner in the family and have children at
    home.
They are disabled.

To illustrate: The majority of persons in the poverty sector are white, but only 10 percent of all whites are poor as compared to one-third of all blacks.

Families with female heads constitute only 12 percent of all families, but not fewer than 40 percent of them are poor.

The proportion of poor among persons 65 years of age or older is 22 percent.

[2] The government estimates of the extent of poverty are based on sample surveys conducted by the U.S. Bureau of the Census. For additional data on this as well as on other aspects of the income distribution, see Miller (1971).

TABLE 2-1

Approximate Distribution of Family Units and of Shares of Income by Four Population Groups in the Early 1970s

Groups	Boundaries[a]	Percent of Family Units	Percent of Aggregate Income
The wealthy	$25,000 and over	5	22
Discretionary-income group	$7,500-25,000	50	60
Lower-middle group	$3,500-7,500	30	15
The poor	Under $3,500	15	3
Total		100	100

[a]Annual money income before taxes and other deductions, as reported in surveys.

Most commonly, poor people are unable to earn enough because of age, physical handicaps, or discrimination. Families headed by women are often discriminated against in their ability to earn a living, especially if they have small children to care for.

Lack of skills and lack of education characterize many of the poor. In modern society specialized skills are a necessary requirement for advancement. Workers without such skills have a low level of earnings and are subject to frequently recurring periods of unemployment.

Since relatively many young and old fall in the third and fourth groups, it follows that the size of the discretionary income group would be greater and its recent growth more pronounced if we had considered only people in their years of maximum earning capacity rather than all people. When American family units whose head is 35 to 55 years old are divided into the four groups, close to two-thirds of them fall into the category either of the wealthy or of those with discretionary income.

Discretionary Expenditures

The second major change, in addition to the change in income distribution, which has permitted consumers to exercise discretion in their spending behavior, has been the invention and widespread use of many consumer durable goods. In the nineteenth century economists commonly considered business investment—the outlays of business firms for plants and machinery—the one element of the economy with wide fluctuations that reflected and even brought about periods of economic upturn and downturn. Beginning early in this century government operations were seen as another factor making contributions to cyclical fluctuations or their absence. Since World War II consumer expenditures for residential housing and durable goods represent a third such element, often of greater importance than either of the other two. Today annual expenditures on household tangible assets—residential construction and household durables—exceed those on business tangible assets—likewise consisting of construction and such business durables as machinery and equipment. Expenditures on durable assets both of households and of businesses are highly volatile.[3] Household expenditures on new cars are the most volatile of all. At several crucial times such consumer expenditures moved earlier and to a larger extent than business investments, so that they were first to indicate the beginning or end of a recession.

Table 2-2 shows the frequent and substantial changes in consumer purchases of durable goods from one year to the next. Actually, the cyclical fluctuations were larger than indicated because the beginning and the end of the movements did not coincide with calendar years.

Consumer outlays for durable goods represent only a small part of their total expenditures, but have grown substantially both in absolute amounts and in relation to other expenditures. In most years prior to World War II they amounted to less than 10 percent of the total; they rose to about 14 percent by 1960 and 18 percent in the early 1970s.

These expenditures share many features with business investment, among which one should be mentioned right away. Both business expenditures on plant and machinery and consumer expenditures on durable goods are commonly made on credit. Credit is of course involved in most purchases of one-family houses for owner occupancy. These are generally considered as investments and not included among consumer expenditures. Where to draw the line, in other words, what to consider as investments in enduring capital goods and what as

[3] See Katona (1964a, p. 20), and Juster (1966, Chapter 4).

TABLE 2-2

Annual Changes in Durable Goods Expenditures and in the Number of New Cars Bought

Year	Expenditures on Consumer Durable Goods in Constant Dollars	Number of New Passenger Cars Bought*
	Change from preceding year in percent	
1964	+ 2.4	+ 3.9
1965	+12.9	+14.8
1966	+ 7.7	− 4.3
1967	+ 1.7	− 7.6
1968	+11.7	+15.8
1969	+ 5.2	− 0.1
1970	− 2.7	−12.3
1971	+10.0	+21.9
1972	+12.6	+ 6.8

*Data on change in 1964, 1965, and 1966: domestic cars only.
Source: U.S. Department of Commerce and Council of Economic Advisers to the President.

expenditures, is far from clear, a point we shall discuss further in the next chapter. Money spent for modernization, improvement, repair or upkeep of housing all fall into an intermediate category.

Traditionally, consumer expenditures are divided into expenditures for durable goods, for nondurable goods, and for services. Spending for services has increased to the largest extent in the last few decades, but probably with less effect on the total economy than spending on durable goods. This is so since many service expenditures are linked with expenditures for food, clothing, and nondurables in general because they are seen as necessary at a given time (e.g., utilities, beauty care, upkeep for durables) and because they depend primarily on income level. On the other hand, most expenditures for durables are outlays of choice: The consumer has great latitude in undertaking such an expenditure at all and especially in its timing. A new car can be bought long before it is really needed in the sense that the old car may still be technically in good condition, or the purchase can be postponed even though the old car is causing a lot of trouble, because the time is not seen as appropriate. On the other hand, some expenditures on cars

28

and appliances are not discretionary. For example, a person may buy a car because his car has been stolen or because he habitually buys a new car every two years. But these are exceptions—just as some exceptional purchases of clothing and food may be discretionary rather than necessary.

Many other consumer expenditures share the characteristics mentioned with durable goods. The latter are just the most conspicuous among the outlays of choice and the only ones for which reliable statistical data are available. In our quantitative studies, therefore, we shall deal with consumer expenditures on durable goods—automobiles, appliances, and furniture—or, alternatively, with what has been called consumer investment expenditures, which include durables, houses, as well as additions and repairs to houses. Purchases of homes for owner occupancy are frequently connected with an array of discretionary expenditures, such as additions and repairs, and purchases of furniture and appliances.

Discretionary expenditures, including those on travel and vacations, and on a variety of luxury items often connected with recreation and hobbies, are characterized by the following three features:

1. There is no compelling need to make these expenditures at a given time. Most purchases of automobiles and large household appliances are replacement purchases and are usually made before the old item becomes unusable. Articles in fairly good condition and even in excellent condition are replaced by newer and better ones, the timing of replacements being a matter of discretion. Even when the occasion for a purchase is the inadequate functioning of an old piece of equipment, the consumer usually has the choice of either repairing or buying. First purchases of automobiles and first purchases of traditional household appliances, usually made by young people, are likewise often discretionary in their timing. Purchases of newer durable goods—room air conditioners, garbage disposals, or clothes dryers, for instance —depend by their very nature on something other than compelling need.

2. Discretionary expenditures are usually not governed by habit. Since habits generally derive from frequently repeated performance and most durable goods are usually bought once in several years, this point needs little elaboration. In the case of vacations, their timing and desti-

nation may be habitual, and yet there is usually considerable discretion regarding their nature and duration, which determine the amounts spent.

3. Discretionary purchases are usually not made on the spur of the moment, but rather after considerable deliberation and discussion among family members. The planning period may, of course, be fairly short. Usually several months, rarely as long as a year, elapse between the arousal of the idea and the conclusion of the purchase. When there were much shorter intervals between first thinking about buying a car or a refrigerator, for instance, and actually buying it, it was found that either the purchase was not discretionary or there were special opportunities for making an advantageous purchase. Exceptional circumstances characterize most transactions in which a single visit by a salesman or one advertisement are successful both in awakening a need and in clinching the sale. Also, relatively inexpensive items—a piece of occasional furniture or a table radio, for instance—are often bought without any extensive planning period. Yet the question, "Should I or should I not buy?", the decision about which of several conflicting desires should have priority, and above all, concern about the timing of the acquisition occur in most purchases of major durable goods. The same is true of improvements and additions to the house and of the purchase of a number of expensive luxury items, such as a yacht, a motorboat, a summer home, or power tools.

Discretionary expenditures, then, are not inevitably necessary, not habitual, and not made on the spur of the moment. It follows that there is no clear and direct relationship between the circumstances or occasions of such purchases and the purchases themselves. Intervening variables mediate between the stimulus and the response. The buyer, as a result of his past experience, his personality, and his group belonging, plays a role both in evaluating the circumstances and in shaping his reactions to them. It therefore becomes essential to study changes in motives, opinions, attitudes, and expectations in order to understand changes in discretionary expenditures.

Consumers have discretion not only regarding many of their expenditures but also the amounts they save. But some amounts saved are contractually set and do not require making a new decision. The repayment of mortgages, of installment and other debts, as well as the payment of life insurance premiums, when the debts and the insurance policies are already in effect, are major examples of contractual outlays which may not depend on developments during the period of the payments. Only under catastrophic conditions does the possibility of choice and decision making arise (should I or should I not pay the amounts due?). Defaults in such payments are rare, even during most recessions. Similar contractual payments, classified as expenditures rather than savings, are represented by a multitude of dues and charges, as well as by rent and by real estate taxes and interest on the part of homeowners. Discretionary saving consists primarily of the results of decisions to increase or decrease financial assets (savings deposits, bonds or stocks).

Expenditures on necessities are in many respects similar to contractual obligations. Basic outlays for food, clothing, and shelter will continue to be made except under catastrophic circumstances. The same applies to payments for such services as gas and electricity and for many medical expenses. In other words, the leeway of consumers to restrict a great portion of their money outlays is severely limited. Limitations exist also in the possibility of a substantial increase in these expenditures, partly because some of them are not indefinitely expandable and, more importantly, because expenditures on food and clothing and many other things are frequently habitual. Some consumer outlays are subject to the influence of habits that are relatively enduring and change but slowly, while others are not. We thus arrive at the following fourfold division of consumer money outlays:

Classification of Major Consumer Money Outlays

Kind of Outlay	Spending	Saving
Outlays determined by past decisions or habits	Necessities, convenience goods, habitual and contractual expenditures	Contractual and habitual saving
Outlays of choice	Discretionary expenditures	Discretionary saving

31

Spending and saving determined by past decisions or by habits are less variable and easier to predict than outlays of choice. Of money spent on food or rent and of money saved by repaying debt or paying life insurance premiums, the outlays made in one period represent a fair prediction for estimating the outlays in the next period. There will, of course, be some differences from year to year in the amounts involved, but the changes will depend primarily upon changes in income. These two segments of our classification are, typically, a function of income. It is not here then that we can look for a clue to consumers' contribution to promoting or impeding economic activity.

Today in America and increasingly in other affluent societies as well, a large part of consumer expenditures is no longer a function of income alone. Some expenditures also depend on available liquid asset holdings, which have grown greatly in the past fifty years, and on the availability and acceptance of credit, the use of which has become increasingly favored. Above all, discretionary expenditures depend on people's willingness to buy and therefore on psychological factors.

Finally, it is important for any consideration of the greater influence of the consumer on the economy to note that the economic intelligence of the American people has increased greatly. Through the mass media, people all over the country and in all walks of life now receive some economic news. News, whether good or bad, spreads rapidly and, because of the centralized nature of news sources, fairly uniformly. Consumer discretion could hardly be exercised in such a way as to influence the economy if broad masses of people were entirely uninformed about economic events.

3
THE MODERN HOUSEHOLD

Thus far we have not specified the sense in which we use the term consumer, nor have we described the areas of consumer activity with which we are concerned. For our purposes the consumer is the family or the "family household." Most purchases of consumer goods and services are undertaken in behalf of the family living together in the same dwelling. While consumer expenditures per capita are relevant for certain statistical purposes, decision making is usually a family affair with the family member who actually makes the purchase taking the responsibility for the entire family. How many family members there are is important, as are stages of life cycle and income, in determining the quantity of goods bought and the adequacy of the available means to cover the expenditure requirements. There are of course one-person family units as well as dwelling units containing persons not related to the main family living there and nevertheless belonging to the same household. Furthermore there are some expenditures that are personal and individual, regularly undertaken by the user himself. There must also be families with sharp conflicts among their members and separation of spending decisions. All of these are exceptions that do not alter the basic picture. Regardless of what aspects of spending or saving are considered, most decisions may be treated as joint decisions of the family or the household.[1]

The role of family composition in determining consumer behavior is studied by distinguishing stages of the life cycle. By

---

[1] Whether either husband or wife is the major decision maker or whether husband and wife decide together are matters of importance for market research, which is concerned, for instance, with specifying the person at whom the sales appeal for specific goods or services should be directed. This question will not be discussed in this book.

considering age, marital status, and the presence or absence of children, major differences in spending or saving behavior can be identified. We may follow Lansing and Morgan (1955) who distinguished six stages of the life cycle into which American family units, not living in institutions, could be divided:

1. The bachelor stage; young single people.
2. Newly married couples; young, no children.
3. The full nest I; young married couples with dependent children.
4. The full nest II; older married couples with dependent children.
5. The empty nest; older married couples with no children with them.
6. The solitary survivor; older single people.

The dividing line between younger or older families—the first three as against the last three stages—is usually set at age 45.

The average income was shown to be much lower in stages 1 and 6 than in the other stages. Families at stages 2 and 3 were found to be the largest purchasers of durable goods, with purchases on the installment plan being most common in stage 3. Additions to liquid savings were most frequent in stages 4 and 5. We shall come back to some of these differences in the course of discussing spending and saving decisions. At this point it may suffice to say that such considerations as these bear out the necessity of considering the family as the basic consumer unit.

What does the consumer do? The simple answer that the consumer consumes requires a definition of consumption. A large American dictionary (*Webster's New International Dictionary,* 3rd edition) presents the following four definitions of the verb "to consume":

1.   —to destroy or do away with completely; cause to waste away utterly;
2a. —to spend wastefully, to squander;
2b. —to use up;
2c. —to utilize in the satisfaction of wants.

The first three definitions give a negative connotation to consumption and even definition 2c, indicating the meaning of the term in economics, does not do justice to the greatly changed functions of consumption in today's economy. The definitions given are based on the notion that production is an active and consumption a passive process.

Theories that were true in the nineteenth century but are no longer true today still exercise a great influence on economic thinking. Language habits persist. The belief that consumers consume, that is, use up and destroy what agriculture and industry produce serves to elevate business investment to the dominant position in economic policy and to relegate the consumer to a minor place. True, lip service has always been paid to the consumer. He was called "king" in the nineteenth century, and the statement that the end of production is consumption is as old as economics itself. But traditional economic analysis did not postulate that consumer wants and consumer demands represented major forces in the economy. Even the "sovereign" consumer whose wishes allegedly determined the direction of production remained a user rather than a chooser. The consumer was considered incapable of generating income or determining its allocation. It was assumed that consumers on the whole spent the income they received from business and government at a fairly steady rate.

Of the three sectors of the economy—business, government, and consumers—only the first two were recognized as exerting an autonomous influence on economic developments. The business sector was thought to be able to do so by raising or lowering the volume of business investment and the government sector by expanding its expenditures, often financed through deficits. But the consumer sector, by spending what it received from the other two sectors at a stable rate, was viewed as an unimportant transmitter of income.

Prior to fairly recent major changes in the economy, this may well have been a correct description of economic processes. In feudal societies a few landlords, and in early industrial societies a few entrepreneurs, represented the major forces bringing about change. The government's role in shaping economic processes has increased in most countries of the world during the last one hundred years. At the same time, consumers remained close to the subsistence level except for a few whose principal influence on the economy was in their role of entrepreneur.

Today the consumer must be seen in an entirely new light. Families and households even if they are not engaged in business partake in economic activities far beyond the consumption of goods and services. The usual sharp distinction between business behavior and consumer behavior can no longer be maintained. Consumers, as we have shown in Chapter 2, are in a position to exercise discretion, just as businessmen do. Moreover, both consumers and businessmen make investment expenditures.

Some of the money outlays by individuals, which in the previous chapter we labeled as consumer expenditures, could with good reason be considered as investments. As we noted earlier, one-family houses are counted in the national statistics as investments—not so, however, automobiles or any other durables. Yet, since a car is not consumed in the year of purchase, it may logically be argued that only the amount of depreciation—admittedly rather substantial in the first year —should be reckoned as consumer expenditure for that year. Whatever accounting system we adopt, consumer durable goods clearly constitute a separate category by themselves since they do not fit completely into the category either of expenditures or of investments.

Saving obviously differs from consumption and the saving unit may not be identical with the consumer unit. Saving involves concern for the future. It may sometimes relate to needs that are expected to arise in the next year or two, while sometimes, as, for instance, in the case of saving for retirement, it may reflect long-range planning. Often there is no time limit to the need saving is intended to fulfill, and it is motivated simply by the belief that the future is uncertain.

The saving unit may consist of everyone living in the same dwelling, as, for instance, in the case of payments for owner-occupied houses. But the ownership of savings deposits or securities may vary from family member to family member. On the whole, however, real conditions in the field of saving, as of buying, are most nearly approached by studying the actions of the entire family living together rather than of the individual members.

The term "investment" is generally used for purchases by individuals of stocks or real estate (other than the family home). The distinction implied in common parlance between such forms of saving and depositing money in bank accounts is usually of little significance. Purchases of stocks are sometimes undertaken with very little thought or care and compete with depositing funds in banks. Whatever the situation is, an

36

analysis of various forms of saving and of motives to save constitutes an important part of behavioral economics.

Investing as an economic concept represents the creation of enduring wealth or capital. As such, it has long been held to be the exclusive province of business. Until recent decades this was indeed so and amounts saved by individuals were used for investments by business and government. Today, however, families or households play a major role in creating enduring wealth. There are now three forms of private investment: business investment in plant and machinery, consumer investment in tangible assets, and investment in human capital.[2]

Private capital or private wealth consists of (1) the productive facilities of the nation including, in addition to natural resources, factories and mines, such business assets as trading, banking, and insurance facilities without which production would not be possible; (2) the housing of the people, supplemented by their durable wealth in such long-lasting goods as home appliances and automobiles; (3) the health, education, and skills of the people.[3] Rich countries differ from poor countries, and the wealth of the present American economy differs from that of the economy of earlier years, not in the first factor alone but in the second and third as well.

What consumers spend on buying and improving their homes and on automobiles or appliances adds to the enduring wealth of a nation. The tangible assets of households, the sum total of household structures and household durables is now as large as, or larger than, the value of the tangible assets of businesses, consisting likewise of structures and durable goods (machinery, and so on). The role of households in capital formation, that is, in the creation of tangible assets has increased greatly since World War II.

What to some extent consumers, and to a larger extent governments, spend on education and health represents another most significant addition to national resources. The sum total of skills and education of the people, as well as their health,

---

[2] The term *investment* as most commonly used includes what is called here business investment, residential construction, and change in inventories. The last of these is not a permanent addition to wealth.

[3] In addition to private capital there is, of course, government capital, consisting of office buildings, schools, hospitals, highways, recreational facilities, etc.

represent economic assets even though their significance goes far beyond economics.

Expenditures in all three areas are future-oriented and enduring, although just as business machinery wears out or becomes outdated in a fairly short period of time, so do the durable goods bought by consumers. Expenditures in all three areas add to productivity. To increase productivity we need skillful, well-educated, and healthy people—and therefore investment in human capital. We need well-equipped factories and businesses—and therefore business investment. We also need a population that is well-housed, within easy commuting distance from home to place of work, and in possession of labor-saving devices—and therefore consumer investment.[4]

The traditional concepts of capital and capital formation are not logically consistent. What was derived from nineteenth-century conditions should be reconsidered in the light of mid-twentieth-century developments. The parallel between capital formation by business and by consumers may be illustrated by studying the opposite process, namely, the destruction of capital (often called capital consumption). Kuznets (1961) correctly states that "consumption of producers' durable goods" is due primarily to economic obsolescence rather than to physical wear and tear. Obsolescence occurs because of technological progress and changes in taste or desirability. Factories remote from raw materials are abandoned even when in good condition; machinery loses value when more efficient machinery is invented; office buildings in fair condition are replaced by new buildings having more desirable features. Similarly, one-family houses in decaying neighborhoods are not kept up and lose value; automobiles and appliances are scrapped when newer ones are desired. Obsolescence and insufficient upkeep destroy capital—business as well as consumer capital. Consumption of food and even the wear and tear of clothing represent different forms of dynamic processes. Truly the consumer is the only one who consumes, but that is not all he does.

Consumer latitude and choice extend to the earning as well as the spending aspects of consumer behavior. Economics

---

[4] Simon Kuznets (1961) in his valuable book, *Capital in the American Economy,* excludes consumers from capital formation by defining capital as intended for use in producing goods or income. This is one of the few differences between business machinery and consumer durables.

38

must concern itself not only with the allocation but also with the acquisition of income. Many families are in a position to choose whether they wish to increase their income. For example, the husband may decide to work longer hours or take a second job, or the wife may decide to go out and work. The process of increasing the income may also take the form of changing jobs or acquiring additional education and skills. When it is fairly easy to have some kind of a job, the pursuit of a higher income is channeled toward getting a better job. The features valued and sought as representing a better job may consist of shorter working hours, security and fringe benefits or, alternatively, of providing an opportunity for advancement and the realization of one's capabilities. Whether or not people are motivated to seek advancement is, at least to some extent, dependent on felt consumption needs. When people are highly motivated to improve their standard of living they frequently find means to raise their incomes. Neglecting the constraint supplied by absence of opportunities, there is then justification to reverse the traditional equation: Instead of expenditures being a function of income, income becomes a function of consumption.

Decisions by adults about the acquisition of skills, education, or training as well as the extent and form of the education of children are of crucial importance in our society where the extent to which knowledge is used may make a very great difference to the economy. The knowledge industry, devoted to the acquisition, transformation, and dissemination of knowledge, has become one of the fastest growing industries in affluent countries. The extent and direction of its growth is not a function of the availability of new technology alone. The utilization of computer hardware and software, for instance, depends on the decisions of people who must first perceive the need and usefulness of the new technology. The decisions about what kinds of skills, training, and information to acquire determine the extent to which individuals will participate in the society and its economic growth.

References to these many and varied activities serve to indicate how far-ranging is the interrelationship between economics and psychlogy. Indeed, so broad is its scope that we must necessarily neglect many areas of economic affairs where psychological considerations certainly play a role. We shall, for example, omit the study of income acquisition, geographic or occupational mobility, and educational achievements and aspirations.[5] Nor shall we include the areas of work behavior, human relations at the place of work, or organizational effectiveness, although in the study of these areas, closely related to economics, psychological principles were applied at an early stage. Motivation to work has been shown to depend on a variety of considerations beyond material wants alone, even though wages and salaries remain of major importance.[6]

Finally, even in the area of the allocation of income, several aspects of market research, as distinguished from economic research, will remain outside the concern of this book. To explain the distinction with the help of an example, the question of whether, when, and why families strive toward having two cars constitutes part of economic research because the answers influence economic growth, cyclical fluctuations, as well as inflation or deflation. But whether the second car will be a General Motors or Ford product, whether brand loyalty prevails and why, these are considerations of a different nature. What contributes to the growth in the size of the pie may differ greatly from what influences an individual producer's share in the pie.

Within the fields of psychological economics proper that are to be considered, we want to point out once again that we are concerned with activities of the modern household and not just consumer activities. This is particularly true when we turn to the analysis of public policy and its influence on the economy. Households do not respond to policy measures merely as consumers but in as many varied roles as businessmen do, for instance, as investors, savers-borrowers, and taxpayers. Furthermore, their response depends on their understanding of economic processes and is subject to learning. The crucial psychological factor, to be taken up in the next chapter, is the extent and form of the learning process. What and how, not one or the other individual, but millions of people learn about inflation or taxes or deficits, for example, represents a central question of psychological economics. It may be discussed as a problem of consumer psychology, although it far transcends the analysis of consumer behavior in the narrow sense.

[5] See the analysis of these processes in Katona et al. (1971a).
[6] See Katz and Kahn (1966) as well as Kahn (1972) and Katz (1972). For the psychology of organizations, see Likert (1961) and (1967).

4
THE RELATION OF PSYCHOLOGY AND
SOCIAL PSYCHOLOGY TO ECONOMICS

In this chapter we shall attempt to explain the psychological concepts and principles used in the analysis of economic behavior. Psychological economics is positive rather than normative; it deals with what is, rather than what ought to be. Empirical findings based on the systematic observation of economic behavior take the place of dogmatic statements or of pure reasoning. Unlike pure theorists, psychological economists do not assume at the outset that rational behavior underlies economic behavior. They study the latter as they find it.

It is commonplace in modern economics to distinguish between macroeconomics and microeconomics. The former deals with processes in the entire economy or in its major parts, based on such aggregate data as national income or total retail sales, while the latter studies individual behavior, primarily the behavior of the typical consumer or the typical business firm. Irrespective of this twofold nature of economic studies, the aims or goals of economics are always macroeconomic in the sense that economics strives to understand and predict what will happen to the economy and not what individuals will do. To give two simple illustrations: Economics is concerned with an increase or decrease in the total number of cars bought, or to be bought, in a given period, but not with whether or not John Smith or Joe Doe bought or will buy a car. Likewise, the change in the proportion of all families with rising incomes, but not the income gain of any one individual, is relevant for economic trends.

In contrast to the concern of economists with aggregates, it is the individual who represents the starting point of psychology, including the psychology of the group, for psychological processes reside in the individual. It is the individual who thinks, feels, and learns. The reconciliation of the divergent points of view of economics and psychology will occupy us in the second half of this chapter. First, let us look at the basic psychological principles that are incorporated in psychological economics.

Psychology is founded on the conviction that it is possible to establish scientific principles of behavior. Behavior is susceptible of analysis and measurement. Furthermore, some principles of behavior have already been established. To be sure, the principles currently known and accepted are not final. Every scientific discipline is at all times in a stage of growth and development. We can confidently expect to achieve greater knowledge and understanding in the future. On the other hand, psychology is no longer by any means an infant discipline.

There are those who may object: The trouble is not that there is no psychology, but that there are many psychologies. Different schools of psychology emphasize different aspects of behavior and propose different, often contradictory, principles. What is correct in this opinion again characterizes any growing discipline. Several paths may lead to the same mountain peak; it is useful to start the exploration of the peak from all sides. Moreover, the differences between psychological schools are greatly overemphasized. Sometimes such overemphasis may be useful for the sake of clarifying the differences. There are, however, certain fundamental agreements among psychologists that are of great import to psychological economics.[1]

Basic Principles of Psychology

1. Psychology is an empirical discipline. It allows one, and only one, way of establishing whether a psychological statement is correct, namely, by means of empirical evidence. Statements not susceptible of empirical validation have no place in psychology.

The term "empirical research" has a specific meaning. It involves, first, controlled observation. Armchair speculation

[1] Much of our discussion of psychological principles makes use of generally accepted principles of psychology. In certain instances, however, it is based on the viewpoint of the specific school of psychology known as Gestalt.

42

and what is believed to be common sense or a matter of common knowledge do not constitute scientific evidence. Likewise, casual observation and observation possible only to one individual are ruled out. Controlled observation, and especially its most developed form, experimentation, produce results that can be checked by other scientists. Controlled observation consists of identifying and singling out factors that prevail in many, apparently different, situations.

Second, empirical research involves the relating of many different controlled observations to one another. It does not consist of a description of a bit of experience here and another bit there, or a planless procedure of observation in a given situation. Empirical research must be guided by hypotheses or theories. It progresses by testing hypotheses through controlled observation, setting up new or changed hypotheses on the basis of that observation, testing them again, improving them further, and so on. Hypotheses must be valid for more than one set of observations. Instead of being constructed to explain one observation, they must be applicable to a variety of diverse facts and enable the research worker to deduce new facts.

2. Behavior is characterized by plasticity within broad limits. Disregarding wear and tear, one can say of machines that they do the same thing over and over again. In this sense, human behavior is not repetitive. Doing the same thing the second time may differ from doing it the first time. There is maturation and there is learning. In studying economic behavior we need not concern ourselves with reflexes that may be established by the neurophysiological structure once and for all. This structure itself is plastic. It is affected by previous actions. Therefore, a major subject of study in psychology is change in behavior.

The human organism acquires knowledge, emotions, and forms of behavior through experience. What has happened does not necessarily belong only to the past and is not necessarily lost. It may or may not exert influence on present behavior. Under what conditions and in what ways past experience affects later behavior is one of the most important problems of psychology.

To be sure, there are limits to the plasticity of behavior. Certain limits are clearly set by the neurophysiological structure. For instance, human beings cannot learn to run a mile in two minutes. The quantity of knowledge we are able to acquire is not infinite, and the speed of learning likewise has definite limits. Within rather broad limits, however, the possible variations are tremendous in number and kind, and these variations and their regularities represent the subject matter of the analysis of behavior.

In studying economic behavior, we need not concern ourselves with that perennial bogey of psychology, the question of what is innate and what is acquired behavior. Economic behavior is learned in the sense that it develops and changes with experience. Not the limits of plasticity and learning, but rather the variations in making use of experience, represent the main issues in the analysis of economic behavior.

3. Psychological analysis makes use of intervening variables. The basic scheme of psychological studies is:

Stimulus—Organism—Response

or

Change in the environment—Intervening variables—Overt behavior.

Change in the environment, or information received, serves as a stimulus and influences the organism or the person who responds. Intervening variables that represent the contribution of the organism or the person mediate between stimuli and responses. Because of the input of intervening variables two people may perceive the same change in their environment differently and may react to it differently. Personality traits as well as past experiences are reflected in the intervening variables.

Motives, attitudes, and expectations constitute intervening variables of great importance for the study of economic behavior. Motives are the forces that pull the organism in a certain direction, toward certain ends and goals. They represent the answers to the question why: Why did I go to a certain meeting? Why did I write this book? Attitudes represent generalized viewpoints that make us regard certain situations with favor and others with disfavor. The general points of view that influence our perceptions and behavior over extended periods need not have the feature of affecting us pro or con. When that feature is lacking, the general point of view may be referred to as the frame of reference or the context.

The terms used and their exact definitions are not very important. Often it does not matter much whether we speak of motives, attitudes, or frames of reference. I hear of a plan to introduce an excess-profits tax on corporation earnings. I view this proposition with favor (or disfavor) because I am motivated by "social" considerations (or by opposition to interference with "the profit motive"), or because my attitudes are procontrol and prolabor (or anticontrol and probusiness), or because my frame of reference consists of the "prevailing large business profits" (or of need for larger business investments).

We have at all times a time perspective. The time perspective extends backward as well as forward. Our "life-space" (to use a term of Kurth Lewin) as of a given moment encompasses some of our past experiences, our perceptions of the present, and our attitudes toward the future. The psychological field, of individuals as well as of groups, includes expectations, aspirations, plans, hopes, and many other forward-looking attitudes. Expectations are attitudes which, like other attitudes, may shape behavior.

Not all our past experiences affect us at a given moment because memory is selective. Sometimes the organization is such that our time perspective extends far into the past, while sometimes fairly recent events appear to be wiped out. There are great differences in the forward extension of the time perspective as well. Under certain circumstances we may live for the moment and our aspirations and expectations may play no effective role. The demands of the immediate situation alone may determine our behavior, for instance, in an emergency. Or, to mention a situation more significant for our purposes, in selling a shoddy product to a stranger I may charge an unjustifiedly high price, without considering the effect of this action on my reputation or on future sales. I may, however, in setting a price or in bargaining, be governed by considerations that extend far into the future.

The presence of intervening variables may be deduced from differences in the response of different individuals to the same stimuli or from differences in the response of the same individual at different times. The presence or absence of a correlation between certain circumstances and certain responses often serves to reveal the nature of the intervening variables. This method of analyzing correlations is generally available, while motives may be elusive, memory fallacious, and attitudes biased. Nevertheless, insights of value may be obtained by simply asking people—respondents in sample surveys, for instance—about the circumstances of their decisions and actions. In this manner information has often been obtained on motives, attitudes, and expectations that prevailed among very many people at a given time and not at an earlier time.

Motives, attitudes, and frames of reference influence the organization of perceptions of the environment as well as reactions to the environment. Human action is response within a field and not an automatic, mechanical reaction to stimuli. The letter O in the schema St-O-R stands not only for organism but also for organization.

Let us take two human beings confronted with the identical situation. We may say that their "geographical environment" is the same, but the "behavioral environment" of the two people may not be the same. The geographical environment is represented by the external factors present, the behavioral environment by what the two people themselves see, hear, smell, feel. People do not see all that is given, and they do not necessarily see an object as it is given. Their perceptions are organized. What a person perceives—and therefore what affects him—depends on the organization of his perception.

Organization of perceptions, as well as of behavior, results in unified wholes. All items or parts are influenced by the whole to which they belong. The whole is different from —though not necessarily more than—the sum of its parts. The change in one item or part may or may not affect the whole or the other items and parts, depending on the role and function of the part within the whole. An organization has structure, often a focus or central feature, and it has one or many peripheral parts. In a broad sense, the psychological whole is represented by the field of behavior. Behavior takes place within a field, is influenced by its field, and, in turn, influences the field.

We may express these principles as intervening variables or in the form of the following schema:

$$A\big/{}_X \longrightarrow B \qquad A\big/{}_Y \longrightarrow C$$

Item A—a stimulus or a specific change in the environment —seen in context X differs from the same item A in context Y. In the first case, it elicits the response B, in the second case, the response C. As an example, we may refer to our brief discussion of consumer response to inflation in Chapter 1. The perception of price increases within the framework or context of a gradual creeping inflation induces people to postpone purchases and spend less. Similar price increases in the context of rapid inflation induce people to buy in advance, to stock up and hoard in order to beat the inflation.

Two Forms of Learning

In studying change in behavior, we shall be concerned with change due to learning and disregard maturation and growth as well as decay and injury, which of course also produce changes in behavior. Learning results in a change in behavior potential. It has two forms: we may learn through stamping in (memorizing, drill, conditioning) and through problem solving and understanding.

We learn to tap the typewriter at a certain place for S and at another place for T. We then form a connection between certain movements and their results. By frequent repetition of this connection we learn something in a mechanistic manner. Similarly, we may learn telephone numbers by heart or, as is done in psychological experiments, we may memorize pairs of nonsense syllables. By establishing such a connection, habits are formed and routine behavior established, especially when the experience or the behavior is reinforced by being rewarded or by appearing satisfactory and successful.

A second form of learning is through solving a problem. When in psychological experiments a problem is presented, the psychological field consists of two parts, the starting situation and the unsolved question, between which there is a gap. Understanding results from a reorganization of parts so that the gap is closed. When this process has been successfully concluded, the behavior potential has changed.

Learning by understanding may be illustrated by a variety of processes in ordinary life as well as in psychological economics. At this point it will be illustrated by considering how expectations are formed, an area to which the psychology of learning offers major clues.

Some expectations are based on repetition. A person may expect those things to happen that have happened before, and the frequency of his past experience—the number of reinforcements—as well as their recency may determine the

47

strength of his expectations. Having experienced the sequence *a-b-c-d* several times, the occurrence of *a-b* may arouse the expectation that *c-d* will follow. Listening to the first few words of a familiar poem arouses the expectation of the next few words. The more frequent and the more recent the past experience, the stronger the resulting expectation.

What happened yesterday, we expect to happen tomorrow as well. This principle of life enables us to proceed without constantly thinking, deliberating, being in a quandary. Only under unusual circumstances do we feel the need to deviate from this principle, which is embodied in the first form of learning, and to expect something to happen that differs greatly from what happened before.

Problem solving may enter into the process and result in an understanding of certain relationships, which may then produce the acquisition of insights not previously present. If and when a person perceives himself to be in a crossroad situation, he may try to solve the problem and to understand what is going on and what will happen. As a result of these processes he may arrive at expectations that do not represent extrapolations of past occurrences.

An important instance of problem solving consists of the reorganization of a situation as the result of major new developments, which make habitual behavior questionable or inappropriate. In such circumstances one may expect a reversal of ongoing trends or developments that have never before been experienced. Expectations people derive from established principles and theories may be viewed as indirect results of problem solving undertaken by others.

The outbreak of a war or the end of a war may be mentioned as extreme examples in which a reorganization of the psychological field is called for, and people's expectations will commonly result from attempts to understand the consequences of the new developments. Many lesser events, concerning the people themselves or the general situation, may also provide the impetus for reorganization and problem solving. Insightful learning may occur suddenly, without any reinforcement, or slowly and gradually. Its results will be important in determining collective economic behavior if the impetus affects very many people at the same time, that is, if the precipitating circumstances are widely known and perceived as significant.

To refer again to the problem of inflation: If inflationary expectations could be formed in no other way than by repetition, their strength would depend on the frequency of past experiences with price increases. The longer an inflationary period lasted and the stronger it was, the greater would be the expected price increases. But it does occur that even after a long period of price increases people do not expect inflation. It also occurs that after a period of stable prices, people do expect inflation. The outbreak of the Korean War, for instance, made some people think about its probable consequences and conclude that shortages and price increases would result from large-scale government expenditures on armaments. This is an example of the second form of learning.

A new understanding and the arousal of changed or new expectations do not happen without reasons of which people are aware and which they consider valid. True, people's understanding of what causes what may be erroneous, and the expectations may be without justification when considered by experts in the light of their knowledge of manifold circumstances of which people in general are not aware. The extent of human intelligence involved in problem solving should not be overestimated. Problem solving makes use of shortcuts and stereotypes and the search for reasons may be superficial and inadequate. The formation of new expectations is not always based on a careful consideration of all facets of a situation.[2]

The Individual and the Group

Up to now our analysis has been conducted in terms of the psychology of individuals. Are the principles of social psychology different? When we speak of groups, instead of individuals, must we look to psychological principles of a different kind?

A textbook of social psychology gives the following clear-cut answer to this question: "To understand [social behavior] we must study both individual life and group life, in terms of a single body of coherent concepts and principles" (Newcomb, 1950). True, psychological processes occur only in the individual; but the individual does not think and act in the same

[2] See George Katona (1940), (1951, Chapter 4), and (1972a). We shall return in Chapter 12 to the discussion of how expectations are formed.

way irrespective of whether he is or is not a member of a group. Action in groups—social behavior—may differ greatly from individual action, but must and can be explained by the same psychological principles. The cue to the understanding of group behavior is that the group plays the same role that was assigned earlier in this chapter to the whole situation or the context. Just as a stimulus is part of its whole or field, so is the individual part of his field, usually of his group.

We are then in a position to derive certain important principles of social psychology from our previous discussion. First, an individual item may be part of several different wholes and may differ according to the whole to which it belongs in the given situation. In terms of social psychology, this means that the individual may at certain times of the day be a factory worker or a student, in other words, he may belong to the group of workers or students. At other times, the same individual may be father and husband, his whole situation or group being represented by his family. At still other times, he may be a club member or a member of a political party.

Membership in a group refers to belonging in a psychological sense. In this sense, we are not family members, and not Americans, when we are fully engrossed in our work at the factory or in the classroom. The individual has a different role and function according to the group (whole) to which he belongs. It is not to be expected that the individual will behave the same way in different group situations.

The schema presented on page (46) on the relation of items or parts to the context in which they are perceived may be applied here as well. The capital letter A may stand for an individual rather than an item, and X and Y for the group to which the individual belongs, rather than the context.

In the group situation it is meaningful to speak of "group forces" or "group motives" (though groups do not have motives, group members may share motives). Conscious identification of an individual with his group is one instance of the effectiveness of such forces. Being subject to the same stimuli and the same requirements of the situation is another instance. The soldier marching in a group need not identify himself consciously with the other soldiers in his group for behavior to be group-determined. Similarly, buying by consumers or pricing by businessmen may be group-centered without identification with the group and without imitation. Imitation

50

and suggestion are phenomena that may reinforce the group situation and group coherence but are not necessary conditions of belonging to, or acting as a group. Reciprocal reinforcement of motives of different individuals belonging to the same group, "social facilitation," is a common phenomenon—in economic as in any other interpersonal behavior.

In addition to groups to which one belongs, there are "reference groups" from which an individual may derive standards for his behavior. He may measure his performance with reference to that of a certain group even when he is not a member of that group. Or a group situation as perceived by an individual may determine his attitudes even though he does not belong to that group. For example, a person moving to a wealthy part of the city, inhabited by people to whom he does not belong and by whom he is not accepted, may nevertheless adopt the opinions and behavior of his neighbors. Both group belonging and reference groups play a role, for example, in consumption expenditures.

Group belonging and group-centered motivational forces are usually most pronounced in groups composed of interacting members who are united in a face-to-face situation. Somewhat weaker forces result from belonging to a group in a general or imagined sense. The group that most commonly overrides the individual in determining action is the small group with which one is associated daily—the family, the work crew, the colleagues, or, in the case of an executive or an official, the corporation or agency. The broader groups of all workers, all businessmen, all government officials, or all Americans, or the reference groups, are less conducive to group feeling or group action.

Macro- and Microanalysis

While social psychology may be seen as not fundamentally different from individual psychology, some major regularities of macroeconomics do not apply to individuals. Most importantly, in the entire economy the amounts saved by all sectors are necessarily equal to the amounts invested; but on the individual level the equality does not hold because any individual person or firm may be saving and not investing at all, or may be investing borrowed funds far in excess of the amounts he has

51

saved. An individual's expenditures do not affect his own income; but in the aggregate, increased or reduced expenditures do expand or restrict the income flow. Macroeconomics develops regularities and establishes statistical laws that relate to aggregates only and not necessarily to individuals.

Yet aggregate data that refer to the entire economy as a unit, or to certain large parts of it as units, do not present a complete picture of the economy. They must be supplemented by microeconomic data, that is, information in which individual families or firms each represent a unit. Aggregative, or macroeconomic data give not only an incomplete but often a misleading account of an economic process or situation. Aggregative statistics may tell us, for example, that the national income—the income of all the people in the United States —rose from 600 to 630 billion dollars in a certain year. This is an increase of 5 percent of total income, or a 5 percent increase of average family income. It is possible—but very improbable—that in this case the income of every family rose by 5 percent. It is also possible that the income of half of the families rose by 10 percent and that of the other half remained unchanged, or that the income of a small number of families increased greatly while that of most families declined. Aggregates do not tell the whole story. They do not indicate what changes have taken place or what the current situation is. We need to know whether relatively few families received most of the 630 billion dollars, or whether the aggregate income was quite evenly distrubuted among all families. Information about the distribution of aggregates and of the changes in aggregates can serve to correct misleading impressions and to avoid false conclusions.

This is, however, only part of the argument. Microeconomic data—information on how aggregate income, savings, profits, etc., are distributed among individual families or firms—have still another function. They provide the link with psychological variables and the basis for a dynamic analysis of what happened and why it happened.

Our aim is to analyze behavior—decisions and actions of consumers and businessmen—and the motives, attitudes, and other factors underlying and determining behavior. Does the national economy "behave"? Can we study the motives and attitudes of all businessmen or all steel producers as a unit? Yes, provided "psychological groups" exist, the members of which are all subjectively in the same situation and therefore react uniformly. But this is not always the case and even when it is, it is not known in advance. Psychological analysis must therefore always be directed toward the individual unit. The decision formation of individual persons must be studied in order to determine the differences as well as the similarities, the individual as well as the group factors involved. Psychological data referring to individual units must be compared with economic and financial data—income, savings, sales, profits, etc.—referring to those same units, not to aggregates.

Two quotations may illustrate this point. In his analysis of the history of the 1920s, Joseph A. Schumpeter (1946) said at the 1945 meeting of the American Economic Association: "If, in a given year, one industry makes 100 millions and another loses 100 millions, these two figures do not add up to zero or, to put it less paradoxically, the course of subsequent events generated by this situation is not the same as that which would follow if both had made zero profits. This is one of the reasons why theories that work with aggregates only are so misleading." And Arthur F. Burns (1946) wrote in his annual report as director of the National Bureau of Economic Research: "Although bread index numbers or aggregates give useful summaries, they tell nothing of the processes by which they are fashioned."

The processes by which aggregate data are "fashioned" include the processes by which consumers and businessmen arrive at economic decisions, the end products of which add up to statistical aggregates. The analysis of the formation of these decisions—for example, why people reduce their rate of saving or firms increase their capital expenditures—can be conducted only at the level of individual families and firms. The situation that generates subsequent events—to use Schumpeter's words—is represented by microeconomic data, not by aggregates.

The Law of Large Numbers

Our discussion must be interrupted by a counterargument. Certain objections to our line of thought are important, not only because they are widely held, but also because they have a sound core and serve to clarify the meaning and use of microeconomic data.

You just can't mean what you say, some people may object. In studying economic behavior, it is just not possible to be concerned with individual families or individual firms as such. Suppose you analyze carefully the spending and saving of John Smith. You find out everything about his past and present, his income, his occupation, his family relationships, his health, his tastes, and so on; you make an inventory of everything he has—money, home, automobile, and so forth—and you get a full explanation of why he spent so much and saved so much. Suppose you even do this time-consuming job with many individuals, what do you have then? When economists say that they are interested in the principles of economic behavior, they do not mean the individual circumstances that make every single case different from every other. They are interested in the regularities persisting in very many or all cases.

The objections, then, become more general. Granted that individual families and individual firms do not behave in an automatic, mechanistic manner, still, so runs the argument, that does not matter for the economy as a whole. There is an "inertia of large numbers." Individual differences cancel out. Differences in motives and attitudes, and even the freedom of every single person or firm to act differently, are then of no interest and can be disregarded. The actions of very large groups of people or of all the people as a whole can be predicted from the given circumstances. The regularities of large numbers, which are the only ones that interest the economist, are susceptible to analysis without regard to the psychological differences and uncertainties prevailing in individual cases.

From this thesis follow specific statements on prediction. We are told: What an individual will do is uncertain, what thousands of individuals will do is not equally uncertain. Reliable predictions can be made on the probable actions of thousands of individuals but not on the probable actions of a few individuals, for, with respect to thousands of people or the entire economy, past relationships will repeat themselves. It is not possible to predict how each single person will use his money, but without knowing which individuals will buy cars or will save money, it is possible to predict how many cars will be bought and how much money will be saved jointly by all the American people. The law of large numbers is the basis of economic analysis and economic predictions, and aggregative economics alone is important and possible. Why should we lose our way in innumerable unimportant details?

Let us set down the true core of that argument. Consider first the simple case of tossing a coin. If I toss a coin once, I cannot tell whether it will fall heads or tails. The chances are equal; I may be right or wrong when I predict. But if I am going to toss the coin 1,000 times, I can make a number of well-justified predictions. I may predict, for instance, that I will not get 1,000 heads; the chances that my prediction will be wrong are very, very slight. I may further predict that of the 1,000 tosses there will be between 490 and 510 heads, and I can calculate the probability of that prediction.

These principles form the basis of actuarial tables. Life insurance companies cannot predict how long any individual will live. They can, however, predict how long a very large group of people, of equal age at present, will live on the average and can therefore calculate the life expectancy of an individual.

A second example to illustrate the application of the law of large numbers will serve also to point out the major condition of its validity. If an investor puts all his money into one single bond issue, he cannot predict with certainty that that issue will not default. Suppose, however, he diversifies his investment and purchases a bond of each of 100 different issues. Does this give him greater assurance? Can he say that total loss of his money—the default of all 100 bond issues—is less probable? Yes, under one condition. Insofar as the different bond issues are acted on by independent causes, the total loss of money invested in 100 issues is much less probable than the loss of money invested in one issue. If, however, the same cause—war or inflation, for example—affects all bond issues, the large number will not help. The same is true of tossing the coin. Or, to change the simile, if the dice are loaded, my prediction that I will not shoot number 6 one hundred times in a row may not come true. Actuarial tables apply only if each person's life span is determined independently of every other person's, and the same cause—say, an atomic bomb—does not wipe out all the people at one time.

More generally, the law of large numbers applies to economic situations if only random factors prevail. If the decisions of thousands of families or firms are due to independent causes, it is true that what thousands will do is more certain than what one will do. But if the same factors influence very many people at the same time in the same direction, the deviations add up instead of canceling out.

To be more specific: If it were true that changes in the proportion of consumers with optimistic or pessimistic expectations depend on random factors alone, there would be good reason to disregard these expectations. If, however, as will be shown in this book, waves of optimism or pessimism spread over very many people at about the same time because of the influence of systematic factors, a very different situation would prevail.

The systematic factor that brings about a fairly uniform change at about the same time among very many people may be readily identified. It is the acquisition of information. Because the same information, or very similar information, reaches millions of people at the same time and is apprehended by them in a similar manner, changes in attitudes resemble contagious diseases rather than movements in different directions, which cancel out.

We may develop the following general model of a change in attitudes and expectations. Such a change may be due to (*a*) information transmitted by mass media and comprehended by masses of people in a fairly uniform manner, or (*b*) personal experiences of individuals, or (*c*) random factors (including errors of measurement).

At any given time there will be individuals who are influenced by personal experiences (*b*) in one direction, and others who are influenced in the opposite direction. On the other hand, most commonly, public information (*a*) is either noninfluential or operates in the same direction with very many people.

If variable *a* is not influential, aggregate changes in consumer expectations will usually be small because the changes in individual expectations cancel out. Observing on successive occasions substantially unchanged distributions, the researcher cannot assume that most individuals have maintained their previous expectations; on the contrary, it is probable that among individuals there have been frequent changes in both directions (due to different personal experiences or to vacillation on the part of many people).

If variable *a* is effective and important, the aggregate changes in expectations will tend to be substantial. In this case

56

it is likely that contrary effects of personal experiences will be suppressed or lessened. Substantial aggregate changes in expectations may therefore be attributed to public information. They tend to occur without the presence of numerous cross-shifts in attitudes.

We have discussed the basic flaw in the assumption expressed above that what an individual will do is more uncertain than what thousands of individuals will do. The same factor influencing thousands of individuals may make it as difficult to predict mass action as individual action. One further question may be raised in this connection: Is it always true that what an individual will do is uncertain? Suppose the one person in question is myself, the writer, or you, the reader. It so happens that I can predict with great assurance whether or not I will buy a car during the next year. You may be able to predict whether you will marry next year, whether you will have an increase or decrease in income, whether you will buy a house. To be sure, in one or the other instance you may be uncertain, and one or the other of your predictions (expectations) may not come true. But it is not correct to say that there is no basis whatsoever for predicting what individuals will do. Individuals know or believe they know many things that will happen to them. And we—the social scientists—can question them. Furthermore, people are often not only able but also willing to give honest answers. Predictions about the future behavior of a few individuals are by no means certain, but it is questionable whether they are always more uncertain than predictions about the future behavior of many individuals. Because it is useful to ask individuals about what they have done, will do, and why, there are good reasons to use sample interview surveys as a major methodological tool of psychological economics.

What, then, is our purpose in investigating the behavior of individual families and firms? It is true that what we are ultimately interested in are regularities, that is, correspondences prevailing under similar conditions. But it is only by studying individual families and firms that we can learn whether or not regularities prevail, and under what conditions and in what groups of people they prevail. By means of such an analysis of the financial position and the decision formation of individuals it becomes possible to place the individual cases into homogeneous groups so that the law of large numbers can be applied. When large numbers of individual instances are found to be similar—when the same reactions are found under the same circumstances—we no longer run the risk of adding indiscriminately apples, pears, and oranges.

Since the objective of microeconomic analysis is not the description of individual cases, microeconomic data are presented as "distributions." Data about aggregate national income, for example, are supplemented by data on the distribution of income, that is, by information on the proportion of those who receive high, medium, and low incomes. Similarly, data on changes in income are expressed in terms of the frequency of those who had income increases and decreases (within the high-, medium-, and low-income groups).

Many microdata are of a psychological nature: In surveys we may determine, for example, which respondents feel better off than a few years earlier or which ones expect to be better off within a few years so that their behavior may be studied separately. Each group of respondents must consist of many individual cases—the more the better. The law of large numbers does apply and a "cell" (a homogeneous subgroup of individuals) consisting of many persons is greatly preferable to one consisting of only a few persons.

We conclude that a major requirement of present-day economics consists of the collection of microdata that serve to enrich our knowledge of macroprocesses. As an aside, it may be said that the situation with respect to psychology is just the reverse: psychological analysis of macroprocesses is needed to broaden the study of the psychology of individuals. We shall see in Chapter 13 that the collective learning of millions of individuals differs from individual learning. Therefore, what may be called social learning or the macrolearning process needs to be included, and the term macropsychology introduced into the discipline of psychology.

PART II
THE INFLUENCE OF ATTITUDES AND EXPECTATIONS IN THE SHORT RUN

5
THE USE OF ATTITUDES FOR THE PURPOSE OF PREDICTION

Instability of the economy is still one of America's most pressing problems.[1] In certain years during the 1950s and again during the 1960s there was a fairly general consensus that depressions and even recessions belonged to the past. Then in 1958 and again in 1970 sharply rising unemployment and declining incomes caused great suffering to some and made millions of people uneasy and anxious. Rapid inflation in the early 1970s also indicated that the endeavor to keep the economy on an even keel had failed.

At the same time the tools at the disposal of the government to stabilize and even to manage the economy became more numerous and more powerful. First of all, in an era of high rates of taxation and large government expenditures there exist "automatic stabilizers." Tax receipts go up in good times and down in bad times, which means that taxes help either to dampen a boom or to promote recovery by adjusting purchasing power according to the need of the times. Some government expenditures, such as unemployment benefits, likewise flow in a countercyclical pattern and may be increased or decreased when policy makers so desire. The flow of information to the policy makers has multiplied many times, so that there should be no problem about their becoming aware of the need to act. They are then in a position to initiate appropriate measures of fiscal and monetary policy—the former primarily through a change in tax rates, the latter through a change in the rate of increase in the money supply. In the 1960s even the

---

[1] Western Europe was subject to fewer and milder postwar recessions than the United States and, among others, Shonfield (1965, pp. 61 ff.) rightly emphasized the fact that economic growth was steadier there than in the past. Nevertheless, even in Western Europe recessions still do threaten.

expression "fine tuning" was used to describe what it was thought might be done by way of adjusting government policies to meet the needs of the economy.

The high hopes reposed in government efficacy were misplaced, not because they were premature but because they had no justification in fact. The government alone does not and cannot "manage" the economy. Millions of other decision makers—businessmen as well as masses of consumers—acting in unison need not and, repeatedly in the last twenty-five years, did not act in a countercyclical manner and indeed often countermanded the intentions of government policy. Then, too, the policy itself was frequently, and at crucial times, faulty. The availability of greatly increased amounts of economic statistics proved of no help because some of the statistical data tended to contradict each other and their interpretation as well as their theoretical basis remained controversial. Reliable economic forecasting remains a most important unfinished task and one in which behavioral economics will have to play a large role.

On the Theory of Forecasting

Not only policy decisions but most economic activities of business firms and consumers involve some forecasting. Even in ordinary life many of our decisions relate to the future and therefore contain assumptions about what will happen. The assumptions may be implicit and imprecise or they may be explicit and even expressed in precise numerical values. Scientific methods aim at replacing hunches, guesses, and implicit predictions by objectivity, replicability, and precision.

The first and perhaps oldest method of forecasting is projection. In the simplest case, the trend of one given variable during the recent past is plotted and the line is extended into the future through freehand extrapolation. The projection technique, of course, encompasses many variations. For instance, it is possible to omit certain past data in making the extrapolation because of their "unusual" nature, or to take into account the acceleration and deceleration of the past trend.

The method of projection becomes complicated and more useful when the projection is based on several variables and their interrelation. This may involve a complex task of analysis. For instance, in trying to predict the future population trend we may decide that we should not simply project the past trend, but rather take into account the three factors of mortality, fertility, and immigration or emigration. These three factors are then studied individually and projections are made concerning each.

The procedure is divided into three broad sectors —consumer, business, and government. The relations among the sectors are expressed in structural equations. Some major variables are projected on the basis of regression equations, which express the most appropriate relations between those variables and explanatory variables—for instance, the relations between business investment and profits or consumer expenditures and income. A major and fully justified function of solving several such equations simultaneously is to make quantitative estimates of how certain assumed changes in one variable would influence other variables or the entire system. Thus the repercussions of an increase in income or in tax rates on consumer expenditures or on the rate of unemployment may be calculated on the assumption that there are no other disturbances. In addition to this use, regression equations commonly serve to predict GNP and other broad aggregates. The exactitude with which these forecasts can be, and often are, expressed operates to blur the fact that the projections are valid only if the past relationships continue to prevail.

A second method of predicting is by analogy. Suppose we had asked ourselves in 1945 about production or employment trends during the first few years after World War II. Using the method of analogy we would have begun by studying the economic trends following World War I. Similarly, in order to foresee developments that are expected to occur after an inflationary period, we would study what happened following previous inflationary movements.

The business-cycle indicators compiled originally by the National Bureau of Economic Research may be viewed as analogy forecasts. Having identified past business cycles and the timing of peaks and troughs, a large number of statistical series are sorted into leading, coincidental, and lagging indicators according to their usual past performance. When most leading indicators show a decisive change, a similar change in the cycle is predicted. This prediction is valid only if it is possible to rely on the forthcoming cycle's being analogous to the average past cycle. Since this is not necessarily the case, the statistical

63

indicators, while representing a valuable tool in analyzing the large amount of data available every month, cannot provide a dependable method of forecasting. The mechanical use of changes in some leading indicators to predict other economic changes is rarely warranted.

Monetarists' predictions of changes in demand following changes in money supply are likewise based on analogy. Their weakness has been revealed by experience with great variations in the lead time of either the expansion or the contraction of the money supply before a similar change in demand followed.

Does a fundamentally different method of forecasting exist? It should be characterized by an absence of reliance on the notion that the past will repeat itself. Even though this is commonly the case, there are times when something new occurs or when discontinuities run counter to old-established relations. Behavior is often repetitive, but not always.

A third category of economic forecasts is based on anticipatory or *ex ante* variables.[2] Certain economic data represent past occurrences and at the same time indicate future happenings. Residential building permits are well-known data that fall into this category. A statistical agency collects, from courthouses and similar sources, information on these permits, which reflect past happenings, solid and reliable as many other series of past data on, for example, sales or taxes. While an upward or downward trend of past sales or prices does not necessarily signal the future trend, building permits are directly connected with subsequent building activity. To be sure, construction during the next period will be based not only on past but also on some future permits, and some permits may even be canceled. Nevertheless, trends in building permits do usually foreshadow future trends in residential construction. Unfilled orders for steel or machinery, for instance, also represent anticipatory variables.

Some past business data foreshadowing future trends are of a contractual nature, while others are less firm. Taking capital expenditures on a new factory as an example, contracts with builders or producers of machinery represent anticipatory data that may be tapped by statistical agencies. Yet, before con-

---

[2] They have been discussed before in Katona (1951, pp. 171 ff.) and (1960, pp. 59 ff.).

tracts are entered into, appropriations are made by directors or committees of corporations; even earlier, budgets, plans, and estimates are usually prepared and their records may be available. Still earlier, key decision makers may be contacted and asked about their intentions, expectations, or even guesses. When a representative sample of top executives is interviewed and the capital expenditures they expect to undertake are found to be higher than they were six months earlier, for example, there is good reason to expect the flow of business capital expenditures to grow.

Over the past twenty years much work has been done to extend the availability of this sort of information. Collection of data on budgets and plans, as well as on intentions, appears worthwhile, even though there is a greater probability of realization in the case of contracts entered into than in the case of plans either approved by directors or existing only in the minds of business executives or consumers. The statistical series of capital-expenditure plans, collected by the SEC and the Department of Commerce, as well as, separately, by McGraw-Hill's Economics Department, represent forecasts based on *ex ante* variables. These series were found to be successful predictors of aggregate trends during the postwar years.

Business expectations are also collected about what will happen rather than what the informant or his company will do. For instance, the U.S. Department of Commerce collects and publishes data on the sales expectations of business firms. Nevertheless, in the United States this kind of information is seldom used for systematic forecasting. It is different in Europe, where the IFO organization in Munich, Germany, and numerous related groups in other countries have for many years successfully used for forecasting purposes information obtained from samples of business firms about the direction of past and expected changes in sales, inventories, or orders. Data are collected on whether sales have gone up, remained unchanged, or gone down, but not on the magnitude of the change.

How about the consumer sector of the economy? Contracts or written records of what will be done in the future are not frequent in consumer affairs. Nevertheless, the notion is incorrect that the *ex ante* approach may be used with business firms that plan ahead and not with consumers who are far less sys-

65

tematic. In fact, anticipatory data were collected first from consumers. Intentions to buy major goods—homes for owner occupancy, automobiles, refrigerators and other large appliances—were determined in consumer surveys toward the end of World War II, when information on the size of pent-up demand was of great interest and the method of sample interview surveys became available.[3]

The planning period even for major consumer durables is frequently fairly short. The consumers' expressed buying intentions consist of some instances in which the transaction is already far advanced and of others in which survey respondents express nothing more than their desires and hopes. Nevertheless, a comparison of the frequency of such intentions as determined at a given time with those at earlier times may yield an indication of the direction of change in actual purchases.[4]

Most buying intentions represent a relatively late intercept in the process extending from first becoming aware of a felt need to the consummation of the purchase. Furthermore, reliable forecasting can hardly be based on the projection into the future of any single variable. Conclusions are more effectively drawn from a variety of explanatory variables and their interrelation. Such a variety of consumer *ex ante* variables was derived from psychological hypotheses about willingness to buy and intervening variables. If attitudes represent predispositions to action, they should point to future behavior. If, furthermore, the attitudes of masses of people change in a systematic manner, differences in the distribution of certain attitudes obtained in a sample survey conducted at Time Point 3 in comparison to those obtained in a survey at an earlier Time Point 2, or at a still earlier Time Point 1, should indicate a change in the predisposition to spend—willingness to buy—by very many consumers. In simplest terms: The goal of psychological economics was to improve economic forecasts by determining the presence or absence of waves of optimism and

[3] The first surveys on consumer buying intentions were devised in 1944 by the Division of Program Surveys in the Department of Agriculture, the predecessor organization of the Michigan Survey Research Center. They were sponsored by the Federal Reserve Board. The author of this book served as Project Director for the economic surveys of the Division of Program Surveys.

[4] Success or failure of this procedure will be discussed in the next chapter.

confidence as against waves of pessimism and mistrust among the entire population. If it were possible to introduce suitable measuring devices, namely, interview questions, in a series of successive surveys conducted with representative samples, the goal appeared realizable.

These considerations led the author of this book to devise, shortly after World War II, periodic surveys conducted by the Survey Research Center of The University of Michigan. The experience with these surveys will be related in the following chapters. At this point it suffices to say that change in consumer sentiment served as an *ex ante* variable contributing to the prediction of one important cyclical factor, consumers' expenditures on durable goods and their discretionary expenditures in general.

Changes in the direction in economic activity—cyclical turning points—constitute the greatest difficulty for forecasts based on projections of past relationships. Forecasting through *ex ante* variables is particularly suited to ascertaining whether or not at a given time the prospects are for the continuation or the reversal of the prevailing trend.

Explanations of Change in Consumer Expenditures

In order to use consumer attitudes and expectations for the purpose of forecasting it is necessary to measure these subjective variables or their changes. Before discussing the problems of measurement, the question of whether or not attitudes are needed to explain consumer behavior must be raised again from an angle somewhat different from before, for John Maynard Keynes (1936) provided a theoretical approach which, if correct, might explain the consumption function without resort to attitudes or expectations.[5]

The functional relation between the disposable income of the community and expenditures on consumption out of that income is called the propensity to consume. This is, thus

[5] Analysis of Keynes's theory of lags in consumer demand in the light of modern psychology played a substantial role in the development of psychological economics (see Katona, 1951, Chapters 7 and 8). Even though that analysis was more timely in 1951 than in 1975, a summary of the earlier discussion is included in this book because it helps clarify several important issues.

defined, an aggregative relation and, although it would be possible to speak of the propensity of individual units to consume, we shall reserve the term for the relationship prevailing in the entire economy. Keynes, in introducing the concept, defines the propensity to consume in terms of wage units rather than money, thus eliminating from the discussion fluctuations of the purchasing power of money income. He then presents his proposition that "the propensity to consume is a fairly stable function so that, as a rule, the amount of aggregate consumption mainly depends on the amount of aggregate income" (1936, p. 96).

What is the basis for that statement? Keynes admitted that the amount a community spent on consumption might depend not only on income but also on other considerations, both objective and subjective. Among the former, he recognized the role of fluctuations in prices and changes in tax rates but obviated the necessity of considering them by virtue of having defined income level as disposable income in wage units. Other objective circumstances, for example, the prevailing interest rate, are found to be of secondary importance. The subjective and social incentives, on the other hand, he assumed could be ignored because they were believed to change slowly. Motives to save and to consume were thought to depend on institutions, conventions, and education and, therefore, to differ in different cultures, but not to account for short-term changes in consumption. It was therefore argued that in the short run consumption must depend mainly on the rate at which income is earned.

Keynes viewed the central issue of the consumption function as being consumers' reactions to changes in their income. He coped with this problem by his discovery of a "fundamental psychological law":

> The fundamental psychological law, upon which we are entitled to depend with great confidence both a priori from our knowledge of human nature and from the detailed facts of experience, is that men are disposed, as a rule and on the average, to increase their consumption as their income increases, but not by as much as the increase in their income (1936, p. 96).

Similarly, according to Keynes, people decrease the amounts they spend as their income decreases, but not by as much as the decrease in their income. Let us repeat the thesis, in the form of three questions and answers. (1) When, under what conditions, is a community willing to widen or to narrow the gap between its income and its consumption? Answer: Only when its income increases or decreases. Except for this circumstance, the propensity to consume will remain stable . (2) If there is a change in the income-consumption relation, what will be the direction of that change? Answer: When income increases, the gap between income and consumption will be widened; when income decreases, it will be narrowed. (3) What will be the extent of the change in the income-consumption relation? Answer: People will spend a smaller part (and save a larger part) of their income when income increases, and spend a larger part (and save a smaller part) when income decreases. The marginal rate of increase (decrease) in consumption will not be as large as the marginal rate of increase (decrease) in income.

The first answer reiterates Keynes's thesis about the stability of the propensity to consume. The second, he says, is "obvious" and "beyond dispute." "When our income is increased, it is extremely unlikely that this will have the effect of making us either spend less or save less than before" (Keynes, 1937, p. 220). That we will spend the same after our income is increased is also unlikely, since we will have more money at our disposal. Will we, therefore, spend all that we gained in income, or will we increase the amount we spend so that the proportion of income spent will be the same at the new level as it was before, or will we spend a smaller proportion of the higher income than of the previous lower income? In due time, we will reach the spending rate characteristic of the new, higher income level. But the adjustment to that new income level, according to Keynes, is slow.

For a man's habitual standard of life usually has the first claim on his income, and he is apt to save the difference which discovers itself between his actual income and the expense of his habitual standard; or, if he does adjust his expenditure to change in his income, he will over short periods do so imperfectly. Thus a rising income will often be accompanied by increased saving, and a falling income by decreased saving, on a greater scale at first than subsequently (1936, p. 97).

The argument is presented in terms of individual families. It is a psychological statement that cannot be true of the aggregate economy unless it is true, as a rule, of individuals. Here, then, we find a psychological principle of behavior of which psychologists were not aware until it was propounded by an economist.

It follows from the considerations just presented that economic analysis need not be concerned with disturbances originating in consumer behavior, because increases or decreases in consumer spending can be derived from changes in other economic magnitudes. Consumers spend either the same proportion of their income as before or, if they change their rate of spending, they do so in response to changes in their income in a way that is regular and predictable. It is in business investments alone, and in government surpluses or deficits, that changes in the income flow must originate. "In Keynes' scheme investment is a free variable, while consumption is rigidly and passively tied to income."[6]

Contradiction of a theory, or its refinement through the incorporation of additional considerations, is possible on two levels. One, the empirical test, that is, the confrontation of the theory with reality, constitutes a slow process. Keynesians in general have pointed to a confirmation of the theory in some rather distant past instances and tended to disregard the frequently noted "wanderings" of the consumption function during the Great Depression of the 1930s, World War II, and its aftermath. Three decades after World War II, to be sure, evidence of the instability of the consumption function in the United States has become overwhelming.

A different level of scrutiny of a theoretical proposition consists of its analysis. Three major counterarguments may be raised against the Keynesian position. First, Keynes's view that habitual practices influence all consumer expenditures may have been correct a hundred years ago when incomes were spent mostly on nondurables and services, but today in the United States expenditures on durables are important and are usually not habitual. Possibly, then, these expenditures should behave in the same manner as savings are assumed to behave: An increment in income, not used for habitual expenditures, would then be used either for durable goods or for saving; when income declines, habitual expenditures are not im-

[6] See Burns (1947).

70

mediately adjusted downward and therefore less money remains either for durables or for saving. In other words, it might be held that amounts either saved or spent on durables would increase disproportionately when national income goes up and decrease disproportionately when it goes down. Such a view, which would represent a substantial departure from Keynesian principles, would not differentiate between money spent for durable goods and money saved.

The second major objection to Keynes's psychological law is that adjustments to income increases cannot be considered as merely the reverse of adjustments to income decreases. The effects of reward are usually not just the opposite of the effects of punishment. It is conceivable that delay in adjusting habitual expenditures to income changes may prevail in the one case, but not in the other. Part of the Keynesian argument appears well supported by studies of noneconomic behavior: habits are sticky under the impact of adverse developments; it is a hardship to abandon pleasurable practices which have become part and parcel of a person's manner of living. Therefore it would be understandable if adjustments of usual spending patterns to declines in income, subjectively a most difficult process, were delayed as long as possible. When, however, income goes up, habits acquired during a period of previous lower-income levels may not be sticky. Upward adjustments of living standards are pleasurable and easy. Such adjustments may be instantaneous or may even occur prior to the income increases as an effect of expectations. This possibility brings us to our third objection to Keynes's psychological law.

Keynes, who assigns great importance to the expectations of businessmen in shaping their policies, does not take expectations into account as influencing aggregate consumer behavior. He does list consumer expectations among the "objective factors" that influence the propensity to consume but asserts:

> *Changes in expectations of the relation between the present and the future level of income.*—We must catalogue this factor for the sake of formal completeness. But, whilst it may affect considerably a particular individual's propensity to consume, it is likely to average out for the community as a whole. Moreover, it is a matter about which there is, as a rule, too much uncertainty for it to exert much influence (1936, p. 95).

71

The notion that expectations usually cancel out may have again been justified in an era when most people who were not entrepreneurs were uninformed about business developments and were not subjected to fairly uniform news transmitted by mass media. Today, however, changes in consumer expectations tend to be uniform and to spread rather than to cancel out. It is thus no longer acceptable to explain fluctuations of durable goods expenditures by means of past income changes alone and to ignore expectations. And if expectations are taken into consideration, they must be seen as something more than simple extrapolations of past happenings. There are good reasons to believe that today expectations influence both individual and mass behavior and frequently do so in a manner different from the influence of past developments.

Measurement of Expectations

The concept of expectations was introduced into economic theory many years ago, primarily by Swedish economists. Nevertheless, analysis of cyclical fluctuations made little use of expectations. The principal reason for this neglect was the failure to develop means of quantifying and measuring expectations. Without resorting to measurement, it is not possible to test hypotheses about the influence of expectations on spending-saving behavior. Toward the end of World War II, however, the development of the sample interview survey made it possible to measure the change in the frequency of different kinds of consumer expectations. The process of arriving at the point of knowing what kinds of attitudes and expectations would provide indications of changes in consumers' willingness to buy was long and painstaking.

The starting point was the notion that fluctuations in spending and saving can only derive from psychological predispositions that are subject to fairly frequent variations. Neither the Oedipus complex nor differences in childhood upbringing because of either stern or permissive parents could be expected to contribute to an explanation of changes in sentiment, say, from times of prosperity in 1928 to times of depression in 1930. Fortunately, a variety of attitudes and expectations were available that were not of early origin and not inflexible.

All attitudes have situational determinants as well as a personality basis. In the case of some attitudes, however, either the situational or the personality aspect predominates. All at-

72

titudes tend to become habitual, reinforced by repeated action or reiteration. Yet some become deeply ingrained habits while others, held for a short time, may easily be changed. Honesty, punctuality, or conservatism, for instance, are personality traits that give rise to attitudes in the former category. No doubt, such attitudes may be influenced by changing conditions or new experiences, but to a much smaller extent than other attitudes.

It has been demonstrated that some attitudes relevant, for instance, to political behavior and voting—such as conservatism or liberalism, favoring the Republican or Democratic party—are acquired fairly early in life and may remain in force through an entire lifetime. But obviously, with some people at least, the events that occur before an election or the personality of a candidate may give rise to new attitudes that may influence their action.

Certain enduring attitudes have become part of the psychological makeup of practically all businessmen at a given time and in a given country (honesty or concern with profits, for instance). Other attitudes differ from person to person—as, for example, attitudes toward risk taking and speculation —though they, too, may be acquired in childhood or during early business experiences and may endure over long periods of time. Finally, there are attitudes that vary from time to time and develop in response to changes in the environment.

The concern of psychological economists was with attitudes that were variable because they were influenced by economic developments—both on a personal and on a national level —and that, in turn, influenced reactions to these developments. Expecting or not expecting inflation or recession would belong in this category, even though they are associated with more enduring attitudes as well as with such personality traits as being of a basically optimistic or pessimistic disposition.

The concept of intervening variables was first applied to economics in connection with the study of reactions to changes in income. Relating major consumer expenditures to one year's income appeared unjustified because of the known variability of income.[7] Taking into account, in addition to current income,

---

[7] See Katona (1949a). The discussion in that early paper is to some extent related to the differentiation between permanent and transitory income by Milton Friedman (1957), but differs from Friedman's concepts, which have no psychological connotation.

the income of the previous year or of several previous years likewise appeared insufficient because of the possibility of radical differences in the subjective meaning of an increase or a decrease in income. An income increase may be subjectively unsatisfactory if it is considered temporary, that is, if it is expected to be followed by a decrease, or if it amounts to less than what is expected, or what seems justified, or what members of a reference group have been getting. Contrariwise, an income decline might appear satisfactory under certain exceptional conditions. Willingness to buy was assumed to be influenced not by the income change alone but by the subjective meaning of the change. Therefore it appeared necessary to find out, through questions addressed to a representative sample, how people felt about their personal financial progress and what changes they expected in personal finances, both in the short and in the long run. [8]

Those questions proved to be more appropriate than questions about income even in periods of fairly stable prices. It was found, for example, that for many blue-collar workers, direct questions about income expectations produced little relevant information. Moreover, most workers understood the questions as pertaining to wage rates which, in their opinion, either rose gradually or remained unchanged but could not conceivably decline. Information about the number of hours to be worked and therefore about prospective changes in total income was not available to most workers, and they often had not even vague expectations on these matters. Thus, lengthy questioning about personal financial prospects frequently failed to indicate people's feelings of security and degree of confidence. A somewhat similar situation was found among many white-collar workers in steady positions, such as government employees and teachers. To some extent even employees of large corporations were found to be unable to envisage the possibility of financial setbacks and differentiated only between faster and slower advancement. Thus, many of these people, too, proved rather insensitive to questions about income expectations.

---

[8] The decision to substitute questions about changes in the personal financial situation for questions about income changes and income expectations was thus taken in the early 1950s without considering the impact of inflation. The relation of price changes to past and expected changes in the personal financial situation will be analyzed in Chapter 12.

Restricting the study of consumer sentiment to personal financial attitudes appeared unjustified on other grounds as well. Since people live in groups rather than in isolation, not only what happens to themselves but also what happens to their relatives, friends, and neighbors, and even to their community and country, influence their attitudes. Finally, for methodological reasons, clues to affective as well as cognitive changes had to be sought in several different ways rather than in one way only. Asking questions about other people's prospects or the prospects of the economy was expected to produce insights beyond those obtained from respondent-oriented questions.

These considerations led to survey questions concerning peoples' information about, attitudes toward, and expectations of business-cycle developments. What people know about recent changes in economic trends, and the news they have heard and can recall, obviously represent highly variable items of perception and cognition. Expectations about what will happen in the economy may be thought of as clues to feelings of confidence and security or lack of confidence and uneasiness.

Survey questions about these matters have frequently been misunderstood. The question "Do you think the next five years will be years of unemployment and depression, or of prosperous times, or what?" was once ridiculed by the comment that the Survey Research Center "asks Southern sharecroppers and unskilled laborers to make five-year business-cycle forecasts!" Indeed, all members of a representative sample are asked this question—business leaders and economists, as well as laborers. Many people say at first that they don't know or "Who am I to say?" but most of them can be induced to express an opinion. At certain times a large and at other times a small proportion of the people reply in an optimistic manner. It is the changes in the distribution of optimistic or pessimistic replies from one time to the next that are sought as clues to changes in willingness to buy. The question is not intended to induce people to make a forecast; it represents an indirect way of probing whether at the time of the interview people feel more or less confident about the economy. Intervening variables that shape people's responses must often be studied in such an indirect way.

An inquiry about the extent of economic improvement or

75

deterioration that respondents expected was found to be of little value because answers to such questions fell outside the range of most people's way of thinking. The findings on expected business conditions, obtained with samples interviewed at different points of time, could be compared in two respects. First, the degree of uncertainty could be measured. The proportion of a representative sample of all consumers, and also of such major segments of consumers as age and income groups, that could not be prompted to express an opinion on the direction in which the economy was moving proved to be an important indicator in itself. Uncertainty is not just a neutral factor, expressing indifference or absence of information. In most instances, being uncertain about what will come represents a feeling that dampens initiative. Thus an increase in the proportion of uncertain people proved an adverse indicator.

Disregarding uncertain respondents, the relation of those who expected improvement to those who expected deterioration in business conditions could be ascertained. Changes in the ratio of the two answers provided the second useful measure.

The wording of the questions about economic trends also caused problems. Answers to the question whether business and the economy would be better or worse, for example, a year later than they were at the time proved difficult to interpret, since they depended on opinions about the current situation. The highest frequency of the answer "Things will be better a year from now" was obtained during recessions. The most fruitful question, chosen after much experimentation, simply asks whether, speaking of business conditions as a whole, the next year will be good or bad. If the question is asked once, the answers are of little value. Many people do not like to complain, and at certain times there may prevail an underlying optimistic bias in our society. But the extent of the difference in the number of people answering "good" or "bad" has undergone substantial and often rapid shifts from one time to another. These changes are taken as indications of greater or lesser optimism and confidence and are studied regarding both short-range and longer-range economic trends.

A third and final area of relevant attitudes, beyond attitudes toward personal finances and business conditions, concerns the market situation. In this respect, again, information on external conditions may or may not be available to consumers

76

and may or may not alter attitudes. Yet satisfaction or dissatisfaction with prices and market conditions and the assortment of goods offered can be studied to discover favorable or unfavorable changes. Studies carried out over several years revealed that a simply worded question served the purpose of indicating changes in people's sentiment. "Is this, in your opinion, a good time to buy or a bad time to buy (cars, appliances, houses, etc.)" has been asked to reveal consumers' underlying attitudes rather than to obtain their rational judgments. A follow-up question, "Why do you think so?" provided significant additional information. Reactions to recent past and expected price trends greatly influenced the answers to this question and the frequency of favorable or unfavorable mentions of price trends could be determined. On the other hand, questions about expected price movements and their magnitude, taken in isolation, proved to be of no value in measuring changes in consumers' willingness to buy. As will be shown in studying the psychology of inflation (Chapter 9), the relation of price increases to spending and saving is rather complex.

Methods of Measurement

In the late 1940s the Survey Research Center of The University of Michigan conducted two surveys each year in which a variety of consumer attitudes and expectations were determined. In the 1950s there were three such surveys each year and beginning with 1960 the surveys were conducted at quarterly intervals. Parts of the questionnaires used in these surveys were identical, including inquiries about personal finances, business trends, and market conditions. In addition, in most surveys unique questions relating to information about and attitudes toward new specific developments were inserted. For instance, questions were asked about the stock market or interest rates following substantial movements, or about political events, domestic and foreign, when they were particularly relevant.

Some thirty to forty questions were asked in each survey, and the need for a simple summary measure of consumer sentiment soon became apparent. An *Index of Consumer Sentiment* was constructed in 1952 and has been published at regular intervals since 1955. Following some changes made in the first few years, the *Index* has consisted of five questions asked in identical form in all surveys. Two questions relate to personal finances: whether the family is financially better off, worse off, or in the same situation as a year earlier, and whether it expects to be better off, worse off, or the same a year hence. Two questions concern business trends: whether the next twelve months and the next five years will bring good or bad times for the economy as a whole. A fifth question regarding market conditions asks whether it is a good or a bad time to buy durable goods. (Similar questions are asked about automobiles and houses separately but are not included in the *Index*.)

The answers to the two questions on business trends were found to fluctuate to a larger extent than those to the other three questions and were thus responsible for a sizable part of the predictive value of the *Index*.[9]

The answers given by respondents to each of the five questions were grouped into three categories: (1) up, better, or good, (2) same, no change, or uncertain, and (3) down, worse, or bad. The *Index* was constructed by deducting the proportion of responses of the third type from the proportion of responses of the first type (and adding 100 in order to avoid negative values). This method of calculation is identical with giving a weight of 2 to responses of the first type, a weight of 1 to responses of the second type, and a weight of 0 to responses of the third type. The *Index* is published for all families as well as for high-income families separately after selecting a base period, which is made equal to 100.

All attitudinal questions asked, and not just the five *Index* questions, will be used in the subsequent discussion. No doubt the *Index* itself is far from ideal; perhaps it should have been expanded or revised in the 1960s or 1970s. This task was not carried out because the payoff obtained from a variety of attempted revisions proved to be insignificant.

The construction of the *Index* was worthwhile insofar as it greatly increased the publicity given to periodic measures of consumer attitudes. For instance, the major government publication of data on economic fluctuations, *Business Conditions Digest*, includes the *Index of Consumer Sentiment* among the

[9] This was first demonstrated by Adams (1964). Regarding common factors in the index components, see Curtin (1973).

data it regularly publishes. On the other hand, some students of economic trends had the impression that the only information provided by the Survey Research Center's studies was the *Index*, and used it without regard to other data or its theoretical foundation. It should be emphasized that the attitude measures have a dual function. They serve not only to provide predictions of probable short-run trends in consumers' discretionary expenditures but also to indicate the reasons for the trends. Information about why consumer expenditures have increased or decreased in the recent past and why they are expected to increase or decrease in the near future contributes to an understanding of economic developments. Chapter 7 will be devoted to the discussion of these findings.

One fairly simple question introduced in the 1950s that has not yet been mentioned helps greatly in determining the reasons for changes: "During the last few months, have you heard of any favorable or unfavorable changes in business conditions?" More people answer this question in the affirmative than are able to reply to the follow-up question, "What did you hear?" (The answer "I forgot" or "I don't recall" helps those respondents who do not wish to appear ignorant.) The proportion of American people who give a substantive reply to this question and mention economic developments is in itself an interesting indicator. In addition, the news mentioned by respondents is classified as either favorable or unfavorable. Changes in the proportion of these two groups serve as significant indicators.

The most important clues about what makes consumers become more optimistic, or more pessimistic, at a given time are derived from the interviewing methods used by the Survey Research Center.[10] This organization conducts conversational interviews in which rapport is established with the respondents, who are encouraged to answer the questions in their own words. Two types of questions are used, closed and open. The former may be answered by yes or no, true or false, or by choosing one of several alternatives presented (multiple choice). Simple factual questions are usually asked in a closed form (e.g., "Do you own a car?") and many attitudinal questions are asked in the multiple-choice form (for instance, the *Index* questions cited above). Open questions can only be answered in the respondent's own words, which the interviewer takes

---

[10] More about these methods will be found in the Appendix to this book.

down verbatim (or as closely verbatim as possible). The question mentioned above about business news—"What did you hear?"—may serve as an example.

Most productive of the open questions is the simple probe that follows all attitudinal questions of the multiple-choice type (including the *Index* questions). Whatever respondents answer about expecting to be better or worse off or about times being good or bad to buy durables, for instance, they are asked "Why do you say so?" or "Why do you think so?" Replies to these questions not only clarify and sometimes even rectify the answer originally given but also yield quantifiable data, the changes of which from one period to the next may be most revealing. The frequency of references to prices, government measures, political events, and the like, point to developments that, at a given time, are so salient that they are mentioned without direct questions about them.

Before turning to survey results, a final introductory remark must be made. The Survey Research Center publishes all its survey data, as well as their interpretation, so as to submit its findings to the scrutiny of scholars.[11]

For many years the Survey Research Center was alone in collecting and publishing information on change in consumer attitudes. Some such information—primarily about intentions to buy—was provided later also by the Bureau of the Census and by private market research agencies. The best known among the latter is the Sindlinger organization, which conducts very frequent brief surveys over the telephone but unfortunately does not regularly publish its complete findings.

The use made by the Survey Research Center of survey data on consumer attitudes and expectations spread to many foreign countries. Canada and several countries in Western Europe initiated frequent consumer surveys.[12] Then, in 1972, a development occurred that cannot fail to enhance the impor-

---

[11] The quarterly reports are sent originally only to survey participants whose financial contributions make the surveys possible. Brief press releases are issued promptly and full reports including all data are published later. In the 1950s the survey reports were published in the *Federal Reserve Bulletin*. Later, when private business and grants from foundations paid for the surveys, the Survey Research Center itself was the publisher of the series of monographs entitled *Survey of Consumer Finances* (annually, 1960 through 1974). For over twenty-five years the attitudinal surveys were interlaced with financial surveys conducted once a year.

[12] See Shapiro and Angevine (1969) and Strumpel et al. (1970).

tance of psychological economics. The top governing board of the Common Market Organization initiated the collection of attitudinal data at regular intervals in order to contribute both to the diagnosis and to the prediction of consumer demand. Following the example set in the United States, periodic data are collected on attitudes toward personal finances, business trends, and market conditions. The project began by using uniform questionnaires in France, West Germany, Holland, Belgium, and Italy with large representative samples. Scientific progress is bound to profit from the availability of comparable data in many countries.[13]

Expectations and Forecasting

Before closing our discussion of methodology, we shall take up again the question of the relation between expectations and forecasting. In a negative way, the relation has already been characterized. It has been pointed out that attitudes and expectations would not serve the purpose of forecasting if it were true (a) that most attitudes were fleeting and elusive, depending on the mood of the respondent, so that data obtained from the same person on successive days might differ greatly, (b) that most attitudes constituted unchanging personality traits acquired in early childhood, (c) that changes in attitudes among different individuals and groups would usually cancel out, and (d) that past trends of income and prices could serve as appropriate proxies for income and price expectations. It has also been indicated that none of these assumptions is correct.

No doubt, the predictive value of expectations would be diminished if the typical change in expectations consisted of small fluctuations in one direction in one period and in the reverse direction in the subsequent period. Moreover, the use of expectations for the purpose of forecasting would be of little value if aggregate spending-saving behavior were to change at the same time as the change in expectations because it takes several weeks to conduct and evaluate surveys in which expec-

[13] The data are regularly published by the Commission of European Communities in Brussels. In 1973 Australia instituted surveys that use the Survey Research Center questions and methods.

tations are measured. But neither of these conditions was found to be the rule in consumer behavior.

The most important positive aspects of the use of psychological factors as tools of economic forecasting may now be expressed as follows: The predictive value of expectations increases when (a) the observed change in expectations is substantial and lasting, and (b) the observed change continues in the same direction during the subsequent period for which predictions are made. Both circumstances were observed frequently though there were also times when the changes in sentiment were minor or fluctuated from one period to the next.

In general, the predictive value of expectations is based on the following proposition: When a trend of changed expectations is established, it will be reversed only slowly and gradually—unless major unexpected developments take place. The first part of this proposition is derived from the theorem that social learning takes place slowly and gradually. It takes time, usually at least several months, for news or information different from that prevalent in the preceding period to spread to many people and be reinforced by word of mouth.[14] This slow, gradual acquisition of information by millions of people may result in a substantial and enduring change of expectations. Such an improvement or deterioration of collective attitudes is commonly followed by a plateau or by insignificant ups and downs before it is reversed. The reversal is hardly ever sudden or quick when it consists of an improvement following a period of deterioration and stagnation. But shocking news, which creates misgivings and fear among millions of people, may represent an exception to the generalization that the response to new information is slow and gradual.

Attitudes and expectations themselves do not represent forecasts. They are but the ingredients of forecasts. Consumers' discretionary demand is a function both of ability and willingness to buy. Attitudes and expectations indicate changes in the latter. Major developments in the former may either reinforce or counteract the indications derived from measures of attitudes and expectations. The same is true of substantial changes in supply conditions, interest rates, or measures of government as well as business policy. Forecasting remains a difficult task and represents to some extent an art rather than a

[14] This point will be discussed further in Chapter 13.

82

science, because it calls for the integration of several ingredients. Most commonly, such integration depends on the judgment of the forecaster. It remains to be seen whether in due time an incorporation of anticipatory variables in equation systems representing the functioning of the entire economy will be successful and will serve to make forecasting more scientific.

6
PREDICTING ECONOMIC FLUCTUATIONS

Three stages of research on the predictive value of attitudes may be distinguished. The first consists of the development of a set of hypotheses concerning willingness to buy as an intervening variable that mediates between information received (stimuli) and discretionary purchases (responses). The development of methods and tools that may serve as measures of change in willingness to buy constitutes the second stage. The third stage consists of testing the hypotheses under varying conditions—upswing, downswing—as they actually occurred. In fact, of course, the three stages were far from separate, although the first began much earlier than the other two and some progress in the second had of necessity to precede the third. But empirical tests were conducted long before the first two stages were completed and the results of the tests changed to some extent the hypotheses as well as the methods used.

Our present concern is with the major form of the third stage, namely, with what has been called the aggregative or time-series test of the predictive value of attitudes. The question in this instance is: Did our measures of change in the attitudes and expectations of the American people foreshadow their discretionary purchases? What is studied is what may be called "macrorelations," that is, the relationship between attitudes and actions of all consumers. This relation alone is important for forecasting economic trends. The relation of individual attitudes to individual behavior, studied in the "cross-section test," will be discussed briefly later (Chapter 12) because of its theoretical importance.

Which aggregate expenditures and purchases would provide the best test of the predictive value of attitudes? As said before, there are no reliable data on total discretionary consumer expenditures. We had to be satisfied with data on durable goods and looked, in the main, at three dependent variables, namely,

number of new cars purchased,
dollar amount of consumer expenditures on durables, and
dollar amount of installment debt incurred (mainly on
durables).

These data are, admittedly, far from ideal because some
purchases of cars and other durables (especially small durables) are not discretionary, because business purchases of cars
cannot be excluded, and because important discretionary expenditures on travel, hobbies, and services are excluded.

When, in what kinds of periods, is the predictive value of
attitudes best tested? One may differentiate between (1)
periods in which no major new developments occur and the
prevailing trend continues and (2) crucial periods characterized by turning points. In the former, a "naive model," postulating that "tomorrow's weather will be the same as today's
weather," would yield correct predictions. Even then, scientific
forecasting has an important function because it is known only
after the fact that there was no change in the economic trend.
Nevertheless, it can be demonstrated only for periods of substantial change and especially for periods in which the direction of consumer activity undergoes a change that attitudinal
data do foreshadow large changes in the economy and are indispensable for that purpose (because the changes cannot be
predicted from an analysis of such traditional economic variables as income, inventories, past purchases, or liquid assets).

In studying the performance of attitudinal measures in crucial periods we must be aware of circumstances that may detract from their usefulness. First, major unexpected developments may impair the predictive value of expectations. If the
period to which the expectations relate should witness the unexpected outbreak of a war, for example, it is clear that all bets
would be off. Incidents in the cold war may also change the
outlook suddenly, as was the case at the time of the U-2 incident. Abrupt changes in expectations may also result from
such events as riots, or an unexpected proposal to change income taxes. Finally, and obviously, a prediction made for automobile sales in a certain quarter may prove false if a large
strike should occur in that quarter in the auto industry.

Secondly, one could envisage a situation in which government measures would be taken to counteract unfavorable
trends indicated by surveys of attitudes and expectations. The

86

success of such measures could be considered the greatest accomplishment of a prediction while at the same time it would result in preventing the prediction from coming true.

Finally, the opposite outcome may be the consequence of self-fulfilling expectations. If the prediction of a recession, for instance, should be widely publicized and induce consumers and businessmen to postpone many of their desired expenditures, the result would be to increase the probability that the prediction would come true.

All these difficulties in testing the predictive value of attitudes must be viewed as rare occurrences that hardly detract from the possibility of testing propositions in crucial periods. Major developments are rare almost by definition and most usually they are not unexpected; thus, they are reflected in people's anticipations as determined in the surveys. Furthermore, acceptance of attitudinal surveys by government, business, and consumers is far from universal. At least at the present time effective countermeasures are not initiated as a consequence of the survey findings, nor do people follow the survey data to an extent that would make them self-fulfilling.

The data on the predictive value of attitudes and expectations will be presented in two sections. The first consists of an analysis of crucial periods. In considering the major turning points during the twenty-five years following World War II as determined by hindsight, we ask how the attitudinal measures performed at those times. For example, we may look at the performance of the attitudinal data before, during, and after the major recession that began early in 1970.

This sort of study is obviously not sufficient. Attitudinal data might provide false leads by disclosing turning points that did not occur, thus detracting from their usefulness. Therefore, in a second section we shall look at what the attitudinal measures indicated at all times, abandoning the distinction between crucial and noncrucial periods. Another reason for this procedure is that it is the one commonly used by most econometricians.

We shall look primarily at *what* was predicted at different times—that is, whether such measures as the Index of Consumer Sentiment went up or down—and reserve for the next chapter the discussion of the reasons for the improvement or the deterioration in attitudes. Yet it was not always possible to draw a clear distinction between the what and the why, the nature of the former often being related to the latter.

There were periods, especially at the time the attitude measurements began and the methodological tools were incomplete, when only anticipatory data on the reasons for probable trends were available and explicit forecasts were fragmentary. Therefore, those early findings, particularly during the immediate postwar developments (1945–46), will be discussed only in the next chapter. All that can be said here is that an analysis of available attitudinal data made the author and his colleagues doubtful about the validity of the prevailing forecast of that time, namely, that there would be a substantial recession immediately after the end of the war. Until 1954, forecasts based on attitudinal data continued to be imprecise and will be discussed only briefly.

Predictions Made at Crucial Times

The major survey finding in 1945 and 1946 was that consumers were highly optimistic. The optimism persisted in the next two years and enabled the survey directors to make and publish a forecast which at that time surprised even the sponsors of the surveys. The forecast was that the widely heralded recession of 1948–49 would not extend to major consumer purchases. Even early in 1949 when employment and income trends indicated some slowdown, consumer optimism persisted. A decline in prices was thought at that time to be the major factor that would usher in a recession. Consumers on the whole agreed with economists and businessmen in expecting the prices of things they bought to go down, but they were found to rejoice in this prospect. The expectation of price declines could be shown to be associated with the expectation of good times for the economy as a whole. Intentions to purchase automobiles and large household goods were 14 and 7 percent higher, respectively, early in 1949 than early in 1948. The survey prediction proved correct: consumer buying remained strong all through the year 1949. This experience permitted the drawing of three conclusions, which served as guides for the study of consumer behavior in subsequent years:

1. It is possible for the consumer sector to exert a decisive influence on economic trends.
2. Consumer attitudes and expectations need not follow the

88

trend of incomes; they may develop contrary to the direction of income changes.
3. Expected price reductions may favorably influence consumer attitudes and may stimulate consumer buying.

Surveys conducted in 1950–51, during the first year of the war in Korea, contributed greatly to the understanding of consumer reactions to inflation. In 1950 inflationary expectations induced consumers as well as businessmen to stock up and buy in advance of their needs. The situation was entirely different in 1951 when consumers reported being worse off than a year earlier and the majority thought that high prices made it a bad time to buy automobiles and household goods. Following the acceleration of demand in 1950, survey data indicated a slowdown in 1951.

Habituation to prices developed in 1952. The presidential election of that year gave rise to some optimism. Neither the traditional business cycle indicators nor the attitudinal surveys pointed toward any major change until the fall of 1953, when a recession set in. A year later it proved to be one of the shortest and mildest recessions in American history. Consumer attitudes did deteriorate in 1953, but in the light of the fragmentary data available it cannot be determined whether the movement of attitudes was coincidental or leading. (The *Index of Consumer Sentiment* stood at 100.0 in January–February 1953, and at 92.3 in September–October, 1953, with no survey having been conducted between those dates.) It appeared probable that the recession in 1953 stemmed primarily from the behavior of the business and government sectors.

Regular and frequent data were available for the first time for the year 1954, in which year recovery from the recession was indicated. The movements of the *Index* in that period—as well as in 1957, that is, prior to the next recession—are contrasted in Table 6-1 with quarterly data on sales of consumer durable goods. It is shown that consumer attitudes improved in 1954 long before the sales of durable goods began to advance; the improvement in attitudes foreshadowed the sharp advance, especially in automobile purchases, which started in the first quarter of 1955 and extended to the subsequent quarters.

Similarly, there was a very substantial decline in consumer attitudes and expectations in the first half of 1957, followed by

89

TABLE 6-1

Movements of Index of Consumer Sentiment and of Durable Goods Sales in Two Crucial Periods

| | | Durable Goods Sales | |
Time of Survey	Index Fall 1956 = 100	Quarter	Current dollars (in billions)
Jan-Feb. 1954	93.6	1954 I	31.2
June 1954	95.1	II	32.2
October 1954	98.7	III	32.3
		IV	33.9
		1955 I	38.2
Nov-Dec. 1956	100.3	1957 I	40.3
June 1957	94.4	II	40.3
Nov-Dec. 1957	86.0	III	40.9
		IV	39.7
		1958 I	36.9

Note: Durable goods sales expressed in constant dollars differ little from those expressed in current dollars because price movements were rather minor in these periods.

a further large decline in the second half of that year, while sales of durables remained stable for three full quarters of 1957 and the recession did not set in until 1958.

As shown in Table 6-2, reports on income changes were less favorable in 1954 than in 1953 and yet the attitudes expressed about the respondents' personal financial situations were practically unchanged. A substantial improvement occurred in expectations about business developments and in the evaluation of conditions for buying durable goods. Intentions to purchase cars rose sharply as early as in June, 1954. As is well known, 1955 proved to be a better automobile year than any up to that time.

Early indications of what proved to be the sharpest recession in the first twenty years after World War II were likewise provided first of all by the notions of people about the business outlook (see lower part of Table 6-2). Both 1956 and 1957 were very good years witnessing a considerable expansion of business investments, personal incomes, as well as discretionary expenditures even though, as Table 6-2 indicates, income gains were less frequent in 1957 than in 1956. Chart 6-1 shows that three important series—new car registrations, ex-

TABLE 6-2
Change in Specific Attitudes in Two Crucial Periods (Changes between indicated periods in percentage points)*

Attitude or Income	A. Upturn in 1954	
	June 1954 Compared with October 1953	October 1954 Compared with October 1953
Change in income	−9	−10
Being better or worse off	+3	+1
Expecting to be better or worse off	+1	−1
Business outlook for next 12 months	+1	+10
Business outlook for next 5 years	+7	+15
Good or bad time to buy household goods	+12	+19
Good or bad time to buy automobiles	+15	+24
Intentions to purchase automobiles	+24	+50

	B. Downturn in 1957	
	June 1957 Compared with December 1956	December 1957 with December 1956
Change in income	−5	−11
Being better or worse off	−7	−17
Expecting to be better or worse off	−1	−7
Express financial worries	−13	−27
Business outlook for next 12 months	−14	−35
Business outlook for next 5 years	−23	−36
Good or bad time to buy household goods	−7	−22
Intentions to purchase automobile	−7	−16

*For each attitude an index was constructed by deducting the unfavorable responses from the favorable ones. The figures in the table show the difference in percentage points between the indices at two dates.

penditures for consumer durable goods, and extensions of installment credit for automobiles—remained stable at record levels all through the year 1957, including the fourth quarter. These three indicators of consumer demand, and many others, slumped in the first quarter of 1958 and remained at a very low level for at least nine months. The movement of the *Index of Consumer Sentiment* stands in sharp contrast: It had already declined in the first half of 1957.

91

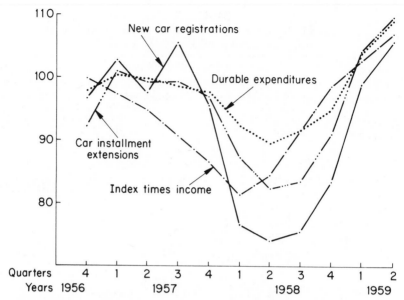

CHART 6-1   Consumer Attitudes and Behavior: Recession of
1958 (Seasonally adjusted data: Index and Income: 4th quarter
1956 = 100; other data: first half 1957 = 100.)

In line with the proposition that discretionary expenditures
are a function of both ability and willingness to buy, Chart 6-1
presents a joint measure of the *Index* and of changes in income. The Index alone, as shown in Table 6-1, provides indications of the forthcoming direction of changes. The joint measure, tentatively plotted by giving each component the weight
that achieves the optimum fit with the movements of durable
expenditures, serves to indicate that it is possible to quantify
advance indications and provide some measure of the magnitude of the predicted changes.

Chart 6-1 shows the recovery from the recession of 1958 as
well. The lead time of attitudes appears much shorter in the
recovery phase than in the downturn phase. Possibly, consumers had a great impact in bringing about the recession, while
measures undertaken by the government were primarily responsible for the onset of the recovery.

A recession occurred late in 1960 and early in 1961. The
Index of Consumer Sentiment declined from 98.9 in
January-February, 1960, to 90.1 in October-November of that
year. Following a sizable deterioration in the first half of the
year, the worsening of attitudes was insignificant in the second

92

half, in sharp contrast to the experience in 1957. Thus the findings pointed toward a short and mild recession—which was the case—but they still underestimated its extent.

In the years 1963–65 extensive studies were carried out about attitudes toward and reactions to the substantial cut in income taxes proposed by President Kennedy and enacted after his death early in 1964 (see Chapters 7 and 13). Consumer demand was not found to be influenced by the tax cut until late in 1963 and early in 1964 when attitudes improved. Only at that time did very many consumers believe that the tax cut would be enacted, which expectation stimulated installment buying. The years 1964 and 1965 proved to be a good period in which income increases were the major factor shaping consumers' attitudes. The *Index of Consumer Sentiment* reached its record value in August 1965. Nevertheless, it may have failed to predict the full size of the increase in discretionary demand.

Consumer attitudes declined in 1966. As shown in Chart 6-2, the downturn of the *Index* in that year extended over a shorter period than prior to two other recessions and the level of the *Index* remained relatively high throughout 1966–67. Much later, developments in 1967 were dubbed a mini-recession. This designation is in line with survey findings, especially if it is considered that incomes continued to advance in 1966 so that the decline of a curve constructed for "Index Times Income" remained fairly insignificant. Nevertheless, such a decline did take place and foreshadowed a reduction in new car registratioñs and installment extensions early in 1967.

The recovery from the mini-recession, as indicated by attitudinal data (see Chart 6-2, top line), was far from complete. There was no consumer boom in the period between the mini-recession of 1966–67 and the recession of 1970.

In 1969 there occurred the sharpest decline in consumer sentiment until that time. As early as the spring of that year consumers turned uncertain and pessimistic. The movements of the *Index of Consumer Sentiment,* also shown in Chart 6-2, are contrasted with indicators of consumer activities in Chart 6-3.

Personal auto expenditures, sales of new cars, and installment credit extended for the purchase of cars remained close to record levels during the entire year 1969. They fell sharply in the first quarter of 1970 and remained low throughout that year. Personal incomes continued to advance in 1969 and also

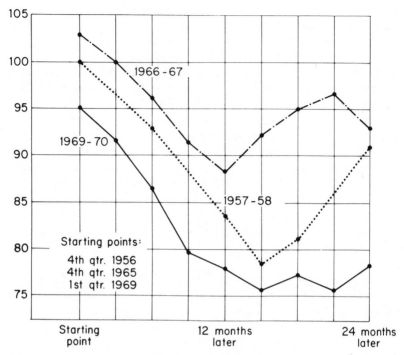

CHART 6-2   Change in the Index of Consumer Sentiment in Three
Periods (First Quarter 1966 = 100).

in 1970, albeit in real terms to a smaller extent than at earlier
times. Therefore, in that period, the movement of the joint indicator, "Index Times Income," differs greatly from the
movement of the *Index* alone. It is shown again, and this follows from the manner in which the *Index* is constructed as
well as from the underlying theory, that the *Index* alone serves
to indicate the direction but not the magnitude of discretionary
purchases. The charts indicate that there was a long lead time
between the decline in attitudes and the decline in spending
and also that it could be predicted that the recession to come
would last longer than the one in 1958. Regarding predictions
about the recovery from the recession, however, the performance of the *Index* was less satisfactory. The advance in the
Index did not begin much earlier than the upturn in demand.

How to summarize the performance of attitudinal measures
in predicting major turning points? If one looks exclusively at
the onset of the first two large recessions in the postwar period,

94

CHART 6-3   Consumer Attitudes and Behavior: Recession of 1970.
Income, personal automobile expenditures, and debt in constant dollars
seasonally adjusted. Number of domestic new car sales, from the *Survey of Current Business*, seasonally adjusted. Because of the automobile strike, the average data for July and August 1970 are shown as
the third quarter of 1970 data. All data: 1st quarter equals 100.

1958 and 1970, the record is remarkably good.[1] Yet the lead time
provided for other recessions as well as for recoveries from the
recessions, with the exception of the upturn in 1954, is less
satisfactory. It appears that the contribution of the consumer
sector in bringing about turning points is more substantial at
certain times than at other times. The contribution of consumer
sentiment to behavior may also vary at different times, and the
attitudinal measures themselves need to be improved. It cannot

[1] The same is true of the prediction of the recession of 1974, made in 1973,
as will be discussed later.

95

be questioned, however, that psychological economics has provided new and valuable ingredients to forecasts of cyclical fluctuations.

Econometric Studies

For practical purposes it is only predictions made at specific times that matter and not the average predictive performance of the *Index of Consumer Sentiment* over long periods. Nevertheless, as we have said, both to present a more complete picture and to conform to customary practice, we shall study the latter as well. Comprehensive measures of the forecasting record of consumer attitude surveys were first presented by Eva Mueller (1963a) who, together with the author of this book, was instrumental in devising the *Index of Consumer Sentiment* of the Survey Research Center. Her calculations, presented on the occasion of the tenth anniversary of the attitudinal surveys, are based in essence on the principle that discretionary consumer expenditures are a function of both ability to buy and willingness to buy. She used income level as a proxy for the former and the *Index* as a proxy for the latter. Two of her most important regression equations are presented on the left side of Table 6-3.

A year later Mueller's findings were confirmed in an important paper by F. G. Adams (1964). He concluded, on the basis of fourteen equations, that "Regression analysis of the attitudes and of buying plans as predictors of consumer durable expenditures show that attitudes make a significant contribution to forecasting durable expenditures."

The statistical significance of data depends, among other things, on the number of observations. Therefore, it is not surprising that in years prior to Mueller's calculations the significance of attitudinal data could not be demonstrated and that a few years later the demonstration became even more striking. This is shown on the right side of Table 6-3. In Chart 6-4 a graphic presentation of estimated durable goods expenditures over fourteen years, in comparison with actual expenditures, illustrates the predictive value of attitudinal data. The chart shows the great "successes" reported in the preceding section, as well as some minor and inconsequential fluctuations representing incorrect leads, and some divergence between estimated and actual values in 1960–61.

TABLE 6-3
Predictive Time Series Regressions

Number	R^2	1952–1961, 22 observations*	Number	R^2	1952–1966, 40 observations**
1	.76	$D_{+1} = .18 \, Y_{-1} + .40 \, A - 48.0$ $\qquad\quad (.03) \qquad\;\; (0.6)$	1A	.91	$D_{+1} = .15 \, Y_{-1} + .47 \, A - 51.6$ $\qquad\quad (.01) \qquad\;\; (.06)$
2	.77	$E_{+1} = .18 \, Y_{-1} + .31 \, A - 49.4$ $\qquad\quad (.02) \qquad\;\; (0.6)$	2A	.91	$E_{+1} = .16 \, Y_{-1} + .37 \, A - 56.8$ $\qquad\quad (.01) \qquad\;\; (.05)$

*As published in Mueller (1963a).
**As published in Katona (1967).

$A \ =$ Survey Research Center's Index of Consumer Sentiment.
$Y_{-1} =$ Disposable personal income, seasonally adjusted annual rate, deflated by CPI and the number of households; during six months prior to survey.
$D_{+1} =$ Consumer expenditures on durables, seasonally adjusted annual rate, deflated by CPI and the number of households; during six months after survey.
$E_{+1} =$ Extensions of installment credit for cars and other durables, seasonally adjusted annual rate, deflated by CPI and the number of households; during six months after survey.

Standard errors are in parentheses.

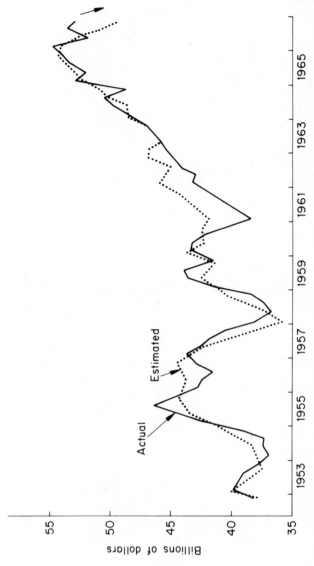

CHART 6-4 Actual and Estimated Durable Goods Expenditures, 1953-1966. (Annual rates adjusted for seasonal variations and for changes in prices and population.) Actual: Dept. of Commerce, quarterly expenditures at the indicated dates. Estimated: Projected expenditures, calculated on the basis of Equation 1A (Table 6-3) using survey data and prior income data available at the indicated dates. Reproduced from Katona (1967).

The equations presented in Table 6-3 suffer from the presence of autocorrelation of residuals. E. Scott Maynes (1967) recalculated the first equation according to first differences and then found no autocorrelation, while the influence of change in attitudes and change in income remained highly significant.

It may also be mentioned that Mueller, in the article mentioned above, was the first, and Adams the second, to demonstrate that the predictive value of the *Index of Consumer Sentiment* far surpassed that of available measures of intentions to buy. She also showed that the predictive value of the *Index* was high for the first two quarters following the measurement of attitudes—that is, for seven to eight months—and declined sharply in the third quarter.

An extensive series of equations was tested by William C. Dunkelberg (1969) over a period from 1951 to 1967. He concluded that

> Tests of the usefulness of SRC anticipations data in this study indicated that the sentiment measures made significant contributions to the explanation of past expenditure variations both as a leading indicator of spending changes and as a predictor in several expenditure models. . . . The *Index of Consumer Sentiment,* a composite, was found to be more highly correlated with automobile expenditures than any of its components.

Ray C. Fair (1971) also used similar equations but substituted lagged GNP values for disposable income. On the basis of 50 observations in determining durable expenditures, he concluded that "the Michigan Survey Research Center *Index of Consumer Sentiment* was significant in explaining short-run consumer behavior" (p. 241).

Finally, S. H. Hymans (1970) demonstrated through a series of simple equations involving income, change in income, and a strike-period variable that were fitted to explain consumer expenditures on automobiles that "in each case the lagged *Index of Consumer Sentiment* was a significant additional variable."[2]

Juster and Wachtel (1972b) compared anticipatory models with objective models and concluded that "the much simpler

[2] See S. H. Hymans (1970, p. 176). See also the *Communication* by George Katona (1971b).

anticipatory models outperform their counterpart objective models" (for the period 1960–67; see p. 574). Both the *Index of Consumer Sentiment* and the Census Bureau intentions to buy data contributed significantly to the performance of the anticipatory models.[3]

In the late 1960s econometricians proceeded to fit anticipatory variables, including the *Index of Consumer Sentiment*, into the structure of their newly developed extensive models. (This was done especially by L. R. Klein and the Wharton model.) The task has not yet been fully accomplished. It is difficult partly because the *Index* was constructed as a trendless variable. The extent of the contribution made by anticipatory variables to a model depends on the specifications used in the model, because some of the variables in a model may serve, at certain times, as proxies for attitudes.

A further aspect in which econometricians are interested appears to be less justified. Attempts have been made to explain and therefore to predict and even to replace the anticipatory data by a variety of objective data. Hymans (1970), for instance, claims success in explaining a large share of the variations of the *Index* by earlier changes in real disposable income, in consumer prices, and, above all, in common stock prices (taken together with the lagged *Index*).[4]

The basic problem raised by such attempts concerns the relation of St to I in the schema

$$St \rightarrow I \rightarrow R$$

where St stands for stimuli or precipitating circumstances, I stands for such intervening variables as attitudes and expectations, and R stands for the response, primarily in the form of discretionary consumer expenditures. While the topic of discussion in this chapter has been the relation of I to R, some

---

[3] Fair (1971, p. 241) finds that the Census Bureau's "Index of expected new car purchases"—a probability model devised by F. Thomas Juster and based on large samples—"was also significant when considered separately, but it did not appear to contain information not already contained in the consumer sentiment index."

[4] S. H. Hymans (1970), p. 176). The contribution of the stock market to explaining changes in consumer attitudes is rather doubtful. True, it has happened that major stock movements have anticipated the movements of the *Index*; it has also happened that movements of the *Index* have "predicted" later stock movements; finally it has also happened that the two movements were uncorrelated. Changes in unemployment rates have also been used to predict the *Index*, but in some instances they appear to perform as lagging rather than leading indicators.

100

major conclusions from extensive studies about the relation of *St* to *I* may be stated here:

1. Major changes in collective attitudes do not arise without good reason.
2. The origin of the changes may be determined only after the fact; information on all objective changes at a given time does not permit the prediction of the resulting change in attitudes.
3. The specific items of experience or news that are primarily responsible for a change in attitudes vary from time to time; therefore, the constellation of objective variables that is found to be successful in explaining attitude change at any given time may fail to do so at another time.

Thus it is necessary to rely on the people themselves to provide information on how precipitating circumstances and information received have influenced their attitudes and therefore their responses. The search for objective data that would replace attitudinal data disregards the pliability of human behavior due to man's ability to learn. Apparently, a major reason for this search is the desire to shove human beings and psychological variables off the stage of economic research.

Attempts to predict future movements of the *Index* are related to the commendable goal of lengthening the forecasting horizon. Yet the longer the time for which a forecast is made, the more probable it is that new unexpected developments will occur and impede the fulfillment of the forecast. Psychological economics is in a position to provide help in the assessment of the impact of new developments because its methods yield material for conditional forecasts.

Two examples may illustrate the use of such conditional forecasts. In the years 1966–70 economic trends depended to a great extent on the progress of the war in Vietnam. However, it was not known (*a*) whether the war would wind up or accelerate and (*b*) whether either trend would give rise to an increase or a decrease in consumer purchases. There was no scientific method available to predict the former. But it was possible to predict how consumers would react to steps taken either to end the war or to intensify it. These predictions were made by analyzing the attitudes and behavior of people with different expectations about the war and their reasons for changing their attitudes. Conditional forecasts of the type "If A_1, then X"

and "If A_2, then Y" are of great practical importance. When government and business are provided with such information, they are in a position to evaluate the consequences of new developments in their early stages.

The same is true of inflation. Whether or not price increases will escalate or slow down in the next twelve or eighteen months is, in most cases at least, very difficult or even impossible to predict. But information on how consumers would react to either possibility was obtained by analyzing the attitudes and behavior of people with different price experiences and price expectations. Again, such advance information is of great practical importance.

7
UNDERSTANDING ECONOMIC FLUCTUATIONS

It is not enough merely to report that consumer optimism either increased or decreased at a given time. Confidence in data on the changes, and in predictions derived from them, is enhanced when the reasons that induced consumers to become more or less optimistic are known and understood. In addition, such understanding helps to clarify the relation between the psychological and economic factors involved.

The quarterly surveys conducted by the Survey Research Center are designed to explore the reasons for changes in attitudes. This chapter and the next consist of a review of findings on these reasons obtained between 1946 and 1973. Thus they contain a brief history of cyclical fluctuations in the quarter century following the end of World War II, as seen by consumers.[1] The emphasis is on the circumstances under which major changes in consumer sentiment have occurred. For the first few years after the end of the war the analysis is less complete than for later years because the earlier surveys were conducted less frequently and contained fewer questions.

After the End of World War II

When the war ended in 1945, the following view of the underlying economic prospects was held by many experts and often appeared in print: For the past few years, economic activity has been sustained by government orders for war materials. They are about to cease, and millions of workers will be dis-

---

[1] The material in this chapter was previously published in the author's *The Powerful Consumer* up to 1959, and his *The Mass Consumption Society* up to 1963. For detailed reports on the 1960–73 surveys, see the annual monographs published by the Survey Research Center under the title *Survey of Consumer Finances*.

charged. At the same time, the labor market will be clogged by millions of soldiers and sailors who will be demobilized. Between 1940 and 1945, prices were driven up because of the high incomes of the war workers and shortages in civilian consumer goods. Although increased production of peacetime goods will give employment to many people, this production cannot compensate for the adverse factors. Therefore, a downward trend in employment, production, and prices is imminent. A few months after the end of the war there will be a depression with several millions of people unemployed.

There were a few dissenting voices. Some economists predicted rapid inflation. During the war an unprecedentedly large proportion of income had been saved. For several years in succession people had saved approximately one-fourth of what they had earned, and most of this money had been put into war bonds and bank deposits, which could be cashed or withdrawn without delay. When people would be spending both their incomes and their accumulated liquid assets, demand would exceed the supply of goods and runaway inflation would develop.

Surveys conducted in 1945 and 1946 revealed that the American people did not think along either of these lines. In contrast to the experts, people on the whole were optimistic about economic developments as well as about their own financial situation. They believed that the end of the war—a most welcome event—could not have any but good consequences. They expected that their incomes, held down by wage controls during the war, would rise when the war was over and that their standard of living would improve. Only a small proportion of people feared a recession.

Nor was rapid inflation expected. After the end of the war there was no inclination to cash war bonds or to use up accumulated savings. On the contrary, most people were glad that they had accumulated some reserve funds; they did not feel that they had been forced to save during the war and did not believe that their liquid assets were excessive. Yet a survey conducted early in 1946 revealed that by then the desire to spend and to acquire consumer goods had become stronger and the desire to save weaker. The widespread desire for consumer goods made it appear probable that the rate of saving would decline, but not that there would be no savings at all. The more optimistic people were, the greater was the expressed desire for durable goods.

104

Needless to say, the predictions of the experts, both about an immediate postwar depression and rapid inflation, proved to be false, and what actually happened was fairly close to what people thought would happen: Rapid increase in consumer demand, increases in income as well as in prices—which were far from excessive—and a sharp reduction in the rate of saving without any net decline in liquid asset holdings.

At that time little attention was paid to consumer attitudes. When consumer demand rose greatly after the end of the war, the increase was usually attributed to demand deferred during the war, not to optimism and confidence.

Makers of wrong forecasts rarely admit that their theories and methods are incorrect. They usually place the blame on accidental factors or on errors of timing. By the fall of 1948 they lifted their heads and predicted that the postwar depression was just postponed and would occur at last. It was assumed that the pent-up demand had been satisfied and business inventories built up to their usual levels. It was therefore expected that the anticipated price declines would finally take place, first in industrial raw materials and then in consumer goods as well. It was thought that the price declines would usher in the long-delayed postwar recession.

In contrast, as reported in the previous chapter, survey findings in 1948–49 revealed a strong association between expecting falling prices and expecting good times to come. At the same time, optimistic income expectations continued to prevail. People generally believed that wage and salary rates could either go up or stay where they were, while declines were inconceivable. In the postwar years, including 1948 and 1949, the most frequent expectation consisted of annual rounds of wage increases. Rumors of a forthcoming reccession did not influence these expectations.

Korea

At the end of June, 1950, North Korean troops invaded South Korea. Within a few days the American people learned with satisfaction that a police action would restore order. Then came a most unusual and shocking experience, news of military setbacks. In the summer of 1950, the American people learned that our armies had been almost driven out of Korea.

105

In the winter of 1950, after the intervention of the Chinese Communists, they learned that our armies had been driven back several hundred miles from the Yalu River.

A survey conducted in August, 1950, revealed that one person out of every four anticipated substantial price increases —increases of more than 10 percent within a year. In contrast, during previous inflationary periods, as they had occurred during and shortly after World War II, most people had envisaged small price increases. Recollections of World War II were revived following the military setbacks, and people expected restrictions of civilian production and shortages. Therefore, many people proceeded to stock up or to purchase goods far beyond the usual rates. Sales records of department stores indicated that buying waves coincided with bad military news. While up to that time the fall had generally been a slow season for automobiles, purchases of passenger cars—remembered as being unavailable during the war—soared in the second half of 1950. Price increases were more rapid than during World War II. Between June, 1950, and early 1951 the index for basic commodity prices rose by 50 percent, for wholesale prices by 16 percent, and for consumer retail prices—including many slow-moving items such as rents, electricity, etc.—by 8 percent.

In 1950, however, both war expenditures and incomes were slow to increase and the advance in demand and in prices was due to anticipated rather than actual developments. Some experts thought therefore that substantial inflation was ahead: If the mere expectation of government spending had had such great effects, how much worse would be the situation when people's purchasing power would actually increase several billion dollars by virtue of the inevitable government expenditures! President Truman requested the reenactment of price controls and Congress speedily complied toward the end of January, 1951.

In 1951 government expenditures and personal incomes did rise substantially, as expected. But other developments did not conform to the predictions made. Instead of continuing their climb, raw material prices fell sharply and rapidly, wholesale prices moderately, and retail prices slightly. The American people reacted by stepping up their saving rather than their spending. A survey conducted at the beginning of 1951 revealed increased pessimism and uncertainty. By that time the front in Korea was stabilized and the acute threat of military defeat had vanished and with it the expectation of a third world war. Instead of expecting rapid price increases and shortages people assumed that inflation would continue gradually and they disliked the prospect.

While in 1951 many experts spoke of a temporary buying lull caused by overbuying during the preceding year, the surveys indicated a fundamental change in consumer sentiment:

1. A new expression spread rapidly and was widely accepted: cold war. It meant for the American people long-lasting conflict and the disagreeable state of affairs of being dependent on what Moscow did. It meant no shooting war, but a state of continuous anxiety.
2. It was believed possible to produce guns for a cold war and butter, too. The expectation of shortages disappeared and resentment of inflation grew. Buying conditions were viewed unfavorably: the majority of people said that high prices made it a bad time to buy automobiles or household goods.
3. Because of the price increases the number of people who felt they were worse off exceeded the number who felt better off. The most common response to questions about the respondent's financial prospects were expressions of uncertainty about the future.

It took a fairly long time until the ups and downs in economic activity in 1950 and 1951 gave way to lesser fluctuations. In 1952 the election of President Eisenhower and the return of the Republican Party to power contributed to the reestablishment of confidence and optimism.

Upturn in 1954 and Downturn in 1957

In 1953, many people had heard the news of a downturn in economic activity, and some people had even heard dire predictions of an impending long period of stagnation. Yet the major survey finding in 1953 and 1954 was that underlying feelings of optimism and confidence had not been destroyed. The majority of people found their financial situations fairly satisfactory; they thought that their standard of living was slowly improving and that their prospects for occupational progress were good. In the confrontation between unfavorable news about economic conditions and favorable personal financial experience, the latter had the greater influence. Feeling better off at a time when the economic news was bad appeared particularly gratifying.

One aspect of the economic news did appear quite satisfactory. In reply to questions about what the prices of things they bought had been doing, the majority said in 1953 and 1954 that prices were fairly stable. Prices were also expected to remain stable. In these years less than 20 percent of all family heads expected prices to go up during either the next year or the next five years.

At the same time, people also greeted a new development with much satisfaction. This development was the widespread establishment of discount houses. The majority of people expressed the opinion that sellers of durable goods were anxious to market their products, that high "trade-ins" and discounts were to be had—in short, that the time was propitious to make "good buys." Consumers' desires to upgrade their durable goods and their living accommodations were revived by the notion that it was a "good time to buy." People were ready to use their own money as well as to borrow to satisfy their desires. In 1954, intentions to buy automobiles increased in frequency long before automobile demand advanced with the introduction of the 1955 models, which proved to be very successful.

By June, 1955, consumer optimism had increased sharply beyond the 1954 levels. While in 1954 many people acknowledged that business conditions were worse than a year earlier and nevertheless expected an upturn, in 1955 practically everybody knew that business had improved and expected the improvement to continue. Many more people reported income increases than income declines in 1955, and the subjective evaluations of personal financial situations improved to an even greater extent.

There can be no doubt that the first phase of the upswing, from the fall of 1954 to the fall of 1955, was of the consumers' making. A substantial increase in business investment expenditures began only late in 1955 and persisted in 1956. The extent of optimism may be gauged by answers received to the following survey question, which was deliberately formulated to induce people to express misgivings: "Do you happen to know about any unfavorable developments which may make the country's business situation worse?" In 1955–56 more than two-thirds of all respondents replied in the negative. A further question "What do you have in mind?" addressed to the minority who had answered affirmatively, yielded references to the international situation and the President's illness. Only relatively few people mentioned economic factors as, for instance, the large consumer debt, low farm incomes, and inflation.

It was different in 1957, when consumer attitudes deteriorated sharply. The increase in pessimism was rather small in evaluating personal financial well-being, although the proportion of people expressing worries rose substantially. People's opinions about overall economic trends worsened to a much greater extent. This was related to experience with and the expectation of rising prices and rising interest rates. A substantial proportion of people were aware of rising interest rates. Not fewer than three-fourths of those with an annual income of $7,500 and over reported this trend correctly and considered it bad news. In scanning economic indicators the year 1957 appears to have been a good year in which policy makers were primarily concerned with combating the boom for the sake of slowing down inflation. Yet the people themselves, when asked about the news they had heard, reported good news only infrequently. Unfavorable business news, on the other hand, even when it concerned only an isolated instance, was given great attention. Failure to see anything that might sustain good times was emphasized by the same people who earlier in the interview had reported gains in their own income. At the same time, to mention a specific important segment of the economy, dissatisfaction with the assortment offered by the automobile industry had become widespread.

Sputniks also contributed to the deterioration of confidence. For most Americans, Communist achievements, the armament race, and international conflict have unfavorable connotations that are carried over into other areas. Instead of thinking that the Sputniks would stimulate the American missile program and thereby make our production go up, the unexpected news that the Russians had put a satellite into orbit brought concern and dismay. Close to one-third of the American people reacted by saying that war had become much more likely. And among those who felt that war was more likely, only 46 percent said in December, 1957, that business conditions

109

would remain "good"; among those who felt that war was less likely, 67 percent said so.

By December, 1957, a substantial proportion of people thought that a recession had already developed. Even though reports on past income changes remained favorable, pessimism spread to the area of personal finances as well.

Minor Fluctuations

Between 1958 and 1962 there were repeated minor changes in consumer attitudes. The reasons for these fluctuations, as revealed in the quarterly surveys, will be summarized here briefly.

In spite of rather pessimistic notions about the short-term outlook, early in 1958 people in general expected good times to return sooner or later. In the fall of 1958 better economic news brought forth slow and hesitant gains in confidence and optimism. The American people remained conscious of the threat of unemployment and of the likelihood of recessions recurring at short intervals.

Disappointment at rising prices and concern with inflation were pronounced in 1959. A long steel strike adversely affected consumer confidence in the fall of that year. Many people were well informed about the strike and argued that inflation would ensue in case of a labor victory, while purchasing power would be insufficient to sustain the economy in case of a management victory. After the settlement of the steel strike, consumer attitudes again improved.

The rise in consumer attitudes from their 1958 low levels was terminated and they began again to deteriorate sharply in the spring of 1960, long before the previous high of 1955–56 had been reached. Least satisfactory among the attitudinal indicators was the long-range economic outlook; people were concerned about the possibility of a recession. In 1960, they saw no factor that in their opinion might serve to sustain continuous good times. Worries about international tensions were also pronounced.

News about the election and the plans of President Kennedy were considered the most important news in the fall and winter of 1960–61. Just as in 1952, the majority of the people derived optimistic conclusions regarding business-cycle trends from

110

the fact that a new man had been elected president. Although they were aware that a recession had begun and that unemployment was rising, consumers expressed no greater pessimism in the fall than in the summer of 1960.

In the spring and summer of 1962 people were found to be concerned with the threat of a recession. They were aware of the apparent inability to cope with unemployment and derived an uneasy feeling from the prevailing international tensions. At the same time there was satisfaction with personal financial trends as well as with the relatively stable prices. Buying intentions for automobiles were so strong that, considering all indications jointly, an early downturn in consumer demand was not indicated. The sharp decline in stock prices did not induce consumers to expect a recession or to postpone purchases.

In November, 1962, gains in optimism were registered. Income gains, better business news, and above all, the quick and, in the opinion of most Americans, favorable solution of the Cuban crisis made for an improvement in consumer sentiment. Attitudes toward the automobile market improved further.

Signs of a possible reversal of the favorable trend were apparent in the spring of 1963. In the absence of new stimuli, there was pronounced concern about how prosperous times might be sustained. In the fall of 1963 confidence in a favorable economic outlook was again strengthened under the impact of an apparent relaxation of international tensions and an optimistic appraisal of the automobile market.

Substantial Improvement in the 1960s

From 1961 or 1962 until 1966 economic trends were favorable. Personal incomes increased greatly and consumer attitudes improved. Consumer expenditures on durables rose substantially. While part of the story concerns the increase in consumers' ability to buy, income trends also had an influence on people's attitudes. The same is true of the relative price stability experienced in those years. The international situation, following the favorable solution of the Cuban crisis in 1962, likewise served to reassure the American people.

One of the most relevant items of economic news of that

period was the substantial cut in income taxes proposed by President Kennedy in the summer of 1962 and enacted, after his assassination, in March, 1964. For more than a year the proposal and its discussion had little impact on consumers. To be sure, they applauded the idea of paying lower taxes, but they did not believe that the plan was realistic or that Congress would pass it. The great majority of Americans thought that large and even increased expenditures by the government were needed in many areas and that it would therefore not be possible to reduce revenues. Public opinion changed very slowly. As late as in August, 1963, only 27 percent of all people (39 percent of those with more than $7,500 income) thought that the tax cut law would be passed. By January, 1964, the proportions rose to 59 percent and 69 percent, respectively. Understanding of the economic impact of the tax cut likewise became more complete in the winter of 1963–64; a rising proportion of the people became convinced that it would stimulate the economy.

Late in 1963 and early in 1964, before anybody had actually profited from the cut, the expectation of paying reduced taxes induced many people to step up their purchases of durable goods and even to borrow money for that purpose. While the anticipation of lower tax withholdings could be shown to have stimulated consumer demand, in the first few months after the actual tax reduction many people responded differently, giving the impression that spending would lag behind an increase in disposable income. The surveys revealed that, compared with the widespread rosy expectations about the many billions of dollars that would be paid out to taxpayers, people were disappointed when they found out by how few dollars their own weekly or monthly pay checks were increased.

In the summer and fall of 1964, however, favorable reactions to the tax cut again became widespread and consumer demand rose substantially. By that time, incomes earned —wages, salaries, profits—had risen substantially, and people did not distinguish between gains in income before taxes and gains caused by the tax cut. For most people the tax cut, just as a rise in salary, was seen as a permanent increase in available funds.

Consumer attitudes improved further in 1965 and in the second half of that year they reached a level of optimism not known up to that time (as well as in the subsequent nine years). What contributed to the improvement in attitudes was, first, the experience and the expectation of income gains, which represented an improvement in the standard of living. With price increases being held at a fairly low level, the advances in income could be translated into improved well-being. In addition, people rejoiced that even the most lagging feature of the economy, the rate of unemployment, appeared to improve and therefore to be subject to change by government action.

The war in Vietnam may also have contributed to the prevailing optimism because in 1965 the majority of Americans thought that on the whole the war had a good effect on the domestic economy. Yet at the same time the majority expected the conflict to become more severe in the future and they did not like the prospect.

The extent of optimism that prevailed toward the end of 1965 is illustrated in Table 7-1. Income gains were reported by a larger proportion (56 percent) of family units than at any time since World War II. Even though the proportion of those who felt better off was much smaller than the proportion with income increases, it is noteworthy how infrequently the opinion "We are worse off than a year ago" was expressed. With respect to expectations, optimism was pronounced both when the question related to personal fiannces and to economic conditions. Again the very low proportion of pessimists—not higher than 1 out of 10 or sometimes 1 out of 20—appears most noteworthy.

Mini-recession without Full Recovery

Following several years of pronounced strength, consumer attitudes deteriorated in 1966. Experience with and resentment of price increases were the first factors to bring about uncertainty and pessimism. Awareness of rising interest rates and even of shortages in money available for loans likewise created doubt about the endurance of good times. News about plans to increase income taxes was also viewed as a threat. With most people being well aware of the beneficial effect of the tax cut, tax increases were considered not only as very unwelcome from the personal point of view, but also as endangering continued prosperity.

113

TABLE 7-1

Economic Attitudes toward the End of 1965

(Percentage distribution of attitudes of all heads of family units at the time of the most pronounced optimism)

Reports	Higher, better, good	Same, uncertain, don't know	Lower, worse, bad	Total
Income received compared to a year ago	56	28	16	100
Income expected a year from now	43	49	8	100
Better or worse off than a year ago	38	45	17	100
Expect to be better or worse off a year from now	52	43	5	100
Business conditions compared to a year ago	57	35	8	100
Expected business conditions a year from now	36	58	6	100
Business good or bad during next 12 months	78	14	8	100
Business good or bad during next 5 years	47	42	11	100
Good or bad time to buy durable goods	61	30	9	100

Finally, in 1966 there began a reversal of attitudes toward the Vietnam war. With an increasing proportion of people being aware of or expecting an acceleration of war activities, not only did opposition to the war increase but the belief that the war had unfavorable effects on the domestic economy also gained credence.

As early as May, 1966, not fewer than 40 percent of all family heads expected Congress to enact an increase in income taxes. At the same time the great majority of upper-income people expressed awareness of rising interest rates and thought that it had a bad effect on the economic situation. Then, too, as a result of price increases, there was a greater proportion of people who felt worse off and of those who expected unfavorable developments. By the end of the year 1966 expenditures on durables were reduced and amounts saved increased. And yet, primarily because of continued sharp income gains, a full-fledged recession did not develop.

There was a partial recovery of consumer sentiment in 1967 that could not be attributed to favorable news. Worries about inflation, high interest rates, and the prospect of a tax increase persisted, but people became habituated to them. The worries, being no longer new, had lost much of their impact. In the course of 1967 it was frequently argued among economists that the rate of consumer expenditures would rise substantially under the impact of an increase in consumer incomes and government expenditures. Survey data did not support these notions; in the absence of good news that was needed to revitalize consumer optimism, the recovery in sentiment had to be characterized as tenuous.

In 1968 both price increases and income increases continued, the two influences partly canceling each other. Yet there was some additional good news. In May of that year peace talks began in Paris, following a reduction and several months later a halt in the bombing of North Vietnam. The impact of this news can best be understood by reporting on the following question asked in the Survey Research Center's survey in February, 1968: "What would you say are the most important things that may influence business conditions during the next twelve months?" In answer, not fewer than 60 percent mentioned Vietnam and the international situation. In contrast, only 25 percent mentioned the forthcoming presidential election and the very low proportion of 12 percent referred to inflation. For a time in 1968 many people viewed the beginning of the Paris peace talks as a hopeful sign. They believed that with the end, or even a reduction, of America's involvement in Vietnam, the domestic economic situation and people's standards of living would improve. The war was seen, not as increasing production, but rather as depleting the country's resources.

The proportion of those who believed in the summer of 1968 that the Paris peace talks would speedily lead to a cease-fire or a reduction in fighting represented only a minority. But this minority had substantially more optimistic views about business conditions than the majority, who expected fighting to continue at an unchanged level or even to increase.

Domestic political developments likewise provided good news in 1968. The nomination of Nixon, the expectation of his victory, and finally, his election were viewed as strengthening economic prospects. The return of the Republican Party to

115

power in 1952, when Eisenhower was elected, had had a strong effect in a similar direction. Kennedy's election in 1960, viewed as the election of a vigorous young president, had also strengthened consumer confidence. Consumer attitudes again improved after the presidential election in 1968, although apparently to a somewhat lesser extent than eight or sixteen years earlier.

One major event of the year 1968 was the passage of a new tax law increasing the rate of income taxes (and immediately effective through an increase in tax withholdings from pay checks). Prior to the passage of the law, in May, 1968, a survey revealed that in one respect public opinion had changed substantially. While in 1967 most people with definite opinions expected an adverse effect on economic conditions from the tax increase, in May, 1968, the proportions of those expecting favorable and those expecting unfavorable effects were the same. After having heard of a forthcoming tax increase for approximately two years, most Americans had become accustomed to the idea. They also accepted the idea that rising income taxes would help in the fight against inflation. Finally, in view of widespread and sizable gains in earned income, they generally were of the opinion that the tax increase would make only a small difference in their financial situations. In sum, the report on the May, 1968, survey drew the conclusion that the major retarding effect of the tax increase had already taken place in anticipation of the measure and would not occur later when disposable incomes were actually reduced.

In the second half of 1968, to the surprise of most experts, the tax increase had practically no effect on economic trends. Nor did it influence consumer sentiment. What should be noted is that, in the case of a tax cut, favorable trends in earned income and the tax measure operate in the same direction; in the case of a tax increase their impact is opposite.

Lest the enumeration of favorable developments in 1968 be misunderstood, it should be emphasized that even in that year consumer attitudes did not reach the level of optimism and confidence that was manifested in 1965. Especially opinions about longer-range economic developments remained guarded and cautious, having never fully recovered from the deterioration at the time of the mini-recession of 1966.

* * *

In reviewing the findings of almost twenty-five years on the reasons for changes in attitudes it becomes clear that survey research has provided a great variety of clues and suggestions. By sifting the data after the fact, when it is known how attitudes and behavior have changed, it appears possible to provide a fairly complete explanation of why this or that happened. But at the time when the predictions were made, the relative importance of different developments and of various items of information was much harder to discern. There were times when consumers and change in consumer demand appeared most influential, and other times when business and government decisions were paramount. There were times when consumer incomes and their changes appeared to be the most powerful factor, and other times when willingness to buy changed independently of income trends.

In studying the cyclical changes we had ample reason to recognize unique factors. It may suffice to point to the Korean war in 1950–51 and the tax cut in 1964. Yet many factors recurred throughout. The acceleration or deceleration of inflationary trends appeared to be influential at practically all times. News about employment or unemployment, about a presidential election and developments relating to the cold war likewise represented ever-recurring themes. We shall return to a systematic examination of the impact of various factors on consumer psychology in Part Four of this book. First, in the next chapter we shall analyze the role of consumer attitudes and expectations before, during, and after the recession of 1970. These developments deserve a special chapter because, in bringing about this substantial recession, in making it one of fairly long duration, and ultimately in overcoming it, consumers played a large role and changes in consumer demand were greatly influenced by psychological factors. A case study of developments at a crucial time may serve in lieu of real-life experimentation.

8
THE RECESSION OF 1970

To understand the onset of the recession of 1970 we must recall the major developments that influenced consumer sentiment in 1968. In that year, as reported before, confidence was strengthened by the cessation of bombing in North Vietnam, by the election of Nixon to the presidency, and by widespread income increases. In 1969 there was reversal in all these respects. The futility of the Paris peace talks became evident. At the same time, opposition to the unpopular war spread and an increasing proportion of people thought that the war expenditures would drain national resources and make for bad economic conditions at home. The Nixon honeymoon proved to be of very short duration. Early in 1969 people came to believe that the President would neither end the war nor initiate policies that would improve economic conditions.

Reasons for Growing Pessimism

The most powerful adverse influence came from the experience of inflation. In fact, prices paid by consumers, far from stable for several years, had already begun to rise at a faster rate in 1968. But in that year news about prices was overshadowed by other news, and income increases generated satisfaction rather than misgivings about not being able to enjoy them because of higher prices. Complaints about prices began to rise in the first quarter of 1969. In the survey conducted in May, 1969, no fewer than 25 percent of respondents complained spontaneously about rising prices when asked to explain their answer to the question about being better or worse off than the year before. The frequency of the "Worse off" answers increased only a little. But those who said "Same

119

as a year ago" frequently explained that in spite of making more their situation had not improved because of price increases. A year earlier about 75 percent of those who said that their income had gone up also said that they were better off; by the second quarter of 1969 the proportion had fallen to 60 percent (in 1970 to 50 percent).

The number of people expecting sizable price increases also began to grow in 1969. Compared with what actually happened in 1970, the expectations must be judged as conservative. Yet it is worth noting that the proportion of Americans expecting the prices of goods they bought to go up by 5 percent or more within a year rose from 30 to 45 percent in the first half of 1969.

Chart 6-2 in Chapter 6 shows the trend of the *Index of Consumer Sentiment* in 1969. When the *Index* fell from its relatively high point of 95.1 in February, 1969, to 91.6 in May of that year, it would have been possible to disregard the decline—even though it was statistically significant—by arguing that a onetime change might be due to accidental circumstances or spurious changes in mood. When, however, the change in the *Index* could be supplemented by information supplied by survey respondents on the impact of the Vietnam War and inflation, the explanation of the deterioration of confidence added great weight to the conviction that the lower rate of willingness to buy would affect consumers' discretionary expenditures.

The movements of the *Index of Consumer Sentiment* in the summer and fall of 1969 strongly reinforced this conclusion and made it possible to predict the recession far in advance. Or, to express the same conclusion from a different perspective: A year later, knowing what had happened, it was evident that a deterioration in consumers' willingness to buy was a major factor in bringing about the recession.

The unfavorable news of the first half of 1969, pessimistic evaluations of the Vietnam War, and experience with accelerated inflation continued to be influential in the second half. In addition, in the summer and fall of 1969 very many people learned that the government intended to fight inflation by reducing the demand for goods and services. Recession and some unemployment might then occur, so many people heard, not because of economic forces the government could not arrest, but as the result of deliberate government policy. The argument that by slowing down the economy inflation would be arrested was not considered convincing. Many people thought that by fighting inflation through reducing demand we would have both evils, inflation as well as recession.

In August, 1969, over half the respondents—52 percent —said that unemployment would increase during the next year; in 1968 only 20 percent had said so. At the same time 40 percent thought that a recession was likely to occur compared with 26 percent in 1968. Finally, the majority of upper-income people were aware of rising interest rates and two-thirds of all respondents expected them to go up still farther. The impact of interest rates on business and, for that matter, also on consumer affairs and installment buying is far from being fully understood by laymen. It suffices to state here that in the opinion of most people high or rising interest rates were bad for business and represented an unfavorable development. While in the first half of 1969 the decline in the frequency with which respondents reported good news they had heard was most noteworthy, in the second half reports of bad news heard increased rapidly.

"It is a bad time to buy automobiles," or houses, or large household goods, said an increasing proportion of Americans, because the prices of these things had gone up and were "too high" and because economic prospects were unfavorable. The expected inflation did not induce people to buy in advance of still higher prices. Most people denied that they had bought anything during the previous few months because they thought they would cost more later. Many argued that the only way to protect themselves against inflation was to economize, to buy less, or to postpone the purchase of various things.

Thus we find powerful economic reasons for a deterioration in people's attitudes and expectations. At the same time there were significant noneconomic reasons as well, in addition to the Vietnam war. When explaining their opinions about economic prospects, especially over the next five years, several respondents spoke of the riots and violence, the racial conflict, the behavior of young people, the continued existence of poverty in the midst of plenty, and the pollution of the air and water. Inner-city riots and disturbances on college campuses, particularly frequent in 1968, apparently had little impact on opinions about business trends during that year. But in the course of 1969, when optimism and confidence were already disturbed, those two areas of concern became influential in generating further economic pessimism. Awareness of the country's inability to solve its great and enduring societal problems—race, poverty, violence, and drugs—impaired confidence in the government and its ability to solve the economic problems of inflation and unemployment.

The Depth of the Recession

The discussion of the considerations that influenced people's way of thinking about economic prospects serves to explain the survey data presented in Table 8-1 (page 125). Various economic attitudes declined to greatly differing degrees in 1969–70. Attitudes about personal finances were only slightly lower in 1970 than at the beginning of 1969. This is hardly surprising because income gains continued to be frequent —even though they were eroded by inflation and reflected smaller real gains. Long-range personal financial expectations were affected very little by the recession, as will be reported in Chapter 12. The deterioration of sentiment was very substantial in expectations about business conditions and the evaluation of buying conditions for durable goods. Regarding business expectations, it should be noted that already early in 1969 they were much less favorable than in 1965. The extent of change over a period of five years is illustrated in Table 8-2 (page 126).

Survey data on economic news heard and reported by respondents show similar changes. In 1965 somewhat more than half of all respondents could not recall any economic news, while most of the others reported favorable news. In 1970 no fewer than 60 percent reported unfavorable news (and 9 percent favorable news), with the unusually low proportion of less than one-third of respondents failing to report any economic news.

Spending less on durable goods at a time of rising incomes led to saving more. First of all, installment buying was greatly reduced at a time of practically unchanged repayments of debt. Withdrawals from bank accounts for the purpose of unusual major cash purchases likewise became infrequent. At the same time, an increased proportion of respondents said that it was more important than usual to add to savings. The expectation of bad times to come may have contributed to this increase in motivation to save.

A few references to traditional economic indicators may be in order. Some of them, highly relevant for our purposes, have already been presented in Chart 3 of Chapter 6. Aggregate personal incomes advanced in 1970, even in real terms, albeit slowly. New car sales and the incurrence of installment debt for purchasing cars—fairly stable at a high level all through the year 1969—slumped in 1970. Consumers' aggregate expenditures on durable goods in constant dollars were lower in 1970 than in 1969, for the first time in several years. The same was true of amounts spent on residential structures as well as of business investment. Gross National Product in constant dollars declined in 1970 for the first time since 1958.

At the same time prices continued to advance. The Consumer Price Index rose from 104.2 to 109.8 in 1969 and to 116.3 in 1970. The increase in prices coincided with an increase in unemployment: On the average, 3.6 percent of the labor force was unemployed in 1968 and 3.5 percent in 1969; in 1970 the average was 4.9 percent. The rate of 3.5 percent prevailed as late as December, 1969, while a year later in December, 1970, it was 6.0 percent.

An additional, most important set of statistical data must be presented. Personal saving in percent of disposable income averaged 5.5 percent in the years 1960-64. In the next five years, 1965 to 1969 inclusive, it averaged 6.5 percent (even though it was over 7 percent in one of these years, 1966). In 1970 the saving rate reached the unprecedented rate of 8 percent and remained at a similar level in 1971.

While in 1969 consumer sentiment was under the influence of the anticipation of bad times to come, in 1970 it was affected by news that the recession had begun and unemployment had risen. Most people became aware of the deterioration in economic trends quite promptly. By May, 1970, in comparing business conditions with those of a year earlier, survey respondents overwhelmingly thought that business conditions were worse. In contrast, late in 1969 the answers "worse" and "better" were about equally frequent and early in 1969 the proportion saying "better" greatly exceeded the proportion saying "worse."

While anticipations resulted in a sharp deterioration of sentiment, the fulfillment of unfavorable expectations induced

123

sentiment to drift somewhat lower. Most of the deterioration shown in Table 8-1 from February, 1969, to the low point of 1970 occurred in the course of the year 1969. By the second half of 1970 a plateau was reached—even though an extended automobile strike made for additional misgivings. The first sign of improvement in attitudes occurred with relation to prices. Many people noticed that the prices of cars and household appliances did not advance to the same extent as other prices. While in 1969 the overwhelming opinion was, "It is a bad time to buy durables because their prices are high," in 1970 some people began to speak about prices of durables being fairly low.

After the Recession

Great differences in the rate of improvement of different attitudes between mid-1970 and mid-1971 may be seen in Table 8-1. The evaluation of buying conditions for durables improved to the largest extent. Short-range business expectations likewise improved while opinions about longer-range economic trends and attitudes about personal finances advanced very little. Absence of change in personal expectations could be explained by the fact that they had not deteriorated much prior to the recession. But this explanation did not apply to five-year business expectations. In 1970–71 there was no change in the rate of complaints about economic and social problems. The recovery of sentiment in the first half of 1971 was not due to any good news that would have restored confidence. It was mainly a result of habituation to bad news, which explains why the recovery was far from robust. Consumer purchases increased at a rate corresponding to income gains but the rate of personal saving remained as high as before.

On August 15, 1971, President Nixon introduced a price and wage freeze. It came as a surprise to most Americans who, however, reacted very favorably to it: Late in August and early in September 76 percent of respondents in a sample survey said that the freeze was a good thing. Only 12 percent thought it was a bad thing, mainly because wages would be held down, while a further 12 percent were undecided. This reaction was expected, because earlier in the same year Americans had expressed rather unfavorable opinions about the government's policies on fighting inflation. Many people had explained their opinion by complaining about government inaction and demanded the introduction of policies that would serve to slow down the price increases. At the same time, most people professed not to know how this could be done, and apparently very few thought of measures such as a price freeze. In September the proportion saying that the government was doing a good job increased although the difficulties confronting the government were widely acknowledged. At that time 39 percent thought that the government's policies would be successful, while 43 percent expressed doubts.

Later in 1971 and also in the first half of 1972 public reactions to price and wage controls reflected features of appreciation and satisfaction as well as of disapproval and dissatisfaction. On the one hand, most people acknowledged the need for controls, and complaints about inflation became less frequent. On the other hand, in 1971 the proportion thinking that the government would not be successful in slowing down inflation rose steadily to 50 percent and in 1972 even to 65 percent of respondents. The majority of respondents also thought in 1971–72 that since the introduction of controls prices had advanced more than wages and salaries. One important function of price controls consisted in altering people's price expectations. Regarding short-term expectations this was accomplished to some extent, but longer-term price expectations were not affected: Most people said that over the next five years there would be sizable inflation.

Immediately after the introduction of the price freeze consumers' willingness to buy was affected only with respect to automobiles. Cancellation of previously announced increases in car prices and discontinuation of the excise tax on cars made many people think that it was a good time to buy a car. In other areas of consumer spending the influence of controls on consumer sentiment was slow to take effect because, in the opinion of most people, the major long-range problems of the society were not remedied by the controls. Nevertheless, in the fall of 1971 a greatly increased proportion of people reported hearing good news about the economy. The opinions and attitudes of higher-income people and of people with college education improved earlier than those of other people.

A substantial improvement in the *Index of Consumer Sentiment* did not occur until the winter of 1971–72 and was there-

125

fore more coincidental with, than an advance indicator of, economic recovery. Early in 1972 a large proportion of respondents reported that business conditions had been improving. In the course of the year 1972 personal financial attitudes as well as business expectations registered considerable gains. As can be seen from Table 8-1, by September of that year the *Index of Consumer Sentiment* recovered to its prerecession level of early 1969. The impact of the recession on consumer sentiment had been wiped out.

The recovery of consumer attitudes was incomplete in one respect: Longer-run business expectations were less favorable in September, 1972, than they had been just before the recession and especially than they had been in 1965. At the same time, when they expressed satisfaction with their own economic situation, people voiced concern regarding problems of poverty, violence, and pollution and related these misgivings to economic prospects over the long run. This dissonance between personal financial satisfaction and societal malaise apparently contributed to ushering in the end of economic recovery.

The story of the 1970 recession would not be complete without mention of the fact that the recovery from it came to a sudden and early end. In the winter of 1972–1973 consumer sentiment deteriorated a little and in spring 1973 a great deal. At that time the experience of very rapid increases in the prices of food, and especially meat, dominated people's thinking. It gave rise to pessimism and posed the threat of a recession, but also had a very diferent immediate effect. Fear of future price increases led to a buying wave, especially in automobiles, the price of which appeared very favorable in comparison to future prices that were expected to reflect large additional costs for emission control and safety equipment. Although the discussion of this buying wave, coincident with a sharp decline in sentiment, is not part of the story of the recession of 1970, it is mentioned here to serve as an aid in understanding the subsequent analysis of the psychology of inflation.

The *Index of Consumer Sentiment* fell from 88.4 in the fourth quarter of 1972 to 75.7 in the fourth quarter of 1973, an unusually rapid decline within twelve months. The survey directors concluded in a press release issued on December 7, 1973, as follows:

"The results of the most recent survey [conducted between

126

TABLE 8-1

Change of Attitudes during the Recession of 1970

(Percent giving favorable or optimistic response minus percent giving unfavorable or pessimistic response, plus 100 for all families)

	Index of Consumer Sentiment*	Personal Financial Attitudes		Expectations about Business Conditions		Buying conditions for large household goods
		Better or worse off than a year ago	Expect to be better or worse off in a year	Next 12 months	Next 5 years	
1965 peak	103.4	121	135	163	136	152
February, 1969	95.1	115	130	148	114	136
1970 recession low point	75.4	99	119	93	78	105
May, 1971	81.6	105	122	114	83	128
Sept., 1972	94.0	116	126	139	106	147

*February, 1966 = 100.

127

TABLE 8-2

Deterioration of Attitudes toward Economic Prospects

Business	During the Next Year		During Next Five Years	
	1965	1970	1965	1970
Will be good	78%	34%	47%	22%
No definite opinion	14	25	42	34
Will be bad	8	41	11	44
Total	100%	100%	100%	100%

mid-October and mid-November] suggest that the onset of a general recession is imminent. Auto sales will be particularly hard hit."

Pessimism was rampant long before the oil embargo clouded economic prospects further in the late fall of 1973. The energy crisis struck when the outlook for two of America's largest industries, automobiles and residential construction, was unfavorable because both in buying cars and in building houses people had borrowed from the future. Even without the energy crisis consumers' discretionary expenditures would have declined considerably in 1974.

PART **III**
THE INFLUENCE OF ATTITUDES AND EXPECTATIONS IN THE LONGER RUN

9
THE PSYCHOLOGY OF INFLATION

The major arguments for disregarding psychological factors in economic affairs have been (1) that, while they may be influential for individuals, they would cancel out for the entire economy and (2) that, while they may be influential in the short run, they would have no effect over the longer run. The discussion of economic fluctuations during the last twenty-five years in the last three chapters may suffice to indicate that the first argument is untenable. Evidence contradicting the second argument will be provided at this juncture by considering the material already set forth but in a different format. Rather than discuss the different periods chronologically, and in terms of their unique characteristics, we shall search out those features common to all periods of prosperity and those common to all periods of recession. This discussion (in Chapters 10 and 11) must be preceded by a clarification of the principles of inflation, which has prevailed throughout all the periods under consideration, both of upswing and downswing.

On Theories of Inflation

Inflation may be defined as a general and sustained increase in the price level. Increases in the prices of individual items are not viewed as inflationary if they occur when most other prices remain stable. Only when the prices of very many different products and services advance over extended periods of time do we speak of inflation and recognize its major characteristic, the decline in the purchasing power of money.

Inflation is a very old phenomenon, which has been known to mankind for thousands of years and has occurred under a great variety of economic conditions. But irrespective of

131

whether the inflation resulted from the debasement of coins, the printing of paper money, large-scale borrowing, or rapid income increases, the theories about it have changed but little. Most popular have been the monetary theories of inflation. In brief, they are expressed by the statement that too much money competes for too few goods. If purchasing power increases more than the available supply of goods, or if supplies are restricted while incomes are not, a gap develops between the two, and the extent of the gap determines the extent of the price increases.

It has long been obvious that this theory tells less than the whole story. The explanation of inflation is one of the few instances in economics where the effectiveness of psychological factors has often been acknowledged. Sometimes their contribution has been thought to be minor, consisting only of making the extent of price increases a little larger or smaller than would be justified by economic factors alone. At the other extreme, inflationary psychology, as a sort of mass hysteria arising without any economic reason, has been seen as the only cause of price increases. The latter notion is clearly not acceptable. Although unjustified rumors may create expectations of price increases and thus result in hoarding or stocking up, such a process will not last over long periods if the rumors are in fact unjustified. (We should not forget that inflation has been defined as a sustained increase in the price level.) A middle position does appear to be justified, as witness what happens in connection with wars. Inflationary price increases have been observed not only in the course of a war, but also in response to a threat of war, or immediately after its outbreak when money in circulation has not yet increased and the supply of goods has not yet been restricted. It is unquestioned that the anticipation of certain developments may drive up prices.

Psychological factors may also manifest themselves in somewhat different ways. Inflation has been described, especially in foreign countries, as a break with past habits and attitudes. While usually people handle their money carefully, tend to economize, shop around, bargain, and take their time before buying, inflationary psychology is indicated by consumers' hurrying to buy, to spend their money with little deliberation before the goods are bought up or the money loses its value.

Clearly, these notions were intended to explain runaway

132

rather than creeping inflation. Experience in the 1950s and 1960s, in America as well as in many other countries, indicated that slow and gradual increases in the price level could prevail over several years without disturbing confidence in the currency or affecting past habits and behavior patterns. Possibly, creeping inflation calls for a different way of theorizing, especially about the interrelationship between economic and psychological factors.

Traditional theories seem not to differentiate between the different kinds of inflation. We may restate the most common explanation of all forms of inflation as follows: When the quantity of money or of incomes grows faster than the quantity of goods, purchasing power exceeds the supply of goods and the general price level is likely to rise. In addition, when they expect prices to go up, rational people (in possession of some liquid funds or able to borrow) buy in advance of their needs and stock up or hoard in order to beat inflation. The more prices have gone up in the past, the greater is the expectation of further price increases. This demand theory of inflation postulates that inflation is brought about and is accompanied by an increase in demand and that it stimulates demand. In inflationary periods consumers substitute goods for money and tend to spend more and save less.[1]

Recent studies of consumer behavior provided different bases for theorizing. Indeed, after World War II, some fairly simple observations about people's psychological reactions to creeping inflation led to quite the opposite proposition, namely, that in inflationary periods consumers tend to spend less and save more.[2] The observations were as follows:

1. Inflation was viewed as a bad thing, both for personal finances and for the economy as a whole.
2. Higher price tags made many people believe that it was a bad time to buy.

[1] The cost-push theory of inflation, popular in the last few decades, says that because of the power of labor there is a trend toward higher and higher wages and that rising costs are then translated into higher prices. This theory expands on the process of inflation, but does not necessarily change the presumed relation between inflation and increased spending made possible by rising incomes.

[2] This theory of creeping inflation was first presented in detail in Chapter 12 of Katona (1960) and was expanded further in Chapter 14 of Katona (1964a).

133

3. When prices were expected to go up people worried that more of their income would have to go for necessities and that therefore less money would be available for discretionary items.
4. Rising prices made for uncertainty, which induced many people to try harder to save and accumulate reserve funds.

It appears that despite all that has been written about inflation, the answer even to such a simple question as "Do consumers react to inflation by spending more or by spending less than before?" is far from clear. There is a good reason why this is so. There is no one generally valid answer to the question. Most commonly during the postwar period consumers' response to accelerated price increases was to reduce the proportion of their income expended for discretionary purposes.[3] But twice, in 1950 and again in 1973, consumers responded by increasing their spending. What triggers Response 1 (spending less) and what triggers Response 2 (spending more)? This is a crucial question the analysis of which will take us a long way toward understanding inflation.

We shall proceed by describing first the findings on people's attitudes and reactions to price increases in periods of creeping inflation and only later the circumstances under which consumers proceed to stock up and hoard and thus step up their rate of spending. Thus, observations made in the 1950s and 1960s will be reported before any discussion of the problems that have arisen in the 1970s. In general, it was possible to compare only periods of relatively slow with periods of relatively rapid price increases. Only with respect to some individual goods, such as automobiles, was it possible to compare the response to stable prices with the response to rising prices.

Resentment of Price Increases

The first noteworthy observation about people's reactions to price changes is that there is a threshold, that is, a point at

[3] The statement about the usual consumer response is made on the basis of survey evidence as related in the preceding chapters. Juster and Wachtel (1972a), aware of the author's discussion of psychological factors, found by fitting regression equations for the period 1954–71 that overall the impact of inflation was in the direction of reducing the rate of consumer spending and increasing the rate of saving.

which an effect begins to be produced. It is not justifiable to assume that any and all changes in prices influence consumer behavior. In the first place, consumers are often not aware of price changes, even though they are a matter of record. Public announcements of increases in automobile prices or in the cost-of-living index may go unnoticed by the majority of consumers. The reverse is also true. At some times many, or even most, consumers may be convinced that prices have increased even though according to the record they have not.

It follows that studies of inflation must begin with a determination of whether there is an awareness or *perception* of price changes. But even generally perceived price changes may be viewed as insignificant. The prevailing *attitude* toward them may be one of no concern. Then we should not expect any reaction to the changes. Similarly, it may happen that many people expect prices to go up or down but feel no concern about it and so do not react.

We may not assume that the threshold is constant. It will vary with experience. Following inflationary experiences, people may become more sensitive and their threshold may be lower. In contrast, following a period of relatively stable prices it may take many months before many people begin to complain about inflation.

A person feels cheated when, for instance, a garment or a piece of furniture in which he or she is interested is found to be priced higher than it was a month or two earlier. That disappointment or even anger represents the root of an unfavorable emotional reaction to price increases. General price increases make people feel worse off; the money they have does not go as far as it once did. The adverse emotional reaction is often expressed in the words "Prices are too high."

Contrariwise, people rely on stable prices. If the housewife thinks that the price of a certain article today is what it has been for a long time, she feels that the price is right. People become accustomed to prices that have persisted for quite a while and gain confidence when they expect prices to remain stable. Absence of anxiety about overpaying creates a climate favorable to purchasing. Generally, the experience that prices have been stable coupled with the expectation that they will remain stable stimulates buying.

"Right" prices or "normal" prices, as well as prices which are "too high," have psychological meaning even though from

135

an economic point of view they are undefinable concepts. If, after prices have gone up and have been felt to be too high, the price advance does not continue, people may become accustomed to the new price level. This process of habituation is slow and gradual. Following inflationary experiences it takes time until reliance on prices is restored and people again come to consider them to be right and just.

Observations on general price declines have not been possible in the last twenty-five years. It can only be said that price reductions in clearance and other sales, or discounted merchandise, were found to be very attractive to consumers. As an example, people feel elated when they find an item of clothing or a piece of furniture priced lower than what they almost paid for the same article a month or two earlier. The feeling of getting more for one's money or of being offered a bargain evokes pleasurable reactions. Lower prices are seen as good for the economy. One major reason for this opinion, as expressed in interviews, is that when prices are reduced people can buy more. Expected price declines bring forth the same reaction. People think they will be better off because prices will go down, and their willingness to buy increases.

Quantitative data about what people consider either a favorable or an unfavorable development were obtained about expected, rather than experienced, price changes. Survey respondents, after expressing their opinion about what would happen to prices of things they would buy during the next twelve months, were asked, "Would you say that these (rising prices, unchanged prices, etc.) would be to the good, to the bad, or what?" Most people did not hesitate to give a definite answer, although the formulation of the question was intentionally vague. What most people had in mind and could report was not a careful judgment about the advantages or disadvantages of inflation for the country or for themselves but an emotional reaction to it. The findings, averaged from several surveys conducted in the 1950s and early 1960s, as presented in Table 9-1, revealed that a large majority felt price increases to be "bad."

Survey findings were quite similar with respect to automobile prices. In the 1950s as well as in the 1960s most of those who said that prices had been and would remain stable also said that it was a good time to buy cars. Rising prices were associated with the notion that it was a bad time to buy. Inten-

TABLE 9-1
Emotional Response to Price Changes

Expected Price Increase Would Be	1956–57	1961–62
To the good	14%	11%
Undecided	18	22
To the bad	68	67
	100%	100%
Expected Price Stability Would Be [a]		
To the good	61%	72%
Undecided	24	17
To the bad [b]	15	11
	100%	100%

[a] In periods later than the early 1960s the observations could not be repeated in a reliable manner because the proportion of people expecting stable prices became very small. Expected price declines could not be studied at all because they were expressed by relatively few people (who usually considered them "to the good").
[b] The prospect of price stability was viewed as "bad" only because the level was already considered to be too high. The usual response in these cases was "Prices are too high, they should go down."

tions to buy new cars were expressed by fewer people among those who thought that car prices would be rising than among those who thought that they would remain unchanged. Price increases resulted at many different times in an increase in the proportion of survey respondents complaining about prices and about the absence of available good buys.

Conservative Price Expectations

Fluctuations of price expectations have been described in the last three chapters. The only times in which a decline in prices was anticipated by a sizable proportion of the people were the years 1948–49 and 1951–52. In sharp contrast, a year earlier, in 1950–51, most people expected substantial price increases. In the entire period 1955–69 the majority of American people thought that prices would be somewhat higher in 12 months, still higher in 5 years and higher still in 10 years. When asked about the extent of expected price increases the responses were rather conservative. To illustrate, the following data represent the averages from several surveys conducted in 1965–67:

44 percent said that prices would go up by 1 or 2 percent in 12 months

14 percent said that prices would go up by 3 or 4 percent in 12 months

30 percent said that prices would go up by 5 percent in 12 months

12 percent said that prices would go up by more than 5 per-cent in 12 months

100 percent = 80 percent of all respondents—those who answered the question about the extent of expected price increases.

It is worth noting that in those years the answers fluctuated very little from survey to survey and were fairly similar in different income and education groups. In 1969, following the acceleration of the war in Vietnam, there were some changes in price expectations, mainly consisting of a decline in the proportion of those who expected price increases of only 1 or 2 percent in 12 months. The median rate of expected price increases rose from less than 4 percent in 1968 to 5 percent in the spring of 1970. But even at that time, when during the preceding 12 months prices had advanced by close to 6 or 7 percent, only one out of every four respondents thought that prices would go up by more than 5 percent. Therefore, in 1970, and also at several earlier and later occasions, the extent of inflation as it actually occurred was unanticipated.

It follows that past developments are not the only determinants of expectations. Specifically, price expectations are not an extrapolation of what has happened to prices in the recent past. Other factors and especially opinions about what the government will do play a substantial role in shaping price expectations. Inflationary expectations can arise in periods of price stability, as was the case most clearly immediately after the outbreak of the Korean War in 1950. Price expectations may slow down substantially following rapid price increases, as happened early in 1951 following the introduction of price controls and following a change in the outlook about the war. During most of the 1950s and 1960s people in general believed that the government would find the means to avoid catastrophic

138

price developments. This notion persisted in 1970–71 and mitigated inflationary price expectations.

At the same time, however, longer-range price expectations remained inflationary. In numerous surveys respondents were asked about what the prices of things people buy would be "5 years from now." In the first decade after World War II price expectations for 5 years were less inflationary than for 1 year; there were some people who thought that what had gone up would come down. In the late 1950s and in the 1960s price expectations over 12 months and over 5 years were quite similar. In 1970 30 percent of respondents said that in 5 years prices would be substantially higher, 30 percent that they would be a little higher, and 20 percent that they might be the same as they were then (20 percent expressed no opinion).[4]

Attitudes toward Inflation

We have already noted a great variety of indications provided by interviews that inflation is seen by most people as an adverse development. We have shown that at various times during the last 25 years people's experience with accelerated price increases induced them to complain about them and to evaluate their own financial position unfavorably. Among those with income gains the proportion who said that they were better off declined, and the proportion who said that they were worse off increased when prices rose substantially. The perception of inflation was also found to be associated with a pessimistic evaluation of business prospects and with a decline in the *Index of Consumer Sentiment*. Consistently over the last 20 years the *Index* turned down, foreshadowing a decline in major expenditures, when inflation accelerated, and improved when price increases slowed down.

The observed impact of inflation is not self-evident either with respect to consumer spending or to expectations about business conditions or personal finances. The notion that business conditions would deteriorate in times of inflation was explained by many survey respondents as the influence of con-

---

[4] Expectations about what will happen in several years are for very many people quite imprecise. Therefore, questions about the extent to which prices will go up over the next five years are answered by a minority of respondents only and were omitted from most surveys.

sumers on business trends: If consumers are worse off, they will buy less and business will suffer. Moreover, inflation is viewed as augmenting uncertainty, which is thought to have an adverse effect on business.

But why should private households suffer in periods of inflation? True, in foreign countries in most inflationary periods before World War II the advance in wages and salaries lagged far behind runaway prices. But between 1940 and 1970 incomes increased more than prices, resulting in a substantial gain in real income and an improvement in people's standard of living. Income increases were particularly large in years of inflation, which for many people were financially the best years of their lives. Since Americans in general are not acquainted with the ravages of runaway inflation that are familiar to the people of many other countries, the adverse opinions about inflation prevailing in the 1950s and 1960s in the United States call for some explanation.

We may ask whether people with large gains in income did not feel compensated for the losses caused by price increases and whether some of them did not even attribute their income gains to inflation. The answer to this question is that most Americans consider income increases and price increases as being unrelated. In Chapter 12 we shall discuss in detail the factors to which income gains are attributed. It may suffice to report here that survey respondents with gains in income were asked the puzzling question, "How come that you make more than five years ago?" In reply most people spoke of their own accomplishments and progress. Only a very small proportion of people referred to inflation. Even blue-collar workers with union contracts specifying cost-of-living increases attributed their gains over five years much less frequently to inflation than to what they themselves deserved to get. People consider inflation bad because higher prices detract from the enjoyment of their higher incomes, which in their opinion are the well-deserved fruits of their labor.

Despite the prevalance of answers indicating that respondents saw no relationship between inflation and higher income, there were other data providing somewhat different indications. We are discussing here the two most pervasive economic experiences of the American people during the postwar period—improvement in their way of living and rising prices. Although, as we said, income gains are attributed overwhelmingly to what a person himself has done, while inflation is attributed to unspecified "others," yet some connection between the two could be found when survey respondents were asked whether they were hurt much, a little, or not at all by inflation.

In 1969 and 1970, that is, at a time when complaints about inflation were very frequent, on the average

14% said that they were hurt very much,
11% said that they were hurt much,
55% said that they were hurt a little,
17% said that they were hurt not at all by inflation, with
  3% "Don't know" answers.
100%

While the answers differed only a little according to the income of the respondents (the poor saying more often that they were hurt much or very much), it was found that those with substantial income gains constituted the bulk of those who said that they were not hurt at all by inflation. Nevertheless, many people with large as well as small income gains were found to give the answer that inflation hurt them a little. The replies indicate that creeping inflation is viewed by most people as bad, but not as a catastrophe. People resent inflation because they believe that it should not and need not happen.

In the 1960s only a few people explained in detail that during an all-out war price increases might have been justified, but in a cold war one could have guns and butter as well; therefore, since there were no shortages, there should have been no price increases either. But even if this rational argumentation was not very common, its affective tone was widespread: In the opinion of most Americans there was no justification for peacetime inflation.

Nevertheless, most people did not place the blame for inflation on any one group of our society. When asked specifically whether they agreed or disagreed that one or another development was "a reason for our having inflation" they overwhelmingly expressed agreement with suggested misdeeds of government, business, consumers, and labor. In 1969, for instance, more than two-thirds of survey respondents agreed that inflation came about because of each of the following suggested reasons:

Business firms raised prices too much.

141

Labor and trade unions demanded and obtained too large wage increases.

The government spent too much on Vietnam.

The government spent too much on other things.

Consumers borrowed too much.

At that time only one of the alternatives mentioned, namely, "The government did not tax enough" evoked any disagreement, and that came from 85 percent of the respondents. It appears that most people resent inflation but few profess to understand how it comes about. Inflation is viewed as one of the evils we have not yet mastered.

The answers received to questions about the kind of people who are hurt most and the kind of people hurt least or not at all by inflation were predictable. Overwhelmingly, people replied that poor people or the little man was hurt most and only one out of five mentioned people with fixed or stable incomes. To the second question the usual answer was that well-to-do people, people with high incomes or businessmen are hurt least by inflation.[5] Practically nobody said that lenders lose and borrowers profit from inflation.

As to what should be done to slow down inflation, most Americans were found to agree with such proposed remedies as, "The government should spend less" or "Consumers should spend less," but to disagree that "Income taxes should be raised" or "Interest rates should be raised." They specifically disagreed with any suggestion to create a recession or increase unemployment in order to slow down inflation. In 1969 they also appeared unwilling to make personal sacrifices to arrest inflation. Wage control or any limitation of income gains were opposed by the great majority while price control was approved by 45 percent of respondents.

During a recession as well as during an inflation most people, irrespective of whether or not they are directly affected, have a sense of reduced certainty and reduced security. Their self-assurance is limited because they feel unable to predict what will happen to them. Thus the prevailing attitudes are frequently similar in periods of recession and of inflation. The same is true of behavior; spending less and saving more have characterized inflations and recessions alike in the 1950s and

[5] Interestingly, both answers were given with about the same frequency by high-income and low-income respondents.

142

1960s. There is little reason to expect that one could serve to rule out the other and that a moderate recession could cure inflation.[6]

How to Protect Oneself against Inflation

At various times survey respondents were asked, "Would you say that someone like you can do something to protect your family against price increases?" In 1969, for instance, 27 percent answered Yes and 56 percent answered No to this question. (The rest answered Possibly or Don't Know; answers a few years earlier were quite similar.) In reply to a follow-up question, "What can you do?" only one kind of answer was given by a sizable proportion of respondents. About 25 percent of respondents said that one should buy less, postpone buying certain things, buy cheaper goods, or economize.

While these answers are in line with the postponement rather than the stock-up theory of inflation, questioning in 1969 and 1970 continued with a specific inquiry about the opposite reaction to inflation. Survey respondents were asked: "Did you or your family buy anything during the past few months because you thought that it would cost more later?" To this question—intentionally formulated so as to suggest an affirmative answer—12 percent of all family heads, and likewise 12 percent of family heads with more than $10,000 family income, answered Yes and 88 percent No. When asked what they had bought in advance, most respondents spoke of occasional purchases of a variety of small items. Some did not remember what they had bought.

Advance buying was observed under different circumstances. The price freeze of August, 1971, was accompanied by a rollback of automobile prices (and the discontinuation of the auto excise tax). Many people said in the fall of 1971 that auto prices were "low"; they thought that the government's efforts to hold down car prices would be temporary and that it was a good time to buy before prices went up again. Similarly, in the

6   Naturally, the author does not mean to say that a deep and enduring depression with an oversupply of goods would not arrest inflation. But there is no foundation to the hope often expressed by policy makers that inflation can be halted by just a slight slowdown in the economy and a small increase in unemployment.

143

fall of 1972, when again announced increases in auto prices were canceled, some advance buying was observed. Even in periods of creeping inflation the desire to beat inflation is not absent but is stimulated primarily by the perception of what are thought to be unusually low prices rather than by rapid past price increases.

Such occasional purchases to the contrary notwithstanding, creeping inflation is generally characterized by a reduction in discretionary expenditures. The perception and expectation of such inflation generate pessimistic attitudes that inhibit inclinations to buy. In addition, a substantial proportion of respondents explained that inflation made them feel worse off because they had to spend an increased proportion of their income, or even all their income, on buying the things they needed. Therefore they could not afford to spend money on things they would have liked to have but could do without.

Inflation and Personal Saving

If it is true that in periods of gradual and slow price increases consumers postpone some of their discretionary purchases, it follows that, other things being equal, they would increase their rate of saving. Abstaining from buying cars and appliances means not borrowing for those purposes, and amounts borrowed would represent negative savings, which are deducted from amounts saved. In addition, it is probable that the general malaise and uncertainty attached to inflation heightens motivations to save. The discussion of the extent of saving in response to good or to bad times must be postponed for a later occasion (Chapter 15). At this point we are concerned with an aspect of the saving process that is specifically related to inflation, namely, the forms of saving people choose when prices go up.

As we shall show in analyzing the saving process, savings deposits (in banks, savings and loan associations, etc.) represent the most common and the most popular form of saving. There has been no change in this respect over the last twenty years. Specifically, in 1969–71, years of substantial inflation, people saved primarily by adding to their savings deposits. Was this the case because people were uninformed and failed to realize that bank deposits were not protected against inflation,

144

or did they behave in an irrational manner? An answer to this question was given by this author in *The Mass Consumption Society* (1964), where he quoted the following interview with a single respondent:

A foreman in an airplane plant was asked, "What have prices of the things you buy done during the last few years?"

"Everything's gone up," he said.

"What do you think prices will do next year?"

"Shoot up further. Seems like there's no limit."

Then the questioning turned to saving. "It is important to have some savings," the foreman explained. "Something unexpected may happen; you've got to save for a rainy day." Asked whether he had saved and in what way, he explained that for over ten years he had had an account with a savings bank and that the account had been growing year by year. "Banks are safe, mighty convenient, and they pay interest besides," he added.

"You spoke of inflation—does that have anything to do with how you feel about your savings account?" he was then asked.

"Oh, I know what you mean," he replied. "The $100 I put in the bank ten years ago aren't worth that much today. Maybe inflation has dropped them to something like $80. But what if I hadn't ever put the $100 in the bank at all? Then I'd have spent the money. . . . Believe me, $80 is a lot better than nothing!"[7]

The argument may be restated in two propositions. First, most people do not see an alternative to saving in banks (savings and loan associations are generally thought of as banks). Stocks are seen as risky and real estate as not being accessible to everyone. In bad times, such as years of inflation, the most important thing is to have one's savings in a safe place, and banks are seen as safe. Second, the loss in the purchasing power of bank deposits is not believed to be substantial. In years of creeping inflation the depositor is compensated, fully or to à large extent, by the receipt of interest.

We spoke earlier in this chapter about the answers survey respondents gave to a question about how people could protect

[7] This is the end of the interview as reproduced from Katona (1964a, pp. 138f).

themselves against price increases. Following this question —to which in 1969 only 3 percent of the sample spoke of buying stocks or real estate—respondents were asked, "Thinking of your savings, do you see any way to protect them against inflation?" Most people answered in the negative and many even failed to see any reason why their savings needed protection. About 14 percent of all respondents and 28 percent of upper-income respondents spoke of putting money into stocks, real estate, or investments that might go up with prices. Thus, even if survey respondents were pushed to relate inflation to a loss in their savings and reserve funds, only a fairly small proportion gave consideration to alternatives to bank deposits. Creeping inflation was thought to hurt only a little, as we reported before, because it was not believed that it could wipe out one's savings. In fact, inflation might enhance the value of what is the most important saving of a very large proportion of Americans, namely, their investment in the home in which they live. Not only have real estate prices advanced in inflationary years, but mortgage debt has also been repaid with cheaper and cheaper dollars. Inflation nevertheless was not thought to be beneficial; rising real estate prices were attributed primarily to good times, and few people were aware of the financial advantages of debtors in times of inflation.

Buying in Anticipation of Price Increases

We recaptiulate the essence of the new psychology of inflation as it developed in the United States between 1951 and 1971: The expectation of slow and gradual price increases creates uncertainty and loss of confidence and therefore reduces discretionary demand. Let us turn now to the traditional psychology of inflation according to which demand increases with rising prices.

We have already spoken of buying an individual product, such as a car, even if not immediately "needed," because its price was seen as "low." A different situation prevails when consumers buy a great variety of goods in advance and in excess of needs. They may do so because they expect shortages, or because they are intent on exchanging their money for commodities. This situation has been known in several foreign

146

countries in which such behavior has been termed "flight from the currency."

In the United States, stocking up, hoarding, and widespread buying waves occurred on the part of consumers and business firms at the time of military setbacks in Korea in 1950. News of military reverses revived the not-too-old memories of wartime shortages and rationing. Businessmen and consumers were energized to act by their fear of specific future developments, namely, large war expenditures and shortages of civilian goods.

Fear of specific threatening developments led to stocking up and advance buying in 1973 as well. In the spring of that year it arose because of experiences in supermarkets. Unprecedented increases in food prices were felt as a threat to well-being. That experience, for which most people saw no good reason, created indignation and the fear of not being able to make ends meet. The largest increases occurred in meat prices. Meat represents the most frequent of all discretionary expenditures to which households pay particular attention. In several interviews women reported their shock on discovering that they did not have enough money to pay for the food they had planned to buy. The rapid price increases came immediately after the transition from Phase 2 to Phase 3 of price controls. The third phase, in the opinion of most people, meant the end of all controls and was viewed as a grave mistake. Faith in the government's economic policies was at a low ebb.

In August, 1973, close to 20 percent of all survey respondents reported that during the preceding few months they had made some major purchase in order to beat inflation. Automobiles were the most frequently mentioned single product bought in advance. The proportion of people expecting prices to increase by 10 percent or more within a year rose to 30 percent of all those who gave a numerical estimate (it was 13 percent in 1970), with the great majority expecting prices to go up by more than 5 percent. The proportion mentioning shortages of food products, and later in the year of gasoline and other oil products, rose rapidly. Under these circumstances fear of future inflation outweighed the resentment of past price increases. In surveys many respondents spoke of "This is a good time to buy because prices will be higher in the future," while just a few months earlier they had said, "This is a bad time to buy because prices are too high." As a result of consumers

147

borrowing from the future, in the first nine months of 1973 consumer expenditures for automobiles and other durable goods were much higher than in the corresponding period of 1972.

We conclude that advance or excess buying represents an immediate response to a specific threat. In contrast, postponement of purchases, the most common response to accelerated price increases between 1951 and 1971, expresses malaise and anxiety as well as resentment of the higher prices. The same stimulus constellation, the perception of accelerated price increases, may bring forth very different responses according to the general context within which it occurs.

In 1973 doubts of the ability of the government to cope with inflation and even mistrust in the policies and purposes of the government were nourished not just by the obvious failure of price controls but also by Watergate. References to Watergate in interviews in which only questions about economic matters were asked leave no doubt that the Watergate disclosures influenced consumer behavior. They contributed to the failure of price controls. How consumers will react to price controls is again something that cannot be predicted a priori because the response may differ greatly under different circumstances. People will accept controls and adhere to them when they feel that controls are required and when they expect them to do the job. This was the case to a large extent in 1971. Then the controls accomplished one of their primary tasks, namely, to mitigate inflationary expectations and thereby insure the persistence of creeping inflation, in which consumers do not step up their demand for goods. In 1973, however, very few people believed in the success of controls. More than 70 percent said in August, 1973, that the controls would not work (and many others said that they did not know enough to answer the question).[8]

In the summer of 1973 the answers to the question about whether inflation hurt much, a little, or not at all differed greatly from the answers received in 1969 or 1970. Not fewer than 35 percent said that inflation hurt them very much (as against 14 percent in 1969–70) and only 3 percent that inflation hurt them not at all (17 percent in 1969–70). Rapid inflation and especially the substantial increase in food prices created real hardship for many people.

[8] We shall return to the discussion of price control in Chapter 21.

148

Two Scenarios

In 1973–74 there was justification to foresee two possibilities concerning the prospects of slowing down inflation—one very pessimistic and the other fairly optimistic. The arguments supporting the former will be presented first.

1. The most unfortunate coincidence in those years was that rapid inflation and the energy crisis struck just at a time when distrust in the government had reached a peak. While in earlier years people in general had believed that the government would find ways to slow down inflation, in 1973–74 in the opinion of most people it was not possible to rely on government action.

2. Pessimism was widespread and was related to the belief that the administration in Washington was untrustworthy. According to a survey conducted in the fourth quarter of 1973 among the over 40 percent of respondents who thought that the government was doing a poor job in its economic policy, 58 percent expected bad and 18 percent good times during the next twelve months; among the 12 percent who thought the government was doing a good job 29 percent expected bad and 41 percent good times. (Close to one-half of all respondents took an intermediate position about government policy.) Bad times meant for most people periods in which prices rose more rapidly than incomes. Pessimism about economic prospects and the expectation of sharply rising prices were interrelated. Early in 1974, among the very many survey respondents who expected bad times to come, 35 percent expected prices to go up by more than 10 percent during the next twelve months; among the many fewer people who expected good times, 10 percent expressed such expectations.[9]

3. In 1973–74 inflation was worldwide. The increase in prices of oil products and to some extent also that of food products was of foreign origin. The devaluation of the dollar raised the prices of goods imported into the U.S., and inflation abroad created demand for American raw materials at rising prices. While many other countries

[9] Sharply rising interest rates enhanced people's pessimistic outlook at that time. They, too, generated attitudes and expectations that contributed to accelerating inflation (see Chapter 21).

149

have long been familiar with "imported inflation," Americans have traditionally paid little attention to foreign economies and international trade and believed, until 1973, that their economic fate was immune to foreign interference.

But in 1973–74 there were good reasons as well for confidence in a return to an era of creeping rather than rapid inflation. The basis for such optimism was as follows:

1. Even though in these years some signs of a break with past habits could be discerned—expectation of shortages, advance buying, and businesses raising prices without fearing adverse reactions by buyers—the extent of substitution of goods for money was quite limited. Among some consumers economizing and even boycotting goods the prices of which rose sharply remained the response to inflation. Confidence in the currency was maintained despite the devaluation of the dollar—as was faith in assets based on the dollar. The American people continued to save large amounts and to put their savings in banks.
2. The slowdown of consumer demand and the turn to pessimism could not be viewed as signaling the onset of a new era of stagnation. There was no reason to believe that the attitudes and behavior patterns that developed between 1951 and 1971—spending less and saving more in response to inflation—would not prevail again and help to restore creeping inflation.

We shall discuss the question about a possible end of the optimistic era toward the end of this book and close this chapter with a few words relating to theoretical considerations.

The clue to a better understanding of inflation is better theory. If we accept the proposition that all there is to inflation is "an insufficient supply of goods in relation to the demand for them at existing prices," then we close the door to a full analysis and real understanding of the subject.[10] In the proposition as stated both the supply of goods and the demand for them are viewed as natural phenomena that must be left to run

[10] The quote is from the Monthly Economic Letter of the *First National City Bank of New York,* August, 1973, p. 3. The article argues that controls cannot eliminate the essential cause of inflation as formulated.

their course. In fact, both are man-made. The supply of goods may be low because producers and sellers (including farmers) abstain from selling in the expectation of obtaining higher prices later. The demand for goods may be high because consumers as well as businessmen stock up and hoard in anticipation of shortages and higher prices. Existing prices must not be accepted as resulting from inescapable forces.

As we have tried to show in this chapter, inflation results both from economic-financial and from psychological factors. Similarly, both economic and psychological measures must be applied to slow down inflation. That goal can be attained only if, in addition to appropriate measures of fiscal and monetary policy, a climate is restored in which business firms know well that indiscriminate price increases hurt their reputation and good will, consumers favor businesses that hold the line, and people have confidence in the government's economic policy.

10
THE PSYCHOLOGY OF PROSPERITY

Prosperity cannot be sustained over long periods unless confidence and optimism prevail. The need for the presence of these attitudes if times are to be prosperous has often been recognized,[1] but the nature of the role they play has been but vaguely understood, if at all. The task in this chapter will be to specify the function of the climate of opinion and therefore of the human element in sustaining prosperous periods.

In good times newspapers and periodicals, in reporting on business trends, often warn that an extended boom would mean saturated consumer markets. In prosperous periods, so the argument runs, very many people gratify their wants and desires; if that process lasts a few years, wants must be exhausted and saturation must bring forth a reduction in consumer demand. Thus prosperity serves as its own gravedigger. The argument implies an inevitability to the periodicity of economic trends. Not only do good times generate saturation and therefore a recession, but in bad years, in which demand is small, slowly more and more unfilled needs and wants are thought to accumulate and ultimately lead to the return of good times.

In contrast to these notions, economic theory usually acknowledges no rigid limits to human wants. But the traditional theory does not say anything about the conditions under which wants are or are not exhausted. This is a crucial question at a time when a wants or aspirations economy prevails rather than a needs economy. Under what circumstances does the gratification of wants give rise to saturation and under what circumstances to the arousal of new wants? We shall find that

[1] For instance, Arthur F. Burns wrote (1957, p. 27), "If prosperity is to flourish, people must have confidence in their own economic future and that of their country."

153

attitudes and expectations determine saturation rather than the rate of past acquisition of goods or the extent of possessions.

Rising Levels of Aspiration

The first theoretical model from which answers to these questions may be derived was presented by the social psychologist, Kurt Lewin. Lewin's principles, supported by experimental evidence with intelligence tests and simple motor tasks, have been summarized by this author as follows:

1. Aspirations are not static; they are not established once for all time.
2. Aspirations tend to grow with achievement and decline with failure.
3. Aspirations are influenced by the performance of other members of the group to which a person belongs and by that of reference groups.
4. Aspirations are reality-oriented; most commonly they are slightly higher or slightly lower than the level of accomplishment rather than greatly different from it.[2]

In simplest terms, then, a beginner in golf sets his goal low; for example, making a score of 100 represents his highest aspiration. If he accomplishes his goal he sets his aspirations higher—not much higher but somewhat beyond the accomplishment level. The greater his success, the higher he aims, and this will be particularly true if his friends and colleagues are ardent golf players. However, if repeated efforts to improve his score fail, our golfer will set his aspirations lower. Frustration may result in contentment and absence of further desires or, if the goal is highly valued in the group to which he belongs, in leaving the group (in this case, resigning from the golf club).

What has been said about golf applies to aspirations about jobs and income. A promotion or a raise for which we strive may appear to us as something which, if obtained, will bring forth satisfaction and contentment. But after the better position or the higher income has been achieved, our outlook may change. The new position may then be seen as a step toward further advancement: gratification may create new ambitions.

[2] See Lewin et al. (1944); also Katona (1953) and (1960, 130ff.).

154

The level of aspiration may be raised with accomplishment.

The principle may be applied to the process of saving. A young family may think that they will be satisfied if they acquire a small amount in the bank, but a few years later, after accumulating that amount, they may consider it insufficient because they have set their sights higher.

The question of saturation with consumer goods represents one of the most important applications of the theorem. It should be noted that saturation with specific goods is not considered because the desire for, as one example, a newer or better car may well disappear after such a car has been bought. Rising aspirations are most commonly the result of the arousal of new wants and desires, after more urgent wants have been satisfied. In studying individual families over several years during the fifties, numerous instances were found in which a desire for a new car—or a house, or new furniture—first dominated the family's thinking. Before the car was bought, the building of a porch or the purchase of various appliances did not appear very necessary. After the car was bought these needs assumed great importance. To quote a psychologist's formulation of this principle of motivation: "The most basic consequence of satiation of any need is that this need is submerged and a new and higher need emerges."[3] We should add only that the new need is not necessarily a higher need.

What has been said thus far tells only part of the story. The connection between past acquisitions and growth in aspiration is not automatic and is not universal. Not all income gains, or increases in savings, or improvements in the standard of living serve as a basis for rising aspirations. Some may even be disappointing because they were smaller than what was aspired to or expected, or because others with whom an individual compares himself are thought to have fared better. Failure to improve one's situation may also be accepted under certain conditions and may not create frustration, which represents a condition fundamental to the feeling of saturation.

How do people react when they feel that they are better off than they were a few years earlier or when they are satisfied with their standard of living? There are two greatly different possibilities. Some people may feel that at last they have made it; having achieved what they wanted, they can now relax and enjoy what they have. Others may feel that they are advanc-

[3] See Maslow (1954, p. 108).

155

ing; they know that things can improve and feel that they must improve further; therefore, they are stimulated to work harder. Similarly, dissatisfaction may also have two meanings. It may signify failure and frustration, or it may provide an incentive to overcome failure.[4]

Persistence of Desires and of Satisfactions

We have sharpened the issue but have not contributed to its solution, which may be found only through empirical studies. First, some descriptive studies will be reported, indicating that high levels of aspiration did occur following the gratification of numerous wants of many people. Studies that contribute to the explanation of the circumstances under which that occurred will be taken up later.

For many years the Survey Research Center has included the following question in some of its surveys, "Now about your wishes—are there any special expenditures you would really *like* to make, or anything you would like to spend money on?" Both in the early 1950s and in the early 1960s somewhat over 60 percent of representative samples answered in the affirmative and somewhat over 30 percent in the negative. Not only was there no decline in the frequency of affirmative answers over many years of large purchases of consumer goods, but the list of unfilled wants and desires given by respondents in reply to a supplementary question even lengthened. While in the first few years after World War II only houses, automobiles, and major appliances were mentioned by many respondents, in the early 1960s it became justified to speak of a proliferation of wants. A great variety of different things, especially those connected with leisure-time activities and travel, or with additions and repairs to houses, were reported by many respondents.

People who denied having a desire for any special expenditures were mostly old or poor. The proportion of negative answers to the first question declined with rising income and increased with advancing age. That older people have fewer unfilled wants than younger people is hardly surprising. (Sixteen percent of those under 35 and 53 percent of those over 65 failed to indicate any desires in 1962.) The relatively few de-

[4] We shall come back to these differences in Chapter 24.

156

sires expressed by low-income people appear to indicate that even our wishes and desires are reality-tested: Among those with less than $3,000 annual income 43 percent, and among those with over $10,000 income 25 percent, indicated no desires. Newer articles or products used by relatively few people and not belonging to the "standard package" are desired primarily by upper-income people who are well supplied with standard goods.

In 1968 the proportion giving affirmative answers to the question about unfilled wants was slightly lower than in 1962 (56 percent against 61 percent) and in 1971, in the midst of a recession, it was still lower (51 percent). The major difference occurred in the proportion of wishes expressed by upper-income people, which declined substantially during the recession. The same was true of the proportion of wishes expressed by older people, including people between the ages of 50 and 65. People in the middle and younger age brackets as well as in the middle-income brackets continued to express a great number and a great variety of unfulfilled wishes.

The frequency of wishes expressed by young married people is of course easily explained by the paucity of their possessions and their desire to participate in the American standard of living. The process of upgrading, however, continues steadily up to the ages of 40 or 50 in which very many people reach their top lifetime income. Newly acquired houses are exchanged after a few years when people can afford larger ones or dwellings in a better neighborhood. The same is true of cars and major appliances. In addition, the desire arises for second cars, second television sets, and even second homes (vacation or leisure-time housing). This movement is most pronounced for automobiles. The ownership of two or more cars by family units rose steadily in the postwar years and reached 28 percent in 1971.

The American people were overwhelmingly satisfied with their economic situation during the postwar period. When asked, for instance, about their occupational progress in 1954, 74 percent expressed satisfaction and 23 percent dissatisfaction; as to their standard of living, 68 percent said they were satisfied and 29 percent dissatisfied; regarding their income, where the question was formulated somewhat differently, 58 percent said that they were getting what they should be getting while 39 percent thought they should be getting more.

In 1962 the findings were slightly less favorable, with 64 percent saying that they were satisfied with their standard of living and 32 percent that they were not fully satisfied. Finally, in 1972, when a seven-point scale was offered to respondents as a frame for answering questions about their satisfaction, 81 percent chose scale positions 1, 2, or 3 reflecting satisfaction when asked about their standard of living and 69 percent when asked about their income. When asked for an opinion about "life in the U.S. today," 67 percent answered by giving scale values 1, 2, or 3 (excellent, very good, good), 24 percent scale 4 (mixed) and 9 percent scales 5, 6, or 7 (various degrees of bad). Likewise, to several additional questions the expressions "good" or "better" far exceeded in frequency the answers "bad" or "worse," thus reflecting an optimistic bias of the American people. Expressions of satisfaction with one's own economic situation are elicited more easily than dissatisfactions. In addition, the data show that a high degree of satisfaction on the part of very many people does persist over many years even in the face of worsening economic conditions.

Persistence of Belief in Progress

Studies designed to provide clues for an understanding of the conditions under which levels of aspiration are raised will be discussed next. The studies related to the arousal of expectations rather than of aspirations. Yet, since the questions pertained to expectations about what would happen in the next four or five years, they necessarily contained a substantial aspirational element.[5]

Between 1967 and 1972 respondents in surveys with representative samples of the American people were repeatedly asked whether they were financially better or worse off than five years earlier. About 60 percent replied Better Off (designated as B_1). A somewhat smaller proportion of all respondents, but a similar proportion of those who gave a definite

---

[5] Short-term expectations, on the other hand, are more realistic than aspirations. For instance, if questions are asked about the income expected during the next few months, the answer is greatly influenced by the respondent's level of information about the situation of the firm for which he works and about the economic conditions of the country as a whole. Long-term expectations reflect desires to a much greater extent.

answer to the question, said that "five years from now" they would be Better Off (B_2). But a substantial proportion of those in the former group were not in the latter. Those in the BB category—giving the answer Better Off to both questions —represented about 60 percent of the B_1 group. Past progress is often expected to continue in the future, or to give rise to optimistic expectations.

An analysis of the composition and the behavior of the BB Group is revealing. We shall show in Chapter 12, where the extent of prevailing optimism and its reasons are studied, that age and income level make for large differences. Younger family heads and those in the upper-income group are overrepresented in the BB Group.

Analyses of recent past purchases and plans to purchase by the BB Group indicate that these are the people who constantly upgrade their possessions, make highly discretionary expenditures to the largest extent, and intend to do so in the future with great frequency. A few of the numerous data collected are reproduced in Table 10-1. It appears that a much larger proportion of BB Group families than of other families purchased cars on the installment plan, bought two cars in the same year, and intended to buy cars.

In the BB Group we isolated people who felt that an improvement in their personal financial situation would continue. The belief in continuous or cumulative progress was found to be associated with several other significant attitudes. Members of the BB Group showed much greater optimism about the chances of fulfilling their wishes and desires than did other people. Most importantly, a much larger proportion of the BB Group than of the NonBB Group believed that what they themselves did would have the greatest influence on their future standard of living. In the NonBB Group a larger proportion than in the BB Group felt dependent on what would happen to the economy in general. Reliance on one's own abilities contributes to the persistence of the belief in personal financial progress.

Similar findings were obtained in a panel study in which the same people were interviewed by the Survey Research Center several times between 1966 and 1970 concerning their purchases of durable goods and the incurrence of installment debt.[6]

[6] See Hendricks et al. (1973).

TABLE 10-1
Differences in the Behavior of Better-Better Group and Other People
(frequency in percent)

	Better-Better Group*	Others
Incurred installment debt in preceding year (1967 data).	53	35
Intend to buy a new car during next year (1968 data)	13	7
Purchased 2 or more cars in preceding year (1972 data)	14	5
(Frequency adjusted for income and age)	(13)	(7)
Intend to buy a car during next year (1972 data)	37	18
(Frequency adjusted for income and age)	(31)	(21)

*Better off than 4 or 5 years earlier and expect to be better off 4 or 5 years later.

NOTE: Some of the differences in the frequency of behavior between the two groups are due to the fact that in the BB Group young people and high-income people are overrepresented. When the unadjusted data presented in this table were adjusted for income and age, the differences between the behavior of the two groups became smaller, but did not disappear, as indicated regarding two items on the table.

Source: 1967 Survey of Consumer Finances, Katona (1968, 1971a, and 1975). These publications contain numerous additional data.

An index was obtained from two questions—being better or worse off than a year before and expecting to be better or worse off a year hence—asked four times in the four successive years. People who gave consistently optimistic answers to both questions in all four years were found to have spent a larger share of their income on major durables than the occasionally optimistic (the great majority) or the pessimistic people. While income trends did not reveal major differences in expenditures for durables, perceptions of changes in the personal financial situation jointly with expectations did make for sizable differences. Larger still were the differences in the borrowing be-

TABLE 10-2
Relation of Felt and Expected Financial Progress over 4 Years to Expenditures on Durables and Outstanding Installment Debt

Index of Financial Progress[b]	Frequency in Percent	Entire Panel[a]		Average Income over $10,000 a Year
		Durables[c]	Installment Debt[d]	Installment Debt[d]
Highly pessimistic	4	6.3	5.4	6.2
−1 to −4	10	7.5	7.6	7.9
0	12	7.9	8.1	7.9
1 to 3	35	8.9	10.1	10.4
4 to 5	21	8.9	11.1	13.2
6 to 7	14	8.9	12.2	13.9
Highly optimistic	4	10.0	13.1	18.2

[a] Low-income families are underrepresented in the panel.

[b] Constructed from 4 successive annual measurements, in 1966–70, of better or worse off than a year earlier and of expecting to be better or worse off a year later.

[c] Mean 4-year ratio of expenditures on major durables to income.

[d] Mean 4-year ratio of outstanding installment debt to income.

Source: Hendricks et al. (1973)

havior of the optimistic and the pessimistic respondents (Table 10-2).

The findings serve to point up the conditions under which aspirations are raised. Having accomplished something does not suffice. Progress or success must not only be experienced but also be felt to be part of a continuing pattern and lead to the desire or the expectation of further progress. Aspirations are raised when both experience and expectations are favorable. Then there is no feeling of saturation; aspirations become independent of the extent of possessions already acquired.

Both in fairly prosperous times and during a recession families who believed that their progress was persisting had higher consumption aspirations than people without that attitude. The size of the BB Group fluctuated little in good and bad times. In 1968, 31 percent of families in a representative sample gave BB answers, in 1970, during the recession, only slightly fewer, namely 29 percent, and in 1972, after the recovery, 34 percent. The extent of discretionary purchases fluctuated much more. In bad times both the BB Group and the NonBB Group reduced their purchases. Therefore, while we answered what may be called the Lewinian question about the origin of new aspirations, we have not yet shed light on the conditions under which prosperous times would endure.

For this latter purpose it cannot suffice to analyze personal financial attitudes. Few people consider their fate to be independent of that of others. In general, people are influenced by what happens to broad groups to which they feel they belong. Therefore, in analyzing the impact of attitudes on demand and in constructing the *Index of Consumer Sentiment,* we took account of attitudes toward and expectations about business conditions in the country, and must do so again.

We again have two survey questions at our disposal. In the first question respondents were asked whether in their opinion business conditions "at the present time" were better or worse than they were "a year ago." In the second question they were asked whether they expected that "a year from now" in the country as a whole business conditions would be better or worse than they were "at present." Answers to each of these questions, taken singly, must be used with great caution. Shortly after an upturn from a recession has started many people note an improvement because the comparison is made with

162

earlier unfavorable conditions. When, however, prevailing conditions are compared with what is remembered as good times a year earlier, the answer "Same" is easily given even though the respondents may be highly satisfied with economic conditions. Only by considering the answers to both questions together is it possible to sort out those who expect a continuation of improvement from those who think the top has been reached or who view the improvement as temporary.

Early in 1965 more favorable answers were received to these questions than at any other time between 1950 and 1970. At that time about 50 percent of those who spoke of improvement in the past expected further gains and the remaining 50 percent said that, following improvement in the past, conditions would remain the same. In 1967, however, only 38 percent and in 1970 only 30 percent of those noting past gains expected further gains and a sizable proportion expected a deterioration. In other words, opinions about past and expected improvement in business conditions show substantial cyclical variations.

The relation of people's expectations about the economic outlook over the next year to the outlook over the next five years provides a further clue to the presence or absence of persisting optimism. In 1972, for instance, opinions about short-range economic prospects improved greatly, while those about the longer-range prospects remained depressed (see Table 8-1). Among all respondents only 27 percent thought at that time that times would be good over the next five years and 35 percent thought that they would be bad. In the BB Group the two proportions were 36 and 31 percent and in the NonBB Group 23 and 36 percent, respectively. The longer-range economic outlook even of the BB Group was rather unfavorable—though more favorable than that of the other people—indicating little expectation that prosperous conditions would persist.

These studies are far from concluded. Additional information is needed before definite conclusions can be drawn. Tentatively, however, we may summarize as follows: Awareness of continuous progress in personal well-being leads to the arousal of new wants. These wants are translated into demand when economic conditions are felt to have improved and are expected to improve further. The BB syndrome of attitudes must prevail both regarding personal finances and economic conditions in order that prosperity be sustained over long periods.

163

Change in Opinions over Many Years

A few words need to be added on the climate of opinion under which prosperity flourishes. The postwar and the prewar eras differed greatly. World War II did not represent a simple interruption after which the economy resumed where it had left off. Psychologically, it was a break with the past. In the minds of the people the depression of the early 1930s and the stagnation of the late 1930s were over. The economic lesson they learned was not that war can make wheels turn and provide employment. They learned that the government can do so.[7] How this conviction developed and what credit may be attributed to New Deal legislation or even to Keynesian economic thinking is hard to tell. What we know is that right after the war, and much more strongly in the 1950s, the great majority of the American people believed that depressions were avoidable. They reasoned that if full employment could be achieved in times of war, when much of the production was destroyed, the same could be done to even better effect in times of peace. They felt that they were entitled to full employment—a conviction shared by Congress, which incorporated this view among the responsibilities of the government in the Employment Act of 1946—and looked with confidence to the government, and to some extent also to business, to give them prosperity.

At various times in the early 1950s the Survey Research Center asked the following question of representative samples of American families: "Do you think that something like the depression of the 1930s is likely to happen again during the next five years or so?" That in those years very many people would consider the recurrence of a severe depression improbable was expected. But the researchers were still surprised by the answers they received. Close to 60 percent of all respondents, and an even higher percentage among those in the upper-income brackets, said flatly that nothing like the depression of the 1930s *could* happen again. Only 13 percent of all people and 8 percent of those with incomes over $7,500 said that such a depression might happen during the next five years; the rest were uncertain or said that it would probably not happen.

[7] We shall return to the discussion of people's belief in the government's power over the economy in Chapter 22.

164

Why did many people think that the depression of the 1930s was a unique occurrence that could not recur? When asked the usual question, "Why do you think so?" only a small minority referred to the prevailing good times, to high incomes, or to the extensive needs of consumers and business firms. Most people expressed themselves in quite different terms, although many found it hard to give clearly reasoned answers. "We know how to avoid a depression" was the most common reply. "We have learned many things since the 1930s" was another frequent expression. What did these people have in mind? Who were "we"? Further questioning revealed that most of them had the government in mind. "The government can avert a depression and would do so if need be," they said. In short, the conviction was found to be widespread that the government had learned that there were means with which to fight a depression and never again would it fail to use those means.

The nature of the means to be used was often expressed in ways that an economist would not consider adequate, but that nonetheless shed interesting light on people's way of thinking. Two aspects stood out clearly. First, references to war and rearmament were rare. Only relatively few people said that a severe depression would not or could not occur again because the production of military hardware would create employment. Second, the most frequent replies concerned public works —schools, highways, and many other forms of domestic expenditure, which the government could and would undertake to create employment opportunities and make large-scale unemployment impossible.

Obviously, the question referring to "a depression such as in the 1930s" was formulated in rather extreme terms. To some respondents the question may have suggested a catastrophe rather than cyclical fluctuations. In the 1960s, therefore, the question was asked in a milder form: "Do you think something like the recession or unemployment we had in 1958 is likely to happen again during the next few years?" The replies fluctuated according to people's economic outlook, but the proportion believing in the possibility of a recession remained substantial throughout the decade of the 1960s. The American people thought that "we" knew how to avoid a depression, but not how to avoid a recession or insure that economic trends would not be interrupted by occasional downturns.

Following the recession of 1970–71 a new factor entered the

picture. Trust in the government's ability to manage the economy was severely diminished. The proportion of Americans saying that the government was doing a good job regarding inflation and unemployment dropped to a low level—6 to 21 percent in 1973 and 1974—and was far exceeded by the proportion saying that the government was doing a poor job. Misgivings relating to the government's ability to slow down inflation were discussed in the preceding chapter and reasons for fearing the onset of a recession will be taken up in the next chapter. While the question studied in this chapter was "Under what conditions will prosperity persist?" the next question to be considered will be "Under what conditions will prosperity not persist?"

11
THE PSYCHOLOGY OF RECESSION

How do recessions come about? In analyzing postwar recessions and especially the two most severe ones, in 1958 and 1970, we had ample opportunity to observe the role of reduced willingness to buy by consumers. Long before the recessions set in consumer sentiment deteriorated and provided a signal of an impending decline in discretionary expenditures. In studying the psychology of recession we must therefore ask, How can it happen that attitudes and expectations deteriorate at a time when business conditions are satisfactory or even improving? The answer was found to be threefold in nature, relating, first, to the tendency of people to become habituated to good news; second, to the function of bad news received at such times; and, third, to certain government policies which, though intended to curb inflation, may serve instead to promote a recession.

Deterioration of Attitudes in Good Times

Shortly after an upturn in economic conditions has started, increases in GNP or retail sales represent great news, reported on the front pages of newspapers and prominently over radio and television. The attention paid to such economic news both by organs of mass media and by the readers or listeners themselves declines, however, as time goes on. Survey questions about economic news heard "in the recent past" indicate that, after prosperous times have continued for a while, there is a significant reduction in the proportion of people who recall favorable news. "Only what is new is news" is a basic principle to which good journalists adhere, knowing well that people

167

quickly become saturated by hearing the same thing over and over again. The third, fourth, or fifth quarterly increase in GNP is not news. Irrespective of whether or not there is habituation to bad news—a matter that is less than certain, because a fourth or fifth consecutive report on rising unemployment, for example, may well be viewed as more threatening than the first—habituation to good news is a well-established fact. Its consequence is that in good times bad news is highly salient. In interviews conducted in times of prosperity, even occasional local adversities of little significance have been found to be remembered and reported by respondents.

Some respondents expressed their cautious attitudes after two or more years of favorable developments by such comments as, "Trees don't grow to heaven." Many people can't believe that good times will last and feel that some adverse development must set in sooner or later.

Habituation to good news may perhaps suffice to generate a plateau, but not to bring about a substantial deterioration of attitudes and a recession. Prior to every recorded recession the American people have heard bad news—not just local and unimportant items but bad news of great significance. This news may have concerned a threat of war, disappointment of hopes for peace, riots and violence, or a government crisis. In practically all recent instances the news also related to inflation or the acceleration of inflation. What was viewed as an unjustified and unexplained increase in the cost of living was felt to make people worse off than they were before and induced them to postpone some of their spending plans and to desire the accumulation of larger savings and reserve funds.

In 1957 and again in 1969 the concern of the government with inflation increased greatly and there was much discussion of steps it would take to slow down inflation: measures directed toward a less rapid growth of the money supply, higher interest rates, lesser government expenditures and/or higher taxes. Some of these measures were initiated prior to both major recessions. Extensive publicity was often given to the changes in economic policy, which were announced as being required in the interest of restoring economic balance. Yet the policy was frequently understood by very many people as one that would bring about a recession. In 1969 and in 1974 many people became convinced that the government consid-

168

ered an increase in unemployment to be a price it was willing to pay for a reduction in the rate of price increases. Fear of recession spread in response to such news, and fear of recession is a most powerful deterrent to willingness to buy.

Interest rates advanced rapidly both in 1957 and in 1969, and again very sharply in 1973–74. In each of these years, the Federal Reserve Banks increased their highly visible discount rates long after the threat of a recession was apparent. The advance in interest rates reflected deliberate policy as well as acquiescence with prevailing trends and reluctance to fight them. In either case the sharply rising interest rates represented the belief, held by Washington authorities, that they would not contribute to a recession or that goals other than avoiding a recession—namely, slowing down the inflation and improving the balance of payments—were of greater importance. Survey data indicate that very many people were aware of the rising interest rates and viewed them as a signal of bad times to come. The unfavorable evaluation of rising interest rates reflects primarily the belief that interest rates represent a cost of doing business. People say that businesses will have to raise prices because interest rates have gone up. In addition, many people associate high interest rates with a decline in construction activity because would-be house buyers are priced out of the mortgage market. In contrast, very few people, when asked about the impact of higher interest rates, mentioned either the higher interest they received on their savings or the higher charges they paid on their installment debt.

Recessions Hurt

What is a recession? Obviously the expression was adopted to denote an unfavorable economic condition less severe and shorter than a depression. Adverse developments in just one or two fields of business do not qualify as recessions. Economic activity must deteriorate in many areas and unemployment must increase to a sizable extent, or very many people must feel a deterioration in their economic situation, before an ordinary person speaks of recession. The definitions of experts are rather similar to the first requirement. Real GNP or the production index that encompasses all industries must decline over a

169

period of at least two quarters before economists usually acknowledge that a recession has occurred.[1]

Recessions may represent fairly small declines in economic activity—for instance, in 1948, 1953, and 1961—or rather substantial ones, as in 1958 and 1974. To illustrate again how extensive the worsening of economic conditions was in one of these recessions, we may cite that in the first half of 1958 the American steel industry operated at 50 percent of capacity, as against 95 percent in the first half of 1957; only 2.4 million cars were sold in the first half of that year compared to 3.1 million in the same period a year earlier; 5.2 million people were unemployed in the spring of 1958 against 2.7 million in the fall of 1957.

Does a decline of such magnitude represent a major calamity? Do recessions hurt many people? It may be argued that substantial fluctuations of prince-and-pauper industries such as steel and automobiles should be taken in stride. Furthermore, rates of unemployment rising to 8 percent of the labor force mean that at the same time 92 percent are employed. Even if it is conceded that the maximum rate of unemployment reached in a recession does not reflect the total number of people who at one time or another lose their jobs during the recession—at any time some unemployed have already returned to work—it is clear that most American wage earners did not experience unemployment during any postwar recession.

Nevertheless, surveys indicate that the recessions of 1958

---

[1] This paragraph was written in 1973 when few experts would have objected to it. In 1974, however, a great debate raged about whether or not there was a recession. Surveys revealed that the majority of Americans already thought at the beginning of the year that business conditions had deteriorated and that they themselves were worse off than before. But government spokesmen denied emphatically even that a recession was in the offing. After GNP in constant dollars showed declines in both the first and second quarters of the year, they still pointed to certain improving areas of the economy. Toward the end of the year, to be sure, nobody had any doubt that a recession, and even a severe recession, had set in.

It is sometimes said that it is merely a matter of semantics whether or not we characterize a given economic trend as a recession. This notion is incorrect. In 1974 many people advocated or accepted restrictive policies in the fight against inflation in the mistaken belief that times were prosperous, and therefore slowing down the economy would not do any damage.

and 1974 were viewed by the majority of people as major disasters. These recessions caused suffering and distress to many people. The explanation of these findings is, first, that many more people feel threatened by unemployment than actually lose their jobs, and such threats are highly distressing. Second, loss of overtime and reduction of working time occur frequently and cause a decline in income earned. Yet the standard of living once attained is usually seen as an absolutely necessary minimum so that a decline in income becomes intolerable. Even foregoing income increases on which one has counted is seen as a great hardship. The number of those who are disappointed or feel threatened is much larger than those who actually experience economic hardship.

As between unemployment and inflation, consistently prior to 1973 a larger proportion of people felt that the former was the more serious problem. Even though rising costs of living hurt practically everyone in one way or the other while the great majority of people were immune to unemployment, more people spoke of unfavorable consequences of unemployment than of inflation. The distribution of opinion as obtained in November, 1971, is shown in Table 11-1. Even among families with fairly high income, almost one-half considered unemployment a greater evil than inflation. This finding illustrates not just the presence of some kind of empathy with the unemployed, but primarily the prevailing evaluation of the impact of recessions. (Opinions changed greatly following the rapid advance of food prices in 1973 when inflation acquired the distinction of being *the* major problem.)

Occasional threats of a recession are inevitable. Bad news does arise in good times, generating fear of a downturn, because many people are then receptive to such news. Yet recessions should not be held to be inevitable because, in principle, businessmen and consumers and, above all, the government may initiate countermeasures and diffuse the impact of pessimistic expectations. Unfortunately, the past record does not permit us to place great store on the power of government policy to arrest threatening or incipient recessions. Far too often threats of a recession have not been recognized by the policy makers. At other times there has been little agreement about the appropriate policy and, when there was agreement, the policy measures were enacted after such great delay that they were no longer effective. We must therefore expect a continua-

TABLE 11-1
Comparison between Unemployment and Inflation, 1971
(Percentage distribution of opinions)

The more serious problem is:	All Respondents*	Income under $5,000	Income over $12,500
Unemployment	50	53	45
Inflation	40	33	49
Both equally	6	9	5
Don't know	4	5	1
Total	100	100	100

*These figures also reflect the opinions of the broad middle-income groups not shown separately in the table.

tion of the present situation in which prosperous times are periodically interrupted by recessions.

Recovery from Recession

The most promising goal of present-day economic policy is to keep recessions, when they do set in, mild and short. To analyze the probability of success in achieving even that goal, let us review briefly the history of how the American economy has climbed out of recessions in the past. The major finding, for all recessions between 1945 and 1972, is that they were not overcome because of policy measures instituted by the government. Such measures were contemplated, proposed, and discussed, but recovery began before the debate was resolved. Developments in 1958 are noteworthy because at that time there was much serious discussion of the advisability of a tax cut to stimulate economic activity. But signs of recovery were visible long before the discussion ended.

How then did the end of the recession of 1958 come about? The first credit must be given to automatic stabilizers. The government did perform substantial service without initiating any new measures. When incomes and profits decline, the tax burden of consumers and business firms drops sharply; at the same time payments to the unemployed and a variety of other government expenditures increase or at least remain at their previous levels. Due to the ensuing deficit, or the ensuing

172

sharp increase in the deficit, additional money is injected into the economy.

The second credit must be given to the impact of consumer behavior. Recessions are widely publicized and very many people become aware of them. Shortly after the onset of a recession the publicity has unfavorable effects by increasing the fear of unemployment and making for pessimistic expectations. But as the months go by there is a gradual increase in the number of people who find that in spite of the recession they are still well off. The great majority of Americans experienced stable or increasing incomes during each of the postwar recessions, many income increases having been arranged in earlier wage settlements or represented regular annual increments. Though the number of those with rising real incomes was smaller than those with rising money incomes, even the former was substantial. There is no expression describing the reverse of disappointment, namely, the satisfaction arising from the absence of expected calamities, but the feeling that the recession caused little damage to the individual, to his friends, and to his community does spread and makes for an improvement in willingness to buy.

The recession of 1970–71 lasted longer than the earlier postwar recessions. Moreover, as mentioned at the end of Chapter 8, soon after the recovery, threats of a new recession arose. Most importantly, both the recession and the recovery from it were periods of sizable inflation. Furthermore, even during the recovery, unemployment did not go down to pre-recession levels and long-range economic expectations remained unfavorable. Under these circumstances the possibility arises that the economic trend in the 1970s will be rather different from the trend in the 1950s and 1960s. While the first twenty-five years after World War II represented a period of economic advance and confidence occasionally interrupted by short recessions, we may ask in the early 1970s: Should we expect a new era of low economic activity, malaise, and lack of confidence, occasionally interrupted by brief spells of recovery?

This expectation is supported by pessimistic opinions about the long-run trend of the economy and by grave concern with a variety of societal problems (persistence of poverty, racial conflict, alienation of youth, violence and riots, pollution of air and water). It receives additional and weighty support from the growing doubt in the efficacy of the government in dealing with or remedying either the economic or the societal problems.

Fortunately, there is another side of the coin as well. The countercyclical features of the government budgets have been mentioned before and must be judged as most useful in an era of large fiscal expenditures and high rates of taxation, with most taxes being collected promptly at the source. In addition, in spite of the mistrust of the government in the early 1970s, the possibility of the effectiveness of new government policies (e.g., a tax cut) must not be ruled out. Antirecession measures have the function of generating both additional income and greater confidence. Even if the measures are not fully appropriate, if they come too late or not at all, mere discussion about them may serve to improve consumer sentiment. This is so because of certain features of consumer thinking that tend to mitigate excesses and stabilize the economy. If and when consumers reduce their expenditures in response to accelerating inflation, they exert an influence in the direction of slowing down the inflation. If and when they feel that "Trees don't grow to heaven," their behavior will tend to minimize a boom and thereby prolong good times.

There remains the one most important argument against the expectation of an era of pessimism and depressed economic activity. It is probable that the major factor that has brought about previous eras of confidence and prosperity will remain effective in the future as well. This factor is optimism about personal financial trends. Very many Americans have experienced an improvement in their standard of living, have aspired to and confidently expected further gains, and have worked toward achieving them. We have discussed these features of consumer behavior in Chapter 10 and will take them up again in the next chapter (and also in Chapter 25). If they represent enduring features, then there is good reason to contradict a pessimistic assessment of forthcoming economic trends.

The foregoing discussion should not be taken as a forecast of things to come. It is not possible to predict forthcoming changes in people's attitudes. Continuous empirical studies are needed to determine them. But it is necessary to be aware of the probable developments those surveys will have to study.

174

12
OPTIMISM ABOUT PERSONAL FINANCES

Income Gains

The entire period from 1945 to 1972 was characterized by income increases. Most commonly, they took the form of annual raises in wages and salaries. In addition, a growing proportion of the population received other forms of income—from overtime, from second jobs or occasional extra work, as well as from interest and dividends. Profits of the self-employed were likewise rising. Mothers returned to work after their children had reached school age, and their earnings added substantially to family income. Occasionally, of course, the upward trend was interrupted for a sizable number of families, not only during recessions but also because of unfavorable developments in the business a person was engaged in, or personal adversity such as illness. The following survey data indicate the frequency of reported income gains and thereby the extent of awareness of an upward trend.

In the 1950s and 1960s, in most of the quarterly surveys of representative samples of the population, heads of family units were asked about their family income and whether at the time of the interview they were making more, less, or the same as a year earlier. The modal distribution of answers was

   45 percent making more,
   40 percent making the same, and
   15 percent making less.

The range of the answers was quite restricted; most of the time, 40 to 50 percent of the sample reported increases, and 10 to 18 percent declines, in income. These data understate the frequency of annual income gains. When the gains were small, perhaps less than 5 percent, survey respondents frequently

177

answered that they were making the same as a year earlier, as reinterviews revealed.

The proportion reporting income gains was higher still in answer to questions about income changes over longer periods. These questions were not asked frequently and answers to them are subject to sizable memory errors.[1] The relation between short- and longer-term income changes obtained in 1967 is fairly typical (see Table 12-1). At that time, 49 percent of the sample said that their 1966 income was higher than a year earlier and 63 percent that it was higher than four years earlier.

Panel studies in which identical respondents were interviewed repeatedly give some information about the income trend over fairly long periods. Between 1966 and 1970, for instance, the average rate of annual increases in family income was 7.8 percent for members of a panel interviewed by the Survey Research Center.[2] At the same time,

12 percent had an income decline of more than 5 percent a year,
27 percent had a change between −5 and +5 percent,
38 percent had an increase between 5 and 15 percent, and
23 percent had an increase of over 15 percent.
100 percent

Thus we find sizable gains over long periods together with substantial variations among subgroups of the population. In presenting these data, extensive short-term income fluctuations are disregarded. A panel study with quarterly interviews in 1964–65 revealed that the income of approximately one-half of the families in the broad middle-income ranges fluctuated more than 10 percent in each quarter. Presence or absence of overtime, change in the number of hours worked,

[1] The memory errors, of course, relate much more to the extent of income increases over long periods than to their direction. The former are usually underestimated.

[2] Hendricks et al. (1973, Table 5-1). The income gains of a sample representative of all family units in the country would have been somewhat smaller because families with heads over 60 years of age were excluded from the panel. (The rate of growth of disposable personal income for the household sector as a whole was 7.4 percent in this period.) In each annual interview with the panel income data were collected by asking several questions. The change data in the text were calculated from data on the income of each year.

and change in the number of family members working accounted for a large part of these fluctuations.

Because people's time horizon extends forward as well as backward, we must supplement the data about past income changes with information about income expectations. As may be seen from Table 12-1, the proportion of family heads expecting increases, both one year hence and four years hence, was smaller than the proportion reporting past increases. This difference is due, however, almost entirely to the fact that to questions about future developments a sizable proportion consistently say that they can't tell, the future being uncertain. When the calculation was restricted to people with definite opinions, the proportion of those with optimistic income expectations was approximately the same as the proportion with favorable past changes.

Less than 30 percent of the sample reported that their income had increased in the preceding year and they expected it to do the same in the following year. When the question was asked to include the four preceding and the four following years, the proportion who had experienced and expected to continue to experience an upward trend over the entire eight years rose to 39 percent. On the basis of the two questions

TABLE 12-1
Experience with and Expectation of Income Gains
(Percentage of all family units)

Income change experience	Proportion of all families reporting gain	Proportion of all families reporting gains twice
Income higher in 1966 than 4 years ago	63	
Income higher in 1966 than 1 year ago	49	40
Expect higher income in 1967 (1 year hence)	41	28
Expect higher income (4 years hence)	51	31

39

Source: *1967 Survey of Consumer Finances;* Interviews conducted with a representative sample of 3,171 family units early in 1967.

179

about longer-range past and expected income changes, the population was divided into six groups, as shown in Table 12-2.

About two out of every five family units reported continuous income gains. This proportion may be shown to be much higher for certain important subgroups than for the entire population. The proportion falling in the group with continuous gains rises from 39 to 54 percent for upper-income people (those with a family income of more than $10,000 in 1966) and to 60 percent for younger families (head under 45 years of age). The relation of the size of the group with continuous gains to the two crucial variables, age and income, is shown in Chart 12-1. The younger the family, the greater is the proportion falling in the group. The slope of the lines reveals that among younger families the size of the income also makes some difference in the proportion experiencing and expecting an upward trend. In the age groups between 35 and 55 income is a major factor; the higher the income the larger the proportion in the group with a continuous upward trend.

Optimistic income expectations were found to be correlated

TABLE 12-2

Four-Year Past and Expected Change in Income, Early 1967

Group	Income now compared with 4 years ago	Income expected 4 years hence compared with now	Description	Percent of all families
(1)	up	up	Continuous gain	39
(2)	up	same	Intermittent	14
	same	up	gain	
(3)	up	down		
	down	up	Reversal	10
(4)	same	same	Stagnation	10
(5)	down	same		
	same	down	Decline	8
	down	down		
(6)	don't know			19
	uncertain			——
	Total			100

For source, see Table 12-1.

180

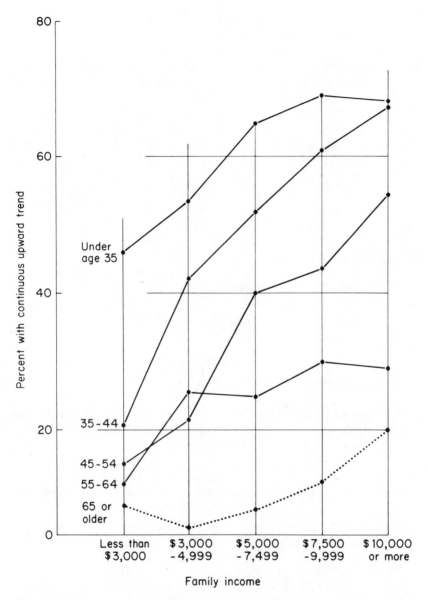

CHART 12-1　Proportion of Age and Income Groups with Continuous Upward Income Trend Four Years Ago and Four Years Hence, 1967. (For source, see Table 12-1).

181

with people's notions about when they would reach their top income. When asked, in the early 1960s, at what age they expected their highest lifetime income, some people in the labor force professed not to know or said that age made no difference in their income. Among the majority who specified an approximate time, one-half said that their peak income would be reached just before retirement or when they were over sixty. Among professional, managerial, and clerical people, the proportion who expected to receive their peak income when they were over sixty was even higher, and among blue-collar workers much lower. As expected, when asked what their peak income would be, most people gave estimates that were considerably higher than their income at that time. The differences were very large on the part of professional and managerial people (median estimate of peak income was over $12,000 as compared with median income at the time of inquiry of under $8,000). Persons with a college degree—another classification in which most people expect income increases almost up to the time of retirement—mentioned an expected peak income of close to $15,000 (median value of estimates) as against an actual income of somewhat over $9,000.

Optimism about Subjective Well-Being

For the purpose of determining the extent of felt progress and optimism, data on income changes and income expectations do not suffice. The following less precise questions provided more appropriate data: "We are interested in how people are getting along financially these days. Would you say that you and your family are better or worse off financially than you were a year ago (4 years ago)?" and "Now looking ahead—do you think that a year from now (4 years from now) you people will be better off financially, or worse off, or just about the same as now?"[3]

Questions about income change over a longer period are difficult to answer because total family income, which fluctuates more widely than the income of the major breadwinner alone, is not a magnitude frequently thought of. Further-

---

[3] The questions were followed by the query, "Why do you say so?" In the text that follows, extensive use is made of answers to this probe.

more, the crucial factor consists of change in real rather than money income, and yet few respondents if any are in a position to answer precise questions about the former. The expression "gains in real income," widely used by economists, relates to gains in money income exceeding the increase in prices. In order to assess changes in real income, precise information on changes in prices would be required. Such information may perhaps be derived from price indexes for the entire economy. But information on the increase in the cost of living is not available for different income groups because the price increases may differ for goods and services bought by upper-income families from those bought by lower-income families. Many individuals have an impression about the relation of the gains in their income to the advance in the prices for their expenditures, but most people are not in position to express this relation in a quantitative manner. These considerations were of crucial importance in the 1970s, but had been significant in the 1950s and 1960s as well, even though in those decades on the average the gains in money income exceeded the rate of price increases.

In contrast to questions about income changes, questions about past and expected changes in the personal financial situation call for nothing more than an affective evaluation of the change. They are concerned directly with what the researcher wishes to ascertain, namely, the presence or absence of a perception of progress and the belief in its persistence.

The questions about being better or worse off are likewise relatively insensitive insofar as the answer "Same" is used not only when there is no change at all but also when the past or expected changes are felt to be small and therefore insignificant. An index constructed from the difference between the "Better" and "Worse" answers, disregarding the "Same" answers, provides the best indication of change from one point of time to the next.

Although the answers given to the question about being better or worse off than a year earlier are most commonly explained by changes in the income of the main bread winner, a sizable number of respondents also refer to contributions by other family members as well as to an improvement or deterioration in the family's asset and debt position, and even to changes in what they need. References to the income of other family members or to assets, debts, and needs are much less

183

frequent, however, than references to the cost of living. At certain times as many as one out of four respondents spoke spontaneously of price increases when asked to explain their answers. The most frequent form of these explanations was, "My income increased but we are not better off (or worse off) because prices went up."

Even though the survey questions ask explicitly whether the family is financially better or worse off, many people do not distinguish sharply between financial and nonfinancial or even nonmaterial considerations. The most frequently noted nonfinancial factor is health. Substantial changes in health do, of course, often have financial implications. Illness of the main breadwinner may, but need not, affect earning power. Illness of any family member usually involves large expenses and thus affects the standard of living by reducing the money available for other needs and wants. Needless to say, recovery from illness has the opposite effect.

There are good reasons to assume that questions on changes in the personal financial situation are understood to relate to changes in the family's standard of living. Most people appear to have some notion about past and expected changes in their way of living. Yet a minority of respondents explain their answers by referring to considerations not directly related to their standard of living. Political problems, social trends, and the like sometimes influence people's opinions about being or expecting to be better or worse off because many people do not consider their fate as independent from that of other people.

The frequency of the optimistic evaluation of personal financial well-being is presented in Table 12-3. As expected, income gains were reported much more frequently than opinions about being better off. Yet, despite the detrimental effects of inflation, there were more "Better Off" than "Worse Off" answers, and the difference was particularly pronounced when the questions covered a four- rather than a one-year time span as well as expected rather than past trends. In spite of many years of progress, expectations of further progress persisted among a large proportion of the population, even in the early 1970s.

Table 12-3 also indicates the size of what was earlier termed the BB Group (Chapter 10), those who had experienced past and expected future improvement in economic well-being over several years. The BB Group is somewhat smaller than the

184

TABLE 12-3
Optimism in Evaluating Past and Expected Changes
in the Personal Financial Situation

	Time	Range	Average
	(Percentage Better Off minus Worse Off plus 100)		
Compared to 1 year ago	1950s & 1960s	94–124	113
Compared to 4 years ago	1966–72	125–140	132
Expected 1 year hence	1950s & 1960s	124–145	122
Expected 4 years hence	1966–72	130–141	136

Continuous Progress: Percent in BB Group[*]

1 year ago and 1 year hence	1950s & 1960s	15–26	19
4 years ago and 4 years hence	1967–72	29–34	31

Four-Year Past and Expected Change in Evaluations
(Frequency in percent, 1972)

Better-better	34
Better-same or same-better	18
Better-worse or worse-better	11
Same-same	9
Same-worse or worse-same, or worse-worse	8
Don't know	20
Total	100

[*]This group consists of those who gave the answer "Better" to both questions, one about past and one about expected changes.

group that reported continuous gains as past and expected changes in income alone (Table 12-2). Nevertheless the crucial findings presented about income hold good regarding personal well-being: Families with continuous or occasional gains constitute the majority of all families. Only 18 percent of a representative sample was shown to fall in the groups "Stagnation" and "Decline" on the basis of income questions in 1967; on the basis of the "Better Off–Worse Off" questions the size of these two groups was practically the same in the period 1967–72, which included a sharp recession and considerable inflation.

While the size of the BB Group was 34 percent for the entire population in 1972, for those with an income of over $10,000 it was 48 percent and for younger families (head of family unit

18-35 years old) even as high as 55 percent. Just as in the case of income changes, age makes the greatest difference and income level a somewhat smaller difference. As shown in Table 12-4, almost four out of every five people falling in the BB Group are under 45 years of age. Occupation and education have a much smaller influence on belonging or not belonging to the BB Group.

On the Origin of Expectations

How do optimistic expectations come about? The emphasis placed in this chapter on expectations that correspond to past experience—as is true in the BB Group—appears to strengthen the case for past trends determining the expectations. Earlier (Chapter 4), however, we presented a theory of two forms of learning and postulated that many expectations are derived from an understanding of new developments rather than from an extrapolation of past trends into the future. The findings relating to income and personal financial well-being indicate that "extrapolative expectations" represent a substantial proportion of optimistic expectations. A consideration of expectations about forthcoming business trends, however, leads to the conclusion that in that area past trends frequently give no indication even of the direction of what is expected. In many instances the majority of respondents expected the direction of future economic trends to be different from those in the past. Moreover, the expected trend was sometimes more favorable and sometimes less favorable than the past trend. Concerning price expectations, past trends appear to play a role regarding

TABLE 12-4
Composition of BB Group, 1972, in Percent

	BB Group	Others
Age under 45, income over $10,000	48	18
Age under 45, income under $10,000	31	19
Age over 45, income over $10,000	16	24
Age over 45, income under $10,000	5	39
Total	100	100

the direction but not the extent of expected trends (see Chapter 9).[4]

It may be that expectations about personal trends differ from most other expectations. We shall find, later in this chapter, good reasons why many people who have been successful in the past expect success in the future as well. The size of the BB Group, still a minority of the population, provides no support for a general acceptance of a "proxy theory," which postulates that expectations are formed exclusively on the basis of recent past changes in income, sales, prices, and so forth, so that the latter may serve as proxies for expectations. A refusal to accept the proxy theory should not, of course, imply that past experience with income or prices should not be considered as one of the factors contributing to those expectations.

The proxy theory is still widely held and has even been called the "rational theory" of expectations.[5] In this theory expectations are made an endogenous variable by postulating that they can be modified *only* by past changes of the same variable coupled with a consideration of past forecasting errors. In the early 1970s monetary economists at the Federal Reserve Bank of St. Louis substituted in their econometric model past price trends for price expectations by assuming that inflationary expectations, which in their opinion had been giving momentum to inflation, derived exclusively from past price increases. Such substitution, while it serves to get rid of subjective data and the human factor in economics, introduces incorrect data into the system, especially at crucial times when trends undergo a change.

Reasons for Optimism

Experience with increase in income and improvement in the standard of living is not the only cause of optimism. Three additional sets of considerations may be recognized as con-

---

[4] Data on the frequency of extrapolative and nonextrapolative expectations are presented in Katona (1972a).

[5] This view probably originated in Phillip Cagan's study in which "the expected rate of change in prices . . . is assumed to be a function of the actual rate of change" (1956, p. 35) and "the expected rate of change in prices is revised . . . in proportion to the difference between the actual rate of change in prices and the rate of change that was expected" (p. 37).

187

tributing to the optimistic frame of mind in the post-World War II era: first, the major occupational shifts in the twentieth century, consisting primarily of an increase in white-collar rather than blue-collar jobs; second, the substantial increase in educational attainment, with high school graduation becoming the rule and the proportion of people with higher education rising greatly; third, widespread notions about progress reflecting personal achievement.

Early in this century farmers and blue-collar workers constituted the majority of the labor force. As recently as 1950 there were more blue-collar than white-collar workers in the United States. Yet, by the late 1960s, major occupational shifts resulted in white-collar workers exceeding blue-collar workers by over 20 percent. Mobility from farms to towns was so extensive by then that farm operators constituted only 5 percent of the labor force. It is probable that the process is still continuing. The reduction in the number of blue-collar workers resulted not only from automation in mines and factories, but primarily from a lesser growth in production than in distribution and service facilities.

Farmers and unskilled blue-collar workers reach their peak income early in life. For perhaps two decades their earning power remains high, but begins to decline as early as their forties or, at the latest, their fifties. In contrast, after leaving school white-collar workers and especially those engaged in professional or executive careers start with low salaries, which are expected to increase year after year in a process of continuous promotions toward better and better positions. The peak lifetime income of these groups of people is reached late in life, often just before retirement. We have indicated before that this is well known to the people themselves. The finding that among young people the proportion expecting income gains is larger than among middle-aged or older people is thus fully explained.

The recent sharp increase in the number of jobs in service industries may have slowed down the effect of white-collar careers on optimistic expectations. By the late 1960s the majority of the labor force was employed in what is classified as service industries. Yet many service jobs, for instance in the retail trade, are badly paid and offer little chance for a career. It should be noted, however, that the largest number of so-called service workers are government employees and espe-

188

cially teachers and that the financial situation of teachers made marked improvement in the 1960s.

Educational shifts are closely related to occupational shifts. In 1900, only 15 percent of high-school-age young people graduated from high school. In 1940, 38 percent of those 25–39 years of age were high school graduates; in 1970, 75 percent. About one-half of high school graduates go to college; altogether, close to 40 percent of youths 18 and 19 years old were enrolled in colleges in 1970. This educational accomplishment is exceeded only by educational aspirations. When in surveys fathers of school- and preschool-age boys were asked about how much schooling they expected their sons would have, two-thirds thought that their sons would go to college.

Statistics on the income earned by people with different educational attainment indicate that the higher the education, the larger the average income. Similarly, among high-income people those with a college degree are by far the most frequent, and among low-income people those with less than eight years of education predominate. All this does not prove that education is a profitable investment. Calculating the payoff of higher education is rather complicated and its outcome depends on how future earnings are discounted and earnings foregone by staying in school are assessed. But the results of such calculations are much less important than what people believe to be true. The association between educational attainment and optimism is well grounded in the American people's belief systems.[6]

Personal Accomplishments

The belief that education or the acquisition of skills makes it possible to increase one's income is probably not unrelated to

---

[6] For a summary of the economic impact of higher education, see Strumpel (1971). He shows that a major consequence of higher education is that persons with such education hold jobs and occupations that are less strenuous and expose them to fewer risks of income loss. For the prevailing great differences in educational attainment and aspirations between the United States and prosperous West European countries, see Katona et al. (1971a).

people's confidence that their income gains have been due to their own efforts. This last conclusion was derived from direct questions addressed to representative samples of families. Respondents were asked first how their income compared with that of four years earlier in order to identify the great majority of people who in the prosperous and inflationary years of the 1950s and 1960s were aware of rising incomes. These respondents were then asked to say why they were making more than four years earlier. Although many people were puzzled by the question, most of them found an answer after some hesitation. Some, to be sure, said no more than "I got a raise" or "My salary went up." But other respondents said, "I did a good job," "I deserved more," or "I advanced in my job," and indicated by these and similar replies that their own work was responsible for progress in their careers and for their higher earnings.

Table 12-5 presents the tabulation of the answers to the question about the reasons for income increases for all families as well as for two important subgroups. In surveys conducted in 1968 and 1970 close to one-half of all respondents made reference to their own efforts or indicated "ego involvement" in their income increases. References to such external causes as improved business conditions, efforts by trade unions or the government, as well as the impact of inflation occurred much less frequently. An answer completely denying a person's contribution, "Everybody got a raise," was quite rare.

Obviously these inquiries shed no light on the true causes of higher earnings. Nor did the analysis of people's belief systems penetrate below a rather superficial level. But the observed difference between what people think has happened because of external causes and for what they feel they themselves have been responsible is revealing. If I believe that my past progress and advancement are due to what I am, what I know, or what I have done, I have every reason to expect that the same considerations will be effective in the future as well and therefore my progress will continue. The optimistic predispositions of a substantial proportion of Americans are explained to a large extent by their belief that they have received what they deserved.[7]

---

[7] It is shown in Katona et al. (1971a) that ego involvement in income increases is much less frequent in Western Europe (especially Germany) than in the United States. Correspondingly, references to government and trade unions as well as inflation are more frequent in Europe.

TABLE 12-5
Reasons Given for Making More Than Four Years Ago
(Percentage distribution of families with income increases; average data
1968–1970)

| | | Families | |
Reasons	All Families	With incomes over $10,000	Head college educated
References to own efforts:			
Did good job, worked hard, deserved increase	7	9	6
Advanced in career, acquired more skill, experience	13	18	18
Changed job to a better one	16	12	15
Other reference to own effort*	8	11	10
Total	44	50	49
"Neutral" answers:			
Other family members started working	13	10	14
Received a raise	31	35	34
Total	44	45	48
References to "external" causes:			
Wages rose because of inflation	6	8	2
Everyone has higher incomes; union got us more	12	7	8
Business conditions better	7	7	6
Total	25	22	16
Proportion of those with income increases	63%	81%	75%

*Related primarily to success in own business.

†Total exceeds 100 percent because respondents gave two reasons.

Sources: Katona et al., 1971a, p. 56, and 1970 *Survey of Consumer Finances,* p. 241.

191

Consequences of Optimism

In numerous studies attempts have been made to trace the behavioral consequences of gains in income and subjective well-being, or of optimistic expectations. This section contains references to a few of these studies.

Striving for higher income may be assumed to be related to past income gains, optimistic expectations, and consumption aspirations. Demonstration of a connection is, however, difficult in the case of individuals or groups of optimists. When respondents were asked about desiring to work more or less, some association was found between optimism and wanting to work more. In the past few decades there has been no further decline in the number of hours people worked, and the proportion wanting to work more has exceeded the proportion wanting to work less. Overtime and second jobs became widespread and were aspired to by many. This was the case to a larger extent in the United States than in Western Europe, and optimism was likewise found to be more pronounced in the United States than in Europe. Wives returned to work after their youngest child reached school age, again to the greatest extent in America. This process was observed in all income groups, including many upper-income families, except for the very highest. The majority of married women 45–54 years of age were working in the United States in the late 1960s—a proportion not approximated in other prosperous countries. All these movements reflect striving toward higher income. So do many changes in jobs and occupations as well as steps taken to acquire additional education or to learn additional skills for the sake of improving one's career.[8]

The effects that income gains had on the allocation of income were studied by Katona and Mueller (1968) by means of quarterly interviews with identical respondents. The Keynesian answer to the question, postulating a lag in stepping up expenditures following income increases, was contradicted by the finding that in response to sizable income gains consumers made both anticipatory expenditures (increased expenditures triggered by the expectation of income gains) and concurrent discretionary expenditures, especially on durable

---

[8] For a detailed account on which the discussion in this paragraph is based, see Katona et al. (1971a). On wives returning to work, see also Chapter 25.

192

goods. In addition—and this is in line with Keynes's postulates—amounts saved also increased in the same quarter as income advanced, while the increase in everyday expenditures was found to lag behind the income increases. These responses were strongest when the income increases were viewed by the respondents as enduring or sustainable rather than temporary, and when they were substantial (20 percent or more) rather than small.

Response to an upward income trend, defined as income increases in several consecutive quarters uninterrupted by income declines, was also analyzed in the same study and was found to be similar to the short-term response. Families with an upward trend stepped up their purchases of durable goods and added to their liquid savings to a larger extent than other families. Thus an upward income trend was found to be associated with devoting an unusually large share of resources to two of the most highly valued material goals families have, durables and savings.

The study of the behavioral consequences of personal financial attitudes and expectations began in the 1950s under adverse circumstances. One-shot studies and even panel studies based on two consecutive annual surveys with the same respondents failed to show any significant differences between the expenditures of optimistic and pessimistic individuals. In comparison with the demonstration of macroeffects of attitudes on demand, indicated by changes in aggregate expenditures on durables following changes in the *Index of Consumer Sentiment,* the failure to demonstrate microeffects of attitudes was called "the cross-section paradox."[9]

[9] The following is a more complete formulation of what was called a paradox in the 1950s: While with attitudes and expectations the outcome of aggregative time-series tests is positive and of cross-section tests negative, with buying intentions the outcome is negative in aggregative and positive in cross-section tests. Regarding buying intentions, it should be noted that the negative outcome of aggregative tests was confirmed in 1969–70, while in the 1960s the probabilistic approach and large samples yielded somewhat better predictive indications. The much praised cross-section performance of buying intentions was far from flawless. True, about 80 percent of expressed intentions to buy cars during the next year were found to be fulfilled, while among nonintenders only about 20 percent bought. Nevertheless, the majority of cars bought in a year were bought by nonintenders. This was the case because intenders represented only 15 to 20 percent of a representative sample and nonintenders 80 to 85 percent.

193

The failure apparently resulted partly from insufficient specifications in the early investigations, but mainly from difficulties in measurement on the individual level. The measurement of the effect of attitudes on the purchases of individuals requires the exclusion of the effects of a great number of other variables that likewise influence purchases. Moreover, interpersonal comparisons are unreliable at best. Finally, some optimists whose behavior is compared with that of pessimists may not buy durables at a certain time because they bought them earlier when they were already optimistic.[10] In spite of these difficulties several later studies demonstrated some impact of attitudes on the individual level.

On the basis of a panel study conducted between 1960 and 1962 the Survey Research Center constructed an optimism index for individuals and found that the median expenditure on durables of optimists was somewhat higher than those with middle attitudes, who in turn spent more than the pessimists (see Chapter 2 of Kosobud and Morgan, 1964). W. C. Dunkelberg (1972) constructed an index of consumer sentiment for each individual interviewed twice, in 1967 and 1968, and found that attitudes played a major role in determining variations of expenditures among individuals. In that study expenditures were defined as including spending not only on durable goods but also on additions and repairs to homes, vacations, and sports or hobby equipment.

Two studies highly relevant in this connection have already been discussed in Chapter 10 (see Tables 10-1 and 10-2). One of these studies is the four-year panel, 1966–70, which supplied data on the impact of personal financial progress, past and future, on the purchase of durable goods. The other set of studies was conducted by this author who analyzed the behavior of the BB Group, which expected an improvement following earlier advances.

The major conclusion of Chapter 10 was: When people feel that they are making progress and when they are optimistic regarding their own and the economy's prospects, new wants arise. In the light of the discussion in this chapter, we may add: There are good reasons why the proportion of those who are optimistic about their personal financial progress has been substantial and is expected to remain substantial. It must,

---

[10] These arguments were presented in Katona (1960, pp. 254 ff.).

however, be kept in mind that this is not the whole story because people's economic attitudes and expectations extend beyond personal concerns. The difference between personal optimism and societal discontent will be studied in the last three chapters of this book.

13
SOCIAL COGNITION

Optimism as a major specific feature of consumer psychology as it has prevailed in the United States during the last few decades has been examined in the preceding chapter. We turn now to the analysis of certain general psychological principles that govern the economic thinking of consumers and—as we shall indicate in connection with the discussion of business behavior (Part VI)—of businessmen as well. The principles involved may be termed the cognitive principles of economic behavior.

Cognition is the process of acquiring information and knowledge. The term knowledge is used in the sense of having information about what has happened in the environment rather than in the sense of exact or scientific knowledge. In the original sense of the term, cognition is contrasted to emotion and volition. It is commonplace to say, however, that there is hardly any knowledge lacking affective connotations. Most of the significant information we acquire, we usually either favor and approve or oppose and disapprove. Still, cognitive processes have a specific meaning. These are the processes through which both an individual and a people acquire their images of the environment both in fairly general terms regarding the relation of a person to his world and in specific terms regarding the meaning of such economic phenomena as prosperity, depression, inflation, or deficits. These images result from a selective crystallization of past experiences as influenced by attitudes and expectations. The manner in which the cognitive processes are organized will be the main concern of this chapter.

Learning and cognition are concepts of individual psychology. In a certain sense these terms are rightfully restricted to the individual. He alone is capable of learning. Saying that a group learns is a metaphor, implying that there is some uniformity in the learning of all individuals belonging to the group. These uniform features of the learning process among millions of consumers are, however, of paramount concern to psychological economics.

In several earlier publications the author designated the acquisition of new attitudes and behavior patterns by masses of people as social learning.[1] In the recent psychological literature the term social learning is used in a much more restrictive manner as denoting learning as influenced by face-to-face groups. In order to distinguish the processes studied here, it would be possible to call learning by the masses societal learning. Because this expression is somewhat cumbersome we shall continue to use the terms social learning and social cognition, but shall also speak of macrolearning processes to indicate the crucial distinction between microprocesses relating to individuals and macroprocesses that prevail when very many individuals are aggregated. As stated before, the introduction of the term "macro" into psychology is long overdue.

The principles of social cognition regarding economic matters that will be enumerated and illustrated in this chapter are far from final. They represent a first attempt to bring order to a difficult and much neglected area. The findings discussed here are mostly the same as those presented in the previous chapters. What is new is the organization of the findings. Therefore, in presenting each of the principles of social cognition, we shall refer to instances of supporting evidence that we have already discussed.

We shall describe five principles of social cognition. Only the last three deal with the presence or absence of acquisition of information, while the first two may be thought to transcend the realm of cognitive processes. Yet, what makes the learning processes of millions of people fairly uniform is the identical emotional or affective component attached to what is learned. Therefore, it is fitting to begin the discussion of organization in cognition with the principle of generalization of affect.

1. GENERALIZATION OF AFFECT

The first principle of social cognition concerns the spread of affect. The operation of this principle was first noted in

[1] See Katona (1960, p. 76 ff), Katona (1964a, Chapter 17), and Katona (1973).

198

1945–46, when surveys indicated that most people considered it inconceivable that the wonderful news of the end of World War II in victory could have anything but favorable economic consequences. In simplest terms, what is considered to be good is seen as having good effects, and what is considered to be bad is seen as having bad effects. More specifically, under the influence of good developments, spirits rise and gratification of wants becomes easier; contrariwise, unfavorable developments make for caution and postponement of purchases.

In listing examples of generalization of affect we start with very big news but mention developments of lesser importance as well:

1. The end of World War II was seen as something that would have to produce good consequences and could not cause such bad things as recession and unemployment.
2. The threat of war or heightened international tensions (e.g., the U-2 incident, Berlin, Cuba) are seen as unfavorable developments that cannot stimulate prosperity. On the other hand, the relaxation of international tensions (for example, the end of the Cuban crisis late in 1962) results in greater reassurance and the feeling of being able to plan ahead or to carry out one's plans.
3. Similar considerations apply to the wars as they occurred in Korea and Vietnam. A war is seen as causing human suffering and wasting resources. For many people it is incomprehensible or unacceptable that war production should make wheels turn and result in reduced unemployment.
4. In the fall of 1957, the first Sputnik was seen as a great achievement of our enemy and, therefore, as unfavorable news. The reaction was one of pessimism rather than optimism that the Sputnik would lead to increased American space efforts and thereby contribute to prosperous business conditions.
5. Inflation is thought to be bad; therefore, in the view of most people, rising prices must have unfavorable effects on one's own as well as on the country's development.
6. News about rising interest rates is seen as bad news, because easy money has long been associated with good times and because interest charges are considered as cost items for business. Therefore, news about rising interest rates contributes to pessimistic attitudes.

199

7. Extensive major strikes, such as the steel strike in 1959 or the automobile strike in 1970, are bad news and give rise to pessimistic expectations about the economic outlook.

It is not assumed that the generalization of affect is operative in every instance. It may sometimes be absent or overruled by other experiences. For instance, in geographical areas with substantial airspace industries, threats of war and the Korean and Vietnam wars were seen as having a favorable impact on domestic economic conditions.

In 1973–74 the great attention paid to the Watergate revelations apparently contributed to a spread of pessimistic economic attitudes. At that time the major reason for the public's turning pessimistic was its experience with rapidly rising food prices. But the political news contributed greatly to distrust in the government and therefore to the belief that the government would not be able to slow down inflation. In addition, Watergate created an atmosphere of unease, doubt, and skepticism. A sizable number of survey respondents spontaneously referred to Watergate when asked about the economic outlook. The statement made both by the administration and uninformed survey respondents that "because of Watergate the government cannot devote its attention to improving economic conditions" makes little sense except insofar as it reflects a spread of affect. Negative feelings generated by Watergate inevitably spread to economic conditions.

2. ORGANIZATION AND POLARIZATION OF NEWS

Isolated items of information are rarely influential and are quickly forgotten. Information that is influential with many people over longer periods is organized around some major issue or around its affective tone. Rarely do many people mention both favorable and unfavorable business news at the same time; according to whether they feel that business conditions are improving or deteriorating, only good news or only bad news are salient to them.

Instead of noticing a number of diverse economic developments, people usually organize the news around a central point. There were times when inflation served this purpose, and economic news was salient only when it had that as its focus. At other times unemployment had the organizing function. International tensions or presidential elections, when in the center of attention, tend to suppress other news.

The organization of information received may also be expressed as a process of congruence or of absence of dissonance. A psychological theory set forth by Leon Festinger (1957) assumes that there prevails a strong urge to establish noncontradictory belief systems. We tend to overcome dissonance, which is defined as the presence of two cognitions from which obverse consequences follow. It is possible to fit many instances related in this book to this principle. Most of the time in the 1950s and 1960s optimistic notions about personal finances corresponded with optimistic notions about the general economic trend and the same consequences followed from both opinions. Or, to mention a specific case, very many people argued incorrectly that what was true of personal finances applied to government finances as well. They overcame a feeling of dissonance by believing that neither they personally, nor business firms, nor the federal government could live with deficits over several successive years.

In many other instances, however, dissonant views are tolerated. An acquisition of the understanding that government finances are different from private finances may of course qualify as overcoming rather than tolerating dissonance. Learning that a tax increase may be good for the country even if it is bad for the taxpayer himself may be another instance of coping with dissonance. On the other hand, at certain times, for instance in the 1970s, optimism about personal financial trends prevailed side by side with pessimism about economic trends in general.

An interesting instance, which sheds light on the organization of belief systems, is people's desire both to spend more and to save more. Even though saving is not spending, many people fail to see that they want A and nonA at the same time. This is so because in times of rising incomes, which many Americans consider to be a fact of life, both amounts spent and amounts saved can be increased. In this case it is hardly appropriate to speak of dissonance being overcome. Conscious attempts to overcome dissonance are rare in comparison to instances in which belief systems are so organized around a central focus that all parts fit.

201

One additional principle of organization may be cited. People tend to abhor uncertainty and to overcome it. Uncertainty in the sense of news received that is unclear, puzzling, or incomprehensible gives rise to a search for information. Uncertainty in the sense of assuming that either of two different or contradictory outcomes is equally probable occurs but rarely. For instance, we seldom believe that both an increase and a decrease in our income are probable. Uncertainty is tolerated and maintained over long periods when it is equivalent to a pessimistic view. Many people, when they say that the near-term outlook is uncertain, mean to say that it is unfavorable. Regarding developments in the more distant future, lack of knowledge (as expressed, for example, in Don't Know answers to survey questions) is acceptable; when dealing with something that has no immediate consequences, uncertainty may not be bothersome.

3. HABITUATION

One form of change in attitudes or opinions, that is, one form of learning, is getting accustomed to things. Habituation to higher prices was first observed in 1951–52. In the second half of 1950, following the outbreak of the Korean War, rising prices were big news and were reacted to by hoarding; after a while, when prices did not continue to advance rapidly, people got accustomed to the new price level and ceased to complain about "high prices." Little needs to be said about the frequent later instances of habituation because they have been extensively discussed in earlier chapters. The basic principle can be formulated in very simple terms: Only what is new is news; when the same kind of news continues over prolonged periods, it ceases to be news. The major examples we found of habituation to economic developments were:

1. *To higher prices.* Observed, for instance, in 1951–52 as well as in 1962–63, but not in 1973 following the sharp increase in food prices.
2. *To good business news.* Records of GNP, national income, retail sales, and so on, were widely noted in 1955 and 1964, but were no longer salient news a year or two later. Habituation to good news contributes greatly to ending a boom.

3. *To bad business news.* During the recession of 1958 some
habituation to unfavorable news and even to the threat of
unemployment was observed. In 1969–70 this was hardly
the case, but the finding that consumer attitudes did not
deteriorate further in 1970 and recovered somewhat in
the first half of 1971 could be attributed, in the absence of
good news, to the lesser influence of the old bad news.
There is much stronger empirical support for habituation
to good news than to bad news.

4. SLOWNESS AND GRADUALNESS OF SOCIAL LEARNING

The acquisition of new attitudes and new behavior patterns
by masses of people most commonly occurs gradually over
fairly long periods. In principle, sudden learning should be possible. Among individuals, it occurs through an abrupt reorganization of their cognitive map in response to information or
experiences of great importance. Yet, in the case of large numbers of individuals, there is only occasional evidence of sudden
learning. It appears doubtful, for example, that the economic
behavior of the American people was suddenly altered after
Pearl Harbor. Information is available about the absence of
sudden learning following the end of World War II, or the outbreak of the Korean war, or the beginning or end of the Vietnam war. In all these instances masses of people changed their
economic opinions, attitudes, ad behavior only slowly and
gradually. A quick response was noted, however, to rapid
inflation in 1950 and 1973, as discussed in Chapter 9 where the
response in the form of advance buying and hoarding was
characterized as exceptional.

There are good reasons why social learning is slow and
gradual. It may take several months or even years until masses
of people become cognizant of important news or of information about the consequences of such news. Mutual reinforcement through exchange of information among peer groups by
word of mouth, a major condition for the emergence of a uniform response to new stimuli by very many people, is a slow
process. The slowness in the acquisition of major new insights
may be indicated by many examples that are significant in our
economy and society.

1. *Expected price movements.* During the first few years after World War II the majority of consumers expected prices to rise for a short while but to return later to their original level. The reasoning that "what goes up must come down" was characteristic of that period. Public attitudes changed gradually between 1952 and 1959, and slowly the new notion of an inflationary age developed. People learned that they were living in a period in which prices were advancing, that five years later prices would be higher than they were, ten years later still higher, and so on. Slowly, people became aware that certain enduring features of our age kept pushing prices up, even though it was not clearly understood what those features were.

2. *Impossibility of a deep depression.* It took from 1945 to 1955 for American consumers to be convinced that a depression like the one in the 1930s could not happen again. Gradually, more and more people came to believe that the government was able to avoid a deep depression.

3. *Probability of recurring recessions.* After the recession of 1958 consumers learned that "recessions are with us" and that "we don't know how to avoid them." The relatively short intervening time before the 1960–61 recession and the fairly high rate of unemployment between the two recessions accelerated the learning process.

4. *Belief in the power of the government in economic matters.* Little is known about the origin of people's belief in the government as a powerful force in economic affairs. When in the early 1950s people's economic opinions were first studied, the notion that remedies to inflation, recession, and unemployment were to be found in the government's "doing something" was already widespread. Even skeptics rarely believed that the government would not be able to influence economic processes.

Doubts about the government's ability to deal with societal problems began to spread after 1966, following the acceleration of the war in Vietnam, and regarding inflation and unemployment after 1969. But even after the recession of 1970 the extent of trust in the government was substantial. This became clear in August, 1971, when price and wage controls were introduced. In the following two years confidence in the government's ability to manage the economy was gradually eroded. In the summer of 1973 more than 70 percent of all adult survey respondents said without qualification that the government would not be successful in reducing either inflation or unemployment.[2]

The slowness and gradualness of social learning can be documented not only regarding belief systems that concern major economic issues but also regarding opinions and attitudes toward specific matters of spending and saving. It will be shown in Part Five that

> Attitudes toward buying on the installment plan improved gradually in the first ten or fifteen years after World War II. (Part of the improvement may have resulted, not from acquiring new information, but from the fact that opponents of borrowing, being mostly older people, gradually passed away.)
>
> Attitudes toward investing in common stocks improved slowly in the 1960s and then deteriorated slowly following the recession of 1970.

Observations of market researchers regarding the slowness of changes in attitudes toward brands may be mentioned in passing. The acceptance of innovations has likewise been slow and gradual in most cases. The relatively quick penetration of television must be viewed as an exception, greatly different from the slow process of acceptance of most other household appliances, for instance, room air conditioners, washers, and dryers. Finally, interest in small cars and compact cars arose first in a small group of sophisticated people who were looking for something different, then among people with limited resources attracted by lower purchase prices, and only slowly and gradually among people favoring the smaller size itself and lesser gasoline consumption. It is an interesting footnote that during the same period there also prevailed a gradual increase in the attraction exerted by expensive "extras" to be added on to the new cars, small as well as large.

We may note that the acquisition of higher income, and of more consumer goods or financial assets, is also a gradual process for most people. The development of new wants and desires likewise follows gradually, because people's level of aspi-

---

[2] But even this process of erosion was far from complete, as may be deduced from findings, which will be reported in Chapter 22, that a large degree of support for major government fiscal programs continued in 1973.

ration, when raised with achievement, is somewhat higher but not much higher than their actual level.

5. PERSISTENCE OF STEREOTYPES

Absence of learning is usually a misleading expression. Even though we often speak of change as being universal, most things do not change over short periods, so that there is no need or stimulus for learning. The instances in which absence of learning becomes meaningful and worthy of note are those in which old beliefs continue to be widely held irrespective of whether they are appropriate.

Believing in and holding on to stereotypes represents a valuable time-saving device. Instead of considering a piece of information as giving rise to a problem that calls for deliberation, we file the information as belonging in the category of well-accepted knowledge. Stereotypes are simple statements of great generality that appear self-evident and require no confirmation. A number of such stereotyped items of belief were found to have been held by the great majority of Americans practically without any change during the twenty-five years following World War II. People believed that

inflation is bad,
recessions occur periodically,
international tensions have adverse consequences for the domestic economy,
deficits (of the federal government) are bad.

We reported earlier that most Americans entertain the almost unshakable conviction that inflation, even one with moderate price increases, has an adverse effect on the welfare of individuals as well as on the economy as a whole. Although many do not believe that inflation is inevitable, most people agree that we know too little to arrest it. Recessions and therefore periods of fairly high unemployment are also widely considered to be parts of our lives that cannot be avoided. A third general value judgment of an enduring nature is that heightened international tensions have an adverse effect on domestic economic trends. This opinion is of more recent origin, but in the 1950s and early 1960s many more people were convinced of it than of the contrary.

206

These three beliefs are related to what most people see as the essential feature of good times: Times are good when standards of living are rising and when people can look forward to still higher standards of living in the future. Bad times are those in which there are no gains in (real) income or in the standard of living.

The results of work and effort on the part of individuals are thought to be hampered by the adverse developments: Inflation is seen to entail loss of purchasing power; recession involves unemployment; war and international conflict are viewed as deterrents to planning ahead and improving one's life; deficits mean to many people that sooner or later they will have to pay, probably through higher taxes. The first two beliefs have already been amply discussed; a few more words must be said about the last two.

The belief that international conflict has an unfavorable economic impact appears to have two roots. One is the abhorrence of uncertainty about the future. We pointed out before that for most people uncertainty represents a disturbing situation in which they are threatened by disagreeable surprises and cannot plan ahead. The cold war, for example, means for many people that our future depends on or is greatly influenced by what the Soviet leaders will do. Periods of heightened international tensions occur when uncertainty about the unpredictable adversary increases, and periods of relaxation in international affairs occur when the future course of Soviet action seems more predictable.

Secondly, people distinguish sharply between defense production and civilian production. The total capacity of the economy is thought to be limited—if the production of guns increases, the production of butter declines, and vice versa. Relatively few people are aware of underutilization of productive facilities or think of the possibility of expanding those facilities. Other more sophisticated people speak of disruption of civilian production by increased defense production and of higher taxes or inflation as a result of large defense expenditures. In either case, the chances of acquiring more and better consumer goods appear to worsen.

The existence of deficits is less generally known than that of inflation, recession, or international conflict. When respondents in nationwide surveys were asked whether or not the government was operating at a deficit, both early in the 1960s

207

and early in the 1970s only 45 to 55 percent of respondents said they knew that there was a deficit. A greater proportion of respondents subscribed to the notion that deficits have adverse consequences.

The great majority of people see no difference between the budget of the government and that of business firms or individuals. Prudent people are supposed to balance receipts and expenditures by adjusting the latter to the former. Relatively few people realize that the government, in contrast to firms or individuals, may also use the reverse procedure, namely, to increase revenues when spending increases or must be increased. Deficits are accepted when there is an emergency. The resulting debt is viewed as a burden that must be repaid sooner or later. Few people think of debt as representing assets and wealth in the possession of creditors and bondholders. These beliefs changed but little in 1964–65 when people learned a great deal about government finances in connection with the tax cut introduced at that time.

The Macrolearning Process

The process by means of which millions of people acquire similar new attitudes and behavior patterns at approximately the same time was analyzed by collecting data from repeated surveys, frequently with identical respondents, at times when the American people received significant new information. The acquisition of information was studied primarily

1. following President Kennedy's proposal of a major tax cut in 1962–64,
2. following the start of public discussion on the need for increasing income taxes in 1966–67, and
3. following the acceleration of inflation, which began in 1969.[3]

Even though survey respondents could not be subjected to experimentation and the time spent with them was rather limited, it was possible to gather a fairly comprehensive set of data not only about their level of information, opinions, and expectations, but also about the reasons for their beliefs and

[3] The discussion in this section is based on Katona (1973). Fiscal policy will be analyzed further in Chapter 21.

attitudes. Though extensive, these data are still less than complete and do not yield adequate information for a full-scale analysis of the learning process of individuals. With respect to an analysis of changes in collective attitudes and the process of social learning, the situation is different. It is the basic assumption of these studies that social learning is simpler and more selective than individual learning.

The macromodel of behavior is much simpler than the micromodel. Extensive differences among individuals, as well as great variations in the information acquired by individuals, may be neglected when social learning and changes in the attitudes of all consumers are studied. What many people learn at a given time represents only a small part of what individuals learn. This discrepancy is not attributable simply to idiosyncratic elements in the acquisition of information by individuals. More importantly, similarities in the information transmitted to large numbers of people and in the information to which many people have access relate only to certain parts of the information received by individuals. Mutual reinforcement among many people extends only to some rather than to all features of environmental change. A unifying characteristic of social learning consists of the affective connotation of what is learned. Practically everyone in a country may learn at a given time that the economic news is good or bad, that business trends are favorable or unfavorable, pointing to an upswing or a downswing. At the same time, the knowledge of manifold details about what has or will become better or worse varies from individual to individual, depending upon the individual's prior knowledge, his personal experience, and the group to which he belongs.[4]

The psychology of learning is concerned with an analysis of both the results and the processes of learning. A few words may suffice regarding the results:

1. Millions of people learned in 1963–64 that a massive tax cut might be of help not only to individual taxpayers, but also to the entire economy. An association was formed

---

[4] It should also be noted that survey data on changes in collective behavior and group attitudes are more reliable than survey data relating to individuals. The latter are subject to greater reporting errors and may even be influenced by changes in the mood of the person questioned. Errors and biases of individual data may cancel out when data from many respondents are aggregated.

between a tax cut and an expected improvement in business conditions. (This association did not prevail prior to 1963, in contrast to the association between a tax cut and an expected improvement in personal financial conditions.)

2. What was learned about the impact of a tax cut propagated a belief in the adverse effect of tax increases on the economy. Nevertheless, in 1967–68, many people acquired the opinion that a small tax increase might be "to the good," because it might help to redress the economic imbalance.

3. The American people learned: (a) that they were living in an inflationary age in which price increases were continuous, (b) that price increases would be slow and gradual, and (c) that it would be unwise to withdraw money from the bank in order to beat inflation by hoarding goods. (In 1973 people's opinions and attitudes changed again under the impact of sharp increases in food prices, but this is a different story.)

Three successive stages appear to be involved in the learning process:

A. The emergence or recognition of a problem.
B. The acquisition and processing of information.
C. Problem solution and theory formation.

A. *Problem recognition.* Little information is available on problem emergence and recognition from the traditional problem-solving experiments in which the experimenter presents his subjects with something explicitly designated as a problem and the subjects are externally motivated to solve it. By contrast, in the instances studied in this chapter, the emergence of a problem or a crossroad situation was found to be far from automatic following the impact of new stimuli. Inertia and old established habits appeared to exert a strong influence toward classifying the new stimuli as familiar ones, so that old response patterns remained applicable and people were not motivated to deliberate and choose.

The recognition of a problem was slow with respect to the acceleration of inflation in 1969 (instance 3, as mentioned on p. 267). Toward the beginning of that year a few survey respondents said, in essence, that prices were rising much faster than before, which was greatly disturbing to them; other re-

210

spondents indicated an awareness of somewhat more rapid price increases but showed no concern; others appeared to have noticed nothing new. It took six months of a variety of experiences with prices and with information received until the majority of Americans became personally concerned.

The tax increase proposal (instance 2) did not appear puzzling to the majority of people who had heard of it in 1966 and in 1967. They registered it as unfavorable news for themselves as taxpayers as well as for the economy, having classified the information as the opposite of a tax cut, which was known to have beneficial effects.

President Kennedy's tax cut proposal (instance 1) was promptly recognized as something new by those who had heard of it. But the information was dealt with simply as impractical, as purely political, or even as impossible, and therefore was not viewed as a matter of personal concern. A year or more passed before many people began to recognize the existence of a pressing problem.

Awareness of a problem does not necessarily lead to desiring and searching for additional information. In some cases, definite answers to the questions that were raised emerged almost at the same time as the problem. This was often the case with respect to the affective connotation of the new situation. For instance, the tax surcharge was viewed as bad right away, even by many people who were puzzled about its having been proposed soon after the tax cut and advocated as something good for the country. Whenever a difference emerged between beneficial or harmful effects for oneself and for the country, there was a tendency to recognize the problem.

The question "What will happen next?" commonly emerged earlier than the question "Should I do anything myself?" A response involving prompt action immediately following the recognition of a problem was observed only rarely.

B. *Information processing.* In problem-solving experiments, the recognition of a problem is followed by a process that has been commonly described either as trial and error or as rational deliberation, consisting of listing possible alternative courses of action and weighing their appropriateness. In contrast, the process of social learning as it has been observed in the three instances cited above may be characterized as: (*a*) serial processing of information received, supplemented by (*b*) selective search for information, usually leading to (*c*) a

211

clarification of the problem, and resulting either in (d) shortcuts representing a temporary, superficial solution, or alternatively in (e) uncertainty and growing uneasiness.

In all instances, the original news was repeated frequently, in greatly elaborated form and by persons viewed as authorities or experts over the TV, radio, and in print. Concerned people among survey respondents also reported having discussed the matter with friends or colleagues, and these reports often indicated the recognition of a problem. While information flows serially, its apprehension and processing is highly selective. People usually listened to news that was in line with their initial perceptions and expectations. The selection of information depended to a large extent on the groups to which the listener belonged.

The outcome of the initial stages of information processing is either a clarification of a problem or a superficial solution. The first type of outcome involves a disclosure of gaps in the information, of missing links and question marks. The other type of outcome involves an apparent closure, usually in the form of a superficial subsumption of the new information under familiar rubrics.

A major indicator of the first outcome is an increase in "Don't Know" statements, especially on the part of bettereducated respondents. Insofar as the tax cut is concerned, in contrast to uninformed people whose initial response was frequently "Don't Know," upper-income respondents appeared to know the answer in the first few months after learning of President Kennedy's proposal. But, as time went by, these people grew increasingly puzzled. When asked what they thought of a tax cut some replied, "Formerly, I thought that it was merely a proposal to get votes; now I don't know; many good people say that it would help the economy." They responded similarly with respect to inflation: "A few months ago I was not much concerned, although my wife complained about rising prices; now I don't know; prices are rising so fast that something must be done, but it is not at all clear what could or should be done." (In both quotations we have paraphrased a variety of reports found in interview transcripts.)

As the problem became more acute for some people, motivating them to search further, other people arrived at easy solutions. Only part of the available information appears to have been used when some respondents reported, "Experts say

212

that the tax cut will make for more purchasing power (for larger consumer demand) so that business conditions will improve." Or, when questioned about inflation, some responded, "The government will do something to slow down price increases," while others stated that "The government can't do anything; there will be unemployment and bad times, and prices will continue to go up." In numerous answers of this sort there were few indications of curiosity, or even of uncertainty. People reported definite expectations about good or bad consequences.

But shortcut solutions may be unstable because new information continues to be received. In some cases, the new information is shrugged off; in other cases, the serial information processing is resumed. The process of social learning continues until the great majority of people acquire a uniform belief system in which there are no gaps or question marks.

This uniformity of opinion among the majority of people, which constitutes the final solution of a problem, is an unexpected finding. In the instances of the tax cut and the surcharge, the process of social learning continued until this uniformity occurred. In the spring and summer of 1964, some people thought that the tax cut was rather insignificant, while others believed that it would stimulate economic recovery. The opinions and attitudes of the first group continued to change under the impact of new information received, until in the fall of 1964 they resembled those of the second group. Late in 1964, close to three-fourths of a representative sample spoke exclusively of the beneficial effects of the tax cut. The change was similar in response to the tax surcharge: In the summer and fall of 1968, there was general agreement that it had only insignificant adverse effects on personal finances and that it was acceptable with respect to general economic trends.

C. *Theory formation.* An analysis of the final stage of the learning process, the solution of the problem, sheds additional light on information processing. The information that is received is not just serially registered; it is organized so that it represents a step toward the solution. Problem solving constitutes a continuous process of reorganization that ends when all of the pieces fall into place. An individual may reach this end point when he is in agreement with others in his sphere of contact (face-to-face group) and feels that he is in agreement with most others in the country. Another indication of a solu-

213

tion is a uniformity of affective connotations. As long as one feels that a new development is partly good and partly bad, tension persists. The same condition exists when the development seems beneficial (or harmful) to oneself but harmful (or beneficial) to the country. The resolution of contradictory effects represents an important part of a cognitive solution.

The development of a theory may be said to constitute the end result. The emergence or formation of theoretical notions is the most satisfactory conclusion of the process. It is not enough that question marks disappear; new schemata must emerge that integrate various pieces of information and enable the individual to cope easily with additional information. This is the traditional function of a theory, to integrate what is known, and at the same time to go beyond the available data by providing the means to answer other questions that may arise.

The schemata or theories that are constructed in the process of social learning are rather simple. Numerous complexities, puzzling or contradictory in earlier stages, disappear. Clarity results from the simplification and even the suppression of information. This process is, to some extent, analogous to the major stages of theory formation in science, which are abstraction and generalization. However, the analogy between the theories formed by the American people concerning tax changes or inflation and scientific theories is far from complete because in the first case the simplification was usually accomplished by forming superficial theories. The shortcuts that were used disregarded complexities rather than integrated them; satisfaction with the final conclusion was achieved by overlooking various aspects of the problem. Naturally, there were great individual differences in this respect, but what emerged as the result of social learning and what was subject to mutual reinforcement must be characterized as containing a few unifying generalizations rather than representing an all-encompassing theory. The answers given earlier about the results of the learning process may all be viewed as oversimplified and even one-sided theories.

The absence of a solution creates uncertainty and usually results in a "wait-and-see" attitude. Problem solution, on the other hand, results in action, because definite expectations arise and induce many people to change their spending-saving behavior. The emerging theory provides answers to questions about what will happen and about what the individual himself

214

should do. When expectations are derived from problem solving, they may differ greatly from personal past experiences.[5]

The oversimplified nature of the theories held by people helps them to overcome the adverse effects of information overload. It is well known that the quantity of scientific information which has been produced, and therefore the amount of information with which scholars must cope, has increased greatly during the last few decades. Similarly, people are generally subjected nowadays to a much larger number of items of information than in earlier times. It has been argued that there are limits to the amount and variety of information that people can tolerate. According to the extreme formulation presented by Alvin Toffler (1970), the American people are subjected to overstimulation and overchoice, creating a "future shock," that is, a distress which results from overloading their adaptive system and their decision-making processes.

Portions of this chapter, which apparently support this argument, may be recalled. While technological change and even social change appear to have been rapid during the last few decades, social learning was found to be slow, and adaptation to changes in the environment must have become more difficult than in earlier times. But is this problem the same as the problem of information overload? The latter problem is derived from finding that the organism can apprehend, retain, and use only a limited number of bits of information. Therefore, as our analysis shows, people order and organize the variety of information impinging on them into a limited number of schemata or theories. Toffler speaks of "glutting a person with more information than he can process." We, on the other hand, noted that people find means to cope with complex material. Sensible learning represents the process of creating order, by integrating manifold detailed items of information into a few major, and often far too simple, schemata. The resulting theories are oversimplified, perhaps to their advantage rather than to their detriment.

---

[5] The description of the learning process was not interrupted by references to psychological literature. It may suffice to mention that the author borrowed primarily from the ideas of Max Wertheimer (1959) and other Gestalt psychologists, as well as of Herbert A. Simon (1971) regarding information processing and Jerome S. Bruner (1971) regarding theory formation.

14
RATIONAL BEHAVIOR

The principle of rationality occupies a central position in traditional economic theory. It states that the rational man aims at a specific end—the maximization of utilities—by employing well-defined means, namely, the weighing of available alternatives. He first lists all conceivable courses of action and their consequences, then ranks the consequences, chooses the best, and sticks to his choice in a consistent manner.[1]

In many theoretical discussions impulsive or whimsical or even ununderstandable behavior is considered *the* alternative to rational behavior. Then a constant flow of rational calculations would appear, not just the ideal case, but also the typical form of purposive and intelligent behavior.

Economic theorists in general acknowledge that the principle of rationality is not realistic in the sense that it certainly does not apply to all economic behavior. But this is hardly relevant, they believe. It comes about because there are people of limited intelligence and foresight and there are bad businessmen who do not proceed rationally. The laws of economics need not apply to them. Businessmen with nonrational motives who make use of nonrational procedures will fail rather than survive. Behavior that reflects human frailty is classified as a short-term aberration that has little impact on economic developments over the long run.

Behavioral economics concerns itself with studying the extent to which rationality actually determines behavior on the part of consumers as well as businessmen. An understanding of the ends toward which economic men strive as well as of the

---

[1] The last point includes the transitive ordering of choices: If I prefer A to B and B to C, I also prefer A to C. For a modern description of the principle of rationality, see Arrow (1951a and 1951b). Parts of this chapter are based on the author's article (1953).

217

means they apply represents a necessary part of behavioral studies. These studies must not be restricted to finding out whether or not the principle of rationality, as described above, prevails in economic life. They must be broader and extend to a search for various forms of purposive and circumspect behavior.

Is the consumer rational or is he irrational? This is not the right question to ask. The consumer is a human being, influenced by his past experience. His sociocultural norms, attitudes, and habits, as well as his belonging to groups, all influence his decisions. He is apt to prefer shortcuts, follow rules of thumb, and behave in a routine manner. But he is also capable of acting intelligently. When he feels that it really matters, he will deliberate and choose to the best of his ability.

We begin by recalling evidence in support of the proposition that consumer behavior is purposive and intelligent. Our analysis of cognitive processes in Chapter 13 and of problem-solving behavior in Chapter 4 indicates that sensible processes play a major role in gaining an understanding of what is going on in the economic sphere and how best to respond to it. The psychological process of problem-solving—from the emergence of a problem to the accomplishment of congruence of parts and fitting them into a unified whole—is not identical with the economists' description of rationality and yet resembles it in several respects. The main alternative to such behavior was found to be habitual behavior and not impulsive, capricious, or whimsical behavior. This finding strengthens the case of rationality, because what is at a given time habitual and routine may have emerged much earlier as the result of deliberation and the weighing of alternatives. Finally, psychology, just as economic theory, refuses to acknowledge the existence of irrational behavior in the sense of behavior that is incomprehensible.

On the other hand, weighty arguments may be recalled in opposition to an identification of economic behavior, as it has emerged in our studies, with rational behavior. Problem-solving behavior is a relatively rare occurrence, which prevails under the impact of strong motivational forces. Habitual behavior occurs much more frequently and, whatever the origin of our habits, they do not exhibit the major features of rational behavior. People act as they have acted before under similar circumstances, without deliberating and choosing. Routine procedures and the application of rules of thumb by consumers as well as businessmen exclude the weighing of alternatives. The impact of group belonging—acting in the same way as others in our group, or following the leader—likewise results in behavior that may be appropriate but that differs greatly from the postulated forms of rational behavior.

Buying Behavior

In order to analyze the process of weighing alternatives and of deliberate decision making it is not enough to study consumer choices regarding the rate of spending or saving in good and in bad times. Instead of reviewing consumer behavior over the business cycle, we shall devote our attention to individuals as they are engaged in spending and saving. Saving decisions will be studied in the next few chapters. At this point it may suffice to state that a large share of the amounts saved at a given time is due to decisions made much earlier (contractual saving) or to decisions about not spending (residual saving). Nevertheless, conscious and purposeful decisions to add to reserve funds do occur. Similarly, when we now embark on the study of buying behavior we shall find that routine procedures, with an almost complete absence of making any choices, are common. So are, however, circumspect and deliberate decisions based on searching for alternatives and weighing them.

It might be thought that any act of purchasing is a complicated process. After having decided what article to buy (for example, a car or a piece of furniture) consumers must make decisions about the brand or make, the quality and price range, and the store or retail outlet. In studying the circumstances under which deliberate or even rational decisions are common, we shall not consider the process of purchasing necessities, which may be assumed to offer little discretion, nor the purchase of products bought very frequently because they may be assumed to have become largely routinized. We shall report on studies conducted by Katona and Mueller (1954) in the early 1950s on the purchases of major household appliances (TV sets, refrigerators, washers and dryers, stoves). These goods are expensive and enduring; they are bought fairly infrequently at the discretion of the buyer, for whom the purchase is important. The major findings obtained may be summarized first in negative terms. The authors did not find that most purchases of large household goods were made after careful consideration or deliberation, that most such purchases required a long planning period, or that they were preceded by extensive information seeking or shopping around.

If careful deliberation were defined as comprising all the features of decision making that were included in the study —consideration of alternatives and of consequences, discussion with family members, information seeking, as well as concern with price, brand, quality, performance, special features, and gadgets—the conclusion would emerge that almost all people proceed in a careless way in purchasing large household goods. This conclusion is, however, not justified. Deliberation may be strongly focused on one aspect of the purchase to the exclusion of other aspects. Therefore, it may be considered as careful deliberation if some, but by no means all, of the features of problem solving and thinking are present. By so doing, about one-fourth of the purchases of large household appliances were found to have lacked practically all features of careful deliberation. On the other hand, close to one-half of the purchases contained several features.[2]

The instances in which people purchased major household goods without taking alternatives into consideration and with practically no information seeking or discussion were not determined by the age, education, or income of the buyers. Three other considerations became apparent as greatly restricting deliberate decision making.

The first was the presence of a special opportunity to make a purchase, as perceived by the buyer. Availability of a desired article through friends, or through "sales," or through a persuasive salesman are examples of situations in which some people proceeded without careful deliberation. The reverse was, however, not necessarily true: people who gave very careful consideration to their purchase often bought at "sales."

---

[2] Katona and Mueller (1954) contrasted the purchase of major appliances with that of men's sport shirts, a product likewise of some interest to the buyer, not purchased very frequently, but much less expensive. They found that features of deliberation were absent much more frequently in purchases of sport shirts. For related studies, see Ferber (1955), who confirmed that a substantial part of durable purchases were carried out without advance planning, and Newman and Staelin (1972), who obtained results similar to those of Katona and Mueller in an analysis of automobile purchases.

Urgent need was another situation in which an absence of careful deliberation was found. When people felt that they could not afford to wait, their purchasing process differed substantially from decision making under other circumstances.

Finally, satisfaction with a similar article previously used led often to a quick purchase without much discussion and information seeking, while dissatisfaction or lack of experience was associated with hesitating and choosing.

The last instance is of particular interest. Satisfied purchasers with ample experience were found to proceed purposefully and intelligently without using the procedures postulated by the theory of rationality. Because of their past experience purchasers are sometimes in a position to refrain from rational calculations. They reserve searching for alternatives and choosing the best for those rare occasions when they are confronted with problems. Information seeking and choosing is apparently more common among people with little experience and may therefore in some instances indicate absence rather than presence of intelligence.[3]

Deviating from a habitual course of action represents one of the major features of genuine decision making. The circumstances under which careful consideration and choosing among alternatives take place, or which are likely to elicit such behavior, are not fully known. On the basis of fragmentary evidence it is possible to present the following, possibly incomplete, list of expenditures and conditions that cause consumers to reflect and make what we have called genuine decisions before making a purchase:

1. Expenditures that are subjectively thought to be major and that are fairly rare. Many of these expenditures are large (for example, a house or, in most but not all cases, a car), but some may be small and yet of great importance to the buyer (as, for instance, a dress or a present for a special occasion).
2. Unsatisfactory past experience, especially disappointment of expectations.

[3] It is the motorist who does not know the way who searches for information (looks at a map, asks questions) and weighs the appropriateness of alternate routes. The scholar knows, or is supposed to know, that even great familiarity with a problem should not inhibit search behavior and deliberation. The economic man appears to resemble the motorist or the ordinary man more than the scholar.

221

3. Some (by no means all) purchases of new products or the first purchase of a product.
4. Awareness of a difference between one's customary behavior and that of the group to which one belongs or an important reference group.
5. Impact of strong new stimuli or precipitating circumstances; these stimuli may consist of general news (threat of war, inflation, and so on) or of news regarding specific products, which may be transmitted by advertisers.

Except in instances such as these the buyer preserves his energies. He deliberates and chooses only when past experience does not offer clear and unambiguous guidelines.

Is the Consumer Well Informed or Ignorant?

Obviously, the information available to businessmen as well as consumers is always limited, rather than complete. Even the rational man is not in a position to take into account alternative courses of action which are not known to him, or about which information is not accessible to him. Therefore, it is important to find out how much the consumer knows or what kind of information he is in a position to consider when he is deliberating and choosing.

Having determined that buying behavior was frequently characterized by a rather limted process of search for information about brands, stores, prices, and quality, we direct our attention to the presence or absence of information about the economy as a whole. The answer to the question, "Is the consumer well informed or ignorant," was found to depend on the kind of information we had in mind. It is possible to develop tests that will indicate that the average consumer is quite ignorant; yet it is also possible to provide evidence for the opposite conclusion.

If respondents falling in a representative sample are questioned about their knowledge of specific economic facts, and especially if numerical data are requested, the results are rather dismal. It is hardly surprising that the size of GNP or of federal expenditures or the number of automobiles sold in a year are known only to a very small proportion of the population. The absence of precise information extends to matters that should be of personal concern: Even people who are accustomed to buying cars on credit are often not able to say what the minimum requirement for down payment or the costs of credit are when buying on the installment plan. Lack of information on life insurance is extensive, for instance, about the differences among different kinds of policies and their costs (see Maynes 1972b and Mandell 1973).

On the other hand, questions about recent changes in the economy are usually answered accurately by the majority of respondents. We may begin by noting a rather surprising correspondence. Over several decades the Survey Research Center asked the following question in its quarterly surveys: "Would you say that at present business conditions are better or worse than they were a year ago?" The answers to this question (in the form of the proportion saying "Better" minus the proportion saying "Worse") were placed on a graph for the decade ending in 1963; a second curve was constructed from fluctuations of the production index of the Federal Reserve Board (percent change in American industrial production during the preceding year). The two curves were found to be practically identical; not only did their turning points and directions coincide but the extent of changes was also very similar.[4] In other words, the average American, who of course does not know anything about the production index, has a good feel for the direction and rate of change in economic trends.

The majority of consumers have been found to have information about major changes in the economy, which information usually corresponds to what available data show. In good times and in bad times the majority knew whether unemployment had increased or decreased in the preceding months, whether profits or retail sales had gone up or down, and also whether interest rates had risen or fallen—without knowing how much larger or smaller any of these magnitudes were. In inflationary periods the proportion saying that prices of things they bought had gone up substantially has been much larger than in those years when the price increases were fairly small. Yet information about the extent of price increases was not precise among most consumers.

Expectations cannot be checked for accuracy, but it can be determined later whether or not they have been fulfilled. On

---

[4] See Chart 5 in Katona (1964a, p. 122). In the ten years following 1963 the correspondence between the two curves has been less complete, but still substantial.

223

the whole, during the quarter century following World War II, personal financial expectations have been more optimistic and price expectations more conservative than what actually happened. Expectations about forthcoming economic trends served as a major component of the *Index of Consumer Sentiment*. Problem solving and deliberation often made these expectations deviate from past developments and contributed to the predictive value of the *Index* at crucial times.

Survey information is available about people's knowledge of stock market movements. Findings repeatedly made between 1950 and 1972 may be summarized by the following statement, which is hardly surprising: In those weeks and months when stock prices move substantially upward or downward many people know what has happened on the stock market, while in periods of small fluctuations very few people know. "Many people" in the preceding statement means about one-half of all family heads and the great majority of upper-income family heads. These findings may be explained by the nature of information transmittal. Only very large stock movements produce big headlines in newspapers and extensive and repeated reports on TV. Therefore, one may conclude that people know only what is repeated often and in a highly salient form. But a somewhat different explanation of the findings can hardly be ruled out: Only what matters to a person is known to him. Only large stock movements are relevant to the average investor who is not playing the market, and only large stock movements may affect business trends or employment opportunities.

It follows that information available is incomplete because the search for information is selective. Only at the roulette table is it possible to have complete information and calculate the odds for all alternative courses of action. While some theoretical statements in economics read as if Monte Carlo were the prototype of rational behavior, purposive and sensible economic behavior appears to differ greatly from what is possible—though in fact, it rarely happens—in certain forms of gambling.

Maximization of Utilities

Our discussion of the similarities and differences between the processes of consumer behavior and of rational behavior casts light on the goals and ends of the consumer as well. If and when a weighing of alternatives is absent, it is no longer possible to choose the best and to attempt to maximize one's advantages. The theory of maximization of utilities, as well as of maximization of profits by businessmen, may be attacked on other grounds as well. In many versions the statement that a person seeks to maximize utilities represents a tautology: Whatever a person does is considered his best choice, and the only way to find out what he prefers is to look at what he does.[5] If his preferences or behavior are found to vary from time to time, then the theoretician assumes that his tastes have changed, and this change is excluded from economic analysis.

Maximization constitutes an instance of a one-motive theory, to be contrasted with the assumption regarding the multiplicity of motivational patterns. If it is postulated that there is just one motive to a certain kind of human behavior, then the introduction of the concept of motive into analysis becomes useless. Motives represent a construct that serves useful purposes if it is possible to demonstrate that the existence of different motives corresponds with differences in behavior—either over time by the same person or business firm, or at the same time among different kinds of people or businessmen. The variety of prevailing motivational patterns may be discussed more appropriately with respect to business firms than consumers. Their study will therefore be relegated to Chapter 18.

At this point it may suffice to list the major considerations that must be taken into account in order to modify or at least to clarify the assumption that a "betterment function"–"everybody does what he thinks is best at the time" (Boulding 1972)—represents a basic feature of decision making. First, striving for doing the best or for improvement is not a constant mode of behavior. Very frequently, behavior is simply habitual with no genuine decision making whatsoever. Second, the aim of improvement may relate not only to one's economic position but to self-fulfillment and nonmaterial satisfactions as

---

[5] A leading theoretician, Fritz Machlup (1946, p. 526), expressed this thought as follows: "If *whatever* a businessman does is explained by the principle of profit maximization—because he does what he likes to do, and he likes to do what maximizes the sum of his pecuniary and nonpecuniary profits—the analysis acquires the character of a system of definitions and tautologies, and loses much of its value as an explanation of reality."

well. Third, people are often satisfied with small steps toward what they consider desirable goals, without an extensive search process and without trying to achieve the optimum. Finally, progress or improvement may relate not only to personal needs and wants but also to those of groups to which one belongs. It is possible for a broad "We" to take the place of the "I" and for the aim of betterment to be directed, for example, toward better schools and hospitals, or toward such goals as progress in the fight against poverty, racial discrimination, and pollution.

Adaptive may be a more suitable expression than rational as a designation of consumer behavior. Adjustment to changing circumstances, rather than adherence to earlier rigid plans, is the prototype of intelligent behavior. The term adaptive may be applied both when behavior is purposive, deliberate, or circumspect and when it is habitual or routine. The consumer adjusts his behavior to changing conditions when he feels that an adjustment is necessary, rather than constantly or regularly. Psychological economics studies the circumstances under which motives and goals are changed instead of emphasizing their consistency, or the transitive ordering of choices.

PART V
SAVING

15
TO SPEND OR TO SAVE?

A few words may suffice to remind the reader of the importance of the process of saving to the economy. Saving represents that part of income which is reserved for future use and
may therefore serve to create enduring wealth. Business firms
and the government may also save, but in the aggregate they
usually borrow, so that in most years it is the household sector
alone which, by spending less than its income, provides the
funds for investment purposes.

The rate of personal saving, the saving of households, was
fairly stable in the 1950s and 1960s but fluctuated greatly in
the early 1970s. In the recession years 1970 and 1971 aggregate personal saving amounted to 8.1 percent of household income after taxes as against 6.0 percent in 1969. In 1972 the
proportion of income saved fell back to 6.2 percent. A change of
one percentage point in the rate of saving amounted to a
7-billion-dollar change in consumer expenditures in those
years. In other words, by raising their rate of saving consumers
withheld considerable amounts of money from the market
place and by reducing the rate provided the market place with
substantial additional funds. Even though the amounts saved
may be utilized by those who receive the funds—mostly banks
or other "financial intermediaries"—the utilization is rarely
either prompt or complete, so that the economy is retarded or
accelerated by changes in collective saving decisions.[1]

Under these circumstances answers to the questions, "Who
saves?" and "Why do people save?" or "Under what circum-

---

[1] In spite of their importance, data on amounts saved belong to the least
reliable of all economic statistics. The figures quoted above are from the
national income accounts prepared by the U.S. Commerce Department
and are derived (essentially) by deducting consumer expenditures from
personal income. Other more direct methods of measurement of amounts

229

stances do people save more and under what circumstances do they save less?'' are of crucial importance. Nevertheless, traditional economic studies have provided rather incomplete and unsatisfactory answers to these questions.

Economists usually begin their analysis of consumer behavior with the equation $Y = C + S$: Consumer income is equal to consumer spending (consumption) plus consumer saving. The equation implies (1) that there is an unequivocal difference between spending and saving, and (2) that the major consumer choice consists of deciding how much to spend and how much to save out of income. When we turn to the question of how consumers themselves see the alternatives available to them, we find that neither of the two assumptions seems to fit. From the point of view of consumers, a third related proposition, namely, that saving consists of refraining from spending and thus represents a form of abstinence,[2] is likewise invalid.

What Is Saving?

Let us begin by listing the various major items that are usually included under personal saving in the presentation of the nation's economic accounts and indicate what those items represent to the average American consumer.

First, there is *contractual saving*, resulting from fixed contractual obligations. The payment of life insurance premiums and repayment of debts (mortgage debt, installment debt, etc.) are the major forms of those contractual obligations that are considered as saving. They are fulfilled as a matter of routine requiring no new decisions. To be sure, the consumer may default on his obligations, but this happens so rarely that it need not be considered in a discussion of present-day consumer behavior.

saved were developed in the 1950s and 1960s, but several items entering into total saving still represent estimates. In most aggregate data, funds of unincorporated business, pension plans, and foundations are not separated from those of households. Survey data on individual saving and also on assets and wealth are likewise among the least reliable of all survey data (see Appendix). They indicate probable orders of magnitude, but should not be assumed to represent exact information.

[2] J. M. Keynes, for example, has stated that "saving consists . . . of refraining from spending the whole current income on consumption" (1930, Vol. I, p. 172). As will be shown shortly, refraining from spending is recognized as one among several forms of saving.

The repayment of installment debt is viewed by most debtors as an expenditure. By buying a car on time people feel that they are paying for it out of income—to be sure, out of the income of two or even three years. Life insurance is likewise viewed by the great majority of people as an expenditure rather than a saving, namely, as a fee paid for the sake of being protected against unexpected adversity. Only a small minority carry life insurance as a form of saving. Repayment of mortgage debt is seen by some people as equivalent to rent payments and therefore as an expenditure, although many are aware of the fact that by repaying their mortgage they enhance their assets. Even so, this accumulation of assets is usually distinguished in their mind from saving money.

When consumers buy a house with a mortgage debt, or durable goods on the installment plan, they make genuine decisions. Usually these are decisions to buy or to spend rather than decisions to borrow. In the national accounts, of course, the incurrence of consumer debt appears as negative savings. Since the value of durable goods bought is not added to savings, in periods when many cars are bought on credit and credit extension exceeds debt repayment, substantial dissaving is shown.

Social security taxes and private pension accumulations, whether paid by an individual or his employer, are rarely considered to be money saved. In most cases the employer's share is entirely disregarded when personal finances are considered. This is not generally true of the individual's share. Yet frequently the take-home pay, which excludes the amounts withheld from wages and salaries for taxes, social security, and pensions, constitutes the starting point for considering how much money shall be spent.

There remains what may be called *discretionary saving,* which most people do consider saving. Additions to deposits in banks, savings and loan associations (which are seen as banks by most people), and credit unions, as well as income used to purchase bonds (including United States Savings Bonds) and stocks or shares of mutual funds represent, in the view of most people, the means of accumulating reserve funds. Withdrawals from those liquid assets, for any purpose other than transfer to another asset, are seen as a diminution of reserve funds or savings.

231

Respondents in representative samples were asked repeatedly: "During the last twelve months or so did you people save any money, or did you decrease your savings, or did you just break even?" Those who said they had saved or decreased their savings were asked what they had done. In reply, most people referred exclusively to what was described above as discretionary saving (or dissaving). Very few respondents mentioned life insurance, repayment of debt, or incurrence of debt.

It does not follow that every addition to bank deposits is considered an amount saved. When respondents were asked what they would do with some "extra money," or when they were asked in 1962–63 what they would do with additional cash resulting from a tax cut, their replies indicated that checking accounts, and sometimes savings accounts as well, are often seen as temporary depositories of funds, prior to their use. "I'd bank it until I decide what I want" was a fairly common answer to the question on the probable use of money from a tax cut in 1963. The use of the term *save* to represent a short-term action may be illustrated by such answers as: "We would save it toward a vacation next year"; "Leave it in the bank to use for travel to see my children"; "I need new teeth; I'll save the tax money for that."

Parts of checking and savings accounts represent, then, funds of maneuver rather than savings or reserve funds. Many people who are not familiar with the abstract concept of liquidity nevertheless have some notion about not wanting to be without some readily available money. Others want to have their savings less readily available, so that they will not be so easily tempted to spend. In whatever form the savings, a large share is subjectively earmarked for specific purposes and is therefore not considered liquid. These considerations have little to do with the technical definition of what is and what is not liquid.

It follows that some part of the amounts saved in banks constitutes *residual saving*, money that the owner failed to spend. The amounts of residual saving are probably larger in bad than in good times, and larger on the part of pessimistic than optimistic people. If discretionary saving were to be defined as the result of decisions to save, residual saving ought to be deducted from increases in bank deposits. Yet this cannot be done in studies of the extent of discretionary saving. What can be done is to treat amounts borrowed and debts repaid differently from changes in bank accounts and securities.[3]

Investment in real estate other than in one's personal residence also constitutes an important form of discretionary saving. Especially people living in small towns or rural areas frequently put their savings in lots or income-producing real property. For most inhabitants of cities, lack of familiarity restricts this form of saving to purchases of second houses or lots in recreational areas, which increased greatly in the 1960s and 1970s. We shall use the expression *financial saving* for discretionary saving in banks and securities, thus excluding saving in real estate.

The Purposes of Saving

People in all walks of life talk freely about the purposes for which they save, for which they would like to save, or for which they feel they ought to save. Although they express themselves in many different ways, most of the reasons they give for saving may be classified in one of the following categories:

1. *For emergencies.* Upper-income as well as lower-income people say that the future is uncertain, rainy days may come, something may happen which will impair one's earning potential or require large expenditures. Therefore reserve funds are thought to be necessary. But even when unemployment occurs or large medical expenses have to be paid, savings are used grudgingly, because the worse the current situation, the greater looms the need to maintain reserves for future emergencies.

2. *For retirement.* Concern with retirement or with money needed for one's old age is frequently expressed even by people in their thirties. The frequency does, of course, increase with age.

---

[3] Some saving in banks and in securities may resemble contractual saving in that it may reflect earlier decisions. During and shortly after World War II, payroll deductions for war bonds constituted a fair share of amounts saved. In spite of many people's expressed preference for automatic saving methods, the amounts saved in banks or securities due to earlier decisions became fairly insignificant in the 1960s.

233

3. *For children and family needs.* Some people mention the education of their children specifically, while others say that in a family with children there are always years with large expenditures, and it is therefore necessary to have money in reserve.

4. *For other purposes.* Some people save to buy a house, to buy a business, to buy durable goods, or to pay for vacations and other trips.

Table 15-1 indicates the frequency with which these purposes of saving were mentioned in surveys conducted by the Survey Research Center with representative samples. The differences in frequencies obtained at different times are probably of little significance.

The data should also be studied from the point of view of what they do not contain. First of all, references to saving for the purpose of later consumption or improving one's standard of living at a later date are infrequent. Only a very small proportion of respondents mentioned saving for the sake of purchasing large and expensive durable goods. On the whole, Americans believe in buying consumer goods out of income. Durable goods are commonly purchased on the installment plan, which means to most people that they are being paid for while they are being used from the income earned at that time. We shall discuss later that these attitudes characterize particularly the American people, while in West Germany, for instance, saving for consumption purposes is very common and installment buying unpopular.

Secondly, hardly any consumers mentioned saving for the purpose of earning additional income in the form of interest or dividends, or in order to bequeath money to their heirs. It does not follow that people are not concerned with the interest or dividends they receive, but it is apparent that most people do not save for the specific purpose of enhancing their income in later years. Nor do they accumulate assets with the intention that they would be inherited by their children—with the exception of a few very rich people whose behavior will be mentioned later.

On the whole, surveys revealed that the accumulation of savings constitutes a highly valued goal. The American people do not speak of saving as a negative act—as refraining or abstaining from using money. Savings are associated with important values and are seen as a goal for which it is worthwhile to

234

TABLE 15-1
Purposes of Saving (frequency, in percent, of purposes mentioned by more than 3 percent of respondents)

Purposes	All family units		Family units with incomes of $10,000 or more	
	1960	1966	1960	1966
Rainy days (emergencies, illness, unemployment)	46	45	45	39
Retirement, old age	27	31	39	46
Children's needs (primarily education)	25	22	33	32
Buying a house	8	8	6	6
Buying durable goods	6	7	4	7
Total	*	*	*	*

*Total adds to more than 100 percent because some respondents mentioned more than one purpose.

The questions were: "Different people have different reasons for saving. In your case, what are the purposes of saving? Anything else?"

strive. Not saving is regretted and sometimes considered morally wrong. The high value attached to thrift has puritan undertones that persist among many people despite the much-lamented "thing-mindedness" of our age.

The extent of the prevailing desire to save is indicated, not only by questioning people about their attitudes toward saving, but also by studying their expressed intentions. Regarding most large consumer goods, many fewer people say they plan to buy them in the following year than actually do buy them, because many things are bought without advance planning. Regarding saving money, the opposite is true—more people say they plan to save in the following year than report the next year that they actually did save. Plans to save often represent good intentions that are not carried out at a later date.

Saving versus Spending

No one can deny that there is great concern with material goods in our society. We have stressed the prevalence of striving toward a better standard of living, which consists of a continuous process of upgrading a variety of possessions. Are the new findings about the positive value attached to saving and the accumulation of reserve funds in conflict with the concern with more and better consumer goods? Not in the eyes of most American consumers. Larger reserve funds are viewed as part and parcel of a better standard of living. People strive for a better home and car, more durable goods, occasional travel, fun and enjoyment, as well as security through the accumulation of savings. Most people are not aware of a sharp distinction between owning many things and owning financial reserves; they want both and take steps toward both goals.

Different ways of using one's money are often in conflict. Determining priorities among several goals constitutes a crucial decision, even for affluent people. To buy a new car and to build a second bathroom, for instance, may both be urgent wishes of the family; or both a better and larger refrigerator and increased reserve funds may be pressing desires of another family. The point is that conflict between spending and saving plays the same role as conflict between two expenditures; the first type of conflict is neither more common nor more fundamental than the second type. Consumer thinking in general is not correctly described by asserting that people first decide how much to spend and how much to save, and later decide on what to spend.

Many people are not aware of a conflict between spending and saving, although they do want to increase their savings and are at the same time eager to acquire more and newer and better consumer goods. Some fail to see a conflict because, as they readily acknowledge (with regret to be sure), they believe they are unable to save. Not only low-income people, but also some people in good financial condition report that buying what is absolutely necessary for them exhausts all that they earn. Extensive contractual obligations, including repayment of mortgage and other debt and life insurance premiums, are included in the necessary expenditures.

More important than this pushing aside of the conflict are other methods by which consumers resolve the problem of desiring both to save more and to buy more. One resolution is to do both. This often becomes possible through an increase in income. Part of the income increment is used to buy durables, frequently on the installment plan, and part to increase savings.

236

The notion that there is an inverse relation between saving and spending is derived, of course, from the simple equation that income equals spending plus saving. New possibilities arise if we rewrite the equation as follows:

Income + amounts borrowed = discretionary spending + other spending + discretionary saving + contractual and other saving.

It is possible, for instance, for both discretionary spending and discretionary saving to increase at the same time, because these two most highly valued goals are favored jointly, and for everyday expenditures to decrease.

In one important respect, however, there is validity to the view of those who see materialism of present-day society as having an adverse influence on saving. The result of the perceived urgency of numerous wants for consumer goods, as well as for such services as travel and recreation, is that the desire to save is frequently pushed into the background and saving becomes residual. Some people wait to see how much remains after diverse other wants have been satisfied before they save. Because some motives to spend are more immediate than the motives to save, saving is postponed, and the postponement may be repeated over and over again. But it should not be forgotten that there are other people with plans to save, which they carry out.

Who Saves?

The answer to the question about the demographic characteristics of the savers depends to some extent on the definition of saving. When discretionary saving is considered, the answer is: Most saving is done by middle-aged people with relatively high income. By "middle age" is meant those between approximately 35 or 40 and 60 years of age, by "relatively high income," an annual income of more than $12,500 (as defined in the early 1970s). Only when the broadest possible definition of saving is used do frequent savers include younger married people in the middle-income groups who accumulate assets by buying houses, automobiles, and appliances on credit and repay their debts.

Evidence will be provided later for the incidence of credit buying and also for the demographic characteristics of asset holders. Data available on accumulated assets are more reliable than on amounts saved. Regarding the latter, a great amount of information is available, which, though far from precise, is impressive because it has been very similar over several decades. The answers to a question, quoted before, about subjective notions of having saved over the preceding year varied greatly among different income and different age groups. In 1969–71, for instance, the proportion of those who said they had saved increased rapidly with income. At the same time the proportion of dissavers remained practically unchanged in all income groups—up to $15,000 income when it fell off sharply. To quote an additional set of data: According to extensive saving studies in 1962, conducted in connection with an appraisal of the impact of private pension plans on saving, in the income group $3,000–6,000, 25 percent reported that they had saved, in the income group $6,000–10,000, 44 percent, and among those with over $10,000 income, 65 percent.

The fact that the frequency of dissaving—both of reducing bank balances and of borrowing—is practically independent of income was pointed out as early as shortly after World War II (see Katona 1949b and 1951). Spending more than income results from one of three different circumstances: (1) inability to meet necessary expenditures out of income, (2) unwillingness to keep usual expenditures at the level of income, and (3) willingness to make unusual expenditures. While the first circumstance prevails primarily in the low-income group and the second is not related to income, the third, usually involving large amounts, is most common among high-income families and least common among low-income families.

Regarding the relation of financial saving to age, findings over two decades have indicated that the annual accumulation of bank deposits or securities of families whose head was younger than 35 or 40 years of age was negligible. The same is true of retired people as a group. There are, however, many individuals over 60 years of age who save substantial amounts.

Data on the saving performance of income groups and age groups conceal a variety of substantial individual differences. Especially with respect to the incidence of dissaving, these differences are great because both borrowing and reducing savings accounts occur intermittently. In studying the repeti-

238

tiousness or variability of consumer behavior (Katona, 1959) it was found that the most frequent behavior pattern was to dis-save every third or fourth year. Such sequences as SSDSSD (each letter denoting one year's performance of either Saving or Dissaving) appear to be more common than sequences of the type of SSS or SDSD or SDDSDD. With the great majority of American families, the pattern has been one of an occasional year of dissaving interrupting years of saving.

Personal Saving in Periods of Prosperity and Recession

In discussing the recession of 1970 we called attention to the sharp increase in the rate of saving. The increase came as a surprise to most experts. They believed, in accordance with observations made during the Great Depression of the 1930s, that recessions were periods of low rates of saving. If saving consists of refraining from spending, it is to be expected that in bad times, when incomes are low and declining, a much larger part of incomes must be spent on necessities than in good times, when incomes are large and growing, so that less remains for saving. On the other hand, those considering psychological factors may argue that felt needs for savings would grow when a recession threatens. The heightened motive to save will result in larger savings at least among people whose income has not, or at least has not yet, declined.

Different forms of saving must be considered separately. In periods of recession characterized by lesser purchases of durable goods, installment buying and therefore the total amounts borrowed are reduced (while repayment of installment debt incurred at earlier times remains high for a considerable period). In addition, unusual cash purchases, such as down payments on large durables, expenditures on small durables, travel and vacation expenditures, are often financed by drawing on previously accumulated assets. The frequency of these transactions likewise declines in periods of recession when, therefore, withdrawals from bank accounts are reduced. These reductions may cancel increased withdrawals necessitated by income losses.

The effects of changes in installment buying and in unusual

239

cash purchases represent two factors listed in the scheme presented on the next page. In the area of decisions about saving, we list first the factor of change in income, considered in traditional analysis as the major factor. Second, we list the psychological consideration of a change in the strength of the motive to save.

As noted above, for most people the principal reason for saving is to be prepared for rainy days. Possible adverse developments for which people wish to be prepared include illness or accidents, the threat of which does not appear to be connected with the stage of the business cycle. But threats to one's job or one's income appear most pronounced when a recession is expected to come, or when it has already started but has not yet affected the individual.

The scheme presented below provides no definite answer to whether we save more during a period of upswing or of

ASSUMPTIONS ABOUT
CHANGES IN PERSONAL SAVING IN GOOD AND BAD TIMES*

Factor	During a Recession	During an Upswing
1. Installment buying	Net saving grows because not reduced by extensive credit incurrence	Net saving declines because reduced by extensive credit incurrence
2. Unusual cash expenditures	Net saving grows because not reduced by extensive withdrawals from bank accounts	Net saving declines because reduced by extensive withdrawals from bank accounts
3. Frequency and size of income increases	Net saving declines because income increases less frequent and less substantial	Net saving grows because income increases frequent and substantial
4. Strength of saving motives	Net saving grows because people strongly motivated to save	Net saving declines because people less strongly motivated to save

*This scheme was first presented in Katona, 1974.

240

downswing. Conceivably, the third factor, the income effect, is powerful enough to cancel the effects of the three other factors. It is also possible that one or the other factor is not effective at a given time. Yet, at any given time, knowing the circumstances then prevailing, it is possible to derive definite answers from the scheme.

In 1970–71, for instance, the adverse income effect was insignificant because money incomes continued to grow in spite of the recession. At the same time the prevalence of unusually strong saving motives was confirmed by survey findings according to which people attached great importance to savings at that time.

In 1972 Factor 1 and probably also Factor 2 were effective in reducing net personal saving. Borrowing increased because a larger number of automobiles were bought. At the same time, income gains were very large in 1972, probably resulting in an opposite effect on net saving. Saving motives may have weakened because in that year the American people became aware of a substantial improvement in economic conditions. The proportion of survey respondents choosing the alternative, "It is more important than usual to add to savings," declined from 51 percent late in 1971 to 41 percent late in 1972.[4]

In 1973 and 1974 saving motives were again strengthened because rapid increases in food and fuel prices as well as political developments (Watergate) created uncertainty and distrust in the government. As a result the rate of saving increased greatly. (The increase was augmented in the winter of 1973–74 by a sharp reduction in automobile purchases, and, therefore, in the incurrence of installment debt.)

At earlier times the impact of good or bad times on savings motives was apparently less pronounced and the income effect very powerful. For instance, during the prosperous years 1964–65 the sharp cut in income tax rates dominated people's thinking. It could be shown at that time that the gains resulting from the tax cut as well as from increases in earned income were used primarily to satisfy the two most highly valued goals, namely, to improve the standard of living—mainly by

---

[4] The rate of saving in 1972 was confounded by the introduction of an excessive rate of income tax withholding. Surveys revealed, however, that most taxpayers were not aware of the overwithholding which, therefore, could not have influenced their saving decisions.

buying durable goods—and to add to available reserve funds. Therefore saving was high in those prosperous years. (At the same time, everyday expenditures and spending on necessities lagged behind the increases in income, as shown by Katona and Mueller, 1968.) The coincidence of increased spending on durable goods and increases in financial saving (not of total saving because of the impact of borrowing) was also observed repeatedly in the 1950s. At that time this coincidence was noted especially in the case of families whose income was increasing and who also felt better off (see Katona, 1960, Chapter 7).

Hypotheses about the impact of income trends on discretionary spending and discretionary saving may be presented in the following scheme:

When Income		
in the preceding period has gone	in the next period is expected to go	Then Discretionary Spending is
Up	Up	Unusually high
Same or down	Same or down	Unusually low
		And Discretionary Saving is
Up	Down	Unusually high
Down	Up	Unusually low

Income gains, jointly with the expectation of further gains, analogous to the Better-Better syndrome (Chapters 10 and 12), are assumed to be associated with the highest rate of discretionary spending, especially on durable goods. Continuous income declines or income stagnation (absence of any stimulation) are assumed to be associated with the lowest rate. Discretionary saving should be highest under conditions of temporary income increases, when an income increase appears not to be sustainable and is expected to be followed by an income decrease. The reverse situation, a temporary income decline, that is, losses to be followed by the expectation of gains, is thought to justify drawing on assets or saving very little. Thus subjective notions about the permanence of income increases or decreases are assumed to affect the rate of saving.[5] Empirical data indicate that people's behavior does indeed coincide with these assumptions, although the evidence is fragmentary, primarily because of difficulties in measuring amounts saved.

Inflation and Saving

The relation of faster or slower rates of inflation to amounts saved has already been discussed in Chapter 9. It was pointed out there that during most of the post-World War II period heightened inflation augmented pessimism and uncertainty and therefore retarded spending and stimulated saving. The primary consideration with a great majority of people was expressed in such terms as, "Because of inflation I shall need more just for the necessities of life," and resulted in an increase in saving. Prior to the early 1970s only people in the top-income or top-wealth brackets were found to be inflation-conscious in making decisions about saving.[6] Exceptions to this generalization were observed in 1950 and again in 1973 when the expectation of rapid price increases and especially of shortages created advance buying. People's attitudes toward inflation and therefore the impact of inflation on saving may and probably will change further in the future.

Interest Rates and Saving

Until the mid-1960s, throughout a long period of easy money, the changes in interest rates were so small that their impact on people's saving performance was difficult to study.

---

[5] This conclusion is not the same as that derived from the abstract concepts of permanent or lifetime income as introduced by Friedman (1957) and Modigliani (see 1971; he presented his theory much earlier as well). If the essence of those theories is seen as consumers endeavoring to achieve a preferred distribution of consumption and saving over very long periods or their entire life, the assumption must be characterized as not reflecting conscious consumer behavior. If the more modest assumption is made that consumers endeavor to smooth their consumption expenditures irrespective of fluctuations in their income, then the assumption may be viewed as applying to everyday expenditures (not to major discretionary expenditures).

[6] See the section on top asset holders in Chapter 16.

At that time, only changes by 1/2 of 1 percent, or by 1 percent at most, were even conceivable, and these changes appeared unimportant in comparison with other considerations that influenced spending-saving decisions.

Awareness of the extent of available interest rates, for instance on U.S. Savings Bonds and also on savings accounts, was rather widespread during the entire postwar period. Advertising by banks and savings and loan associations probably contributed to people's high level of information about changes in interest rates on savings in the 1960s and 1970s. When interest rates rose sharply in 1966 and repeatedly thereafter, the impact of the changes on people's behavior was studied and yielded the following conclusions:

An increase of interest rates by one or two percentage points induces some people, especially large asset holders, to switch their saving deposits from one place to another (especially to certificates of deposit). Differences in interest rates obtainable have an influence on where new savings are held. On the other hand, any influence on the rate of saving is, if it exists at all, rather minor.[7]

It follows that if all institutions paid the same interest, saving performance would hardly be influenced by interest rates. There are more important considerations than changes in interest rates that determine the rate of saving.

Saving for Retirement[8]

The desire to make ends meet and even to live comfortably during retirement was mentioned by very many people as a

[7] Supporting data are presented, among others, in the volume 1966 *Survey of Consumer Finances* (pp. 238 ff.). In answer to the direct question asked in a survey conducted in December, 1966, "Since the first of this year, did you do anything because of the change in interest rates?" only 7 percent of those with $1,000 to $10,000 financial assets and 12 percent of those with $10,000–25,000 assets answered in the affirmative. These two groups represented 30 and 7 percent of all family units, respectively. Among those with more than $25,000 financial assets (likewise 7 percent of all units) 32 percent said "Yes." Most of those with affirmative answers replied to a supplementary question that they had switched some of their assets. Practically no respondent answered that he or she had saved more than before. (The increase in interest rates was well known to most survey respondents with assets.)

[8] This section is based on the author's monograph (1965) and on Chapter 19 of Katona (1964a).

major purpose for which they saved. Therefore, the possibility arises that saving motives would weaken when, as has been the case all over the world including the United States, the government assumed the task of making arrangements for retirement, or trade unions induced large employers to form company-financed pension plans. This assumption has often been made, for instance many years ago by Milton Friedman, with respect to the spread and increase of old age benefits under social security.[9] Other economists argued similarly in the 1960s when private pension plans supplementing social security were introduced for more than one-third of American families. It was not possible to study this problem with respect to social security benefits because all members of the labor force were entitled to them and no "control group" was available. In the early 1960s, however, it was possible to compare the saving behavior of two broad groups of families, those covered and those not covered by private pension plans.

The study aimed at a comparison of two contrasting hypotheses. In line with the assumption that a rational man would reduce the amount of his individual saving by the amount contributed by him and his employer to collective security arrangements, the first hypothesis was formulated as follows: Being assured of some resources after retirement, people will spend more freely on the good things of life and concern themselves to a lesser extent with saving for retirement. This hypothesis takes no account of psychological assumptions about rising aspirations following accomplishments, and about effort being intensified the closer one is to one's goal (goal gradient hypothesis). Attainable concrete rewards serve as incentives as formulated in the following second hypothesis, which postulates the opposite outcome: Being assured of some, for many people insufficient, funds after retirement, the attainment of adequate funds for one's old age no longer appears an insurmountably difficult task; being closer to the goal stimulates people to work harder to achieve the goal, and therefore collective retirement plans promote individual saving.[10]

The study was extended beyond an analysis of the impact of private pension plans to the following more general question:

[9] "The availability of assistance from the state would clearly tend to reduce the need for private reserves and so to reduce planned saving" (Friedman, 1957, p. 123).
[10] See Katona (1965, p. 5).

245

Is the saving behavior of people who expect to be well provided for during retirement different from that of people with much less favorable retirement expectations? As dependent variables in addition to measures of saving-mindedness and subjective recollections of recent past saving performance, the proportion of income saved was used, assuming that answers to several survey questions addressed to a large sample (over 5,000 respondents) would make it possible to distinguish between "large savers" and "small savers."

The results of the investigation indicated that the first hypothesis was not supported by any data. The notion that people tend to reduce the amounts they voluntarily save by the amounts they are compelled to save through their own and their employer's contributions to pension plans was flatly contradicted by the findings, as was the contention that the expectation of retirement income from pension plans weakens the motivation to save and induces more liberal spending. In fact, people enrolled in private pension plans were found to have saved somewhat larger amounts than people who were not enrolled.

The studies also indicated that people expecting to be well provided for during their retirement, either because of private pensions or because of having saved much in the past, saved somewhat more than people who foresaw financial problems during retirement. Of course, it is not possible to draw a conclusion about cause and effect from the association between an optimistic view about retirement and relatively large saving performance.

The apparent stimulating effect of pension plans on individual saving may not persist under changing conditions. If benefits from pension plans were increased so as to provide much larger amounts than was the case in the early 1960s, their impact might be different. At the time the study was conducted very many people thought that the payments they would receive jointly from pension plans and social security would not suffice to enable them to live comfortably after retirement.

Rarely do two investigators who decide to study the same problem at the same time, and work with different methods and know nothing about each other's work, obtain the same findings, contradicting traditional assumptions. This was the case in the study of the impact of pension plans on saving.

246

Phillip Cagan (1965) investigated the question with data from a panel of Consumers Union subscribers, that is, with rather sophisticated people who, in contrast to this author's sample, were not representative of all American households. Cagan found that those covered by pension plans had saved slightly more than those not covered (contributions to pension plans were not considered amounts saved). Cagan's explanation of his findings is not quite the same as ours. He argued that a "recognition effect"—increased awareness of retirement needs because of coverage by a pension plan—induced people to step up their rate of saving when they became covered, while we linked the findings to the established principles of rising levels of aspiration and the goal gradient hypothesis.

Wealth and Saving[11]

Being entitled to benefits from social security or private pension plans represents a form of wealth. Therefore, the preceding section may be viewed as the analysis of one instance of the relation between wealth and saving. Other aspects of the problem call for further study.

Financial wealth in the possession of private individuals has grown greatly during the twentieth century. In consequence, economists have turned their attention to the question of the impact of increased wealth on consumption and saving. World War II stimulated such discussions, since in many countries the war was financed, partly at least, by the sale of government bonds, which increased the amount of liquid wealth available to the people. Since, in principle, consumer expenditures may be paid either out of income or from liquid assets, it was a simple matter to change the traditional equation $C = fY$ to read $C = f(Y, W)$: Instead of saying that consumption was a function of income, economists postulated that it was a function of income and wealth. It was for most economists a self-evident conclusion that wealth, like income, would be positively correlated with consumer expenditures: The greater the income or the wealth, the greater the consumer expenditures and the smaller the amounts saved.

[11] This section is based on Katona (1951, p. 167 ff., 1961, and 1964a, p. 213 ff.).

247

Several arguments have been used to explain such an influence of total wealth or of liquid wealth on consumer expenditures. First, in an apparently obvious analogy to the principle of diminishing marginal utility, incentives to save were supposed to weaken with an increase in wealth: The richer the family, the smaller the need to add to its wealth. According to a priori considerations, the only two purposes for liquid assets in the possession of households are to be available for investment opportunities and to be used for expenditures. The share of liquid assets earmarked for the first purpose may vary greatly, but some assets would usually remain over and above the reserves held for investment opportunities, and they would stimulate spending. "Money burns holes in people's pockets," or substantial liquid assets make it difficult to resist the temptation to spend—thus have run the arguments in favor of the assumed relationship. Many economists thereupon postulated that, given unchanged income, the greater the liquid assets, the larger the proportion of income spent. This appeared to be so indisputable that sometimes even the need to obtain empirical verification was denied. J. E. Meade, for instance, contrasts an individual with £1,000 tax-free income in two situations, in Situation 1 having £10,000 and in Situation 2, £5,000 worth of property. He asserts that "The amount which he would spend on goods and services would almost certainly be considerably greater in Situation 1 than in Situation 2" (1958, p. 166).

From a psychological point of view the only one of the preceding arguments that can be accepted is that available liquid assets do represent enabling conditions for consumer expenditures. Even in this respect, it should be kept in mind that a large part of the so-called liquid assets represents what people consider to be permanent savings, and subjective liquidity is not the same as legal liquidity. The contention that increased wealth reduces the strength of motives to save must be contrasted with the principle of levels of aspiration, which says that the more we accomplish, the higher we raise our sights. Should the latter be the operative principle, the felt need for greater liquid assets may even increase with the accumulation of such assets.

Probably the most important consideration is the enduring nature of dispositions to save. Thriftiness as a personality trait and the habit of saving contribute substantially to the accumulation of financial assets, since inherited wealth is relatively

248

uncommon. Most holders of large assets have been large savers in the past, and it should be assumed that they will continue to be large savers.

Only empirical tests can determine the outcome of the various and partly conflicting influences. As a preliminary step, consumers' alleged saturation with large asset accumulations was studied. After determining the approximate size of financial reserves, representative samples of savers were asked whether or not the amount they had saved was too little or adequate for their purposes. In reply, both in the 1960s and early 1970s the majority said that they did not think they had enough savings. The replies differed only slightly between those who had fairly small and those who had middle-sized savings. Only families reporting that they had liquid savings exceeding $15,000 in the early 1960s or $25,000 in the early 1970s thought overwhelmingly that their savings were adequate.

The crucial question, the saving performance of people with different asset holdings, was also studied in several instances. The most complete data, presented in Table 15-2, were derived from a panel study in which the same respondents were interviewed three times at annual intervals.

The saving performance of panel members with some initial liquid asset holdings during a 24-month period was grouped in three categories. The first contains the large savers—those who added 20 percent or more of their income to their savings. The other extreme category contains the large dissavers —those who dissaved at least 10 percent of their income. The middle category contains the small savers and those who broke even, as well as the small dissavers.

Table 15-2 shows that the middle category predominates among those who had small assets to begin with, as well as among the majority of all people. Large dissaving is fairly rare among families with less than $2,000 in liquid assets; large-scale saving is likewise uncommon among those families. In contrast, one-third of the holders of sizable liquid assets add large proportions of their income to their assets, while another one-third of the same group do the opposite. It appears, then, that larger liquid asset holdings have a twofold effect on subsequent saving—they are associated with both high positive and high negative saving-income ratios.

Further statistical analysis indicates that the differences be-

249

TABLE 15-2
Relation of Initial Liquid Asset Holdings to Subsequent Rate of Discretionary Saving

	Liquid asset holdings in early 1960†			
Saving-income ratio, 1960–61*	$1–499	$500–1,999	$2,000–4,999	$5,000 and over
20 percent or more	14%	14%	21%	32%
Between −9 and +19 percent	76	69	50	37
=10 percent or less	10	17	29	31
Total	100%	100%	100%	100%
Number of cases	274	258	148	143

*The amount of discretionary saving was determined for the two years 1960 and 1961 and is expressed in percent of average income in those two years.

†Amounts in checking accounts, savings accounts, and United States government savings bonds.

Source: Katona 1964a, p. 216.

tween the saving performance of families with small and those with large initial assets are not a function of income. When, for instance, only the middle-income families are considered —eliminating from the study both the high and the low-income groups—the differences between the saving performance of people with large and small initial assets become greater still.

We may conclude, then, that for some people at certain times the proposition presented by economic theorists is valid. Liquid reserves are accumulated in order to be used during one's lifetime, and when the time of use arrives, dissaving may be substantial. As important as this effect of sizable asset holdings is the opposite effect. The relatively high percentage of large savers among those holding sizable assets may be explained by the persistence of habits of saving and the principle of rising levels of aspiration.

These studies are not complete. They provide no information about the circumstances under which large asset holders will either save or dissave substantial amounts. We may assume that good or bad business conditions, income changes and income expectations, as well as the rate of inflation may account for the observed differences. But the studies reported in this section do yield some clear-cut conclusions. They confirm that many people with substantial asset holdings continue to save large amounts year after year. Increased liquid asset holdings, or greater wealth, do not necessarily reduce personal saving.

Americans in general are security-minded as well as thing-minded. They place great value on having reserve funds and therefore desire to save. But again and again in the course of time needs or opportunities for spending arise and call for drawing on accumulated savings. This is frequently done, albeit with regret. Because people feel that they have acted contrary to one of their major goals, namely, to have reserves for rainy days and for retirement, they are usually eager to restore the amounts withdrawn from savings.[12]

[12] See Mueller and Lean (1967), whose study will be cited again in the next chapter.

251

16
ASSETS AND INVESTMENTS

The result of saving is the accumulation of assets. For most Americans, it can also be said that their assets are the results of their saving, and therefore the size of the assets they own depends on how much they themselves have saved. The two other possible ways of accumulating assets—by inheritance and by capital appreciation—apply to a minority of families only. Only a small proportion of families have inherited sizable assets[1] or made substantial capital gains. It is primarily among the well-to-do that the advance of values in real estate and common stock over several decades resulted in substantial gains in assets. Capital appreciation was a more important factor creating wealth in the 1960s than in the early 1970s because of changes in stock market trends.

A few statistical data may serve to introduce the discussion of the influence of psychological factors on the selection of assets. Reports on the value of assets and of wealth are taken from the most comprehensive survey available, conducted by the Federal Reserve Board in 1962; for data on the extent of ownership of different assets, reliance is placed on more recent as well as older surveys by the Survey Research Center.[2]

When wealth was defined broadly to include all kinds of assets, the value of owner-occupied homes net of mortgage debt constituted 27 percent and the value of businesses, farms, and professions, including closely held corporations owned by a

---

[1] In the entire population 19 percent reported in 1962 that they had inherited some assets, but only 4 to 5 percent that inheritance accounted for a substantial proportion of their current assets. Among those with an income of over $50,000, however, 12 percent said that their fortune was entirely or mostly inherited.

[2] See Projector and Weiss (1966), Katona and Lansing (1964b), Katona (1964a), and the annual monographs, *Survey of Consumer Finances*. For a discussion of methods of collecting asset data, see the Appendix.

small number of individuals, 18 percent of all personal wealth in 1962. In addition to some miscellaneous assets there exist two major forms of financial assets, namely, liquid assets (primarily in savings accounts) representing 13 percent and investment assets (primarily common stock) representing 33 percent of total wealth.

Relatively few families own a major share of all wealth in private hands. When families were ranked by the size of their wealth, the top 10 percent were found to own 60 percent and the top 20 percent close to 80 percent of all wealth. When families were ranked by their incomes, the top 10 percent owned 40 percent and the top 20 percent owned 60 percent of all wealth. These data, obtained in 1962, indicate the substantial correlation between income and wealth, which relation has apparently changed little over the past few decades. Low-income people have practically no financial assets, whereas the assets of those with high income exceed their annual income by five or ten times. In the broad middle-income brackets, typically financial assets are equal to one year's income.

The rate of concentration of different kinds of assets differs greatly. By far the most concentrated is the ownership of common stock; the distribution is most egalitarian with respect to owner-occupied homes; savings accounts are in the middle. The difference between the value of a rich man's home and a poor man's home is very much smaller than the difference in the value of their financial assets.

The most recent study indicates that in 1965 the share of the richest 1 percent in total assets was 27 percent and in corporate stocks 61 percent. Data for that year are typical for many other postwar years but in 1969, the latest year for which information is available, the rate of concentration was somewhat lower (see Smith and Franklin, 1974).

Income is one of the two major factors that determine the size of assets. The other is age. The older a person is the more years of saving are represented by his assets. It is shown in Table 16-1 that among family units whose head is younger than 35, there are only 2 percent with substantial wealth, and not fewer than one-half have practically no wealth. Following many years of saving, families in the age bracket 45 to 54 are well off in accumulated assets and families in the bracket 55 to 64 better off still. There is apparently little decline in wealth among families over 65 years of age. This group consists of two

254

segments that differ very greatly. A sizable segment has substantial reserve funds and another segment of similar size has practically no reserve funds at all.

Financial assets were owned by relatively few families before World War II. During the war, however, saving rates were high and were used to repay most of the existing personal debt and to accumulate sizable liquid assets. Close to two-thirds of all families acquired some war bonds in those years. Even though the number of holders of U.S. Savings Bonds declined sharply in the subsequent years, the proportion of asset holders continued to grow steadily and substantially in the 1950s and 1960s. The increase in the rate of ownership is shown in Table 16-2 to have occurred both in assets of substantial value (common stock, homes, other real estate) and in assets representing a relatively small part of total wealth (checking accounts, life insurance, automobiles).

Home Ownership

Home ownership constitutes the single asset of substantial value that is widely diffuse among the population. It is represented even among many lower-income families for whom the gradual repayment of mortgage debt constitutes their major form of saving out of income. At the same time, home ownership is an asset that has greatly increased in value over

TABLE 16-1
Relation of Size of Wealth to Age, 1962
(Percentage distribution of wealth in different age groups)

Age of Head of Family	Less than $1,000	Between $1,000 and $25,000	More than $25,000	Total
Under 35	50	48	2	100
35–44	23	66	13	100
45–54	18	61	21	100
55–64	15	56	29	100
65 and over	19	56	24	100

Wealth includes value of own home, automobile, business, profession, liquid assets, investment assets, and a few miscellaneous assets, less the debts secured by these assets.
Totals do not always add to 100 because of rounding.
Source: Projector and Weiss (1966), Table A-2.

TABLE 16-2
Spread of Ownership of Personal Assets
(Ownership by family units in percent)

Assets	1947	1962	1971–72
Home	45	57	62
Other real estate	16	NA	20
Automobile	51	73	83
Liquid assets	74	79	84
Thereof: Checking account	38	59	74
Savings account	43	59	66
Certificate of deposit	—	—	13
Bonds	58*	28*	28
Common stock	8	16	27
Life insurance	77	NA	80
Number of family units in millions	37	52	66

NA = Not available.
*U.S. Savings Bonds only.
Sources: Survey Research Center, Surveys of Consumer Finances for 1947 and 1971–72; Projector and Weiss (1966) for 1962.

the last few decades. The value of owner-occupied one-family houses is as large as, or even larger than, the value of all tangible capital of business firms.

While shortly after World War II there were less than 20 million American families living in one-family houses they owned, twenty-five years later there were 40 million such families. The increase is due both to a growing proportion of home owners and to the increase in population (see Table 16-2).

During the 1960s more than two out of every five home owners had no mortgage debt at all. The median value of owner-occupied homes rose between 1960 and 1970 from $11,000 to $18,000 according to the estimates of home owners, which were shown to be fairly reliable, while the median mortgage debt increased only from $6,000 to $8,000. The net equity, therefore, rose substantially and amounted to $12,000 in 1970 for the middle-most home owner.

The increase in the number of home owners slowed down beginning with the late 1960s, as a result of the recession and two new developments. One was an increase in the number of families living in mobile homes or trailers and the second, an increase in the construction of apartment buildings—including luxury apartments. It was, however, primarily very young as well as older families who chose to live in rented quarters. For middle-aged families with children, the attraction of home ownership continued unabated.

Every year about 5 to 6 percent of all families purchase homes, a majority buying old and a minority newly-built houses. Studies of the reasons why people purchase houses[3] disclosed that only a minority of home purchases are accounted for by the two most obvious reasons, namely, (1) to provide a home for newly formed or growing families shortly after marriage or the birth of children and (2) to provide living quarters in a different community (usually when the family has moved because of a job in the new place). The most frequent reason given for home purchases was the desire to own a better house, or a more suitable one, or one in a more suitable location. Thus the process of upgrading appears to have been responsible for most of the frequent moves from one house to another that characterize American home ownership. With rising income as well as with the children getting older, the kind of home people desire changes. Moves into suburbia and from suburbs to more distant and less congested areas characterize many home purchases.

Payments by home owners on their mortgage debt as well as on real estate taxes are similar in size to rent payments of renters in comparable income groups. But in addition, many home owners regularly spend substantial amounts on repairs, modernization, or additions to their homes. Surveys revealed that in the 1960s the majority of all home owners made such expenditures each year, with $400 a year being the middlemost amount spent. These substantial outlays again reflect the continuous process of upgrading as well as the great value Americans attach to the quality of the homes in which they live.

Expenditures by home owners on household appliances are likewise larger than similar expenditures by renters, especially in the first year, or the first few years, following the purchase of a home. Altogether, close to one-half of all families spend

[3] See Paxton (1955) for the first Survey Research Center study of this problem as well as repeated volumes in the *Survey of Consumer Finances* series.

money every year on the purchase of a durable household item and 40 percent of the purchasers use credit for that purpose. Yet from the point of view of the value of assets owned, appliances must be counted as insignificant—partly because of their small resale value; the same is true of automobiles, even though they can be readily sold.

In the early 1970s about 28 percent of family units owned two or more cars and 55 percent one car. (The remaining 17 percent had no car.) The proportion of multiple-car owners doubled between 1958 and 1971. The multiple-car owners are responsible for a disproportionately large share of all car purchases. On the average approximately 20 percent of family units purchase a used car every year and 11 percent, a new car. Among the used-car buyers roughly one-half, and among the new-car buyers 60 percent, purchase on the installment plan.

Life Insurance

Life insurance also constitutes an asset representing a rather insignificant part of personal wealth. The proportion of Americans carrying life insurance was already very high during World War II and has changed little since that time. In the 1950s and 1960s the increase in amounts of life insurance owned likewise showed little gain over the increase in incomes in those years. Life insurance is viewed by most Americans as a necessary expenditure—as money spent to provide protection against adversities. Only a small proportion of Americans think of it as a form of saving. Those who do so, and think of life insurance as providing retirement income or money for their children's education, carry larger amounts of insurance than people who do not have saving purposes in mind. It should be noted that in the past twenty years there has been no increase in the appreciation of life insurance as a means of saving. As we shall see in connection with our study of people's attitudes toward savings accounts, inflation could not have been the major cause of the relative lack of interest in this aspect of insurance. Gains in term insurance likewise confirm the survey finding that for most Americans life insurance is viewed as indispensable and not as a way of spending or saving money that is either attractive or popular.

258

The Composition of Reserve Funds

We reported in the previous chapter that Americans on the whole are eager to accumulate reserve funds and to enlarge the funds they have. Neither the substantial assets invested in their homes nor the relatively small assets in durable goods or life insurance are included in reckoning their reserve funds. The obvious reason for excluding these assets is that most people feel they would not turn to them for cash in case of need.[4]

Throughout the more than twenty-five years of conducting surveys the Survey Research Center has concerned itself with the forms in which people chose to hold their assets and the subjective reasons for their choices. The latter served to explain the rather slowly-changing pattern of the former. The basic attitudes changed but little between the late 1940s and the early 1970s: The majority of family heads—late in the 1940s about 70 percent and early in the 1970s about 60 percent—considered putting savings into banks or bonds preferable to putting them into stocks or real estate. The major reason for this preference also remained unchanged: *Safety* was emphasized as their principal requirement, and banks (including savings and loan associations) as well as government bonds were considered by far the safest place for savings.

Two considerations, in addition to safety, were frequently mentioned when respondents were asked about the advantages or disadvantages of various forms of assets. One was the degree of their familiarity with them, the other the rate of return. *Familiarity* increases confidence while lack of familiarity makes for distrust and fear of being deceived. Government bonds, which became familiar during World War II, and various forms of savings accounts profited from the consumers' familiarity with them. This was especially true because bank failures were forgotten during the war and the image of banks changed from remote and inaccessible institutions to familiar and friendly places. We shall discuss unfamiliarity with securities as well as other considerations regarding common stocks later in this chapter. It may suffice to say here that very many people abstain from purchases of real estate other than

---

[4] Because of the great reluctance to give up homes even under adverse circumstances, many poor old people live in houses that are far too large for them.

259

their own homes because of unfamiliarity and their belief that only with expert knowledge can real estate investment be successful.

During World War II most people expressed satisfaction with the *interest* obtained on war bonds, bought at $18.75 and redeemable at $25.00 in ten years, which rate they knew to be 3%. But when several years later savings and loan associations, and still later commercial banks, instituted advertising campaigns about the much higher interest rates paid by them, complaints about the interest on government Savings Bonds were frequently voiced. The ads served to channel savings into savings accounts and also increased the attention paid to the rate of return on savings.

The surveys revealed several other considerations to be much less important. One was liquidity or illiquidity, which however was mentioned at certain times by many respondents. In the early 1950s some people complained that U.S. Savings Bonds were not readily redeemable because even though legally they could be cashed any time, the procedure was inconvenient. Others, however, were attracted by this feature of bonds, because it made them immune from use for unnecessary expenditures. Convenience—although it was not often mentioned—is no doubt an important feature in the placement of assets and operates in favor of banks.

When specifically asked about capital appreciation, respondents agreed that it was very desirable. For most people it represents a goal to be achieved only at great risk. We shall discuss interest in speculation shortly in connection with the stock market. Generally, it may be said that many Americans are attracted by gambling, but not with their savings or reserve funds and primarily when there is a chance, however slight, of winning really high stakes rather than adding 10 or 20 percent to the money wagered.

Inflation was another feature rarely mentioned in the 1950s or 1960s as a consideration either for or against choosing certain forms of saving. As we showed in discussing attitudes toward inflation (Chapter 9), creeping inflation was not viewed as a strong enough incentive to overcome the reluctance to put a large part of one's savings into stocks or real estate. In the early 1970s when inflation accelerated, stocks were known to be depressed and there was an increase in the proportion of people saying that the wisest place to put savings was in real estate. Many respondents who said so, however, were found not to have done so. The proportion who had assets in real estate other than their homes did not rise over 20 percent. Those owning income-producing real estate or lots were primarily high-income people or inhabitants of rural areas and small towns who were familiar with their neighborhood. However, ownership of second homes, primarily in recreational areas, did increase in the 1960s.

Top Asset Holders

The asset preferences just described are true of the great majority of Americans, but not of the holders of large assets. The average person is preoccupied with the task of earning income rather than of saving or investing. He prefers assets and investments that may be "forgotten" in the sense that he would not lose money by not paying attention to them. However, studies in which special sampling methods made it possible to interview a fair number of investors with assets of more than $100,000, or even a million dollars, about their investment policies revealed that the saving behavior of top asset holders differed greatly from the average. The major findings are summarized as follows:

1. *Top asset holders are inflation-conscious.* Their investment policy is consciously directed toward the problem of hedging against inflation.

2. *Top asset holders are interest-conscious.* They review their investments frequently and sometimes shift them to take advantage of interest differentials amounting to not more than one-eighth or one-fourth of one percentage point. Government securities other than Savings Bonds—treasury bills and notes, tax exempt bonds, and so on—as well as mortgage loans and foreign investments, practically unknown to the average saver, are familiar to many top asset holders. Considerations of yield strongly influence their purchases or sales of securities.

3. *Top asset holders are tax-conscious.* They devote time and energy to finding investments that serve to minimize income and estate taxes. They are concerned with capital gains and losses as well as with gifts of inflated assets to charity and also with gifts to their children and heirs.

4. *Top asset holders are concerned with leaving an inheritance to their children.* The middle-income saver is hardly cognizant of this motive to save. He thinks of giving his children a good education and possibly assisting them in starting in their business or professional career. He believes that everyone must make his way on his own. The transfer of assets from one generation to the next is, in most cases, accidental rather than intentional. The wealthy, on the other hand, are concerned with establishing and preserving a family fortune. They often set up trust funds in order to preserve wealth for their grandchildren.

5. *Top asset holders devote much time to managing their investments.* The task of management consists not only of extensive reading but also of discussing financial matters with other investors. They also have access to, and make use of, professional advisers. Some, of course, entrust the management of their assets to professionals, but most do not delegate such authority to others.[5]

These findings are important, because holders of large assets, though relatively small in number, control a very substantial part of the nation's wealth, are much more active traders than other people, and exert a great influence on the outcome of monetary policy through their reactions to new measures and regulations. But in some important respects no difference was found between top asset holders and other savers. First, both groups were found to be greatly concerned with the security of their investments. Capital appreciation and high yields as goals of investment policy are surpassed, even among the wealthy, by concern with safety. Usually only a small part of the wealth of top asset holders is available for risky or speculative ventures. Secondly, inertia and past habits play a large role in the decision making of holders of very large, as well as small, assets. When asked about their satisfaction or dissatisfaction with their portfolios, the majority of wealthy people interviewed complained that they had left too large a share of their investments in the same form for many years and that they had not switched their assets frequently enough. The

[5] See Katona and Lansing (1964b) on a survey with top asset holders in one city, and Barlow et al. (1966) on a survey of high-income people in the entire country.

prevailing composition of assets represents a powerful constraint to new decisions. People become accustomed to the given situation, and abstaining from action is the easiest of all decisions. These are human traits which the very rich share with the rest of the population.

It must also be emphasized that the extent to which taxes influence financial decisions was found to be limited even among many high-income people. Even though, as stated in point 3 above, the very wealthy are much more tax conscious than the less wealthy, they too are concerned with taxes in a few of their decisions only. A substantial proportion of wealthy people were found not to take advantage, and even to be unaware, of numerous avenues of tax avoidance.

Savings Accounts

Beginning with the early 1950s various forms of savings accounts constituted the most preferred and the most widely-held financial asset. Savings accounts were favored because they were considered safe, convenient, liquid, and yielded a return that was at most times considered very satisfactory. Their only drawback was a reduction in the value of money due to inflation, and, as we have said, until the early 1970s people in general were hardly concerned with this loss.

Not only has the proportion of families with savings accounts increased steadily throughout the years since World War II (see Table 16-2, above), but the average amounts put into this form of saving also grew fairly rapidly. In 1960 the middle-most account holder had $700 in his savings account, in 1970 he had $1,250. The median amount for all American family units increased during these ten years from $300 to $800.

While in the 1950s savings and loan associations and mutual savings banks were predominant in this field, in the 1960s commercial banks began to compete vigorously and succeeded in drawing substantial personal funds into their time deposits and, later, certificates of deposit. The growth of such certificates, often for substantial amounts, continued on a large scale during the inflationary years of the early 1970s.

One major function of savings accounts consists in providing a depository for long-term reserve funds. This is

263

documented by the finding that each year about 40 percent of account holders report no withdrawals at all from their savings accounts. A second function of savings accounts is to serve as revolving funds for large, unusual expenditures.

We indicated before that Americans in general do not save with the purpose in mind of having funds available for later consumption expenditures. In fact, however, they frequently use their savings for such purposes, not for everyday expenditures but for paying either fully or partly (as a down payment) for their cars, appliances, furniture, home improvements, vacation trips, medical expenses and the like. Eva Mueller and Jane Lean (1967) have shown that about one out of three owners of savings accounts financed such outlays to some extent by drawing on their accounts. But, and this is the most important finding, the withdrawals were temporary. Not only did respondents say that they intended to replenish their accounts, but they were also found to have carried out their intentions. By the end of the calendar year studied, more than one-half of those who had made withdrawals for the purposes cited were found not to have reduced their savings account balances.

Studies cited before about dissatisfaction with the amount of savings on the part of the majority of American savers relate primarily to the amounts held in savings accounts. Fluctuations in amounts saved in the early 1970s were reflected mainly in the rate of growth of various savings accounts.

Concentration of Stockholdings

The very substantial increase in the number of stockholders from approximately 3 million shareholding families in 1947 to more than 18 million in the early 1970s (translating the percentage figures in Table 12-2 into absolute numbers) has often been cited as indicative of a great advance in the public ownership of business. Yet this conclusion is hardly justified, and the financial community has little reason to derive satisfaction from the number of families involved in stock ownership. The additional fact must be kept in mind that the majority of stockholding families have a very small stake in American corporations.[6] In 1969 about one-half of all stockholding

[6] This is one major reason why the data on stock ownership are taken from the Survey Research Center's *Survey of Consumer Finances* rather than from the more comprehensive and more exact calculations of the New

families indicated that the total value of their stockholdings was less than $5,000. A further one-third set the value of their holdings between $5,000 and $25,000. Only the remaining one-sixth of the stockholders, or about 4.5 percent of all American family units, had a major investment in corporations and owned the bulk of all personal shareholdings.

In any consideration of the very substantial concentration of stock ownership, cited earlier in this chapter, it is relevant to note, first, that more than one-fourth of all stockholders were found to own stock in one corporation or one mutual fund only. The former were primarily employees who had accumulated small amounts of the stock of the corporation for which they worked.

Secondly, new stockholders, people who had purchased their first stocks no more than a few years before the relevant survey was made, usually owned small amounts. Most people begin their experience in this form of investment with no more than a very small part of their savings. Thus the bulk of American stockholders did not profit to a large extent from the appreciation of stocks in the 1960s—nor did they suffer substantial losses, in absolute amounts, in the early 1970s.

In the preceding discussion owners of mutual fund shares were included among the stockholders. As recently as 1962 only 5 percent of family units owned shares of mutual funds. In 1969–70, the Survey Research Center found this percentage to have doubled. At this later date all families owning stock were divided as follows:

16 percent - shares of individual corporations only,
3 percent - shares of mutual funds only

York Stock Exchange (which determines names and addresses of a random sample of stockholders and eliminates duplications from lists of the owners of different stock issues). The New York Stock Exchange takes no account of the value of the stockholdings. In addition, it defines stockholders as individuals rather than family units. Husband and wife, if each owns stock, are both listed as stockholders, as are minor children. Therefore, the Stock Exchange data indicate a greater proportion of lower- and middle-income stockholders than do the family data. It has been shown repeatedly over the past several years that the Survey Research Center data on the number of stockholding families were in fairly close agreement with the larger number of individual stockholders (over 31 million in the early 1970s) shown by the New York Stock Exchange (see the references on p. 221 of Katona, 1964a).

_7 percent - both
26 percent (total proportion of shareholders)

People who had only mutual fund shares—or more mutual funds than individual stocks—were usually quite small investors. In the late 1960s, however, a sizable proportion of substantial investors were also found to have placed a small part of their assets in mutual funds.

The great proportion of small stockholders is no doubt related to the infrequency with which stocks are bought, and the even greater infrequency with which they are sold by individuals. Stockholders were divided into four groups according to whether or not they had, in the course of 12 months,

1. neither bought nor sold,
2. occasionally bought, but not sold,
3. both bought and sold, and
4. occasionally sold, but not bought.

Studies conducted between 1968 and 1971 indicated that the majority of stockholders fell into the first category. The fourth group was found to be very small. Less than two out of every five stockholders had purchased stock in the previous twelve months, and among them the majority had only bought (group 2, consisting among others of very many mutual fund owners) and only a minority had both bought and sold (group 3). The finding that less than 20 percent of all stockholders were active in the sense of reviewing and adjusting their holdings to changing circumstances is of importance for an assessment of the function of the stock market.[7]

Before turning to a discussion of psychological factors that will shed light on the above finding, it may be well to summarize the relation of personal wealth to stockholdings in the United States. In considering all personal wealth, with the exception of the value of owner-occupied homes, the best estimate is that 60 percent of American families have very little (less than $5,000). The approximately 25 percent of families who have from $5,000 to $25,000 own hardly any stocks. Among the other 15 percent stockholdings are common, but most families who set their wealth at less than $50,000 report that the value of their stockholdings represents much less than

[7] In 1973–74 more than two-thirds of trading on the New York Stock Exchange was institutional.

266

the value of their other assets. Only holders of substantial wealth (more than $50,000) report that common stocks are their most important asset.

Attitudes toward Stocks

The first data on attitudes toward stocks and the stock market were collected in the late 1940s. At that time the great majority of Americans spoke disparagingly of stocks, with many people recalling the events of 1929. (They mentioned having known one or several "innocent victims" who had been "wiped out" in the fall of 1929.) Survey respondents argued that you can make money on the stock market only if you are an "insider" or get tips from "insiders." The ordinary person buying stocks would pay too much when he bought and get too little when he sold. Such indications of a lack of understanding of the market were widespread. Common stocks were seen by most people as highly speculative and therefore not safe. They were rarely associated with defense against inflation.

The changes that took place in the 1950s and especially the 1960s were the result partially of the gradual disappearance of recollections of 1929, but primarily of rising stock prices. The upward movement of the stock market and acquaintance with a few people who were not "insiders" but just people like oneself and who had made good in the market contributed most to the changes both in attitudes and in behavior. The answers to the two questions, "Do you own any stocks" and "Do you have friends or colleagues who own any stocks" were practically identical. The number of stockholders increased to the greatest extent in periods of bull markets. In the early 1970s when bear markets prevailed, there was no increase in the proportion of families owning stock.

Questioning of savers disclosed some additional factors that helped to explain why people bought stock. Interest in diversification of assets grew with the increase in the size of the savings, and some savers expressed a desire to participate in American industry. But most people continued to be skeptical about capital appreciation: They argued that the risks were great with only a slight chance of getting rich, and speculation remained a bad word. Inflation was not a major incentive to stock purchases any time in the 1950s or 1960s.

267

In 1969 the Survey Research Center carried out extensive studies with fairly large samples (close to 5,000 respondents) on stock ownership and the investment goals of stockholders. [8] Responses to various questions on willingness to take risks, as well as on the desire for capital gains or safety, permitted us to divide stockholders into three groups. The first group, conservative stockholders who desired to avoid risks by holding what they called "safe stocks," constituted not less than 60 percent of all stockholders. Those primarily interested in speculation for the sake of making sizable capital gains, usually younger people, represented another 20 percent, and those with mixed goals the final 20 percent. In fact, even a superficial analysis of the kinds of stock owned by respondents indicated that most of those with stocks in more than two corporations owned both "conservative" and "speculative" stocks.

We have already indicated in Chapter 14 that most people, including most stockholders, have little information about stock market trends except when major upward or downward movements result in big headlines in the papers and extensive coverage over the T.V. When asked about the causes of such major stock market movements, a very large proportion attributed sharp advances as well as declines to "speculation" or "manipulation." Many people of course gave such simple answers as, "Prices went down because they were too high before." Most stockholders also said even about sharp drops in the market in the 1960s that they were of little significance to them personally because their investments were for the long run and their losses were thus only paper losses, which they would recover in due time. Most importantly, the great majority of Americans expressed the belief that stock market movements were of little significance for and had little influence on the economy as a whole.

In the course of the 1960s the proportion of stockholders who thought that success in the stock market was a matter of luck or depended on connections or tips declined greatly. Knowledge of and research about economic trends and the prospects of individual companies were increasingly appreciated. But the proportion of stockholders who said that they devoted much time to such studies was very small even among those with

[8] The author is indebted to Merrill Lynch, Pierce, Fenner and Smith, Inc. for sponsoring the surveys, some findings of which are reported in the text.

substantial holdings. It is hardly surprising therefore that three-fourths of all stockholders—and half of those with stocks worth more than $100,000—said flatly in 1969 that they did not know enough about stocks to invest successfully. Despite the expressed appreciation of the value of knowledge about stocks and the admission that they lacked such knowledge, almost one-half of all stockholders said that "during the last few months" they had neither sought nor received any information relating to their investments. (The proportion was much higher among very small stockholders, and smaller among large stockholders, but still as large as 25 percent among holders of more than $100,000 in stocks.) About one-fourth of all stockholders said that they had received some information and that it was sufficient and satisfactory. A similar proportion expressed a desire for more information. Most of those who had obtained no information said that trustworthy information or advice was not available for people in their situation.[9]

Do people under these circumstances transfer responsibility for their investments to professional management? Purchases of mutual funds point in this direction, but when buyers were asked about their reasons for buying mutual fund shares, interest in diversification was found to be a far more important consideration. Most stockholders and even most holders of mutual funds said that they wanted to participate in the management of their investments.

The studies carried out in 1969 revealed that the average American saver is ill prepared to invest in securities. It appears that in purchasing cars, for instance, the average buyer's expertise is far superior, as is his interest in getting information and comparing products and prices. Although the purchase of stocks involves for most people fairly large amounts of money, it is often done at the recommendation of a friend, a neighbor, or at best a broker, with practically no knowledge about why the particular stock should be bought or how the company is getting along or even what it does.

There is ample reason to believe that increased participation in share ownership by individual families would be a good thing for the economy. It appears that the accomplishment of

---

[9] Brokers are the main source of information on stocks and the stock market. Yet about one-half of all stockholders said that they did not have a broker and many others that their relation to their broker was rather distant.

that goal constitutes a difficult task. It would require a substantial change in the opinions and even convictions of very many people. Information on stocks would have to be more readily available and confidence in the reliability of that information would have to be strengthened.

The absence of a close relation between the saving process and stock ownership does have some advantages. The belief of the majority of Americans that even very substantial stock market movements, upward as well as downward, do not reflect or foreshadow changes in economic trends contributes to stability at a time when such movements can be brought about by waves of purchases or sales on the part of institutional buyers.

17
INSTALLMENT CREDIT

The important role of installment credit in the American mass consumption economy was discussed early in this book. Consumer discretion is greatly enhanced by the possibility of making large purchases at a time when the consumer has but a small part of, rather than the entire, purchase price readily available. Being discretionary, the use of installment credit fluctuates according to changes in consumers' willingness to buy, and the *Index of Consumer Sentiment* could be shown to predict movements in the rate of installment buying. Over the past twenty-five years it has even been possible to demonstrate the influence of consumers' automobile purchases on the American economy by showing that periods in which the repayment of automotive installment credit exceeded the extension of such credit coincided with recessions.[1]

Installment credit represents one of several forms of consumer credit. From the point of view of size, mortgages are the most important form and one which is also fairly widespread: In the 1960s about 38 percent of family units owed mortgage debt. (As reported in the previous chapter, approximately 60 percent of all families reside in owner-occupied homes and about 60 percent of home owners have mortgage debt.) Except for older people who exchange their homes for smaller ones, most people buy their homes on credit. The size of their mort-

---

[1] It was shown in a chart presented on page 230 in Katona (1964a) that repayments of automobile credit exceeded extensions twice in the preceding 10 years, in 1958 and in 1961. There was a small excess of the former over the latter in 1967 and a substantial one from December, 1969, to February, 1971.

Much of this chapter is based on Chapter 22 in Katona (1964a); some of the newer data are taken from Survey Research Center studies by Hendricks et al. (1973) and on credit cards by Mandell (1972a).

gage debt depends primarily on the length of time they have owned their home. Therefore little needs to be said about the use of mortgage credit beyond what has been said in the last chapter about home ownership.

In connection with the study of our major topic, installment credit, some survey questions were asked about the use of credit cards, the newest form of consumer credit. It is true of both installment credit and credit cards that debtors do not think of themselves as being engaged in borrowing money when they incur either form of debt. They see only that they bought some goods and either delayed payment or contracted to pay gradually in the future. The emphasis placed on the convenience of buying on credit by the buyers themselves does not do justice to the importance of installment credit. Without the easy availability of credit, consumers would not be in a position to purchase many important goods at the time they need or want them. Thus without the use made of consumer credit the economy would not be stimulated to the same extent by optimistic expectations, which enhance the urge to improve one's standard of living in advance of earning the money required.

Who Buys on Credit?

Toward the end of World War II American families were practically debt-free, the total amount of installment credit outstanding being as low as 3 billion dollars. Fourteen years later in 1959, 39 billion dollars installment debt was outstanding, and another fourteen years later in 1973 the debt had risen to 148 billion dollars. The growth rate of installment debt is far greater than that of inflation, or of incomes, or even of sales of automobiles and other durable goods. In the 1950s as well as the 1960s consumers tended to finance an ever-increasing share of their major outlays.

Consistently in the 1960s and early 1970s annual statistics indicated that about one-half of all family units owed some installment debt. When periods longer than one year are studied, the proportion of those who make use of credit buying is much larger still.[2] The average amount of installment debt

[2] Survey Research Center data indicate that in the four years from 1967 to 1971 some durable goods had been purchased by 97 percent of a panel and some debt had been incurred by 80 percent (Hendricks, 1973). These data

272

carried also rose steadily over many years to approximately $1,000 per family by 1970.

Debt is far from being equally distributed, however. Whether or not a family buys on the installment plan depends primarily on income and age (or, more correctly, on the stage of the life cycle). Installment debt is primarily a middle and upper-middle income phenomenon associated with younger people. The notion that the well-to-do pay cash while the poor buy on time is incorrect. Low-income people as well as people with very high incomes buy on the installment plan least frequently, and older people less frequently than younger ones. Among younger families with children at home, more than 70 percent were found to have made use of installment credit in both 1963 and 1970. When the amount of debt incurred is considered (see Table 17-1, right-hand columns), the preponderance in the use of installment credit by the middle and upper-middle income groups, as well as by younger families with children at home, is still more striking.

In studying the ratio of installment debt to income, however, neither income level nor stage of life cycle tells the whole story of the use of installment credit. Income expectations were also found to make a great difference: A substantial proportion of families with an installment debt exceeding 20 percent of their annual income (as received in the preceding calendar year) were found to expect sizable income increases. These findings correspond to data presented earlier. It was shown in Table 10-2 that the mean amount of debt outstanding rises sharply when families are ranked from highly pessimistic to highly optimistic and, in Table 10-1, that a much larger proportion of the BB Group (better off than four years earlier and expecting to be better off four years later) incurred installment debt than of the Non BB Group.

A few words may be added regarding the incidence of the use of credit cards. About one-half of all family units said in response to survey questions in 1970 that they had made use of credit cards during the preceding year. Most frequent use was made of cards issued by one seller, such as a department or chain store, or a gasoline company. Charge accounts represent, of course, an old institution. Among the newer forms of

overstate the extent of credit buying somewhat because of the composition of the panel from which older people were excluded.

273

TABLE 17-1
Relation of Installment Debt to Income

Income Groups	Proportion Owing Installment Debt		Proportion Owing Installment Debt of Over $500	
	1963	1970	1963	1970
Under $3,000	32%	19%	9%	4%
$3,000–5,000	53	31	28	15
$5,000–6,000	57		32	
$6,000–7,500	62	52	37	32
$7,500–10,000	63	61	41	43
$10,000–15,000	53	65	35	46
$15,000 and over	30	49	23	39
All family units	50%	50%	27%	33%

NOTE: The differences in the data obtained in 1963 and 1970 are due primarily to inflation. Whereas in 1963 the highest incidence of substantial debt occurred in families with incomes of $6,000–7,500 and $7,500–10,000 (37% and 41%, respectively), in 1970 it occurred in families with $7,500–10,000 and $10,000–15,000 (43% and 46%).
Source: Surveys of Consumer Finances conducted by the Survey Research Center, The University of Michigan.

credit, bank credit cards were used by 16 percent of families and travel or entertainment credit cards by a still smaller proportion in 1970. Less than one-half of users of credit cards said that they owed money on their accounts. The aggregate amount of this form of debt outstanding in 1970 was less than 10 billion dollars. Young married families in the upper-income groups are the greatest users of credit cards.

Attitudes toward Installment Credit

It is possible to demonstrate that people's expressed attitudes toward the use of installment credit correspond with their behavior. Survey respondents were asked whether or not they considered it appropriate to borrow for various purposes. They replied (in 1960 as well as in 1970) overwhelmingly in the affirmative when the question referred to medical expenses or illness; more than three-fourths said that it was proper to borrow to buy a car; about one-half, to pay bills that have piled up; but only 10 percent, to pay for a vacation trip. Hendricks et al. (1973) constructed an index from eight such answers and

274

found a very high correlation between attitudes and actual use of installment credit over a four-year period. (The ratio of outstanding installment debt to income was 5.3 for those with very unfavorable attitudes toward borrowing and rose steadily to 12.5 for those with very favorable attitudes.)

These findings may be interpreted in either of two ways, and probably there is some truth in both interpretations. It may be concluded either that those with favorable attitudes make substantial use of credit in their purchases, or that those with sizable installment debt express favorable attitudes. While the direction of the causation is questionable, the findings indicate without doubt that users of installment credit are not disappointed and do not acquire unfavorable attitudes toward credit. It also follows from the data cited that people's attitudes toward installment buying are fairly deep-seated and worth further study. The latter conclusion is reinforced by the finding that attitudes toward credit improved during the 1950s and 1960s, at a time when its use grew steadily.

The Survey Research Center's inquiries about attitudes toward installment credit usually began with a simple question: "Do you think it is a good idea or a bad idea to buy things on the installment plan?" In the early 1950s about one-half of all respondents said "a good idea"; by 1960, about 60 percent. The question served to introduce a more detailed study of attitudes. We first asked people who were in favor of using installment credit how they explained their attitudes. Some said that they, or their friends and neighbors, would have to go without various necessary and useful articles if they could not buy on credit. Many others emphasized the positive aspects of credit buying. It appears justified, in their opinion, to pay for a car, a refrigerator, a washing machine, and other durables, while using those articles. Many made the analogy with the accepted practice of buying a home with a mortgage. Most people believe that automobiles and durable goods should be paid for out of income. It does not seem right to use accumulated savings to pay for such purchases. (Correspondingly, as we said in Chapter 15, few people mentioned plans to buy a car as a reason for saving.) Installment credit is the method that makes it possible to pay for a car out of the income of two or three years.

Many people are undecided when asked whether buying on the installment plan is a good idea, and even among those who approve, many do so conditionally. Two considerations are frequently noted: the size of the debt and the purpose of it. Some say that the credit is justified only if one does not borrow too much: one should know how far one can go and should never overburden oneself with debt. Others say that it depends on what one buys: they approve of installment credit only to buy important and necessary items.

Opposition to installment buying is supported by three kinds of arguments. First, there are people, representing about 10 percent of the population in the 1960s, who argue that debt is morally wrong. They believe that going into debt should be avoided under all circumstances. Then there is a similar proportion who think that installment buying makes for excessive spending. They say that people do themselves a disservice by "easy buying." The enjoyment of goods is paid for by future worries or even trouble. Third, there are people who think that installment buying costs too much. In the 1960s about one out of every six respondents raised the question of high costs when asked about the advantages and disadvantages of installment buying. We shall come back later to the problem of cost.

We may mention here briefly that attitudes toward the use of credit cards are less favorable than those toward installment credit. Mandell (1972a) found that 38 percent of a representative sample approved and 45 percent disapproved of the use of credit cards. (The remaining 17 percent had no definite opinion.) Again, users thought much more favorably of credit cards than nonusers. (Among users 51 percent approved and 33 percent disapproved as compared to 25 percent approval and 56 percent disapproval among nonusers.) The main argument against credit cards was that they made buying too easy; the arguments in favor were that they made it possible to take advantage of favorable buying opportunities and were convenient.

Borrowing as a Sign of Prosperity

Among old stereotypes that linger on and impede the understanding of new developments is the association between distress and borrowing. Even though this notion is no longer applied to the financing of business investments through credit, some critics think of personal borrowing as an indication of need for money due to illness or unemployment or, in the case

276

of farmers, bad harvests. Many opponents of consumer credit fail to notice the similarity between the use of credit for consumer investment and business investment. They fail to realize that today much of consumer credit, rather than being associated with distress of the borrower or with recession, is not only a sign of, but indeed makes a contribution to, prosperity. Not only do the rates of purchases of durable goods and of installment buying advance in good and decline in bad times, as already discussed in Chapter 15, but installment credit also enables the consumers to translate their optimistic expectations into effective demand.

The changed situation can be seen most clearly in the finding that consumers frequently buy on the installment plan even when their liquid assets would permit them to pay cash. In the late 1950s and early 1960s one-fourth to one-third of installment buyers had enough money in banks and bonds to pay for their purchases. It is, of course, true that families having, say, several thousand dollars in bank deposits hardly ever buy on the installment plan. But most others who would exhaust a large part of their liquid assets if they paid cash prefer not to touch them. It is not true that installment buying is resorted to only when it is unavoidable.

Additional information on this issue was obtained by asking survey respondents the following question (first asked in 1959): "Speaking of buying a car on time, Mr. Smith has done so, although he has enough money in the bank to pay cash; why do you think he bought the car on time?" ("What kind of a man is he?" was a further probe added to this question.) No fewer than two-thirds of all respondents could find an acceptable reason that explained to their satisfaction why Mr. Smith had bought his car on time, even though he had enough money in the bank to pay cash. The one most commonly given was that the money in the bank was earmarked for something else. Bank deposits should be kept for rainy days, many people said. Of interest are three further reasons attributed to Mr. Smith: one is that by buying on the installment plan one establishes credit; another, that by buying on credit rather than paying cash one gets better service, sometimes even a better price; finally, a number of respondents said, in essence, that it is difficult to replace savings. In other words, after paying cash for a car one is under no pressure to replenish the depleted bank deposits. But, after buying on the installment plan, the monthly payments are made out of income; thus, after a couple of years, one owns a car on which there is no debt and still has the money in the bank untouched. Among installment buyers with sizable liquid assets such an awareness of their own frailty was not uncommon.

Derogatory remarks about Mr. Smith, such as calling him a spendthrift or a foolish man, were made by only a small proportion of respondents. Many more people referred to him as a person who planned ahead or even as a cautious or intelligent person.

Consumer behavior in which there is clear evidence of advance financial calculations is quite rare. The majority of Americans today do not prepare detailed budgets for their expenditures. For many, installment buying and incurring other contractual obligations take the place of budgeting. Most people, when they buy a house for their own occupancy, calculate the monthly mortgage payments they can afford to make. The same is true of large installment purchases, and most debtors know how much their installment payments are every month. Others, with several forms of debt, calculate all their contractual obligations—the mortgage payments of home owners or the rent of tenants, plus taxes, social security payments, and life insurance premiums, as well as the monthly installment payments—and relate the total to their income. Many people intentionally set their contractual obligations fairly high. This is the way they make sure that they do not spend their income for unimportant things. The contractual obligations incurred for valuable purposes represent the first charge on income; most of what remains is needed for food and other necessities. In this way some people keep themselves from splurging and wasting money.

People with installment debt have been asked in many surveys whether it would be easy or be a hardship for them to make larger monthly payments. The proportion of those who said that it would be easy fluctuated between 20 and 30 percent; it was relatively high among upper-income people and low among lower-income people. Of primary interest are their explanations for their opinions. Those who said that it would be a hardship for them to make larger payments usually explained that their debt was up to their limit. The others asserted that they were not paying to their full capacity. Most people, in answering the question, revealed that they figured the relation

278

of their installment payments to their income. This is in contrast to the opinion sometimes expressed that it is common practice, when no down payment is required, for people thoughtlessly to overburden themselves with debt.

On the Cost of Credit

Installment credit is expensive. This is not because the lenders are inefficient or noncompetitive, but primarily because of the high costs of operation. The investigation of debtors who borrow relatively small amounts and the collection of monthly payments create high operating expenses. On the other hand, reserves for losses can be kept fairly small in view of the low default rates. On the whole—although, of course, not in all individual instances—American consumers have proved to be conscientious debtors.

Most American consumers are not well informed about how much installment credit costs. This was shown first in a nationwide survey conducted by the Survey Research Center in 1959, in which the following question was asked: "Do you happen to know how much interest or carrying charges one has to pay to buy a car on time? Suppose you need a thousand dollars which you would repay monthly over two years, about how much do you think the interest or carrying charges would be each year?"[3] About two out of every five respondents were unable to give a numerical estimate. Many said simply that they did not know. Among the respondents who gave answers in dollar amounts or percentages, a very substantial proportion cited unreasonably low interest rates. Only 20 percent, or at most 30 percent, of all people indicated by their answers that they had some awareness of actual interest rates.

It was found in practically every area of knowledge or information covered by our studies that people with a college education, or high-income people, were better informed than other people. This finding was not sustained concerning the cost of installment credit. Respondents with high incomes, with college educations, and even many of those with installment debt

[3] Intentionally, the question was not made precise. No attempt was made, for instance, to find out whether the answers related to the amount originally borrowed or the unpaid balance. We tried to formulate a question that would be understandable to broad groups of people.

hardly knew more about the interest paid on such debts than other people.

Studies conducted in later years confirmed these findings and contributed to the passage of the 1969 "Truth in Lending" law requiring lenders to make advance disclosure of the true effective rate of interest. Yet Mandell (1971) found in 1970 that the effect of the new law in making consumers aware of the cost of their loans was negligible. At a time when the cost was substantially over 10%, only about one-third of all people estimated the cost of automobile credit at 10% or more. Among respondents who had purchased a car on the installment plan during the year before the survey, accurate estimates of the interest rate increased from 45 percent before to 53 percent after the passage of the law.

The main reason why few people know about the interest rate on installment debt is that the rate in itself does not interest them. Their concern is with the size of the monthly payments, because the amount they can afford to pay each month influences the decision to buy or not to buy. And who is to say that this attitude of the average American is wrong? He knows the rate of interest he pays on his mortgage debt because in this case a difference of even 1/2 of 1 percent amounts to a lot of money. But on the average small installment debt owed for two years, the difference between paying even 12% or 15% annual interest may rightly be considered unimportant.

The Function of Installment Credit

Even superficial perusal of the literature about installment credit reveals three major lines of attack against its widespread use in the United States. First, the usage is called excessive and is said to intensify cyclical fluctuations of the economy. Second, the easy availability of credit is believed to induce people to buy goods they cannot afford, to create financial difficulty, or even to drive them into bankruptcy. Third, the carrying charges are thought to represent money wasted.

No doubt, there has been misuse of credit, both in the form of borrowing too much and of borrowing for frivolous purposes. But on the whole the American people have used credit in a circumspect and responsible manner. The good record of debt repayment even during recessions supports this statement. In addition, survey findings indicate that most borrowers are well aware of the need to use credit cautiously and that they carefully calculate their ability to meet the monthly payments out of income. To be sure, if incomes were to decline—or even if confidently expected income gains should fail to materialize —the ability of many persons to repay their debts would be endangered. Income declines over long periods, however, represent a contingency that can hardly be expected to confront many wage or salary earners. In any case, installment debt is not an initiating cause of economic instability; it may become a reinforcing influence after a drop in incomes.

Obviously, by paying cash, consumers would save the expense of the carrying charges. It does not follow, however, that abolishing or restricting installment credit would result in the spending of more money for the purchase of goods. The stimulating influence of credit buying must be taken into consideration. In a society in which incomes rise with age, installment buying plays a particularly important role. We have pointed out before that over the past fifty years there has been a shift in the working population from farmers and unskilled workers to white-collar and professional people and that, with the change in the distribution of occupations and with increased educational levels, the peak income is now earned at a later age in life.

Were it not for the institution of consumer credit, young people would have to be satisfied with a lower standard of living. Arriving at a mature age, they might find that they had accustomed themselves to a simple way of life and might have no use for the things they could then afford. It has been said in the past that young people should save for their old age. The new situation is that people, in effect, borrow while they are young, when they benefit most from things bought on credit, and delay the accumulation of financial reserves until later in life. For many people borrowing and saving are not at opposite ends of the pole but activities of different stages of the life cycle. The practice of installment buying does not detract from the desire to save.

Installment credit has made it possible for millions of American families to acquire what they consider necessities at a fast rate, in anticipation of future earnings. Today Americans marry young and have children shortly after marriage. They believe that children should be brought up in a home they own, located in a nice neighborhood, and equipped with a refrigerator, a washing machine, and many other appliances. The question is no longer whether young couples should have children *or* durable goods; thanks to installment credit, they have both.

The influence of optimistic expectations on demand is facilitated and often even made possible by the use of installment credit. In this sense installment buying promotes the growth of a mass consumption economy in which very many people, belonging to different income and age groups, participate in the improvement of living standards. Yet installment credit is not the only possible way to achieve such improvement. This becomes apparent when the use of installment credit in West Germany, one of the most prosperous countries of the world in the 1960s and 1970s, is compared with its use in the United States. [4]

In West Germany in 1967, for instance, outstanding installment debt amounted to $30 per capita as against $400 per capita in the United States. Only slightly more than 10 percent of Germans, compared with 50 percent of Americans, bought on the installment plan each year, and only 25 percent of Germans compared with 60 percent of Americans approved of installment buying. Installment buying was most common among low-income people in Germany, who used it to buy furniture and semidurables rather than automobiles. The proportion of income saved, on the other hand, was much higher in Germany than in the United States, primarily because it was not reduced by large amounts of money borrowed year after year. One of the most powerful forces motivating Germans, including young German families, to save was to have money in the bank to buy consumer goods at a later date, as well as to pay for houses and apartments with money accumulated for that purpose over many years.

Similar attitudes and behavior patterns exist in some other European countries as well, but not in all; Sweden and England are the Western European countries in which buying on credit is most popular.

---

[4] The following discussion is taken from Katona et al. (1971a), which contains many additional data. There may have been some changes in German practices since the late 1960s when the studies were conducted.

Attitudes toward installment credit apparently stem from deep-seated traditions. Because traditional ways of thinking are often reflected in language, it may be noted that the German word "Schuld" means both debt and guilt. The main lesson provided by the German example is that fiscal discipline, resulting in saving in advance for later purchases, may prevail provided it is vested in what has often been called the national character.

A final point must be made in favor of the American preference for paying while using rather than saving in advance. In an inflationary age, borrowing is advantageous while the accumulation of money for the sake of buying goods later may be very expensive. If and when prices advance steadily, the practice of installment buying gains in usefulness and the burden of the carrying charge diminishes or even disappears.

18
BUSINESS MOTIVATION

We shall turn now from consumer behavior to the behavior of the business enterprise or business firm. A business firm is a private (nongovernmental) organization, consisting of a group of interacting individuals, with economic resources that are used to produce and/or distribute goods and services. In today's economy most production and distribution is carried out by corporations and particularly by large corporations the shares of which are sold publicly. Of major interest to us will be the behavior of the corporation in setting production schedules and prices, investing in new plants and machinery, promoting sales, and advertising products. In business behavior again our main concern is with the psychological factors that enter into decisions.

In line with the contention that the business firm represents an organization with a life of its own, we shall speak of the firm as a singular rather than a plural actor. The procedure, appropriate for our purpose of analyzing the antecedents of external actions of the firms contrasts with the procedure of organizational psychology and organizational theory. This latter discipline, which has made great progress in the last few decades, is concerned with the study of the "motivations that induce various groups to participate as customers, employees, owners, etc.; i.e., to assume their roles."[1] Studies of the behavior of people as members of an organization, or of forms of management and organizational effectiveness, differ greatly from the task we have set ourselves of analyzing decisions of

---

[1] The quotation is from "Comments" by Herbert A. Simon which were included in the Social Science Research Council report, *On the Business Enterprise as a Subject for Research* (see Bowen, 1955). Simon goes on to say that studies of organizational behavior can and should be separated from studies of business behavior.

the firm that affect the economy. Some references to organizational psychology do, nonetheless, belong in this book, particularly in the next chapter.

From a psychological point of view it may be argued that there is no need for a discussion of the objectives and goals of business firms. What was established about the motives of households and consumers must apply to business motives as well. A person is not fundamentally changed when he leaves his home in the morning and enters his business office. Irrespective of whether at a given moment his role is that of consumer or business owner or business executive, the same multiplicity of motives must be effective.

On the other hand, it is sometimes argued that when an individual functions as a businessman—owner, manager, or executive—his psychological field is fundamentally different and is always structured in a specific way. He then adopts a more "rational" or more calculating attitude. This argument implies that business decisions are thought through more carefully than consumer decisions; that the former are considered and deliberated, with alternatives weighed and resolved according to some principle or criterion, whereas the latter are frequently habitual, emotional, or whimsical.

Sometimes it is conceded that the second view may not apply fully to small firms or one-person firms where a single owner may often not be able to proceed in the best possible way. But large firms, which to an increasing degree dominate the economy, are said to optimize their course of action by means of rational calculations. They can afford to study all available alternatives and choose among them after carefully weighing their consequences.

We shall find that there is some truth in both points of view. The second view is embodied in traditional economic theory, according to which the objective of businessmen is the maximization of profits: People are in business in order to make profits; businessmen want to make profits and want to make the maximum possible profits. This point of view has not, however, gone uncontradicted. It has been argued that it is one-sided; that sociological, anthropological, and psychological studies have revealed that businessmen do not strive for profits alone; that striving for security, power, and prestige plays an important role, in conjunction with, or even in opposition to, the profit motive. These arguments seem to imply that the first

288

point of view is the more correct one, and that motives remain the same irrespective of whether one is functioning as a consumer or as a business executive.

Evidence to be presented later about the wide prevalence of habitual behavior in business life points in the latter direction. It is not at all certain that genuine decisions play a larger role in business than in consumer behavior. Nor is it certain that goal setting and decision making are more deliberate in large than in small firms. Nevertheless, there can be no doubt that in present-day American business thinking the function and role of profits are substantial. We shall try, therefore, to understand the psychological meaning of profits, of striving for profits, and of striving for maximum profits, before we proceed to the discussion of more complex motivational patterns of business-men.

Profit Motive and Profit Maximization

1. *What are profits?* The concept "profit" must be clarified first. Profits are not objectively given data. After they have been determined for a given period and especially after they have been reported and published, they may assume the role of facts in the minds of people outside the business firm and even of those who determined them. But determining how much profit was made in a given period is not an operation of simple fact finding or arithmetic. It involves subjective considerations and is influenced by the attitudes and motives of the business owners or managers.

The simple definition of profits as the difference between what a commodity costs the seller and what he sells it for does not cover all that enters into the determination of profits, except in certain simple situations that are not typical in business life. Let's say John Jones, a bookkeeper, collects stamps as a hobby. One Saturday afternoon, while he is making the rounds of the stamp dealers to see what he can buy to add to his collection, a dealer offers him $3 for a stamp he once bought for $2. Because John has seen another stamp he would rather own, he accepts the offer, figuring that it has netted him a $1 profit. For John Jones the determination of costs is simple. He does not consider the value of his own time in effecting the transaction, or overhead, or taxes, or the need for maintaining reserves.

When we apply our definition of profit to business life, however, we meet with some difficulties. The price for which goods are sold is easily enough determined, and it is a relatively objective procedure to determine the total amount of sales for a year. But what is the cost of a commodity? What are the costs of producing a Chevrolet car and what are the total annual expenses of the Chevrolet Division?

In determining their costs, businessmen are guided by accounting practices and conventions, which are not rigid and unchangeable and which leave them much latitude. Of course, there are costs that are objectively measured—wages and salaries and the cost of raw materials, for instance. But costs also depend on depreciation rates, on valuation of inventories, on allocation of overhead, advertising, sales, and developmental expenses. Multiproduct firms, dealing in several products, are the rule and not the exception, which means that the cost and profit of a specific product depend on the allocation of joint costs. How to apply the accounting principles, when to deviate from them, whether to transfer some "profits" to special reserve funds or to draw on such funds—all this depends on subjective considerations, on the businessman's frame of reference and expectations.

To be sure, the businessman's latitude is severely limited. Habits are powerful constraining forces. Businessmen habitually determine the excess of their net assets at the end of a year over their net assets at the beginning of the year and make their valuations of their assets in a conventional way. Of course, the facts themselves present upper and lower limits to valuations, and then, too, habits can be given up and new decisions can be made. Often, with regard to cost allocation, developmental expenses, and reserves, decisions must be made. In other words, the exact amount of profits shown depends on business decisions.

Several different uses of the concept of profit have been distinguished. Their function as an indicator of efficient or inefficient operation (a function operative even in Soviet Russia) concerns us little. On the other hand, the incentive value of profits concerns us greatly. Motives, defined as forces pushing us into action, serve as incentives. The distinction between push and pull is entirely formal. The incentive value of future profits is very substantial even if they are not known exactly but represent a vague glimmer on the horizon. The question to be raised here concerns the circumstances under which the incentive value is particularly large and under which it is fairly small.

2. *Profits for whom?* If a man is engaged in a business of his own, if he uses exclusively his own funds and has no employees, the question of "profits for whom" may not arise. It may be said that he strives to make profits for himself and for nobody else. The problem is somewhat more complicated in the case of a large business enterprise in which the owner, the major partner, or the holder of the majority stock is also the principal manager. Still, the two cases are similar. But how about the large corporations, which at present account for the bulk of production and distribution? As a rule, the "owners," that is, the holders of common stock, are widely scattered and there is no individual holder or group of holders who control a substantial share of the capital. Business funds are supplied not only by those who purchase common or preferred stock but also by those who invest in bonds, and by banks as well as by suppliers and customers. Neither the stockholders nor the lenders are, as a rule, the managers of the corporation, nor do they have a substantial direct influence on the management's decisions. The ownership interest of the management itself is usually very small. Yet the management is self-perpetuating and frequently supervises itself by controlling the selection of members of the board of directors or by relegating that board to an advisory position. Although there are marked differences in this situation among American corporations, there can be no doubt that complete separation of ownership and management functions is widespread. Therefore, we must ask: For whom do business executives strive to make profits?

The legalistic answer to this question is: The owners hire the managers to make profits for them, the owners. In sharp contrast to this assertion, one may quote recent statements of a number of corporation executives to the effect that they have responsibilities toward their stockholders, employees, and customers, and strive to strike a balance among these three groups of interests. Psychological studies of group membership, of belonging to, and identifying oneself with groups, lead to a view that appears to be different from both statements.

If all motives were ego-centered, one might argue that the managers strive to maximize their own salaries or remuneration. The objective of getting the highest possible profit for oneself from the corporation's activities, that is, the objective of

291

"milking" the company one directs, may prevail in one or the other exceptional instance, but it is contrary to the institutional patterns prevailing in our society.

Furthermore, this objective is contrary to psychological principles of group belonging. People are not only part of their family, or of groups consisting of their neighbors or business associates, but the group with which they identify themselves may also comprise the business enterprise. As a rule business managers identify themselves with the businesses they manage. Identification with the business in which one is employed may exist even in low-level employees or may occasionally be missing in high-level employees. But usually the corporation or business enterprise has psychological reality for at least the executives. It is perceived by them as acting, as having objectives of its own, and as persisting beyond their association with it. The separate psychological reality of the firm appears to be especially pronounced in the minds of executives when management responsibilities are divided among several persons, as is frequent with many of the large corporations that are not managed by an autocratic president and his subordinates.

Not only executives and employees who belong to, identify with, and share a common fate with "their" firm or enterprise, but also many people who view the firm from the outside believe that the firm has a life of its own, irrespective of changes in its personnel or assets. The firm is not only an organization but also a social entity with a "personality," with traditions, values, and often patterns of action of its own.

It follows that the corporation manager may think of the interests of his corporation without regard to the special interests of owners, employees, or customers. He thinks and acts as if it were his corporation, even if he has no ownership share in it. Improvement in the situation of the business enterprise brings him genuine satisfaction, and deterioration in its situation causes genuine worry, without regard to whether the improvement or deterioration affects his own position.

But group belonging varies from time to time. At a given moment, during a conference with a customer, for instance, a business executive may identify himself with his firm, and a few minutes later he may think and act as a family member to whom social relations with this customer may be important. Ego-centered motives of business executives may then be in

292

conflict with business motives. But usually they are not. Institutional practices may have contributed to this situation. It has been found, for instance, that moderate increases or decreases in corporation profits rarely have a direct effect on the executives' remuneration or on the assurance with which they hold their positions. The personal motivation of the executives—to satisfy their ego, to have power, security, and larger and larger income—may be and often is satisfied through identification with their firms. Rivalry between executives of the same firm exists, but frequently takes the form of striving for a larger share for one's own department. The production vice-president wants larger funds for engineering developments, the sales vice-president wants larger advertising budgets, and so on, because they think that this is in the best interest of the firm. Ego-centered motives may be responsible for the executive's thinking, but they do not detract from his identification with the firm.

It appears, then, that the current widespread split between ownership and management functions provides no valid arguments against the role assigned to the profit motive in our economy. As a rule, a salaried executive will strive for profits for his firm. To speak of the motives of a firm is a metaphor, but a meaningful one representing a situation that is in accordance with psychological principles and organizational life.

3. *Profits–when?* The profits for which businessmen and business executives strive are, of course, future profits. The conception of maximizing future profits is a difficult one even in pure theory, as exemplified by such a typical formulation as "The entrepreneur maximizes the present value of his firm." He may seek to maximize the firm's net worth, for example, by figuring the discounted value of all future receipts minus the discounted value of all future outlays. In setting up a mathematical or theoretical model of the firm, economists have devised several approaches to deal with time preferences and the degree of uncertainty. Sometimes, in the models, past profit rates are substituted for expected profits; sometimes future profits are discounted so that a dollar's worth of next year's profits has a higher current value than a dollar's worth of profits to be made two years hence; and sometimes large uncertain future profits are equated with smaller but certain profits. Are any of these procedures justified in the sense that

they correspond with what businessmen actually have in mind?This question leads us to the study of businessmen's time perspective and their profit expectations.

Survey findings appear to indicate that businessmen as a rule have some profit expectations that concern either specific transactions or the total profits of the firm. In contemplating and discussing large transactions—be they accepting orders, purchasing goods, or making investments—businessmen invariably think in terms of expected profits. Advance budgeting, a common accounting practice, appears to make the profit expectations definite. But often enough the figures written down are considered as illustrations only, or different contingencies are represented by several sets of figures. Similarly, businessmen, if induced to do so for the purpose of presenting their arguments to their bankers, directors, or colleagues, or to answer opinion questionnaires, may estimate that the next year's sales of their firm should be, say, 12 percent higher, and the next year's profits 8 percent higher, than the preceding year's. What is meant, in most cases, is the expectation of an upturn, somewhat larger in sales than in profits, of an order of magnitude approximately indicated by the figures.

We showed above that the determination of profits depends upon subjective considerations. Businessmen have even greater latitude in estimating expected profits than in calculating past profits. Definite opinions about future profits—as expressed in such statements as, "The firm will make $50,000 in this transaction" or "Next year's profits will be 8 percent higher than last year's"—are no doubt held with lesser certainty than opinions about current profits. But the direction of a change in profits, or whether a specific future transaction will be profitable or unprofitable, is often thought to be known with great assurance. The general knowledge that the future is uncertain, or the experience that one has been wrong in the past, is frequently disregarded. Businessmen in their business planning, just like consumers in other kinds of decisions, are found to have definite expectations of the type of "I expect an upward (or downward) trend" or "This should work out well (or badly)," which they hold with great confidence.

On the other hand, it cannot be said of businessmen—any more than of people in other walks of life—that they have definite expectations all the time concerning all matters of interest to them. Such expectations arise only when they have good reason to concern themselves about the future; when there is need for making genuine decisions rather than going on with habitual patterns of business action.

No doubt at certain times the effective time perspective of business managers is rather long and may extend to several years, and at other times it is quite short, being restricted to a few months. Striving for immediate or short-term profits constitutes a very different goal from striving for long-term profits. In either case future profits may serve to motivate businessmen, although they are rarely, if ever, exact data.

4. *What kind of profits?* The term "maximum profits" must be qualified further. The instances in which it has a clear, unequivocal meaning are rarely typical of business life. Suppose I want to sell my house and have three offers for it. The meaning, then, of maximization is clear: I will accept the highest of the three offers. But complicating factors may enter even into such a simple case. Given certain expectations, I may strive toward the maximum benefit by not accepting any of the offers but rather closing up or renting the house and waiting for a higher future offer. In business transactions there is usually even greater question about the best way of making the most profit. There are usually many more alternatives and it is, as a rule, not possible for a businessman to weigh rationally all possible alternatives and to decide which will yield the highest profits.

Does, then, profit maximization mean striving toward the highest known profit? Methods to increase profits may be known and may, nevertheless, be shunned. The typical American businessman is not a fly-by-night trader who charges all that the traffic can bear. This statement means, first, that profits are not sought by any and all means. Certain ways of making profits are excluded by law: Businessmen in general do not attempt to maximize their profits if doing so involves the risk of going to jail. Other means of maximizing profits are excluded by conventions. There are, in most trades, certain things that are just not done. To offend customers, suppliers, competitors, employees, or public opinion in general is usually considered bad business even if it should lead to higher profits. This means that maximization is restricted by the extension both of the ego and of the time perspective. Insofar as businessmen consider the future of their businesses or as they identify themselves with their markets or their customers, they do not produce or sell shoddy goods in order to achieve higher profits. In short, any consideration of business behavior must, among all other factors, also take into account the social norms that guide it. Not only the laws but also the conventions regulating business behavior have changed substantially in the last hundred years—and will probably change further in the future.

Beyond such considerations as maintenance of the firm's good will or the reputation of its brand names some businessmen today feel that the "maximization" principle must be qualified by yet other factors. Unusually high profits, they believe, may lead to the introduction of new taxes or of government regulation and control. They may lead to wage demands on the part of the employees. Or they may lead to the entry of new firms into the business field. Therefore, it may be that less than what is known to be the maximum possible profit is sought. How does it all add up? If businessmen strive for profits but not for maximum profits, what is their aim? There was a time in the distant past when it was assumed that businessmen should make and should strive for "fair" profits. Even though fairness is rarely considered today, there are indications that "satisfactory" profits represent a familiar and cherished goal to many business people.

The concept of satisfactory profits is meaningful only in the presence of accepted standards that determine what is and what is not a satisfactory profit. Standards do exist according to which current and expected profits are evaluated. First of all, the preceding year's profits represent an important standard. Corporations generally publish their profits in comparison with those made the year before. Our newspapers contain daily a large number of reports like "The XYZ Corporation in the last quarter (or the last calendar year) made $3.10 per common share, as against $2.78 a year earlier." Similarly, in internal balance sheets and in budget calculations, profits are usually compared with those made the year before. It may happen, of course, that the standard is set not by the last year's profits but by the average profits or by the highest profits achieved in several preceding years, or by some rate of return on sales or capital. Whatever is the case, one meaning of the term "satisfactory profit" evolves clearly: It should not be lower than the preceding year's profit, or should not be lower than whatever is considered the standard profit. Striving toward satisfactory profits means, first of all, attempting to avoid a reduction in profits. Not to make less money than last year or than whatever is considered "normal" appears to be one of the strongest motivational forces of businessmen.

What else do satisfactory profits mean? How much more do businessmen desire to make than they made the year before, or than they think is their normal profit? It is not possible to give a definite answer to this question, but it appears that regular, gradual, small advances in the profit rate are usually preferred to large jumps. Because of their adverse effect on public opinion, legislation, customers, and labor, unusually high profits are not generally desired or sought.

The standard that gives meaning to the term satisfactory profit may be found in other firms' profit development rather than in one's own. Not doing worse than one's competitors may replace the aim of not doing worse than the preceding year. Doing slightly better than one's competitors may take the place of doing somewhat better than the year before. The meaning of the term satisfactory profits in times of a general business decline may be different from that in times of an upswing. During a depression, profit reductions may be expected and considered satisfactory, provided they are smaller than the profit reductions shown by competitors. [2]

H. A. Simon proposed in 1955 to replace "the goal of maximizing with the goal of satisficing, of finding a course of action that is 'good enough.' "[3] He argued that this solution to the problem conformed to the necessity to simplify the choice process in line with businessmen's uncertain knowledge of the future. Those who satisfice need no consistent preference orderings and no estimates of probability distributions. Simon continues to note that satisfaction is not an all or nothing phenomenon; that there are many satisficing states, not just the maximum; and that when alternatives are examined se-

[2] The discussion of striving for satisfactory profits is reproduced from Katona (1951). The book quotes the following earliest reference to satisfactory profits known to the author: "I suspect that 'satisfactory profits,' as vague as that criterion is, is frequently a more accurate description of the primary objective than 'maximum profits.' This is particularly likely to be true of mature, successful firms" (Gordon, 1948, p. 271).

[3] See Simon (1957, 204 f.). This book also reproduces an article by Simon from the February, 1955, issue of *The Quarterly Journal of Economics*. See also March and Simon (1958).

quentially a unique solution is obtained by selecting the first satisfactory alternative that is evaluated. In solving problems a satisfactory alternative is often chosen if it meets certain minimal criteria. [4]

Diverse Motivational Forces

In Chapter 14 we have presented some major arguments against a one-motive theory of behavior and may expand on them here. Only very rarely, under such extreme conditions as, for example, a threat to life or intense thirst, does a single motive govern our behavior. Usually the psychological field contains diverse forces directing our actions. Some of them may conflict with and some may reinforce one another. If whatever a businessman does is subsumed under the profit motive—by talking about psychic profits, for instance—we lose information. If there is only one motive, it becomes impossible to analyze any change in motives and relate differences in prevailing motivational patterns to differences in behavior —either among different firms or within the same firm at different times.

The investigation of motivational patterns in business may begin with an enumeration of the variety of factors that have been found to enter into these patterns and may then proceed to the question of whether under certain conditions some of the motives become prevalent while others diminish or even disappear. One of the oldest distinctions is between pecuniary and nonpecuniary motives of business. Closely related is the differentiation prevalent in organizational psychology between extrinsic and intrinsic motives. For our purposes, these terms seem less descriptive than the expressions pecuniary and nonpecuniary.

Among pecuniary motives we have already distinguished between striving for short-term and striving for long-term

[4] Recent theoretical studies of the minimax strategy that is to take the place of maximization may be mentioned even though they are of little interest to a psychological analysis of actual business behavior. In explicit formulations of the idea, businessmen confronted with uncertainty are supposed to consider the worst possible outcome of each available course of action and choose the least bad one. Thus business should aim at minimizing regrets. This represents a rather conservative strategy.

profits, which two goals may occasionally conflict with each other. By trying to achieve the highest possible profit in the shortest possible time, the firm may disturb its relations with its customers and may even jeopardize its reputation and good will. The goal of achieving short-term profits may also conflict with the goal of achieving long-term security. Relief from anxiety, a strong motivational force in human affairs, influences pecuniary motives because such relief may be sought through making money. Usually the desire for security implies striving for continuous, regular, and satisfactory earnings rather than short-term maximum profits. The anxiety-security mechanism may be much stronger in the negative than in the positive sense. Avoidance of bankruptcy, avoidance of business losses, and avoidance of a decline in profits may on this level of motivation be stronger drives than those directed toward increasing profits.

One further form of pecuniary motive that is known to enter frequently into the motivational pattern of today's business firms is striving for greater business volume. It has been found that interest in volume often transcends interest in profits. When in some studies top executives of large corporations were asked about their own and their competitors' profits during preceding quarters and years, it was found that they frequently did not have the answers at their fingertips. When, however, they were asked about their own and their competitors' volume of business, and especially about their own and their competitors' share in the total market, exact answers were quickly forthcoming. Such findings are, of course, not conclusive, and it cannot be proved at present that the view to be set forth here is correct. But it is possible that some businessmen gauge their success primarily by their relative volume rather than by their profits. Newspapers and trade journals regularly publish the shares of General Motors, Ford, Chrysler, and other automobile manufacturers in the automobile market; of the various cigarette brands in the cigarette market, and so on. Businessmen in general know their own and their leading competitors' share in the trade, are aware of orders received by their competitors, and direct their business rivalry primarily toward increasing their share in the market.

Striving for volume, attempting to increase one's share in the market, may serve the purpose of securing profits in the long run. In a formal sense—in theoretical models—of course, the aim of "maximum volume" will rarely be the same as the aim of "maximum profit." Regarding the direction of the motivational forces, it appears that the two drives often reinforce rather than conflict with each other. It may, of course, also happen that attempting to increase volume may reduce profits. Yet an increase in volume or the growth of one's firm may be desired irrespective of its contribution to future profits. Growth of the firm may become an objective in itself related to certain social needs and nonpecuniary motives of businessmen to which we now turn.

The phenomenon of group membership makes the desire to occupy an esteemed, a high, or even an outstanding position in one's group understandable. We strive for the approbation of those belonging to our group. We desire prestige among our business associates, neighbors, and fellow citizens; our ambitions are linked with the esteem and opinion of others regarding our position and progress.

The urge for prestige may develop into a desire to influence other members of our groups, to control or dominate them—in short, into a striving for power. There are indications that the prevailing institutional setup has greatly enhanced the desire for power among American businessmen. This desire is closely connected with striving for regular and secure profits. A business firm that rules and dominates its market is usually more profitable and has less to fear from sudden adverse developments than one that is in a weak position vis-a)-vis its suppliers, competitors, and customers. The relative size of a firm in its field, as well as the absolute size of its physical assets and capital funds, is related to its power position. The outstanding and acknowledged quality of the product or the service of a firm and the popularity of its brand name are further means that make for supremacy of the firm over its competitors and customers.

With respect to striving for power, the ego-centered motivations of business executives often coincide with their business or group motivations. The president of a weak firm may be a dictator in his own office but must assume a subordinate role in negotiating with suppliers and customers. The head or executive of a powerful firm may, however, exercise power all around and thus satisfy personal as well as business drives.

The feeling of achievement does, of course, not necessarily derive from the reactions of other people. Satisfactions may be inherent in a job well done without the approbation or even awareness of others. Professional pride may be derived from business activities even if they do not contribute to prestige or power. There are values and satisfactions in self-realization, and there is dissatisfaction in tasks not completed, in failure, in not getting ahead with a task. Desire for progress or for growth may be the joint result of subsistence needs, of social needs, and of the urge toward self-realization. Because of our identification with the business enterprise which we manage, or in which we are employed, these forces again may be centered in the business firm instead of in our own advancement. Self-realization may be achieved through the progress or growth of the business enterprise of which we are a part.

We said before that the business firm is commonly viewed as a living entity in itself. The self-realization of a business concern represents, then, a topic worth further study. A corporation is not conceived by its executives simply as an organization making money or making automobiles. To justify itself, it has to carry out its functions, complete the tasks taken up, and expand. Here may be found one of the most important explanations of the fact that large corporations are continuously expanding in diverse fields that are often foreign to their original activity. For instance, a small investment may be made to study the use of by-products or waste products. When some progress has been achieved, the task once begun is inevitably pushed toward completion. There is a drive, perhaps even a compulsion, to follow through after one has begun. Or materials purchased from other firms are studied, then manufactured experimentally in a pilot plant, and ultimately manufactured on a large scale. Or the technical know-how in the firm's laboratories drives toward self-realization and, ultimately—to give but one example—General Motors becomes the leading producer of Diesel locomotives. [5]

Differences and Changes in Motivational Patterns

The structure that results from the interplay of diverse motivational forces must be assumed to vary greatly under differ-

---

[5] An enumeration of potential business motives other than the profit motive is found in several older books, among which are those by Nourse (1944) and Griffin (1949). The book by Gordon (1945) and the report by Bowen (1955) are also relevant for some of the discussion in this chapter.

ent conditions. The variety of conceivable business motives combine into different motivational patterns. The resulting pattern within the same business firm may differ from time to time, and different firms may be motivated in greatly different ways at different times. If this is the case, the differences in behavior, both of the same firm at different times and of two firms at the same time, may be explained by differences in motives.

We may apply to business motives a well-known psychological principle most clearly presented by A. P. Maslow (1954), namely, that some motives are directed toward lower and some toward higher needs; that basic needs for food, shelter, sex, and the like must be satisfied first and that only then do motives directed toward new and higher needs emerge. The need for short-term profits, which provide survival or subsistence, may be analogous to motives directed toward lower needs. Motives directed toward assuring survival loom large until survival is assured. Later other goals may take over and gain great power.

We may contrast two extreme business situations and try to describe the differences in the motivational patterns that might prevail under the two different sets of conditions. We shall take up first the business enterprise that is in a precarious situation; for instance, a new firm with insufficient capital struggling to stay in business, or any business firm under adverse conditions or severely affected by a depression. Then, disregarding intermediate situations, we shall discuss the motivational forces that might influence a well-established firm operating under prosperous conditions.

The first major difference between the psychological fields in which business firms operate in the two situations is probably in their time perspective. In the first case, what will happen years from now hardly enters into consideration. Long-range transactions that would bring large profits after many years, investments that would pay only after some time, are ruled out. The immediate problems are pressing. The main aim is survival. The means to this end may be sought and found in quick profits, even though they may be lower than possible future profits. Or, they may be found in transactions that contribute to liquidity and solvency. To reduce debts or to build up liquid funds may become the strongest business motive. Under these conditions, not only will the pecuniary motives be of short

302

range, but they will also prevail in preference to nonpecuniary motives. Satisfaction of social needs, self-realization, or the urge for growth will play minor roles.

In the case of a well-established business firm operating under prosperous conditions, the time perspective will usually extend into the relatively distant future. Transactions that may not bring any profit for a number of years and long-range investments may be contemplated. Whether or not they will be made will depend on the businessman's expectations. The nature of the profit expectations, their degree of certainty, and all the factors shaping those expectations will greatly contribute to decision formation.

Not only the time period considered but also the scope of the motivational forces will be extended under prosperous conditions. The company's volume and its share in the market will become important considerations. The good will of the firm or the reputation of the firm's brand name may be given greater weight than the size of liquid assets and profits. Reputation among customers and among suppliers may be assigned large pecuniary value. Beyond the desire to maintain a strong market for his goods, the business executive's interest may extend to the entire country. Maintenance of full employment and avoidance of depression may become goals that influence specific business decisions.

Nonpecuniary motives may loom large in the case of well-established businesses operating under prosperous conditions. Improving the living standards of the firm's employees or even of the town in which the business is located may be viewed as being in the interest of the firm itself. Employee relations and the productivity of the employees may be thought to be improved by such indirect means as building recreational facilities or hospitals, or by slum clearance. Desire for prestige will be interwoven with more specific business motives.

All this adds up to a weakening of the motivational forces directed toward high immediate profits. Furthermore, under these conditions businessmen will be aware of dangers inherent in large profits and will study the vulnerability of a condition that may be viewed by others as representing excessive profits.

We have discussed two extreme situations. Naturally, prevailing conditions are very often neither precarious nor highly prosperous. Not much is known about the motivational pat-

303

terns of businessmen under such intermediate conditions, but it is probable that both the length of the time perspective and the role played by social needs increase as we go farther from the first and closer to the second extreme situation. Furthermore, striving for increased profits may be more prevalent in a situation that is relatively close to precarious conditions, and striving to avoid a reduction in profits more prevalent in a situation that is relatively close to prosperous conditions.

Two paradoxical conclusions emerge. It appears, first, that the worse the situation, the more powerful is the urge toward high or maximum immediate profits, and the less powerful the nonpecuniary motives. Second, whatever the situation, the desire to avoid a decrease in profits may be stronger than the desire to increase profits.

From an analysis of change in motivational patterns over time we turn to a discussion of differences in the motivational patterns among different firms at the same time. It is possible that motives may differ in old versus new and in relatively competitive versus relatively monopolistic fields of business. New industries—for instance, some time ago the aerospace industry or electronics, and somewhat more recently the computer industry—may be characterized by a greater degree of venturesomeness than old industries, as, for instance, railroads or coal mining. Similarly, in business fields in which there are no established leaders and into which entry is easy—as examples, women's dress manufacture or the laundry or the baking industries may be mentioned—motivational patterns may be determined by a much greater degree of uncertainty and a shorter time perspective than in such fields as the aluminum or the automobile industry, where the few established firms occupy a secure position.

The impact of motives on pricing behavior is worthy of special consideration. It was characteristic of some new industries, such as aluminum, successively to reduce the price of their product and thus to increase its use, guarantee a rapid growth of business, and ultimately bring about a substantial rise in profits. Whether or not such behavior occurs only after the industry has established itself and the new product is accepted represents a major question that should be raised in regard to several other new products as well. There may be periods in newer as well as in older industries in which the business leaders are interested only in preserving what they

304

have and other periods in which they strive to expand and gain advantages over competitors.

Those who assume that the motives of executives in old and new industries differ may explain the differences by the traits of the executives themselves. Men of inherently conservative character tend to seek and obtain employment and advancement in old industries, while men of imagination, endowed with an enterprising spirit, may choose or may be chosen to promote new industries. Yet another type of causation, namely, the shaping of personality by the atmosphere and conditions prevailing in the industry in which one works and with which one identifies oneself, also appears possible. On the other hand, in some instances a business executive may give up his position and leave a company because its goals are not in accord with his own motivational pattern.

More information is also needed about the motives and behavior of large as against small business firms. It may be argued that large firms with large staffs tend to be bureaucratic; that not only the day-to-day work but also the decision formation is routinized and follows established rules. Furthermore, in large firms it is necessary to delegate authority, often to middle-level and lower-level executives. Therefore, top management may establish policy guidelines that the subordinates can and must follow. The existence of such guidelines may tend to perpetuate habitual business procedures and to preserve the status quo. Small firms may be more flexible because the number of people involved in decision making is small. Not being subject to bureaucratic restraints, small firms may be thought to be more venturesome than large firms. On the other hand, only large firms are in such a strong position that they may make the really long-range plans needed for new ventures. Furthermore, small firms usually require outside financing for expansion, while large firms often have substantial liquid reserves or can use profits for such purposes. Strings are commonly attached to borrowing money, and the consent of the lenders to any but conservative procedures is rarely obtainable. In these respects, again, the facts themselves are disputed and require study. The question of whether the size of their business is a factor shaping or even determining the outlook, the ambition, and the motives of businessmen is far from resolved.

The increasing importance of large corporations, and of

conglomerates and multinational firms in the last few decades, represents just one of the major changes that a theory of the firm must consider. Most importantly, capitalism as we know it now differs from nineteenth century capitalism. To a larger or smaller degree in various countries, it has been transformed into an apologetic capitalism, a welfare state, or a mixed socialistic economy. If, instead of being proud of profits, businessmen see a need to justify or even to excuse them, motivational patterns must have undergone a change that has great implications for business behavior. The essence of these changes, when they fall far short of socialism, represents an acceptance of social responsibilities by business.

19
BUSINESS IDEOLOGY

Business does not operate in a vacuum. The environment that surrounds the business firm has an impact on prevailing motivational patterns and on the way business is conducted. There was a period in the nineteenth century when the assertion of some philosophers and economists that business best served the purposes of the general welfare by making the highest possible profits was apparently widely accepted and approved. At that time, maximization of profits as the sole aim of business may have coincided with the requirements of the business environment. In the twentieth century, more and more people became distrustful of large profits. At the same time, people began to expect more from business leaders than that they should just manage their companies properly and make profits. What is expected of business and the extent to which businessmen are aware of these expectations influence business ideology and business policies. In recent decades, there has emerged some acceptance on the part of business that it has social responsibilities, that it has obligations not only to its owners or stockholders to whom the profits accrue, but also to its employees and customers, as well as to the community and country in which it operates.

Sources of information on business ideology and the attitudes of business toward its responsibilities are interviews with samples of businessmen, as well as speeches, papers, and reports by business leaders.[1] Most public statements known to the author were made by executives of large American firms. Because of their influence on small firms and because of close contacts among big firms all over the western world, there is

---

[1] For a valuable collection of business proclamations, see Sutton et al. (1956). Further sources of information are Bowen (1953) and Eels (1960).

justification for relying on statements by American business leaders in evaluating the overall climate.[2] It may be objected, of course, that these pronouncements and publications do not represent what business really thinks and how the business firms act but rather indicate what business wants the public to believe about how it thinks and acts. The publications are then considered as public relations or propaganda efforts not deserving serious attention. No doubt there is some truth in this objection; some statements were probably meant to persuade the public about the good intentions of business. But suggestions work best in the in-group, and therefore the suggestive power of the pronouncements of business leaders must have been much greater among businessmen than among the general public. Moreover, there is always the process of self-suggestion; the business leader who begins to make speeches about his social responsibility for the sake of persuading others may eventually come to believe in what he has said!

Today's business ideology has developed over many decades and has numerous antecedents. Certain aspects of business life that have long prevailed and still prevail today should not be confused with what we here call the social responsibilities of business. Business ethics, for example, expressed most simply as "businessmen should not cheat," falls into this former category. The same is true of philanthropy. Corporate giving, for instance to colleges and universities, may be related to but is not the same as responsibility for the welfare of one's employees or of the community at large. Business concern with public relations also long preceded business concern with social responsibilities. When firms consider institutional advertising and the promotion of a favorable corporate image much of their thinking is apparently directed toward narrow business goals, as, for instance, enlarging the market for their products or their common stock. In no way can a sense of social responsibility be viewed as having replaced profits as a major motivational force of business. Yet the emergence of certain new

---

[2] Although the discussion in this chapter is based on studies and observations made in the United States, extensive material is available from other countries as well to support the arguments presented. It may suffice to quote the conclusion of Andrew Shonfield (1965) who argues that in Western Europe capitalism, which appeared a failure in the 1930s, has been transformed so greatly that it became the great engine of prosperity in the postwar world.

ideas and concerns among the public at large must have contributed to the shifts in business motivation that have been described in the preceding chapter.

Forms of Social Responsibility

The changes in business ideology are related to two major developments in this century. First, the fact that the "owners" of big business, the stockholders, are remote and in most cases without influence called for a reconsideration of the functions of business management. The same need for reevaluation was derived, secondly, from the obvious great power of big business over its total environment—not only economic, but also political and social. The conclusion was drawn by informed public opinion and by business leaders as well that powerful big business, not controlled by its owners alone, must consider and respect the rights and interests of its employees, its customers, its community, and its country. In addition to these major constituents some responsibility was accepted even toward suppliers and competitors.

Employees. The long history of relations of business to labor indicating a slow but steady increase in real wages paid and a gradual improvement in working conditions need not be recalled here. Nor is it of great relevance in the present context that attitudes toward labor unions have changed since the beginning of this century from resistance and even aggression toward unions, to recognition given grudgingly, and, finally, to acceptance and in many cases cooperation. According to the new ideology—accepted only partially by most firms—employees, including rank-and-file labor, should be recognized as members of the firm and the consideration of their rights, interests, and welfare should represent a major concern of management. Some of the business decisions dictated by this approach may result in a curtailment of the firm's immediate profits. On the other hand, it is coming into acceptance that satisfied employees who are involved in the shaping of their task represent the condition for greater productivity and thus ultimately for increased profits.

Acceptance of responsibility for the welfare of employees must lead to substantial changes in internal management. Autocratic one-man rule and communication exclusively from the

309

top down then ceases to be viable behavior. Participation in management, even of lower-level employees, two-way communications, and committee rule among executives would become the norm. The actual extent of participation of employees varies from firm to firm and from country to country—in some Western European countries certain forms of participation are prescribed by law. It has been found where it has been tried that giving employees a voice in certain business affairs creates greater worker satisfaction than other more tangible changes. An important aspect of supportive relations between employees and the firm consists in making their work meaningful to the workers ("job enrichment"). In this respect it must be said that progress has thus far been quite limited.[3]

Customers. Emphasis on such goals as creating and maintaining a high reputation for the firm and its products is hardly new. In the first three decades of this century American business was concerned primarily with production. Later, it assigned major importance to distribution, giving those in charge of sales departments an increasing role in business command. After World War II it turned its attention increasingly toward the consumers and research into their needs and wants (see Pratt, 1972).

Orientation toward and concern with the consumer induce business to pay great attention not only to marketing activities but also to marketing research. One major purpose of that research is to find out what consumers want, with the goal of persuading management to adjust production and distribution accordingly. To the extent that a company is aware of its social responsibilities, research directed toward the consumer's interests and desires has greater weight than research with the aim of finding out how the company can increase the sales of the products it customarily sells. We shall return to these two

---

[3] The intellectual ancestors of participative management range from Elton Mayo to Douglas McGregor and Rensis Likert (1961 and 1967). The differentiation between autocratic and participative managements has already had an influence on internal business policies. Likert also proposed an important innovation regarding human resources accounting, which as yet is far from becoming part of American business life. Likert argues that prevailing accounting systems disregard that significant part of the firm's assets that consists of the abilities of its management and its human resources in general. He suggests ways to include such assets or liabilities in the firm's financial reports.

310

potentially conflicting aims of marketing in Chapter 23 when we shall discuss the thesis of Galbraith that big business through its marketing and advertising activities is intent on making consumers subservient to its aims. It may suffice to say here that marketing research has not one but two facets: finding out what consumers want and finding out how the firm's goals can be achieved. Business in general has obviously not accepted the definition once given to this author by a professor of marketing that "Marketing is a process through which business serves human needs." Marketing is clearly intended to serve the needs of business, but it should do so without violating the best interests of its customers.

The same ambivalence that we encounter in the position of business with respect to marketing manifests itself in business attitudes toward consumerism. The latter also will be mentioned only briefly here and discussed in greater detail later. The first reaction of most business firms and organizations to Ralph Nader, as well as to earlier and later private or public agencies involved in testing products and judging sales messages, consisted of opposition and condemnation. Businessmen maintained that their own standards and competition among them would suffice to assure a fair treatment of customers and that interference with the "free market" would only worsen the service normally offered. This position contrasted sharply with growing public acceptance of the idea that business has responsibilities to society, and thus it became increasingly difficult to maintain. It was easy enough to muster the support of the business community against the outright deception of consumers. It has, however, been a difficult, uphill, and not always successful struggle to achieve acceptance of new standards for services given and even for information supplied to consumers.

Regarding the introduction of technological innovations business has been attacked on two rather conflicting counts. It has been asserted that business is to be blamed because it is far too slow in introducing new products and letting consumers benefit from technological progress. As long as the machinery used to manufacture old products is not fully amortized, business is said not to be interested in replacing it with machinery producing new and better products. On the other hand, the automobile industry in particular has been attacked for the artificial obsolescence of its products. Many critics consider that the substantial cost of introducing new models year after year represents deliberate waste, for the sole purpose of stimulating demand, and is of no value to the consumer. No doubt, there have been instances in which one or the other industry has been guilty of either or both offenses. But there are also examples of an expeditious handling of innovations and of model changes that have been most useful to consumers. In general, business practices are altered cautiously and slowly, and therefore a quick change of products is the exception rather than the rule. To what extent the new climate of opinion, requiring that business should serve the interests of consumers, has changed customary practices is not known.

Other responsibilities. As opposed to what was called cutthroat competition in an earlier time, the prevailing cautious and conservative attitude toward suppliers and competitors may perhaps more appropriately be expressed as "live and let live." Over the long run, access to supplies at satisfactory prices is assured only when suppliers are in sound financial condition. Some competitors must likewise prosper if a good image of the industry is to be maintained as well as antitrust action avoided. Therefore, squeezing suppliers by paying them unreasonably low prices or putting competitors out of business has become less and less acceptable as a business goal.

In many instances it is obvious and necessary for the sake of profits that a business be greatly concerned with the community in which it operates. A department store, for instance, may be badly hurt by the decay of the inner city, and civic action as well as large expenditures on urban renewal may be necessitated by profit considerations. Yet involvement in community affairs has sometimes become a goal in itself, particularly on the part of successful businesses. The physical environment of the factory or office, the air or water in the city or town where the firm operates, and the quality of the local government are beginning to be seen as the firm's social concerns because they represent the larger whole to which the firm belongs and with which it shares a common fate.

National affairs are hardly remote from big business, which operates in many parts of the United States and often of the world. Just one aspect of business concern with economic policies of the national government, namely, the avoidance of depressions and of cyclical fluctuations, will be discussed here.

Nothing should be closer to the firm's own interests than the maintenance of the economic well-being of the firm's customers and of the ultimate consumers. A recession causes great economic damage, even to the best-managed enterprise. It might be assumed, therefore, that it would be easy for business to adopt anticyclical policies. In fact, this has proved not to be the case. As a prime example, it may be noted that capital expenditures for plant and machinery have yet to be used as an anticyclical measure. To increase business investment expenditures when a recession threatens or after it sets in, or to decrease them in times of a boom, represents a notion to which lip service has been paid but which has rarely been adopted (see the next chapter). It has proved very difficult to change traditional principles of business according to which the full utilization of capacity, as it occurs in prosperous times, calls for business investments, while excess capacity, as it occurs in times of recession, does not. When "everybody" expands capital expenditures, as in good times, and when "nobody" does, as in bad times, swimming against the current becomes most difficult. Notions about the social responsibilities of business are apparently easier to translate into action when obligations are felt toward specific groups of people, such as employees or customers, than when abstract ideas are at issue.

What Is Expected from Business?

Having described various aspects of change in business ideology, we must remind ourselves of our initial assumption that these changes occurred in response to demands by the environment in which business operates. Do the changes correspond with what people expect from business? Does the new ideology satisfy the people? Do they believe that business has accepted and demonstrated its social responsibility? These are the questions we shall try to answer in the light of findings from surveys with the American people.

A nationwide sample interview survey conducted by the Survey Research Center in 1950 revealed rather favorable attitudes toward big business (Fisher and Withey, 1950). Respondents were first asked what things big business did that were good for the country and what things it did that were bad for the country. The respondents were then requested to make

313

an overall evaluation. In reply, 76 percent of a representative sample of all adults said that the good things outweighed the bad things, while 10 percent had the opposite opinion (and 14 percent thought that the two were equal or said they did not know). Among the good things big business did, the most frequently mentioned were that it created jobs ("hires lots of people"), that it kept prices down ("makes things cheaper"), and that it introduced mass production and mass distribution. Among the bad things just one was frequently cited, namely, that big business had too much power and squeezed out the little man and destroyed competition. Detailed questioning indicated that, in the opinion of the majority, (a) big business paid higher wages than small business, (b) those who worked for big business were more certain of their jobs than those who worked for a small business, (c) big business helped to create jobs, and (d) big business helped to introduce new products. In general, people thought that they trusted the products of big business and that they would be in favor of their children getting jobs with big business.

These attitudes in 1950 are worth describing as an indication that big business was once highly respected in the United States. But since the early 1950s public attitudes have changed substantially. The deterioration of confidence in business and in business leaders was most rapid shortly before and after the recession of 1970. In this period confidence in the government and its economic policies was impaired to a still greater extent. Trusting business less and less coincided with expecting more and more from it and attributing to it great responsibility in economic as well as social spheres.

Some of the changes in attitudes can be traced from the results of successive Harris polls (Harris, 1973). The first relevant question was: "As far as the people running [our] institutions are concerned, would you say you have a great deal of confidence, only some confidence, or hardly any confidence at all in them?" People were asked about their confidence in leaders of 16 institutions. In 1966, 67 percent said that they had a great deal of confidence in financial leaders; in 1973, 39 percent. In 1966, 55 percent said that they had a great deal of confidence in top business leaders; in 1973, 23 percent. Public regard for institutional leadership dropped generally; for instance, esteem for doctors, who are usually held in the highest regard, declined from 72 to 48 percent.

An extensive list of activities was also presented to respondents who were asked (1) whether business should give some special leadership in any of these areas and (2) whether business helped solve any of the problems. The findings indicate that in the opinion of very many people business both should and does provide help in solving a variety of social problems but does less than it should. The gap between the desired and the actual performance widened considerably between 1966 and 1973 (see Table 19-1).

Similar findings were obtained by the Survey Research Center in the fall of 1973. To a question about the desired influence of various institutions in our society, the average person wished the present influence of the President, the federal government, as well as of labor unions to be reduced. Yet the desired reduction of the influence of large corporations was the largest of all. At the same time, when the question asked in 1950 and cited above was repeated, the majority still said that the good things big business did outweighed the bad things, but the proportion dropped from 76 percent in 1950 to 60 percent in 1973.

Clearly, people expect much more from business than economic performance. They appear to expect more than business can conceivable deliver. Business, and especially big business, is thought to have such great power in America that it is held responsible, at least to some extent, for practically all evils whatever their source. When economic or social conditions are felt to worsen, and when some large firms are revealed to have deviated from the right path, there is an inevitable increase in public opposition to and condemnation of business.

Big Business as a Public Institution

It is apparent that in the 1970s business, and especially big business, is not very popular. Widespread criticism and even condemnation of business may or may not be connected with the fact that it is hardly in a position to adopt social responsibilities to as great an extent as people think it should. American business has chosen a middle position—and middle positions rarely win popularity contests. Although business has not accepted all the responsibilities society today considers desirable, it has nonetheless moved far away from the other extreme

315

position, which maintains that business has but one responsibility, namely, to increase its profits by engaging in free competition and that when it has fulfilled that one responsibility it has done all it is supposed to do for society.[4]

At present, opposition to business appears to have little to do with the old debate about capitalism versus socialism. Condemnation of the profit motive is voiced primarily when rising prices and rising profits coincide. The American public shows little interest in either defending or attacking the free enterprise system. The similarities of the bureaucracy in big private business and in government impress people much more than the differences between the private and the public sectors. The two bureaucracies share something which, while objectionable to some people, is also thought to have advantages—their large size. Even though monopoly and concentration of power are condemned, antitrust action is often popular, and the advantages of competition are generally praised, there is little indication of any weakening of belief in the beneficial nature of bigness and its association with efficiency. Nor is the political role of business in the center of the controversy, although some widely publicized misconduct has contributed to the deterioration of the business image.

It appears, therefore, that it is not philosophic issues or matters of principle that have made business unpopular and subject to criticism. People are dissatisfied with the manner in which business has handled specific problems that have become very important to them in the last ten years. One of these problems is pollution, another is the quality of products and services, and a third is their price. In all these respects business leaders appear to be aware of the problems and may make some contribution toward solving them in the future. The climate in which business operates is subject to change. Its deterioration in the late 1960s and early 1970s may not continue. What will endure is that big business is regarded, and is expected increasingly to act, as a public institution the actions of which must be open to public scrutiny.

The largest firms have become multinational or world firms far exceeding in size and influence most national states. These business firms operate all over the world and some even have their homes in several countries rather than operating from a

---

[4] This position was presented by Milton Friedman in the *New York Times Magazine*, September 13, 1970.

single home base. There are now also conglomerates, which operate in several lines of business at the same time. The question is whether and to what extent the changes in the climate of opinion have influenced the ideology of these largest businesses. One possible extreme formulation of what the ideology should be is that multinational corporations have a responsibility to serve the world economy, peace, and cooperation among different countries. At the opposite extreme, it has been argued that the true motivation of world corporations as well as of conglomerates is simply to avoid control and scrutiny by supervisory agencies or the public. Multinationals are then thought to assume the role of a superstate, not responsible to anyone.

Corporations operating in many different countries are, of course, subject to the demands of various governments, and those demands may well be contradictory and therefore impossible to fulfill. Under these circumstances, as for instance at the time of the oil embargo in 1973–74, American-based multinationals may have pursued nothing but their own goals in opposition to legitimate American interests. It is not argued here that an American-based corporation must always operate in the American interest, and a British or Dutch-based corporation in the British or Dutch interest, but it is argued that no corporation should be permitted to be responsible to no one but itself. When corporation management is self-perpetuating and stockholders and boards of directors, rather than controlling management, are dependent upon it, there exists an urgent need to insure that corporations operate in a responsible manner. Ultimately, it is only public opinion that can exert the

TABLE 19-1

Public Opinion about Social Responsibilities of Business (in %)

| | Business Leadership | | | |
| | Has helped | Should help | Has helped | Should help |
Selected Activities	1966		1973	
Eliminate racial discrimination	58	69	50	84
Eliminate economic depressions	75	73	41	88
Wipe out poverty	63	69	35	83
Control air and water pollution	35	69	36	92
Rebuild our cities	76	74	60	85

Source: Harris Poll, 1966 and 1973.

necessary pressure to provide that insurance. But informed public opinion cannot develop unless big business discloses fully all aspects of its operations. (Such disclosure may require new legislation.) Although the abandonment of business secrecy may well result in lower profits, it has become increasingly clear that multinationals, and generally all large corporations, must eventually operate as public institutions with ultimate responsibility to the public.

20
DECISION MAKING BY BUSINESS FIRMS

Let us recall that the assumption of rationality extends to both the goals business pursues and the means by which it tries to achieve the desired ends. The goals and ends have been amply discussed in the preceding two chapters, but little has been said up to now about how business firms proceed in order to reach what we know by now represent a variety of ends. The question will be raised here whether business behavior differs fundamentally from everyday behavior and, therefore, the behavior of consumers, in that business firms, or at least well-managed business firms, proceed in a rational manner. In other words, is American business life characterized by a succession of carefully weighed and deliberated decisions or rational calculations?

In opposition to the assumption of rationality it may be argued that if businessmen were to consider every item of information they receive—every piece of news, letter, or telephone call—as giving rise to a problem that needs to be studied and analyzed, they would have no time to conduct their business. In larger firms, delegation of authority is necessary and rules and conventions must be set up to insure uniform procedures. Therefore, genuine decisions made after careful weighing of available alternatives may be as rare in business life as they are in everyday life. They may occur only under the impact of new developments that are seen as bringing about major changes in the situation.

The characterization of the decision-making process by business firms as rational or nonrational is, of course, incidental to the central task, which consists of the description and analysis of decision making. The reader may be reminded, however, that the dichotomy between habitual behavior or following rules of thumb and carefully deliberated genuine decisions is not the same as the dichotomy between rational and nonrational behavior. Habitual behavior may be as appropriate as deliberated behavior.

The empirical studies related in this chapter will indicate the common occurrence of habitual behavior and of the application of rules of thumb and routine procedures in business life. The same rules may prevail in an entire trade or industry, or they may be restricted to a single firm. In addition, the consideration of personal relations will be seen as being far from foreign to business behavior. Nevertheless, evidence will also be found of major decisions that resemble what has been called rational behavior. Even genuine decisions tend to be similar among very many firms at the same time, as we shall show at the end of this chapter, and thus influence not only the individual firms but also the entire economy.

Which of the many aspects of business decisions merit study? A demonstration of the prevalence of routine procedures in matters that constantly recur may not be of great interest. In contrast, an indication that habitual forms of action are common in determining business investments may be a significant finding because these major decisions are made but rarely and have a wide-ranging influence on future economic developments. Alternatively, the choice of the topics to be considered may be made on the basis of the aspects of business behavior studied by the author or his associates by means of survey research. The two criteria are interrelated. The author chose the topics of the business surveys encompassing pricing, investment, location, and financial decisions primarily because of his interest in infrequent decisions the study of which may serve to modify assumptions made about the rationality of business behavior. [1]

---

[1] Findings of the studies in which the author has participated are to be seen in the following publications: Katona (1945) on pricing; Survey Research Center (1950) on industrial mobility; Katona and Morgan (1952) on factors determining business decisions; Mueller et al. (1961) on location decisions; Mueller and Morgan (1962) on location decisions; Mandell (1972b) on industrial location decisions in the Detroit area; Katona (1957) on financial decisions. On the possibilities and advantages of surveys conducted with representative samples of firms, see Appendix. It would have been useful if the studies had been extended to cover decisions about introducing and marketing new products; unfortunately, this was not done.

320

Price Setting[2]

Within a firm, or within an entire trade, specific pricing rules are often found to prevail. They are applied in a routine manner; major policy decisions would be needed in order to abandon or to change them, but not in order to apply them. A very important form of pricing is margin pricing. A retailer, for instance, buys at price X and sells at X plus some fixed percentage. The markup added to the purchase price may be fixed for all products sold and may remain unchanged over long periods. Or there may be in a single firm several different markup rates, applied to different products or at different seasons. In other instances, instead of marking up by adding a percentage to the purchase price, the reverse system may prevail. The sales price may be considered as given by the supplier, and the retailer purchases goods, if possible, at a certain traditional percentage of the sales price. In the case of a manufacturer operating on a markup principle, he adds a given percentage to his "costs" to determine his sales price. Not only is the percentage of markup traditionally set but the determination of costs is likewise ruled by habitual principles. Most frequently, the so-called variable costs alone are considered as costs, namely, raw materials and labor, while the margin is supposed to cover fixed costs (overhead, depreciation, interest charges, and so on), sales costs, and profits. When margin pricing prevails, price changes may come about through the application of habitual margin rates rather than because of any decision to change prices. Fluctuating or flexible prices may be the result of rigid pricing methods.

Habitual pricing rules may extend to such measures as rebates, markdowns, promotions, and clearance sales. A wholesaler or a department store, for instance, may have a fixed system of reducing by a given percentage the prices of certain products if they are still unsold after a given time. Retailers may have a fixed system of seasonal sales, and the traditional principles may apply both to the range of products that

---

[2] For a detailed discussion of pricing rules, see the volume by the Committee on Price Determination (1943) and Kaplan et al. (1958). See also Part III of Katona (1951). Even in a period of rapid inflation such as 1973–74, many traditional principles of price setting remained applicable.

are subject to markdowns and to the percentage of the markdown.

Very many prices do not emerge in free markets consisting of unorganized sellers and buyers; nor are the prices fixed by an authority (at least in the absence of price control); they are set by business firms. The pricing rules discussed up to now do not suffice to understand how these "administered prices" are set and especially how they are set by big multiproduct business firms. Administered prices, especially of manufacturers, are often kept stable over long periods of time, even though raw material prices fluctuate and therefore a strict application of margin pricing would involve frequent changes in these prices as well.

After studying the price-setting practices of a large number of top corporations and interviewing their executives, Kaplan and his associates (1958) concluded that target pricing represents the most common method of pricing. The large corporations set a target return for their investments. Most usually the pricing objectives prevailed over many years and acquired the status of tradition. Knowing what target return to seek, a division manager needs to use little discretion in setting the price of his product. He adds the necessary margin to his costs to achieve the target and sticks to the price for a long period, expecting that fluctuations in raw material prices will average out.

The pricing of new products may be more complicated but target pricing has the effect of simplifying even that. To mention a complex case in which the process of developing a new product takes several years, reference may be made to Kaplan's analysis of pricing new automobile models. At the beginning, the quality or style of a new car model, to be introduced two or three years later, and its price are the product of joint experimentation. Yet the price is set at a fairly early date on the basis of the target return sought, and the features of the new car are then adjusted to the price. These pricing practices serve to bring about nonprice competition and to promote the goal of changing prices as rarely as possible.

Reliance on target return pricing may often result in not realizing the maximum possible profit. Formulas and rules of thumb take the place of numerous conferences and discussions. No doubt, however, the formulas must be changed under exceptional circumstances. One of these circumstances, discussed by Kaplan, is pricing to improve one's market position, and another is pricing to meet competition. The traditional pricing systems are intended to restrict rivalry, but this goal is occasionally abandoned by major policy decisions of the top command.

It should be added that the introduction of the computer brought automation, which began in manufacturing processes, into the office and into management itself. The computer makes it possible for decisions to be "programmed." While in earlier times a buyer, for instance, had to size up a situation in the light of his opinions and often feelings, today he is aided by the computer's analysis of a very large quantity of data.

It may also be mentioned that long-lasting and substantial inflation may make adherence to pricing formulas difficult. The principle of target pricing then provides a signal that calls attention to the need for a price increase. In business as in other activities of life, the making of genuine decisions involves calling into question the value of habitual patterns of action and realizing that the situation requires a different procedure.

Investment Decisions

The results of decisions by business firms to build plants and acquire new equipment are enduring and nonreversible. The success or failure of the decisions will often not be known for several years. In addition, the decisions usually involve large amounts of money and are unique in the sense of not being strictly comparable to previous decisions. Therefore, in business investments we should expect rational behavior to prevail.

In fact, even casual observation reveals numerous instances in which rules of thumb prevail and business investment appears to be the habitual or even automatic result of certain conditions rather than the outcome of careful deliberation. Accounting rules about depreciation make it easy to replace machinery when it is fully depreciated and very difficult at an earlier date. Depreciation and the customary establishment of reserves out of profits create internal funds the size of which influences both the upper and the lower limits for annual investment outlays. Accounting rules prevalent in an entire industry about the payoff requirements for new machinery also provide standards that are more or less automatically applied.

Of great importance is the "follow-the-leader" principle. In many fields of trade and industry there exists a leader whose decisions are followed by the others in the field. More generally, what other firms in the field and especially close competitors do with respect to the introduction of new technological processes or the utilization of inventions is easily adopted. When the managers of a firm believe that their competitors are about to make use of new procedures, they hasten to do so also. On the other hand, capital outlays for modernization or innovation not undertaken by other firms in the trade represent some of the most difficult and most carefully considered decisions.

The impact of the general business climate on investments was demonstrated when deviations from planned investment outlays were studied. In responding to the SEC-Commerce Department surveys regarding the amount of money they expected to spend on plant and machinery during the following year, individual firms were frequently found to have greatly underestimated or overestimated their actual outlays (while in the aggregate the predictive success of the surveys was substantial). When in some special studies the factors responsible for the errors were investigated, changes in the demand for the product of the responding firm and changes in the general economic trend were found to have made for changes in plans. When the economy improved more than expected, investment outlays were stepped up; when the economy deteriorated, actual investment outlays lagged behind the planned outlays. Improvement in business volume also brings about larger profits and thereby an increase in internal funds available for investment. For most firms, internal funds constitute the major source of investment outlays.

The studies on location decisions conducted by this author, to be reported below, were extended to an analysis of investment decisions. A sample representative of manufacturers in the state of Michigan was drawn (with the probability proportionate to the number of employees) and lengthy interviews were conducted with the top executives of 188 plants in 1950.[3]

[3] The big three automobile companies were excluded from the quantitative tabulations. As will be reported later, the location studies were repeated

Executives of firms that had expanded their plant or equipment in the year prior to the interview, and that entertained such plans for the near future, were asked to relate the considerations that led to their decisions. The detailed answers received could be grouped in four categories. The first category, growing demand or growing orders at the time the decision to expand was taken, was by far the most frequent. It was given by 61 percent of the firms with past, and 45 percent of the firms with contemplated, expansion. In these cases executives frequently denied that they had taken any initiative. This may be seen from such answers as, "The demand for our product was growing: it compelled us to acquire more space," or, "It was not a planned proposition, it followed behind an increase in our sales." Operating at or near full capacity was frequently cited. The threat of having to turn down orders or to delay delivery of products to old customers because of lack of capacity appears to represent the most compelling factor in expansion decisions.

A second type of answer is given by some executives referred to a policy of expansion. "The firm is growing every year," the interviewer was told, or reference was made to earlier policy decisions. Similarly, some executives of firms that had not expanded spoke of a policy of self-containment.

A third category of investment decision includes those cases in which manufacturers explained past as well as contemplated expansion as measures leading to reduced cost of operation or greater efficiency of operation. In some cases this was a carefully planned proposition, while in others the respondents said that they were compelled to expand because their competitors had cut their costs by building more efficient plants.

A fourth category includes those cases in which manufacturers referred to future rather than recent past developments. They said that they expected demand to increase or that they wanted to take steps to increase the demand for their products in the future. In some instances past or contemplated expansion was explained by the introduction of a new product or a new line of business. This was a major, carefully considered decision.

Factors responsible for decisions to expand may be determined not only by asking business executives those factors, as we have just related, but also by means of correlation analysis.

<hr>

with larger samples in 1961 and 1972. For the following discussion, see Katona and Morgan (1952).

In the studies reported here interviewing began by asking several questions about business conditions at the time of the interview and about business prospects for the next few years. The inquiry regarding plans to build new plants or additions to plants followed much later. It appeared that among those who characterized current business conditions as very good, 45 percent entertained expansion plans. Among those who spoke of business conditions as fair, the frequency of expansion plans was 18 percent, and among those who voiced some dissatisfaction with business conditions it was 22 percent.

Scrutiny of how the executives who gave the three different answers about business conditions spoke of expanding their facilities was rewarding. Many of the executives experiencing "very good" business devoted few words to explaining their expansion plans. The decision was self-understood, simple, sometimes automatic. At the other extreme, however, the interviews revealed that a very difficult decision was made after lengthy and careful consideration. The firms had decided to attempt to reverse an existing trend; dissatisfaction with the existing situation or with their competitive position induced the executives to build a new plant or change their products or their production methods. Thus, the analysis shows that some investment decisions are based on the careful weighing of alternatives. Other decisions, however, are probably much more frequent and are routine and habitual in that established procedures are followed. In these instances businessmen often are not aware of having made a choice and expectations concerning future developments play a small role.

Location Decisions

Obviously, the selection of the site of a newly established business firm or of a plant to be built, as well as a change in the location of an established firm or plant, represent major decisions of substantial impact for the success or failure of the firm. Several forms of such decisions may be studied, such as (a) decisions of a new firm in selecting its location, (b) decisions to relocate or to stay, (c) location decisions taken in connection with the expansion of facilities, and, finally, (d) recollections of location decisions taken at the time when a plant was built, often many years prior to the study. No doubt, there are hardly any manufacturing plants that are located in just the right place. Therefore, interview surveys in which executives were asked about perceived advantages and disadvantages of a given location were revealing.

Such investigations may be of practical value regarding the prospects for a specific area. It is important to know of threats of substantial out-movements or, alternatively, to prepare for forthcoming growth. Whether or not promotional activities should be undertaken and how they should be conducted may be determined by surveys of location decisions. Thus, practical problems confronting industry in Michigan, and especially in the metropolitan area of Detroit, induced the Survey Research Center to conduct studies in 1950, 1961, and 1972. On all three occasions the studies revealed the probability of a substantial out-movement of manufacturing plants during the next few years. These predictions were realized in the 1950s and the 1960s. This was the case even though the major reasons for industrial mobility were found to be man-made, and therefore potentially changeable, rather than given by natural conditions.

Location theory has long established the importance of proximity to raw materials and/or markets. The availability and cost of labor as well as differences in taxation are likewise major factors affecting profits and therefore of great influence on the choice of the best possible site. Surveys confirmed that opinions and attitudes of business leaders are derived to a large extent from such objective economic factors. Nevertheless, there are good reasons to study subjective notions and attitudes toward location and industrial mobility.

First, it is difficult to measure the advantages and disadvantages of a location in terms of cost and revenue. This is true even of labor costs because of differences in labor productivity and reliability in different geographical areas. The measurement problem becomes formidable when industrial climate is considered in all its ramifications. Second, objective data, for instance on differences in local tax rates, do not tell us how important the differences are for the manufacturer. Third, it is probable that certain subjective considerations such as the quality of life—opinions about good schools, secure streets, nearness of recreation areas, and so on—would play a major role in location decisions, irrespective of economic differences.

327

One approach to the study of location decisions consisted of showing top executives of manufacturing plants in Michigan a long list of locational factors and asking them to identify those that would be most crucial in locating a plant such as theirs. In 1961 six factors each were rated as being of major importance by manufacturers accounting for 50 percent or more of employment in Michigan. They were, in order of frequency: labor costs, proximity to markets, availability of skilled labor, industrial climate, taxes, and proximity to raw materials. By and large, these are the cost and demand factors stressed by traditional location theory. The one nonpecuniary factor among the six top-ranking considerations was industrial climate, defined in the survey as "attitudes of the state and community toward industry."

The results of a second approach to the same problem were rather different. Executives of plants that had been opened in Michigan since 1940 were asked why this specific plant was located in Michigan. In this context noneconomic reasons were mentioned much more often. Executives of plants accounting for half of the employment in plants established in Michigan since 1940 reported that their plant was located in Michigan by historical accident or because of personal reasons—because the founder lived there, liked it there, or had valuable business connections there. Twenty percent (in some cases the same executives) said that they happened to find a good plant site in Michigan or that they had an attractive opportunity to buy a business in Michigan. The remaining responses related primarily to cost and demand factors, with proximity to customers receiving particularly frequent mention.

The same executives were asked to evaluate the relative importance of proximity to markets and materials on the one hand and "such things as good community relations, favorable industrial climate, good schools, or adequate recreation facilities" on the other hand. Then 26 percent of manufacturers maintained that these intangible matters were more important, another 12 percent that they were equally important, and 47 percent that they were less important than the economic considerations.

In a study of expansion plans, a very substantial proportion of respondents disclosed that the new installations would be made outside the state. This was particularly true of those whose attitudes toward a Michigan location were unfavorable.

In contrast, favorable general attitudes toward Michigan were closely associated with expansion plans in Michigan.

Similarly, in all three studies, plans to relocate were related to nonpecuniary opinions and attitudes. This was disclosed, for instance, by comparing plans and attitudes of executives of 229 manufacturing plants in Michigan with those of 57 in Ohio (1961 study) or of executives of 106 manufacturing plants in Detroit with those of 37 in Chicago and 29 in Atlanta, Georgia (1972 study). In 1972 the expression "quality of life" was introduced and described as

> satisfaction or dissatisfaction with things like education, recreation opportunities, personal safety, housing, neighborhoods, rather than strictly material measures of well-being.

To the question, whether the quality of life had become better or worse in the past ten years,

> in Detroit 21 percent said better and 69 percent worse,
> in Chicago 32 percent said better and 35 percent worse.
> in Atlanta 78 percent said better and 10 percent worse.

When asked whether the quality of life was better or worse in their own city than in another metropolitan area they were familiar with,

> in Detroit 8 percent said better and 23 percent worse,
> in Chicago 48 percent better and 5 percent worse,
> in Atlanta 95 percent better and 2 percent worse.

These opinions may be compared with the answers received to a question in which the executives were asked about the possibility of relocating their plant in a different geographical area during the next five years. Such relocation was called

> in Detroit very probable or probable by 28% and out of the question by 45%,
> in Chicago the percentages were 19 and 57, respectively,
> in Atlanta 15 and 68, respectively.
> (In these tabulations the percentages do not add to 100 because answers such as "Same," "Don't know," or "Hard to say" have been omitted.)

In sum, the location studies reveal that personal factors, the executives' notions and feelings about nonpecuniary trends, as well as their attitudes toward economic conditions, play a large role in location decisions.

Financial Decisions

The major financial decisions made by business firms must be characterized as deviations from established policy or the habitual course of action. Answers to questions about the form in which a business firm will keep its liquid reserves or the conditions under which, and the purposes for which, it will borrow money from banks were sought by asking firms what they had done in the past or what they customarily did. In everyday life problem-solving occurs but rarely and even the need for deliberating and solving a problem arises only infrequently. Similarly, in business life most of the time no problem is seen. But there are instances when the need does arise for reconsidering what one has always done. A study of financial decisions of business firms and of their relations with banks revealed numerous instances of the persistence of habitual behavior and a few instances of its discontinuation.[4]

Table 20-1 indicates that in 1955 about one out of four firms said they did not borrow from banks, partly as a matter of policy and partly because of having ample cash reserves. A somewhat larger group of executives said, in essence, that "short-term credit can be used only for short-term purposes." In general, accounting principles are held to establish inflexible rules; to finance inventories and accounts receivable is the function of bank credit, while plant and equipment are paid for either out of internal funds or by the issuance of bonds or stocks. Yet a sizable proportion of firms, and especially of large firms, acknowledged that they had occasionally financed, or that it was their regular practice to finance, capital expenditures by means of credit from banks. To do so represented a major decision, in contrast to the fairly automatic use of bank credit for working capital. For some firms the use of bank cred-

---

[4] See Katona (1957). This report is based on lengthy interviews conducted in 1955 with treasurers and other top financial officers of a representative sample of manufacturing and retailing firms in the United States—142 "middle-sized" firms with a net worth of 1 to 10 million dollars, and 95 "large" firms with a net worth of more than 10 million dollars—about their financial practices and attitudes toward banks.

it for capital expenditures was intended to be transitory, to be consolidated when long-term financing became possible. Other firms maintained, however, that they always chose the most available and most advantageous form of financing because "money mingles" or because the borrower is in a stronger position than the lender. (It should be noted that these opinions were expressed in the mid-1950s when easy money conditions prevailed.)

The studies about what executives of manufacturing and retailing firms thought of banks may best by summarized by the frequently voiced opinion, "Banks are people." Personal relations to banks are believed to be very important because the major function of banks is seen as giving advice. Different banks are thought to differ not in the performance of their financial functions, but in their ability to give good advice as well as in their willingness to identify themselves and collaborate with their customers. Changing the banking connections is considered a very difficult and highly visible decision. Therefore, and because of inertia, banking connections are rather stable, even in the rare cases when they are not fully satisfactory.

Group Belonging among Business Leaders

We may summarize the evidence presented in this chapter by pointing to the similarities of decision making in business and in other aspects of life. Customs, habits, rules of thumb, as well as personal relations play a great role in both. Whether or not careful deliberation and calculation are more frequent among business leaders than among consumers is hard to tell. In one respect, however, some differences were evident. Business leaders apparently know or think they know what other business leaders do and what their plans and expectations are. They are therefore in a position to shape their own actions according to the behavior of others in the same trade. In principle, the result may be to act differently from competitors; more usually, however, conformity prevails because it represents the simplest and easiest way to proceed.

The mass media reach consumers and business leaders alike. That prompt and fairly uniform information is now provided from coast to coast should presumably have a like

331

influence on both. But it might be argued that the latter also have access to additional and perhaps better information and may be more discriminating in evaluating the news they receive. On the other hand, it might seem that consumers, having incomplete knowledge of economic principles, might well become easy victims of news, rumors, propaganda, as well as manipulation, and might serve as carriers and transmitters of rumors. On the basis of these assumptions, one might expect that business leaders would not be easily swayed by others from their decisions made on the basis of solid knowledge, while the less wise mass of consumers could readily be shifted from one position to another and thus have an unsettling effect on the economy. In fact, our studies revealed practically the opposite to be true.

One significant difference between business leaders and the millions of middle and upper income consumers is that among the former there exist face-to-face groups, while the unorganized masses do not unite in cohesive consumer groups. A business manager frequently meets other business managers, exchanges information and hunches about the economy with them, and tends to form opinions through personal contact. Business groups are fairly cohesive units in which some pressure prevails toward uniform attitudes. Each consumer, of course, knows many other consumers but typically does not discuss economic or financial matters with them. Housewives may talk about sales or bargains with one another and may complain about high prices to one another, but discussions among consumers about the probable course of the economy are infrequent—except under the rare circumstances when radical changes occur or threaten. Even though attitudes tend to change in the same direction among millions of consumers, since they are all subject to similar information transmitted to them, the process of mutual reinforcement tends to be less pronounced with consumers than with business leaders.

Economists have long been aware of the interdependence of business sentiment. In analyzing business cycles, they have often used such expressions as "errors of optimism" and "errors of pessimism." Even though, the future being uncertain, one business leader may err in an optimistic and another in a pessimistic direction, economists have noted that usually the errors of forecast are all in the same direction, most businessmen being overcautious at certain times and overexuberant at

TABLE 20-1
Borrowing Practices Reported

	Middle-sized Firms	Large Firms
Borrow from banks		
for working capital only	44%	31%
also for capital expenditures	24	38
For purpose not ascertained	6	5
Do not borrow from banks	23	26
Total	100%	100%
Number of cases	142	95

Source: Katona (1957).

other times. Clusters of errors help explain cyclical fluctuations. If all businessmen acted in the same way, small causes might have explosive effects.

We have already illustrated an outcome of these considerations by pointing to the difficulties involved in conducting countercyclical investment policy. "What we expect others to do, we must do" was the explanation for his business policy given by a top industrialist in a highly competitive industry. Failing to follow the leader may lead to reducing one's share of the market. The judgment of one business executive, and even the result of his careful studies, are strongly reinforced by knowing that others have arrived at the same conclusion. To follow the leader may not imply collusion, but may result from belonging to the same group. It is apparently the most conservative and least risky policy. In fact, it tends to exaggerate cyclical fluctuations in that an upswing gives rise to optimistic and a downswing to pessimistic views among the executives of practically all firms. In contrast, the old-fashioned opinions of many consumers that "What has gone up must come down" or "Trees don't grow to heaven" operate in the direction of stabilizing economic trends. These early observations about the psychology of business leaders[5] were confirmed by findings in the 1970s: Hoarding and buying in advance of expected price increases were reported much more frequently among business firms than among consumers.

[5] See Katona (1960, Chapter 14).

333

PART VII
ECONOMY AND SOCIETY

21
ECONOMIC POLICY

Following the analysis of the behavior of consumers and business firms, we turn to the third actor on the economic scene, the government and its economic policy. The influence of government policy on economic developments differs of course from country to country and is much smaller in the United States than in most European countries. Nevertheless, the discussion of economic policy in this chapter will be based on American experience alone and will reflect primarily studies of reactions to measures of economic policy undertaken by the American government. When in the next chapter we extend the discussion to such broad problems of our society as people's attitudes toward the economic tasks of the government, there will be still greater need for international comparisons.

Which measures of economic policy are chosen and how and why policy is changed represent political decisions dependent on prevailing ideologies as well as on the power of various interest groups. That this has long been recognized is evidenced by the erstwhile name of the academic discipline, "political economy." We shall be concerned here not with the origins of economic policy, but with its impact and shall argue that in this respect psychological considerations have all too often been unjustifiably neglected. The success or failure of any such policy depends on the response it evokes among consumers and businessmen, and this response is greatly influenced by people's perceptions, attitudes, and expectations. Some of this was recognized during the Great Depression of the 1930s when the impact of governmental pump priming was nullified by reductions in expenditures on the part of the private sector. Unfortunately, the lesson seems not to have been learned.

The consequences of fiscal or monetary policy must be

337

characterized as neither immutable nor even entirely predictable. The causal chain between changes in taxes or interest rates and amounts of money spent, invested, or borrowed is not simple. Measures of economic policy must be viewed as stimuli to which people respond. Variables, we must repeat, such as past experiences, motives, attitudes, and expectations intervene between stimuli and responses and shape the manner in which the former are perceived and what the latter will be. It is important to remember in this connection too that psychological variables frequently operate in the same direction among millions of people. Because of the role of psychological factors a policy measure may be influential long before it is enacted, or even when it is simply proposed and not enacted, so that anticipatory responses must also be taken into account.

To be specific: A tax increase (or tax cut) may reduce (or increase) consumer expenditures far beyond the amount by which it alters disposable income if people view it as an indication of bad (or good) times to come. At the other extreme, fiscal policy may also have "perverse effects." A tax increase may actually stimulate expenditures if it is seen as a means of prolonging good times without excesses; or a tax cut may retard spending if it is viewed as a signal of an impending depression that people believe fiscal policy will be unable to prevent. Among other effects of fiscal policy, the possibility of the absence of any impact at all should not be overlooked because people are often in a position to disregard or discount whatever the government does.

The position taken here is not identical with the notion that a change in economic policy has two effects, one on financial matters and one on attitudes and sentiment (sometimes called the "announcement effect"). But one major conclusion remains the same irrespective of whether we speak of one joint effect or two separate effects: In either case, it is not permissible to restrict the study of the response to a measure of economic policy to an analysis of changes in the demand or supply of goods or money. The questions of whether or not a policy measure is considered significant, or is even noticed by masses of people, and whether it generates optimistic or pessimistic attitudes are not only of great importance in shaping the economic effects the measure will have but can also be determined long before the effects occur. We shall look therefore at findings about attitudinal as well as behavioral re-

338

sponses to different economic policies enacted in the United States in the recent past.

Fiscal Policy[1]

We have already discussed people's attitudes toward the tax cut of 1964 and the tax increase of 1968 while relating the economic history of those years (Chapter 7) and analyzing the learning process among masses of people (Chapter 13). Regarding President Kennedy's major initiative to reduce income tax rates in order to avoid the erosion of purchasing power that would result from the ever-larger tax bite as incomes went up, it may suffice to recall here that the initial response differed greatly from the later responses. During the first stages of discussing the tax cut proposal, in 1962 and most of 1963, there was no response at all in the form of either spending or saving more or less; most people were skeptical and thought the cut would not be enacted. Later in 1963 and early in 1964 there occurred an anticipatory response over a short period, in line with the intended response: Believing that the proposed law would help not only individual taxpayers but also the economy as a whole, many people increased their expenditures on durable goods purchased on the installment plan. For a few months following the receipt of benefits as the result of a reduction in tax withholdings, consumers were not stimulated to increase their expenditures, because many recipients found the actual amounts of tax gains to be disappointingly small. But a few months after the enactment of the reduction in income tax rates, there began a long period of steady increase in demand, brought about by optimistic attitudes resulting from substantial increases in wages and salaries as well as the tax gains. Optimistic views about economic prospects induced business firms as well as consumers to embark on a great variety of discretionary expenditures.

In 1964–65 both the benefits of the tax cut and the frequent and sizable increases in wages, salaries, and profits appear to have exerted an influence on consumer behavior. Since larger amounts were involved in the latter, their impact on spending

[1] See Katona and Mueller (1968) as well as the annual monographs, *Survey of Consumer Finances* issued 1960 through 1970.

was greater than that of the former. This conclusion, however, does not take into account the possibility that increases in wages, salaries, and profits may have reflected an impact of the tax cut and the consequent improvement in the business climate. Evidence that the tax cut, taken by itself, played a part in the increased rate of spending was supplied by the finding that families whose before-tax income remained unchanged, that is, those whose disposable income changed only because of the tax cut, stepped up their expenditures on durable goods when the gains from the tax cut had accumulated over several months.

Following the proposal to increase income taxes in 1966, the anticipatory response set in fairly early. The proposed increase was readily understood as detracting from economic prospects, even if each individual taxpayer were to be deprived of only a very small additional part of his income, so that his personal well-being would be little affected. The threat of a tax increase came at a time when more rapid price increases and rising interest rates (to be discussed later) were also exerting an adverse influence on attitudes about the economy. In 1966 consumer sentiment deteriorated steadily. The result was what has been called the mini-recession late in 1966 and early in 1967: a decline in consumers' discretionary expenditures, especially for automobiles and housing, without a general recession. During the following twelve months the prospect of a tax increase was no longer new. Habituation to the idea plus frequent and substantial increases in income earned largely nullified any anticipatory effect of the threatened tax increase on consumers' willingness to buy.

When in the summer of 1968 the income tax surcharge actually went into effect, it created no observable psychological impact that would have depressed consumers' discretionary spending. Again, the change in disposable income appeared insignificant to most recipients and for very many an increase in wages, salaries, or profits more than compensated for the reduction in take-home pay caused by the surcharge. The great majority of Americans in all walks of life said in the second half of 1968 that the surcharge made no difference in the amounts they either spent or saved. In the twelve months after the surcharge went into effect neither consumers' ability nor their willingness to buy was reduced as compared to the preceding twelve months. (Their ability to buy was of course lower than it would have been without the surcharge.)

On the whole, the 1960s constituted a period of optimism and confidence in which incomes—not only money incomes but also real incomes—were constantly advancing. Rising wages and salaries reinforce the intent of a tax cut and run counter to the intent of a tax increase, thus raising the chances of the former and lowering the chances of the latter to accomplish their respective purposes. However, this generalization may not be valid for a period such as the early 1970s, when rising incomes failed to keep pace with rising prices so that real incomes declined and people were receptive to unfavorable news.

Over a short period consumers' disposable income may be influenced not only by legislative but also be administrative measures. In 1972, for instance, employers were instructed to withhold larger proportions of income for taxes than before; therefore, substantial amounts of taxes had to be refunded the following spring. Surveys disclosed that in 1972 people in general were not aware of the increase in the amounts being withheld. Few people increased the number of exemptions they claimed (a remedy suggested by the government) and few expected to receive higher refunds the following year. Therefore the increased withholdings could not be construed as compulsory savings, which would have induced consumers to lower the rate of their voluntary savings in the expectation of refunds. The increased amounts of refunds in 1973 came as a welcome surprise to some, while many others failed to notice them as anything unusual. Those who were aware of unexpected sizable refunds either saved them or used them for unusual expenditures. On the whole, consumer behavior at that time depended on other news—improved economic trend in 1972 and accelerating inflation in the spring of 1973—and the tax changes in themselves had little influence.

Of course, it would have been possible to publicize the fact of the greater withholdings in 1972 and thereby influence the spending-saving behavior of many taxpayers. Similarly, it is possible to mount a psychological campaign in connection with a proposal to change taxes. Frequently, attempts to persuade consumers to act in a certain manner are derisively referred to as "jawboning" and are characterized as ineffective or even

341

dangerous in the sense that they may backfire. No doubt publicity alone, unaccompanied by any action, is hardly ever effective. But publicity attached to an action taken or proposed is a different matter. Attempts to make the people understand what the government plans to do or what it has been doing are frequently necessary and may substantially promote the desired effect of fiscal policy. Spreading knowledge and destroying stereotypes that are no longer applicable represent a legitimate part of economic policy.

Interest Rates

Changes in prevailing interest rates usually result from market forces—a rising or falling supply of, or demand for, funds—but government policy, including the policy of the Federal Reserve System, may either support or obstruct the trend of the market. There is, therefore, ample justification for discussing the response to sizable changes in interest rates as an important aspect of response to economic policy. Needless to say, the effects that rising interest rates have on borrowing must be distinguished from the effect of shortages or even of the unavailability of funds; the latter are often automatic and predictable. The effects of higher interest rates, repeatedly mentioned before, may be summarized as follows:

1. In the area of personal saving, in 1957, in 1966–1969, as well as in 1973–74 a very large proportion of savers were found to be fairly well informed about the increase in interest rates. As shown in Chapter 15, however, only a small proportion of large asset holders reported switching from one savings medium to another (for example, to certificates of deposit) because of interest rate differentials. A somewhat larger proportion reported placing new savings so as to earn the largest possible interest. Yet even leading questions failed to elicit answers that would have indicated that people were saving more, and thus spending less, because of the high interest rates. Pressures to make a variety of expenditures continued to be much more powerful than the attraction of high interest rates.

2. Consumer purchases of one-family houses for owner oc-

cupancy were restricted by rising interest rates. Among all forms of consumer behavior, this is the one where carefully calculated behavior is most frequently observed. Thus would-be home buyers are aware that an increase in the interest on their mortgage by one percentage point may raise the monthly cost of home ownership—the equivalent of rent—to a large and significant extent. When asked whether it was a good time to buy a house, repeatedly in the 1970s the majority of all respondents, and most would-be home buyers replied, "No, interest rates are too high."

3. Interest rates were found to exert hardly any influence at all on the purchases of cars and other durable goods on the installment plan. An increase in the cost of buying on the installment plan from, say, 14 to 16 percent per annum over a period of two or three years matters much less than an increase in the mortgage rate from 7 to 8 percent over twenty or thirty years. Most purchasers are concerned with the amount of their monthly payment, rather than with the cost of borrowing, and many see great advantages in installment buying irrespective of costs.

4. Regarding the effects of an increase in interest rates on business borrowing, it appears that the considerations that impel business firms to invest and therefore to borrow are usually so powerful that small changes in the cost of money are seldom decisive. Furthermore, in times of rising interest rates most business managers expressed the opinion that the rates would continue to rise in the future. Therefore, following an increase in interest rates some of them said that the time was appropriate to borrow for future needs. Such anticipatory action, which represents a "perverse response," was not observed among the general public.

5. News of rising interest rates was found to have an adverse effect on consumer sentiment. Many survey respondents said that since interest rates were business costs, higher rates would cause business to suffer or to raise prices and thus add to inflation. Rising interest rates frequently evoked or reinforced pessimism about the future of the economy.

Tightening the credit situation has been used or advocated

343

as an anti-inflationary measure in the belief that high interest rates lead to a lesser use of credit and thus to a reduction in the demand for goods and services. But the findings cited above indicate that neither business borrowing nor consumer installment buying is highly sensitive to changes in interest rates and that the impact of such changes on the rate of spending or personal saving is small at best. Thus several times during the postwar period the main impact of sharply rising interest rates was to stifle the construction industry or even to usher in a recession, rather than to slow down inflation.[2]

Changes in Money Supply

Monetary theorists postulate that an increase in the supply of money leads to increased consumer expenditures and a decrease in the supply of money to decreased expenditures. Both the theoretical arguments and past observations differ greatly regarding the length of the assumed time lag. As to the linkage between changes in the money supply and in consumer expenditures, scholars generally point either to stock prices or liquid asset holdings as being influenced by the money supply and, in turn, influencing personal wealth and therefore personal expenditures.[3] Changes in wealth do indeed occasionally alter consumer expenditures, but the impact has not been demonstrated as taking place consistently. A few words may suffice here because the major considerations that detract from a consistent impact on consumer expenditures of either the stock market or growing liquid asset holdings have already been presented in Chapters 15 and 16.

Regarding the impact of the stock market on total spending, we may recall (a) that the proportion of families with sizable stockholdings is very small and (b) that, in the opinion of many stockholders and most nonstockholders, what happens on the stock market is usually unrelated to what happens in the

[2] Particularly unfortunate was the psychological impact of very high interest rates in 1974 when in the opinion of most consumers a recession already prevailed at the time interest rates were advancing sharply. (We shall mention the 1974 developments briefly toward the end of Chapter 25.)

[3] See the volume issued by the Federal Reserve Bank of Boston (1971) and the book by Beryl W. Sprinkel (1971).

economy. No doubt, irrespective of these findings, substantial and enduring movements of stock prices do either facilitate or impede the raising of new capital and influence the feelings of many people. But the connection between stock market movements and either consumer expectations or consumer expenditures is much too tenuous to provide a reliable basis for economic policy. Both the attitudinal and the behavioral response may vary depending on circumstances, which is not surprising in view of the frequency with which ups and downs in stock prices have been known to follow one upon the other.

Consumer response to increased liquid asset holdings was discussed extensively in Chapter 15, where it was shown that most people attributed their financial assets to the fact that they themselves had saved in the past. On the one hand, what has been done in the past is often continued in the future. On the other hand, substantial liquid assets represent enabling conditions for spending and thus may provide a linkage between rising money supply and rising consumer expenditures. Because it is not known which influence will be the stronger one, the foundations of an impact of monetary policy on consumer expenditures appear to be much weaker than those of tax policy.

Price Control

A major task of economic policy is, of course, that of arresting inflation or at least lessening the damage caused by it. Since reduction of demand is the principal means of fighting inflation, the tools most commonly used are higher taxes and higher interest rates, which have already been amply discussed.

A third measure that has been used is the control of prices. In a very real sense price control is a psychological measure. This appears paradoxical because a regulation that prohibits price increases may be thought to operate automatically. But it was shown during World War II as well as during the 1970s, in this country as well as abroad, that price control works only if people cooperate with it. Governments are powerless and enforcement becomes impossible if the majority of people choose to disregard controls, even short of black markets taking over. People cooperate with price control only if they think it is

345

necessary and if they expect it to work. Therefore perceptions and attitudes are crucial determinants of its success or failure. Making sacrifices equitable represents a paramount function of all controls and a precondition for public approval of them.

Moreover, some major functions of price control are specifically psychological. The prohibition of price increases is intended to alter people's expectations. It should induce both businessmen and consumers to expect price stability, or at most a slight upward trend in prices, and to change their behavior accordingly. Price controls should thus prevent the distortion of supply and demand that occurs in an inflationary climate. When they expect rapid price increases businessmen and farmers may withhold goods from the market and thereby create artificial shortages. For the same reason, businessmen as well as consumers may stock up and hoard and thus augment demand. By restoring faith in prevailing prices price control should serve to avoid such developments.

This is hardly new. It was the thesis of a book the author published in 1942 under the title, *War without Inflation*. He wrote then that World War II might be the first great war without inflation if the government instituted suitable economic measures such as financing the war by taxes, if it made the sacrifices equitable through price and wage controls and rationing, and if it made use of patriotism to insure the cooperation of the people. The book also implied that inflation without war was possible, because after the end of the war in the absence of patriotic cooperation price controls would not work.

In the summer of 1971 when the Nixon administration surprised the world by introducing a price-and-wage freeze, conditions were favorable for controls even though the end of the Vietnam War was not in sight. A few months earlier surveys showed that the American people were critical of the government for doing nothing to stop what were considered unjustified price increases. In September, 1971, more than three out of four respondents said that the price-wage freeze was "a good thing" and the proportion approving the government's economic policies increased greatly.

But the favorable attitudes toward controls wore off in time. First, wage control was found by many to be harmful and inequitable. Then, the absence of uniformity in the application of price controls was noticed and criticized. Most importantly, an ever-increasing majority of the people doubted that the gov-

346

ernment would succeed in stopping inflation, and the expectation of success represents a major condition for compliance with controls.

A first requirement of price control has seldom been spelled out because it would seem to be obvious: The price controller should have faith in the controls he administers! But in 1972 and especially in 1973 the American people were told that the President and his top advisers were opposed to controls and intended to abolish them as soon as possible—at which time they expected prices to go up. In addition, price controls did not extend to many very important goods, such as farm products and crude oil, nor to exports and imports. Under these circumstances the chances of price controls working were nil. Thus an important tool against inflation was discredited.

The prediction of things to come represents one of the ways government, and big business as well, may and often do attempt to influence public opinion. For instance, General Motors and Ford used to publish very optimistic forecasts about expected automobile sales in order to convince would-be buyers that the new automobile models would be successful and therefore good products. The government's economic experts often lean toward optimistic views in their forecasts of economic trends in order to strengthen people's confidence (and to indicate that they, the experts, are doing their job well). Forecasts of price stability, or of very small price increases, may have a function in conjunction with price control and may be viewed as a rather innocent device of persuasion. These forecasts may serve to contradict the doomsday predictions all too frequently voiced by social critics, journalists and, alas, even by government officials themselves.[4]

It is the task of the government not just to make economic policy but also to explain it so that it becomes intelligible to

---

[4] In August 1973, the Secretary of the Treasury announced that the public should expect "astounding increases in prices." This remarkable statement on the part of an official in charge of slowing down price increases represents the most extreme example of negating the functions of psychological factors in influencing economic trends. This conclusion would be justified even if the Secretary of the Treasury had made a factually correct prediction. It is of little importance to add for the record that in the fall of 1973 price increases were less rapid than a few months earlier (or several months later as the result of the oil embargo, obviously not anticipated by the Secretary).

347

millions of people. Because what people think influences their response to government actions, every effort should be made to induce them to reflect upon the problem, to understand the government's proposed solution as being in their best interest, and so to provide willing cooperation.

22
ATTITUDES TOWARD THE GOVERNMENT

Public response to specific measures of governmental economic policy depends not only on the manner in which they are understood, but also on attitudes toward the role of the government in economic affairs. How people view these tasks of the government is a function of traditions, sociocultural norms, and ideologies. One may therefore expect such views to be long lasting and fairly stable; this has been found true in some instances, but not in others. In this chapter we shall discuss the opinions and attitudes of the American people about major economic functions of the government. The three belief systems to be discussed have prevailed fairly uniformly among many segments of the population throughout the approximately thirty years of our research studies. The first, however, changed substantially in the early 1970s, while changes in the second and third have been minor and gradual.

1. *Power of the government over the economy.* The belief prevailing among most Americans that the government was very powerful in economic matters was first observed shortly after World War II, although it no doubt prevailed during the war as well. It was strengthened in the 1950s and early 1960s but weakened in the late 1960s. In the early 1970s trust in the ability of the government to remedy economic evils collapsed.

2. *Approval of government spending.* Most of the domestic fiscal programs involving large government expenditures are approved by the great majority of Americans. Only a few programs, and particularly those which are thought to be badly managed, are opposed. In the 1970s, as ten years earlier, people on the whole were inclined to support further increases in government spending.

3. *Acceptance of taxes.* Most people feel that deficits, large government debt, and high taxes are undesirable. But knowl-

edge about these matters is limited and opinions are not strongly held. Over the years there has developed some habituation to deficits and to large debt. In contrast to often noted adverse attitudes toward local taxes, very many people express willingness to pay higher federal taxes to finance government programs of which they approve.

On the Government's Power

We begin by reproducing the summary of observations made in the early 1960s:

Whenever unfavorable developments in the economy are discussed, the American people speak of the responsibilities of the government. The remedies for unemployment, recession, or inflation are to be found, in the opinion of most people, in the government's "doing something." People in all walks of life, including the majority of top-income people, agree that the government has the power to influence the economy.

We earlier reported the conviction shared by most Americans that a depression such as we had in the 1930s could not happen again. Lesser fluctuations, however, and even frequently recurring recessions, were considered probable. The main reason for these notions was found in the belief that the government has it in its power to avert a depression but does not seem to know how to cope with recessions or how to create full employment. Our surveys revealed only a few people who understood how "automatic stabilizers" function or who were aware that taxes took a larger bite from income and profits in prosperous times than in times of recession. Yet many people had the feeling, with which experts might well agree, that the character of the postwar business cycle differed from that of the prewar cycle (specifically, from what had prevailed in the 1930s).

Many people believe that the government can bring about good times if and when it really puts itself to the task. Reactions to the election of new Presidents in 1952 and 1960 provided insights into these attitudes. The election of General Eisenhower made for optimism in the business

350

outlook. When asked whether the election had any significance for business prospects, most people replied that there would be an upturn. Their arguments differed. Some opponents of the new President said the new government was a business government; it was the function of such a government to bring about good times, and it would certainly do so. Some supporters of the new President argued that business confidence would improve under the new administration, and this would do the trick.

Fundamentally similar were people's reactions eight years later. The election of Kennedy to the presidency was greeted by friend and foe alike with the notion that times would improve, and the impending recession would soon be overcome. Some people, to be sure, spoke of temporary improvement due, in their opinion, to inexcusable government spending; others praised the end of a period of government inaction. In either event the reactions indicated many people's belief that it was in the government's power to do something about economic activity.

Surveys conducted shortly after the end of the recessions of 1958 and 1961 yielded similar conclusions. People who in October 1958 or in June 1961 were aware that recovery had begun—a substantial minority at both times —attributed the turn to government action. Respondents were asked whether in their opinion the federal government had done a good job, a fair job, or a poor job in dealing with the problems of recession and unemployment. Only about one in five, in representative samples, said at both dates that they did not know. In October 1958, 23 percent of all people and 21 percent of high-income people thought that the government had done a poor job or had not done enough; in June 1961, 11 percent of all and 14 percent of high-income people expressed these same negative opinions. At both dates, then, the majority agreed that the government had done a good job or a fair job in bringing the recession to an end. Criticism of the government's anti-recession policies was quite rare, even among its political opponents.

It should be noted, however, that the finding gave no indication of identification by the people with the government. In talking of prospective actions by the new President, it was he who was expected to do something to help us or to

351

help the economy. In discussing the recessions of 1958 or 1961, most people spoke of the impersonal government which should act for the benefit of the economy.[1]

This is the end of the story of the high regard of the American people for the government as it was written in the early 1960s. Survey findings obtained in 1974 about trust in the government or approval of its economic policy were very different. The erosion of confidence extended far beyond attitudes toward the economic functions of the government. As we reported in Chapter 19, in the early 1970s, in sharp contrast to earlier years, attitudes toward all institutions—private business as well as professions, the judiciary, the Congress, as well as the presidency—reflected little respect or confidence. Mistrust began to develop in the late 1960s when the spread of violence, racial conflict, and urban decay generated societal discontent (to be discussed in Chapter 24). The recession and the inflation of the early 1970s were of course responsible for the finding that in 1973 three out of four Americans judged the government unable to cope with inflation and the majority thought it unable to deal with unemployment. Then came Watergate. The frequent references to Watergate made in surveys conducted on economic topics indicate that the 1974 findings shown in Table 22-1 were influenced by those revelations.[2]

In Table 22-1 we reproduce data obtained in September, 1971, shortly after the introduction of the price-wage freeze, when attitudes toward the effectiveness of government in the control of inflation and unemployment were as favorable as in 1958, but much less favorable than any time in the early 1960s. In contrast, in February, 1974, a very small proportion of Americans used the adjective "good" in speaking of the government's economic policies. The usually preferred middle position—"only fair"—was likewise rejected by the majority. The table also indicates that upper-income people evaluated the

[1] These six paragraphs are taken from Chapter 15 of Katona (1964a).
[2] An *Index of Trust in Government*, constructed by the Center for Political Studies of The University of Michigan from five survey questions (unrelated to economic matters), stood at 50 percent in 1958, 45 percent in 1964, 25 percent in 1968, 3 percent in 1972, and minus 30 percent late in 1973. The minus figure means that negative evaluations and expressions of distrust were given more frequently than positive evaluations or expressions of trust.

TABLE 22-1
Opinions about the Government's Economic Policy

In regard to inflation or unemployment, the government is doing:	All Families		Families with Over $12,500 Income	
	Sept. 1971	Feb. 1974	Sept. 1971	Feb. 1974
A good job	26%	6%	29%	4%
Only fair	44	41	39	37
A poor job	21	49	27	56
Don't know; not ascertained	9	4	5	3
Total	100%	100%	100%	100%

The question was: "As to the economic policy of the government—I mean steps taken in regard to inflation or unemployment—would you say the government is doing a good job, only fair, or a poor job?"

government's economic policies even less favorably than other people.

It is perhaps worthwhile to note that regarding the power of the government to steer and direct the economy, the opinions of the majority of the American people have been in good agreement with the likewise greatly changing opinions of experts. In 1946, influenced by the effectiveness of economic policy during World War II, the Congress enacted a law that charged federal authorities with the task of insuring full employment. At that time the common man approved of the new law and thought that it was possible to accomplish its intent. When in the 1960s, following years of hesitant activity and limited success, economic policymakers became ambitious and introduced a variety of new measures, the people learned to accept even the term "fine tuning" for what was believed that economic policy might accomplish. In the 1970s, however, the public as well as scholars realized that the effectiveness of government policy in combating either inflation or recession was subject to severe limitations.

Indications of Spending-Mindedness

The past twenty-five years have witnessed a continuous expansion of domestic government expenditures, which have

353

spread to more and more types of activity. Increases in government spending represent an alternative to decreases in taxes as a means of providing funds to the economy—or more correctly, a tax cut is a relatively new and rarely used alternative to an increase in government expenditures, the traditional form of pump priming. Having described in the last chapter public attitudes toward a tax cut, and also a tax increase, we shall now analyze attitudes toward the government's major expenditure programs.

In the case of tax cuts or increases, the people are in a position to take direct action, depending on their attitudes, either to reinforce or to nullify the intended purpose. In the case of government expenditures, however, they can exert only an indirect influence by voting for public officials who are either economy-minded or spending-minded.

By means of survey research it has been possible to determine people's preferences among government fiscal programs. These preferences should, of course, not be seen as mandates that should ipso facto be enacted into legislation. Although in some instances the opinions about spending programs were stable and based on good arguments, in some other instances many people appeared confused and opinions changed over fairly short periods on bases that were one-sided and emotional. Thus changes in public opinion may or may not be enduring, and there is justification for decisions to be made by experts and chosen representatives. At the same time there are good reasons why experts and officials should keep themselves informed by means of survey research of the people's opinions, attitudes, and desires. Knowing which opinions are enduring and soundly based and which stem from shifting emotions may help them in making decisions.

Studies of public attitudes toward fiscal programs were conducted by the Survey Research Center of The University of Michigan in 1961, 1969, and 1973.[3] The methods used in these three studies were quite similar. Although some changes were made in the wording of the questions asked, major findings of the three studies are comparable. Replication of studies is most

[3] On the 1961 studies, see Mueller (1963b); also Katona (1964a, Chapter 15). Regarding the 1969 and 1973 studies, see *1969 Survey of Consumer Finances*, Chapter 15, and Curtin and Cowan (1974). The 1973 study was conducted prior to most Watergate revelations.

helpful because the absence of change in opinions over time tends to confirm the unchanged opinions, and the presence of change provides clues to the nature of changing opinions.

Interviewers in these surveys began by telling the respondents, "The government spends money on a variety of things. I want to ask briefly about some areas of government spending." Then a card listing many programs (11 in 1973) was handed to respondents and regarding each program they were asked, "Do you think the government should be spending more money, less money, or about the same amount on . . . as it does now?" Table 22-2 presents the answers obtained to this type of inquiry in 1961, 1969, and 1973. Relatively frequent answers that the government should spend "the same amount," as well as infrequent answers of "Don't know" or "Can't say" are omitted from the table.

It appears that in 1961 the public favored increased federal spending for seven programs and reduced spending for three. In 1969 increased spending was advocated for five programs, reduced spending for four. (For one program the same proportion said "more" as said "less.") In 1973 increased spending was favored for seven and reduced spending for four programs.

In all these years there appears to have been little opposition to several programs: The proportions supporting increased spending for pollution control, education, as well as hospitals and medical care were substantial in all surveys. Equally substantial proportions advocated reduced spending on foreign aid and space exploration in the three surveys, with the exception of the latter in 1961. Overwhelmingly, spending-mindedness prevailed and indications of economy-mindedness or of concern with large federal expenditures were infrequent. Even for federal programs on which expenditures have increased greatly over the last decade, such as education and medical care, the majority of people favored still further increases.

We find substantially the same distribution of responses with respect to spending on education, low-income housing, and foreign aid in all three surveys and the same distribution with respect to expenditures on hospitals and medical care in 1961 and 1973. (This question was not asked in 1969.) The response to expenditures for reducing pollution and for space exploration was quite similar in 1969 and 1973. Opinions about expenditures on highway construction slowly became less supportive from one survey to the next.

355

TABLE 22-2
Public Attitudes toward Fiscal Programs
(Percentage distribution of answers in 1961, 1969, and 1973*)

	Government Should Spend						More even if taxes have to be raised**
Programs	More	Less	More	Less	More	Less	
	1961		1969		1973		1973
Reducing Pollution	N. A.		64	8	69	8	54
Education	60	7	62	9	57	8	46
Hospitals and Medical Care	54	9	N. A.		57	7	45
Low-income Public Housing	55	9	52	15	49	18	34
Highway Construction	36	10	36	15	32	21	22
Mass Transportation for Cities	N. A.		N. A.		47	15	29
Support for Agriculture	20	26	30	30	38	22	26
Foreign Aid	7	53	4	73	3	74	N. A.
Space Exploration	26	32	8	58	9	64	8
	(Help needy)						
Welfare Payments	60	7	36	29	23	49	17
	(Help old)						
	70	23	(Vietnam war)				
			7	69			
Defense	47	6			15	39	10
			(Other defense)				
			13	35			

The question was: "Do you think the government should be spending more money, less money, or about the same amount on . . . as it does now?" The sequence in which the programs were presented is not the one used in this table. The description of two programs differed somewhat in 1961 and 1969 as indicated by the words in parentheses.

*Do not add to 100 because "Same" and "Don't know" answers are omitted. For instance, in 1973, 23 percent gave these answers when asked about reducing pollution.

* *This column presents the answers obtained to a second question, cited later in the text.

N.A. = Not asked.

But public attitudes toward defense expenditures and welfare payments changed significantly over the twelve years studied. In 1961 an increase in expenditures on defense was advocated by 47 percent and a decrease by only 6 percent. By 1969 military expenditures, especially for the Vietnam War, became highly unpopular and remained so in 1973. At that time 15 percent favored an increase and 39 percent a decrease in defense expenditures.

Attitudes became more and more opposed to welfare payments over the years. Exact data are not available for 1961, but the great majorities advocating spending more to help the old and needy make it probable that in that year a question about welfare payments would have resulted in more favorable replies than in 1969. In 1969 the proponents of increasing welfare expenditures outnumbered by only 7 percentage points the proponents of decreasing them. In 1973 the latter were more than twice as frequent as the former.

In order to clarify the attitudes expressed, in 1973 detailed inquiries were made regarding several government programs. It was found that the attitudes toward programs that were supported by great majorities were simple and, in the respondents' minds, noncontroversial.[4] On the other hand, attitudes toward defense and welfare expenditures were found to be rather diverse, with many people citing arguments both pro and con. Apparently in these two areas the American people are aware of conflicts that are far from resolved. The lack of consistency in people's answers makes it probable that these opinions will change in the future.

The reason most frequently given in favor of reduced government expenditures for defense was the desire that the funds be used for other purposes. But when those people who favored spending less were asked about any disadvantages of such a policy they frequently spoke of the necessity of being "prepared" and of the need for security. Regarding welfare payments, respondents explained their opinion that less should be spent by speaking often of the need for improving the welfare system so that people who were not deserving could not take advantage and would be encouraged or even forced to work. Even though in 1973 many more favored a reduction rather than an increase in welfare expenditures, it was easy to formulate a question that evoked the response from most people that at least certain welfare expenditures should be increased.

---

[4] For instance, the most frequently mentioned reason for spending more government money on medical care was that medical costs were too high for individuals to pay. When asked whether the government should help to alleviate financial hardship caused by very long and expensive illnesses, not fewer than 88 percent of respondents answered in the affirmative in 1973.

When asked whether payments to people who were not able to work should be raised, kept the same, or reduced, 70 percent said "Raised," 21 percent "Kept as they are now," and only 1 percent "Reduced."

Acceptance of Taxes

The survey findings reported thus far might perhaps be dismissed as a popularity contest in which a vote for a popular program was expressed by saying "Spend more" and a vote for an unpopular program by saying "Spend less." In order to find out whether respondents had or had not given some thought to the fiscal consequences of increased expenditures, in 1973 they were asked at the end of the inquiry: "You said the government should spend more money on. . . . If your taxes had to be raised to pay for the additional expenditures for . . ., would you still favor an increase in spending for this item?" The question was repeated with respect to each program.[5]

The results of this inquiry are shown in the last column of Table 22-2. A comparison of this column with the data under "More" in 1973 indicates that a sizable number of respondents revised their opinions in response to the second inquiry. But 60 to 90 percent of respondents who had originally favored spending more stuck to their first answer, even at the price of being willing to pay higher taxes.

The survey thus reveals, contrary to expectations, a rather low degree of sensitivity toward taxes. This is confirmed by several other findings. The question about whether there were disadvantages to increasing expenditures for certain programs provided ample opportunity for the respondents to refer to taxes. And yet opposition to increased spending was most frequently justified by reasons other than taxes. Also, when asked about possible advantages of spending less on defense, 7 percent mentioned taxes (avoiding a tax increase, etc.) while 30 percent said that the government could use the money to better advantage elsewhere.

At the end of the 1973 survey respondents were asked a summary question about their preference either for the

[5] A similar procedure was used in 1961 as well with similar results, although there were some differences in wording.

358

government's doing more at the price of raising taxes or for avoiding higher taxes under all circumstances. The wording of the question was: "Some people say that the government should be doing more in some areas of activity even if it means higher taxes for everybody. Other people are against raising taxes, whatever the reason. What do you think?" In reply,

50% favored increased government activity and higher taxes,

40% were against raising taxes even for the sake of deserving programs.

10% said they did not know or would not take a position.

To be sure, a substantial proportion qualified their answers and argued that taxes should be raised only if an expenditure was really necessary. Many others singled out specific programs for which in their opinion a tax increase would be justified if no other financing were possible. Thus, willingness to pay higher taxes appears to be related to opinions about the merits of the government's spending programs.

Needless to say, the question of the relationship between attitudes toward specific expenditures and taxes is far too complicated to be studied by means of brief surveys. No doubt, the answer of a survey respondent that he would be willing to pay higher taxes to enable the government to increase its expenditures for education does not mean that the same person would vote for higher local school taxes at the next election (in which different local issues might be involved). But the survey responses do illustrate the extent of support for government spending. It is also true in the area of taxes as in other economic areas that what has prevailed for a long time rarely gives rise to complaints or opposition. Although the American people do grumble about taxes, especially when filing their tax reports each spring, and are opposed to tax privileges, no indications of a tax revolt were observed in the 1960s and 1970s.

In a similar vein it must be noted that the idea that preferences for spending programs depend exclusively or mainly on self-interest was not confirmed. True, the proportion who favored increased welfare expenditure was larger among low-income than among high-income people and among blacks than among whites. But on the whole, the higher the education and the income of a respondent, the more acceptable were both large expenditures for a variety of programs and an increase in

359

taxes for financing those programs. Since the widespread distrust of the government in 1973 has already been reported, it is worth citing here that early in that year, in reply to the specific question, 65 percent of those with a college education and 39 percent of those with only a grade school education expressed themselves in favor of an increase both in government activity and in taxes. Among those under 35 years of age the proportion in favor was 57 percent as compared with 32 percent among those over 65 years old, and among those with more than $12,500 income it was likewise 57 percent compared with 39 percent among those with less than $5,000 income.

Turning to attitudes about deficits, we found in response to direct questions that people generally condemned them. The great majority could see no difference between government budgets and personal or business budgets. Prudent people are supposed to balance receipts and expenditures by adjusting the latter to the former. Relatively few people realize that the government, when spending increases or must be increased, may also use the reverse procedure, namely, to increase revenues either by raising tax rates or increasing the tax base. Deficits are accepted by most Americans only when there is an emergency. The resulting debt is viewed as a burden that must be repaid sooner or later.

At the same time information about the extent of actual deficits was found to be scanty. In 1973, for instance, when federal deficits were substantial, 55 percent of a representative sample indicated some awareness that the government was operating with a deficit while 9 percent said there was no deficit and 36 percent said they didn't know. In 1961 the proportion of incorrect answers was much larger. Although most people answered in the affirmative when asked if they were concerned about the government's deficits, replies to other questions did not confirm the presence of any great concern. When in the late 1960s respondents were asked what should be done with money saved through a reduction in some expenditures—for instance, if military spending were to decline as a result of an end to the war in Vietnam—many more people said that the money should be spent for other worthwhile purposes than that it should be used to eliminate the deficit or reduce taxes.

Most people express hesitant opinions rather than firm convictions about taxes and deficits. Therefore changes in opinions may be forthcoming in line with the greatly changing views about the government's power over the economy, which we described earlier. The one attitude that has remained stable over many years is the spending-mindedness of the American people. Americans are in favor of large expenditures by the government as well as by themselves.

It is possible to minimize the differences between American and Western European attitudes toward the economic functions of the government by pointing to changes in American attitudes during the last several decades as well as to legislation enacted in those years in the United States (large increases in social security taxes and payments, broadening of public welfare, Medicare, and Medicaid). In the early 1970s American public opinion even favored governmental assistance for the medical expenditures of the entire population, a proposition that, a few years earlier, was attacked as representing socialized medicine. On the other hand, it should not be forgotten that in Europe social legislation not only began much earlier than in America but it also continued to increase in scope and spread to new areas in several countries during the post-World War II era.[6] No doubt, there has been a narrowing of the differences in the attitudes of the people on the two sides of the Atlantic. Nevertheless, fundamental differences are apparent regarding the meaning and importance attributed to planning and regarding what is seen as the responsibility of the government in the United States and in much of Europe. The American acceptance of large governmental spending for an ever-growing number of programs, and of governmental action against unemployment or inflation, in no way reflects approval of central planning.

[6] See Andrew Shonfield (1965), who describes the changing balance of public and private power in Europe.

361

23
"ARTIFICIALLY-CREATED WANTS"

We have thus far presented our analysis of the present-day consumer economy without reference to different opinions and evaluations as they have been expounded by some social critics. Our presentation would be incomplete, however, were we not to consider some of the arguments of others who have found fault with the consumer economy.

Social criticism is useful and may even be necessary. Although this author has emphasized the beneficial aspects of the consumer economy—a much higher standard of living for masses of people and economic upturns stimulated by the arousal of new wants among optimistic people—critics have every justification for pointing to excesses and waste associated with consumer behavior. Is the consumer economy, as it has developed during the last few decades, good or bad? There is no simple answer to such a question of values. Acknowledging both its beneficial and its detrimental aspects, we nonetheless feel it necessary to contradict those who present only a negative view of recent trends in consumer behavior and their impact on society.

The discussion of problems raised by social critics will occupy us for three chapters. The present chapter will be devoted primarily to the ideas of John Kenneth Galbraith about private wants having been artificially created. The next two chapters will reflect our concern with two important popular catchwords in today's social science, the "quality of life" and the "limits to growth." While GNP and material standards of life have advanced substantially in the post-World War II decades, the extent of happiness and the rate of subjective satisfactions have not. This observation will be related in Chapter 24 to the discrepancy between personal-financial aspirations and societal discontent. The threat of the exhaustion of natural re-

363

sources and the damage caused by pollution have contributed to widespread disillusionment in and condemnation of growth. In Chapter 25 the psychological meaning of limitations of the growth process will be explored.

The Penalty of Affluence

Rarely are new developments, whether social or economic, greeted with rejoicing. With every change, however desirable it may be, there are those who yearn for the "good old days." Traditionally, prophets of doom find a wide audience in times of prosperity. Thus, with the spread of discretionary purchasing power in the United States, affluence was first recognized, not by those who welcomed it as a unique accomplishment of our times and our country, but by social critics who deplored it. In popular books, for instance by Vance Packard (1960), what Galbraith (1958) has called the affluent society became an overabundant society; the wealth of consumer goods was equated, not with the high American standard of living, but with gadgetry and waste.

The first argument we shall consider is that our present-day consumer society constitutes a betrayal of the American Revolution. Arnold J. Toynbee calls the Revolution glorious because "It staked out human rights and staked them out for all men." After thus setting forth this magnificent achievement of the United States in the history of mankind, Toynbee continues:

> Though I am a foreigner, I can tell you what was not one of the aims of the American Revolution. It was not its aim to provide the people of the Thirteen Colonies with the maximum amount of consumer goods per head. . . . It [affluence] has sidetracked America from the main line of her own revolution (1962, p. 150).

There is little question that the great men of 1776 were concerned with matters other than consumer goods. But must we believe that the ideals they staked out were intended to be rigid and fixed for all time?

364

Human rights and political freedom, constitutional guarantees and independence—these were the goals of the first struggle. Then came the struggle for social justice. Finally—and the word *finally* reflects our own myopia since there is no end to the fight—came the struggle for economic democracy. In our early history it was conceivable that equal justice for all might have been provided even if productive facilities were controlled by a few rich people who alone reaped profits and lived abundantly. For the millions of immigrants of the second half of the nineteenth century, freedom from persecution and oppression was its own reward, justifying even the drudgery and poverty of life in the mines and mills of America. Wages remained low and working hours long while a few captains of railroad and industry amassed huge fortunes and the Newport set lived in luxury surpassing that of Europe's aristocracy. But the American frontier provided a livelihood to many, and the success of a few second-generation immigrants sufficed to create the dream of unlimited economic opportunities in a classless society.

The American dream was dreamed long befor it was realized. Until World War II the middle-class bourgeoisie improved their standard of living to a similar extent in Europe and in America. Yet the new middle class shared only some of the amenities available to the rich; money for discretionary expenditures beyond the necessities of life remained in the hands of the few. More important still, the middle class itself was small; the broad masses of the population were still struggling to satisfy subsistence needs.

Although some of its aspects appeared earlier, it was only after World War II that the first great mass consumption society came into existence in the United States. In this instance, the advent of a new kind of society preceded the concept of it even as an ideal. The majority of Americans were freely making discretionary purchases before they realized that they were living in a new era. Central in that era was the belief that economic equality might be approximated by raising the living standards of the masses through means other than by appropriating the wealth of the rich. Europeans soon recognized that the high American standard of living differed radically from the way of life of their own upper classes. The latter—which American millionaires of an earlier era had taken over from

365

their European counterparts—was a life of country estates and many servants, lavish parties, and jewelry and art collections. The former, by contrast, was seen as the standard of the average people, which permitted them to concern themselves no longer with averting hunger but with the amenities of life —cars and washing machines, vacations and savings accounts.

The great change in ideals cannot be better described than in the words of Toynbee himself. Unbelievably, the following passage contains no reference to America. And Toynbee's discussion of America's having abandoned its old leadership contains no reference to the following:

> For the first time since the dawn of civilization about five thousand years ago, the masses have now become alive to the possibility that their traditional way of life might be changed for the better and that this change might be brought about by their own action (1962, p. 40).

Just as surely as America pointed the way to human rights for all in 1776, so did she show the way to material well-being for all in the mid-twentieth century.

Toynbee argues that there is a "penalty of affluence." Affluence cuts people off from the common lot; it insulates the rich minority from the poor majority. There is truth in the observation that the rich are rarely loved. Those who have what others desire or envy are seldom popular. It does not follow, however, that Americans would win more popularity contests or would be better liked by allies and neutrals if they were poor. Toynbee seriously advises America to give up her affluence. We should stop spending, says he, on "unwanted consumer goods" (we shall shortly return to this phrase) and rather devote that money to "meeting the basic and pressing needs of the majority of our fellow human beings." The intention may be good, but the advice is bad, not only because it is not feasible, but primarily because it is based on fallacious economic principles. A redistribution of existing resources is not the solution to worldwide needs. Taking away from the rich to give to the poor has never provided the long-term help needed. The solution to mass poverty is not cutting the pie into different-size slices, but rather exerting every effort to increasing the size of the pie. Growth of resources provides the best hope for the poor.

Unwanted Consumer Goods

Toynbee maintains that America by renouncing her affluence would not really make any sacrifice, because that affluence is, in any event, doomed to perish. What he calls unwanted demand, in excess of genuine wants, is easy to give up since, as he puts it, "We have merely to stop listening to Madison Avenue" (1962, p. 145). He is not alone in believing that our economy is saturated and that it cannot long flourish because the artificial creation of demand for goods not really needed or wanted cannot endure.

We turn to the more sophisticated argument of Galbraith. Like most economists, Galbraith recognizes the error in the belief that there are rigid limits to human needs and wants. But he asserts that "If the individual's wants are to be urgent, they must originate with himself. They cannot be urgent if they must be contrived for him" (1958, p. 152). A brief reminder of the age-old discussion of innate versus acquired behavior may suffice to cast doubt on any notion that economic wants arise spontaneously. Our innate or inherited capabilities, needs, and personality traits are modified by experience. Economic behavior is learned behavior and it develops and changes with experience. This is true even of our most basic needs: Habits of eating and drinking, toilet training, and the like are impressed upon us in early childhood. Sociocultural norms as well as personal experience fashion our behavior. All wants originate both from the person and from his environment; in the present context the distinction between the two is irrelevant.

Before turning to the major problem of wants being "contrived," we may briefly mention that Galbraith links the creation of wants to the creation of debt and warns of the dangers of the growth of consumer credit. His thesis as presented in *The Affluent Society* was once aptly expressed in the late 1950s as: "We are buying goods we do not need with money we do not have." In reply it may suffice to remind the reader of the survey findings (Chapter 17) about the overall beneficial effects of consumer credit on the lives of the consumers—who are helped by installment buying to improve their standard of living at an earlier age than would be otherwise possible—as well as on the economy as a whole.

From his assertion that many of our wants are contrived for us, Galbraith is led to the following major conclusion: "One cannot defend production as satisfying wants if that production creates the wants." According to him, modern advertising and salesmanship have given the American economy a new direction, which he deplores. Nobody attributes greater power to Madison Avenue than its critics. Serious spokesmen of the advertising industry do argue that advertising has contributed to an increase in consumer demand and a change in its composition, but they would hardly dare to credit themselves with being as successful as Galbraith, Toynbee, and Packard claim they are. Let us look first at the assertion that advertising shapes consumer attitudes and "brings into being wants that previously did not exist" (Galbraith, 1958, p. 155).

The Influence of Advertising

One function of advertising is to transmit information. The consumer is provided the means of finding out what products are available on the marketplace. New products are not invented, manufactured, and promoted because the consumer has expressed a desire for them, as witness the automobile, the TV set, and innumerable smaller innovations of lesser importance. The consumer must, therefore, be informed of the existence of new products, of the purposes they serve, as well as of their prices.

This is hardly controversial. Providing information is not what is usually meant by influencing the consumer. The problem becomes more complicated when we consider persuasion and the changing of people's tastes, opinions, and beliefs as possible functions of advertising. Advertising does attempt to persuade prospective buyers, and the constant repetition of brand names and the virtues of specific brands does sometimes take the form of unreasoned appeals. The rule relating to the success of such endeavors is simple: The influence of advertising decreases in proportion to the importance the consumer attaches to whatever is advertised. This follows from the presence of genuine decision making in important matters but can be illustrated even without reference to the psychological principles involved.[1]

[1] For an excellent analysis of the vast literature on what has been called the "mass society," see Bauer and Bauer (1960). The authors cite evidence that the alleged omnipotence of the mass media is a myth and conclude

Surveys have revealed that most Americans hold that the various leading brands of gasoline do not differ from one another in any significant way; this is true even of those who regularly buy one particular brand. Matters connected with the gas station and the people operating it, for example, convenient location, good service, and personality of the serviceman, are primarily responsible for establishing a habit of purchasing at one station and, therefore, of using one kind of gasoline. In the face of such consumer indifference, advertising is important for the seller. The brand name must constantly be kept in the public eye, just because it does not matter to people whether they buy one brand or another. Similar situations prevail, for some people though not necessarily for all, regarding brands of toothpaste, orange juice, and many other products. We let ourselves be reminded and even persuaded because the decision is of no great importance.

Since beliefs and attitudes usually concern important matters, changing behavior is often easier than changing attitudes. But there are certain major forms of behavior that are based on our beliefs and attitudes. In important situations the American consumer is sensible and critical rather than foolish and gullible.

If modern psychology has proved anything, it is that changing other human beings, and especially changing them without personal contact, is a very difficult task. Frequently, husband and wife learn to share each other's tastes and opinions. This may be due to purposive selection (people with similar tastes and opinions marry), as well as to a slow process of change resulting from close contact over many years. Personal interaction and intercommunication also occur at places of work; employees learn to share the attitudes of their colleagues, and sometimes even of their superiors.

Groups to which we belong—trade associations, labor unions, professional societies, and others—exert an influence on us, because we specifically seek the group's influence in joining it, or because group belonging makes for a selection of the communications that reach us. Democrats, for example, tend

that "mass media of communications exercise a distinctive advantage in inverse proportion to the importance of the issues involved" (p. 24). They also suggest that a change in attitudes is more difficult to achieve than a change in behavior.

369

to listen to Democratic campaign speeches; and Republicans, to Republican campaign speeches. In addition, over a long period of time group belonging may result in genuine social learning, that is, in the acquisition of the new beliefs, attitudes, and wants that prevail in the group.

In view of the strong resistance of people to changing their tastes and convictions, it becomes clear that changing the multitude of consumers, through advertising, concerning matters that are important cannot happen frequently. Social influence, which is effective, rarely comes from the outside or from above. We are influenced by the group to which we belong, that is, by a horizontal rather than a vertical process (Katz and Lazarsfeld, 1955).

There is some information available about consumer reactions to advertising (see Bauer and Grayser, 1958). Relatively few people appear to be irritated by advertising or hostile to it. Only rarely does one find either pronounced liking or disliking of advertising. More often people seem to be weary of it, and very often simply indifferent. Millions of people have become adept at discounting advertising claims and some have even developed an ability to disregard advertisements—for instance, to close not only their eyes but also their ears while waiting for the resumption of the interrupted TV program.

Many things are wrong with advertising. First of all, there may be good reason to argue that there is too much of it. Then some advertising involves a waste of money by the seller and a waste of time for the listener or viewer. There may be reason to complain about the form of many advertisements—too much hard sell and exaggeration—which is seldom as sophisticated as would be appropriate in view of the rising educational level of the American people. Advertising may contribute to conformity and may make the development of individual life styles difficult. Most importantly, truthful advertising and full disclosure of all information relevant to the consumer are required but not always provided. However, there is little justification for condemning advertising on the ground that it has changed the consumers or that it has opened the way for control of the consumer by industry.[2]

---

[2] The question may be raised under these circumstances about the value of advertising, either for the advertiser or for the consumer. The following answers may be given to that question:

1. Advertising has an important information function, for instance,

The Management and Control of Consumers

In a second important book, *The New Industrial State*, Galbraith's starting point is very close to our own position. He writes: "High production and income . . . remove a very substantial part of the population from the compulsions and pressures of physical want" (1967, p. 4). From this starting point, however, we have argued that higher incomes for masses of people allow them to exercise discretion in their behavior as consumers. We have maintained that when incomes cover more than subsistence needs, consumers are free to gratify their desires and aspirations, to regulate the timing of their purchases, in short, to be in control of their own actions.

Galbraith, on the other hand, contends that in the absence of physical want consumers' "economic behavior becomes in some measure malleable. . . . Along with prices and costs, consumer demand becomes subject to management" (1967, pp. 4-5).[3] Thus, as opposed to our proposition that affluence makes for discretion in action, Galbraith concludes that "affluence opens the way for control over the consumer."

According to traditional theory, Galbraith states, all power lies with the consumer: "The flow of instruction is in one direction—from the individual to the market to the producer" (p. 211). This "accepted sequence," he continues, must give way to the "revised sequence" in which "the producing firm reaches forward to control its markets and on beyond to . . . shape the social attitudes of those, ostensibly, that it serves" (p. 212).

---

about what is available, what new products or services are offered, as well as about prices. Advertising of prices is particularly important in an inflationary age.

2. Advertising keeps the name of a firm or a brand in the public eye. Advertised products are often seen as "good" products, manufactured by firms with high reputations.

3. Advertising has a function in persuading consumers, especially, as said before, when the choice is not highly relevant to the consumer. Persuasion is a two-way process, from business to consumers, as well as from consumers to business. A firm that stopped advertising would suffer in comparison with other firms that continued to do so.

[3] See also: "The further a man is removed from physical need the more open he is to persuasion—or management—as to what he buys. This is, perhaps, the most important consequence for economics of increasing affluence" (Galbraith, 1967, p. 202).

Yet communication and learning are characterized by interaction. Although we learn from experience with others —from the teacher, from information received by word of mouth and the printed page, or radio and television, and also from advertisements—it is we who do the learning. Conditioning and stamping-in are limiting cases of learning that are most applicable to a situation in which we are not involved (when the choice does not matter) and least applicable to changing social attitudes. The unidirectional form of Galbraith's "revised sequence" represents an exception as does the "accepted sequence." Both sequences negate consumers' discretion and contradict psychological principles of learning (except under circumstances of servitude or compulsion).

The success of producers in influencing their specific product's share in the market, or in insuring the penetration of their brands, is hardly a matter of great importance to the total economy. The extent to which business may be able to manage or regulate aggregate demand is, however, of great significance—and in this respect the record of the effectiveness of big business and advertising is far from good. To mention a conspicuous failure of some of our largest corporations: The automobile industry, which cannot store large inventories of its bulky product, exerts great effort backed by extensive advertising campaigns in an attempt to stabilize, at a high or preferably rising level, the demand for new cars. Yet year after year the industry is surprised by large fluctuations in demand, which necessitate overtime operations followed by layoffs and which are apparently beyond the influence of the industry.

In 1973–1974 the auto industry acted just as Galbraith thinks large corporations always act. It instituted an advertising campaign in order to persuade consumers to purchase large cars (the so-called "full-size cars"), which it desired to sell, rather than small cars, which an increasing number of people desired to buy.[4] This time again the industry found itself unable to shape consumer tastes and preferences.

[4] Surveys showed that the preferences of many people turned away from large cars long before gasoline economy became the major argument in favor of smaller cars. The latter were desired as second cars, for short-distance commuting and for easy parking. For large families and long vacation trips, large cars were preferred. Since cars are seen as a necessity, most people tend to economize with respect to the basic purchase price while they spend more freely on optional "extras," including such expensive items as car air conditioning.

Much of the effort of large corporations goes into finding out in what direction the consumer is moving or what may be acceptable to him. Rather than changing consumer preferences, the results of marketing research are then used to change the decisions of business command in line with consumers' incipient wants. The success of growth industries in enlarging the demand for their products over many years may be better explained by their success in anticipating the direction of consumer demand than by their changing or controlling the consumers.

Persuasion in itself is neither good nor bad. The principal question concerns not even whether the object of persuasion is good or bad but whether those who are to be persuaded have any choice; or more precisely, whether they are in a position to resist. Studies of advertising effectiveness indicate, as has been so often pointed out in this book in other connections, that consumers are not marionettes. No doubt, the consumer's choice is restricted by what is offered to him, and the two-way flow of the learning process involves some management. But restricted choice is not the same as absence of choice. Persuasion goes both from the consumer to business and from business to the consumer. Which is more powerful varies from case to case, with consumers developing an increasing ability to discount advertising claims.

Private Opulence and Public Poverty

The most serious argument against the mass consumption society contends that the consumer exercises his influence in a socially undesirable manner. It is Galbraith's accomplishment to have presented this argument to the American public most convincingly. We do not have enough schools and spend far too little on education; we do not have enough hospitals and spend far too little on the health of our people; there are too many slums that breed delinquency and crime; scarcity prevails in the entire domain of public expenditures, such as highways, parks, and recreation facilities. Such realities represent Fact No. 1. Fact No. 2 is the affluence in the private sector of the economy, the extent to which we are endowed with consumer goods. Galbraith argues that there is a causal connection between the two facts: It is because of Fact No. 2 that we are

373

suffering from Fact No. 1. To reestablish the social balance, he would have us change the allocation of our resources. He would have us cut down on consumer expenditures in order to increase public investments.

Again the argument goes far beyond economics and concerns human values. Social critics deplore our preoccupation with material goods, our gadget-mindedness, and our wastefulness on the ground that they detract from the true goals of man, which are spiritual. In the phrase of Toynbee: "The true end of Man is *not* to possess the maximum amount of consumer goods" (1962, p. 144).

The philosophic and historical basis of the argument is complex, and its roots are not always consistent. To some extent the argument stems from the longing for the proverbial "good old days," which are recalled as having been peaceful and quiet, while modern life is thought to be anxiety-ridden. Puritan notions about the dangers of self-indulgence also play a role. It has been said, in every era, that wealth blunts incentives and makes people soft. Historically the decline of civilizations has often been associated with the acquisition of material goods.

It may be argued that criticism of the American society as being materialistic and money-minded was more justified toward the end of the nineteenth century than it is today. Luxurious living by the rich was no doubt more conspicuous at that time. The esteem of cultural values by a small elite, as it prevailed in earlier times, does no more to stimulate the arts than does the participation of millions of people in cultural activities. The romantic notion that poverty, hardship, or deprivation facilitate the development of great artists is surely false.

The praise of frugality and austerity and the condemnation of extravagance and self-indulgence are part of our religious, philosophic, and artistic tradition. They also conform to generally accepted economic beliefs. Thus, if business investment represents the only source of enduring wealth, as economists have assumed, and if resources are scarce and cannot be expanded, future-oriented activities can be carried out only at the expense of present need-gratification. Consumption must give way if we are to build for the future. Should the present generation consume at too great a rate, it is assumed that the next generation will be deprived of its due. Workers who toil hard and efficiently at low wages are considered to be building for

374

the future of the country. Contrariwise, large-scale consumption expenditures are believed to result in a slow rate of growth of productive facilities. This argument obviously disregards the possibility that some consumer expenditures represent enduring investments and stimulate the economy in the same way as does business investment.

In a certain sense the belief that the public sector of our economy has been neglected is quite surprising. In the years of affluence since World War II, the share of the gross national product spent by the government has been higher than ever before. Yet in most years a larger part of government expenditures has been used for the military than for health, education, slum clearance, and the like. Even this rise in military expenditures stands as proof that consumers, in their role of taxpayers, acquiesce in being deprived of a large share of their earnings to allow the government to use that share. The argument that public poverty is due to huge military expenditures would be more justified than the argument that it is due to private consumption. Were it not for the cold war, the Korean War, and the Vietnam War, America could have and doubtless would have spent much more in such areas as education, low-income housing, and health than it actually did.

The greatly increased cost of welfare expenditures is likewise borne by the affluent customer. Old-age insurance, unemployment insurance, and Medicare represent collective arrangements, all of which support the argument that the mass consumption economy is not devoid of social conscience. Increased governmental expenditures, both for the military and for social welfare, have been financed through progressive taxation that has greatly reduced the private spending of the middle- and upper-income groups. The condemnation of affluence would stand on better grounds if, during the last few decades, the distribution of income had become less egalitarian. Nevertheless, we cannot but agree with Galbraith that we are faced with what we have called Fact No. 1. There is indeed too much pollution of our air and water and too little housing for the poor, for example, and an increase in outlays for curing these and other social ills is of prime importance.

The area of disagreement concerns the question of how to remedy the situation. A redistribution of our present national resources is neither the only way nor even a desirable way of achieving the goal. In fact, such redistribution would have lit-

375

tle chance of being successful. Any attempt to cut down on consumer spending for the sake of increasing public expenditures might easily plunge the economy into stagnation or recession. As we shall argue again in Chapter 25, even maintaining current levels of consumer living standards would not suffice to do the job. It is precisely the wanting and striving for improvement in private living standards that forms the solid basis of American prosperity. Only if prospects of further gains in the so-called private opulence are maintained can we hope to overcome public poverty. The question is not one or the other; it is both or none.

* * *

Having begun this chapter with comments on writings of a great historian (Toynbee) and having devoted much of the chapter to an analysis of the position taken by a great economist (Galbraith), we conclude with a short reference to the adaptation of Galbraithean ideas by a great psychoanalyst. Erich Fromm, one of the leading neo-Freudians, begins his book, *The Revolution of Hope*, with a familiar complaint: "We as human beings have no aim except producing and consuming more and more" (1968, p. 1). This is what he calls the "most ominous aspect at present." He blames the "completely mechanized society," directed by computers, for having transformed man into Homo Consumens, "whose only aim is to *have* more and *use* more" (p. 28). He fails to recognize the discretion and choice available to the modern consumer and calls him passive and constantly in need of new stimuli.

Fromm offers us a way to escape the "hopelessness' characterizing Homo Consumens. He distinguishes between "harmful consumption" and "humanistic consumption," which "serves man's growth and joy" (p. 120). The advice of experts and enlightened public opinion, together with legal restrictions on advertising, should, Fromm argues, be able to redirect production as well as consumption. Again, it must be asked whether or not Fromm overestimates the extent to which human wants can be manipulated. Moreover, there is a question about the price that would have to be paid for changing consumption in terms of freedom sacrificed and incentives given up.

No doubt, there is harmful consumption—even beyond certain drugs and other hazards to health. But the arguments presented up to now do not indicate that an increase in the

376

goods and services demanded by consumers is in itself harmful. Moreover, the remedies for harmful consumption must come from the consumer himself, rather than being imposed on him. We shall continue in the next two chapters with the discussion of potential drawbacks of the consumer economy and how they may be overcome.

24
QUALITY OF LIFE, SOCIETAL DISCONTENT, AND CONSUMERISM

As recently as the 1950s the determination of GNP was considered a major achievement of social significance. When the Gross National Product, the sum total of the value of all goods produced in a country, is known for several successive periods, it becomes evident whether the economy is growing rapidly or slowly or not at all. Rapid growth of GNP was accepted as the goal which, when achieved, would result in better nutrition, better housing, better health, more education, and more leisure.

By the late 1960s it had become commonplace to state that growth might be damaging and that increase in GNP was far from identical with the greater happiness or even the greater well-being of the people. The highly refined statistical and economic concepts and methods, standardized and accepted all over the world, which yielded the GNP data were criticized as giving a distorted picture. It was therefore proposed that in addition to measuring the value of "goods," we should also calculate the value of "bads"—to use a picturesque expression of Kenneth Boulding. Or, as such leading economists as Paul Samuelson and James Tobin have advocated, the total output should be figured without including "negative externalities" or undesirable goods, which concepts were extended to encompass repairs of flood and fire damage as well as military products.[1]

Noneconomists demanded that a second comprehensive set of data be made available in addition to GNP. Many social scientists advocated that the government should prepare and publish at regular intervals not only an Economic Report, but

---

[1] From the extensive recent literature on the shortcomings of GNP, we cite the papers by Nordhaus and Tobin (1972) and Juster (1970).

379

also a Social Report. The latter should contain social indicators that would provide data on changes in the quality of life.

Certain aspects of the request for comprehensive social indicators and the ensuing extensive research endeavors are relevant for our purposes. Both economic and social indicators may be either objective or subjective.[2] As has been shown in this book, measures of GNP exclude economic indicators of a subjective nature, primarily data on change in the attitudes and expectations of consumers and businessmen. Even such basic economic information as the rate of increase in aggregate personal income must be supplemented by microdata indicating the distribution of the income change and the proportion of people who are and expect to be better or worse off. Similarly, objective social indicators must be supplemented by subjective indicators. Objective social indicators are collected on changes in the incidence of crime and violence, the number of physicians or hospital beds per capita, the educational achievement of different groups of the population—to enumerate just a small number of measures relating to different domains of life. But it is hardly possible to find a common denominator for these and a variety of other measures—relating, for instance, to family life or government expenditures for health, welfare, and research—and thus create one social indicator competing with GNP, the economic indicator.

As for the need for subjective data on the quality of life, it may suffice to ask whether an increase in the number of teachers or physicians insures an improvement in education or health, in order to point out that objective data represent just the beginning of an attempt to construct social indicators. While attempts to measure improvement in education would remain controversial in any case, a more modest endeavor promises to be successful, namely, the collection of information on greater or lesser public satisfaction with education or educational opportunities. Such satisfaction—like information we reported in earlier chapters about consumers' satisfaction with their standard of living or savings—is susceptible to measurement. People's satisfaction with various aspects of their life is not only indicative of the quality of life as seen and

---

[2] On objective social indicators, see Moore and Sheldon (1968) and U.S. Department of Health, Education and Welfare (1968). On subjective social indicators, see Campbell and Converse (1972).

felt by those concerned, but is also related to their subsequent actions. Yet the relation of the extent of satisfaction to its antecedents as well as its consequences is far from simple.

Satisfactions and Dissatisfactions

Satisfaction with a product, for instance, a car or a restaurant meal, depends not only on the quality of the product, but also on what the person whose satisfaction is studied expects from the product. Satisfaction with income or standard of living is likewise affected by the person's expectations and aspirations in addition to what actually has happened to him. The relation between the rate of satisfaction and behavior is also rather complex. The presence of satisfaction or of increased satisfaction may mean that a person has achieved what he wanted and therefore feels that he can sit back and enjoy what he has. Alternatively, as discussed earlier in connection with rising aspirations (Chapter 10), increased satisfaction may indicate that a person has made progress and therefore knows that he can advance. Then he raises his sights and strives for more. Two results of dissatisfaction must also be recognized. A dissatisfied person may try hard to improve his situation or, if he feels disappointed and frustrated, he may resign himself to his unsatisfactory situation.

It follows that measures of satisfaction and dissatisfaction alone do not suffice. Gurr (1970) introduced the concept of relative deprivation as the perceived discrepancy between the conditions of life to which people believe they are rightfully entitled and the conditions they are capable of attaining. Strumpel found that two additional measures must be collected, which may help greatly in clarifying the meaning of findings about satisfactions: data on people's expectations and on their rate of self-efficacy or fate control.[3] The following tentative generalizations have emerged from Strumpel's research, in which he has compared the economic satisfactions, expectations, and

---

[3] A person is thought to control his fate when he believes that he is able to change some aspect of his life, plan ahead, and carry out his plans. The data presented in Chapter 12 on many people believing that they themselves were responsible for increases in their income are related to fate control. A further concept, which Strumpel has used, is perceived fairness or equity. See Strumpel (1973a, 1973b, and 1974).

aspirations of different population groups (blue-collar and white-collar workers, blacks and whites, and so on): If aspirations exceed perceived accomplishments, dissatisfaction will lead to goal reduction provided expectations and the rate of fate control are low. If expectations and the rate of fate control are high, dissatisfaction and high aspirations may prevail together and result in behavior designed to eliminate the one and fulfill the other.

For most forms of satisfaction as well as for aspirations, data are available over short periods only. In the early 1970s, in contrast to the increase in GNP, economic satisfactions did not increase. Nevertheless, they were more common than economic dissatisfactions and gave no indication of a radical change.

The available data on satisfactions and aspirations indicate that the rigid separation of social from economic indicators is inappropriate. Subjective indicators are of crucial importance not only for an understanding of economic trends, but also for information on change in the quality of life. According to data on satisfactions collected by the Survey Research Center with respect to approximately 70 different aspects of life, satisfaction with the standard of living is highly correlated with a substantial number of satisfactions in other areas and, in fact, deserves to be put in the center of a correlation matrix including mostly satisfactions with noneconomic developments.

Measures of the subjective well-being of large population groups as determined in survey research are required because they can be shown to influence not only spending-saving behavior, but also attitudes toward social issues, or, as Strumpel has called it, the extent of societal discontent. The conceptual schema of Strumpel is more complex than the one with which this author began in the late 1940s, when he distinguished (a) stimuli or precipitating circumstances, (b) the organism or intervening variables, and (c) response or action. As shown in Chart 24-1, the antecedents of subjective well-being are presented in a manner similar to Kurt Lewin's well-know formulation of $B = f(P,E)$: Behavior is a function of both the Person and the Environment. It is assumed that the extent of subjective well-being influences not only behavior, but also people's response to the system, including the government.

According to Strumpel's model the two outcomes, SD, Societal Discontent or, more generally, attitudes toward the

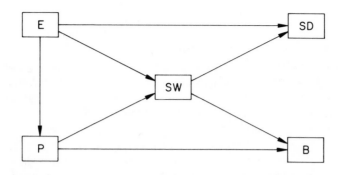

E: Objective environment   SD: Societal discontent

real income per capita
standard of living
assets, debts

dissatisfaction with:
prices
employment
government policies
political system

P: Person   B: Behavior

goals / aspirations
preferred life styles
notions about equity
self-efficacy, fate control

consumption demand
saving
working
occupational choice
education
retirement

SW: Subjective well-being

satisfaction with income,
savings, standard of living
economic attitudes and
expectations
sense of opportunities

CHART 24-1.   Conceptual Model of Burkhard Strumpel.

government and society, and B, spending-saving Behavior,
may develop in divergent directions. This was found to be true
in the early 1970s. We may recall the discussion of two measures in earlier chapters. The BB measure revealed a substantial proportion of people saying that they were better off than
five years earlier and also that they expected to be better off
five years later. On the other hand, five-year business expectations showed a sizable deterioration in the late 1960s and prac-

383

tically no improvement in the year of recovery, 1972. We showed in Chapters 10 and 12 that the belief in personal financial progress that characterizes the BB Group is associated with extensive demand for large consumer goods —frequent intentions to purchase durables, especially on the installment plan, and the arousal of new wants following gratification of older wants. The belief in personal financial progress extended to young families in the labor force. Yet, in the early 1970s, the great majority of Americans, including very many in the BB Group, expressed pessimistic expectations about economic trends during the next several years. This second belief system appears to be related to the more cautious opinions held about recent changes in and prospects for the quality of life.

The two variables constructed by dividing the sample into (a) those in the BB Group and the NonBB Group, and (b) those with optimistic or pessimistic expectations about business trends during the next five years were cross-tabulated with data on expressed satisfactions. In 1972, satisfaction with the following variables showed high association with optimistic opinions about five-year business conditions and low association with optimism about personal financial progress:

Conditions of the natural environment
The way police and courts were operating
The way local government was operating
The way national government was operating
The way political leaders were thinking and acting.

On the other hand, satisfaction with the following variables was found to be more highly associated with optimism regarding personal financial attitudes than regarding business expectations:

Standard of living
Family income
Own job
Personal health
Personal accomplishments.

It appears, then, that pessimistic expectations about economic trends have their origin in economic as well as in social beliefs. Inflation has been the most powerful economic factor, but recession, unemployment, and even high interest rates have also contributed to widespread disillusionment. In addition, the deterioration of long-range business expectations could partly be attributed to lack of trust in the government and its ability to remedy economic and social evils. Finally, as replies of survey respondents to a question about their reasons for having pessimistic business expectations indicated, racial problems, the persistence of poverty among a minority, widespread violence (and riots in the late 1960s) have all contributed to dissatisfactions and discontent.

Consumerism

Among the variety of dissatisfactions that constitute societal discontent, one must be discussed at some length in a book that deals extensively with consumer behavior. There are ample indications, even though few precise data are available, that in the early 1970s American consumers were more dissatisfied with the quality of goods and services available to them than in earlier times. Increased dissatisfaction and a growing number of complaints about poor quality and poor service may have originated in either of two developments: in a worsening of workmanship, lesser durability, and similar objective factors, or in consumers' expecting more from the goods and services than before. It cannot be doubted that concern with the quality of consumer goods and expectations about them has grown. Consumers are no longer content to blame themselves for not having been more careful when they acquire something faulty. In view of the impersonality of buyer-seller relations and the complexity of many products and services purchased, redress has become increasingly difficult. At the same time, consumers came to believe that they are entitled to satisfactory quality and to remedies when they don't get it. These attitudes may have resulted both from consumers' awareness of their great purchasing power and from the consumerism movement. The latter brought forth widespread publicity about poor quality, unsafe products, and deceptive advertising. It remains a question to what extent consumer discontent may have been caused by the actual deterioration in the quality of goods or services and to what extent it may have been the function of consumers' higher expectations. Lesser pride in workmanship and frequent absence of quality control in the process of mass

385

production point in the direction of quality deterioration. But an estimation of the true economic value of a consumer product is hardly possible because it would have to include calculations of the benefits derived from the product during its lifetime, minus the costs involved (including repair costs). Therefore, in this instance, subjective data alone must be relied upon.

Dissatisfaction grows when people see not only the need for but also the possibility of improvement. The latter appears to be the historic function of consumerism, which caught on very rapidly because consumers were ready to seek remedies for unsatisfactory goods or services. Consumerism is the result of rising expectations about better product performance, more product reliability, better service, and more complete and truthful information. The movement attempts to overcome the earlier feeling of powerlessness among consumers.[4]

Consumerism has therefore been defined as "the organized efforts of consumers seeking redress, restitution and remedy for dissatisfaction they have accumulated in the acquisition of their standard of living."[5] The beginning of the movement may be set with the publication of Ralph Nader's first book, *Unsafe at Any Speed*, in 1965. Within a few years the literature of consumerism filled several large bookshelves, and the federal government as well as most states and large cities set up commissions to assist consumers.

In the past the consumer has been ill-served, writes Scott Maynes (1972b, p. 270), and in his opinion "the culprit is consumer information." No doubt, information available to the average consumer is insufficient to enable him to make a fully intelligent choice in a variety of important decisions. For instance, in buying life insurance or in borrowing money the purchaser or borrower is confronted with a great variety of

---

[4] E. Scott Maynes (1972a) speaks of the microimpotence of consumers in contrast to their macropower—the latter expression referring to a major topic of this book and expressed in the title of the author's 1960 book, *The Powerful Consumer*. Whether or not economic conditions will be good or bad next year, as we have argued before, frequently depends on the consumer rather than on business or government. This is a reflection of power exercised by the consumer sector but not by any individual consumer. The individual consumer's inability to do anything when he feels "cheated" represents consumer impotence.

[5] Buskirk and Rothe (1970, p. 62).

prices and qualities that make it difficult or even impossible for him to evaluate the advantages and disadvantages of the services offered. Even discriminating buyers may therefore follow the advice of a salesman, or purchase securities according to the suggestion of a broker, without taking the time and effort needed to study the matter carefully. In everyday shopping, for instance in supermarkets, the buyers often fail to or are unable to study the differences in quantity, quality, and price of the products displayed. They proceed by purchasing what they have bought before or by choosing widely advertised brands that have become well known to them. Therefore, entry into the market by new products, even with distinct advantages in price or quality, has become difficult. Moreover, consumer deception has become relatively easy.

Under these circumstances it has become clear that the consumer needs assistance and even protection, and some progress has been made in this respect. In various countries private agencies have been organized to test consumer products and publish guidelines on prices and quality (e.g., *Consumer Reports* published by Consumers Union in the U.S., and *Which* in England). Government agencies have been set up to test dangers associated with the use of certain food and drug products, or to make it possible for the consumer to seek redress when he feels cheated. Laws intended to make products safer have been passed in various countries.

Obviously, consumers cannot have everything; various advantages and disadvantages must be balanced against each other. A failure-proof product may be of great value, but even if technically possible it may involve initial costs that would be prohibitive. The same is true of extended warranty or complete avoidance of pollution.

Repeated careful surveys of consumer satisfactions and grievances may help to determine the issues most salient to most consumers. Action by government regulatory agencies should of course be vigorously pursued when matters of health or outright deceit of consumers are involved. In addition, the consumerism movement and information on consumers' dissatisfactions may bring about a voluntary improvement of the quality of goods and services by business firms. Firms, when aware of many consumers being greatly interested in certain aspects of product quality, may try harder than before to remedy defects in order to stimulate demand for their products.

387

The principal traditional remedy, competition among sellers, remains very important.

Dissatisfaction with the quality of consumer goods hardly represents a basic change. It contributes to increased societal discontent, but not to a revolt against material values. Disillusionment may have grown in the early 1970s with doubts about the quality of life increasing, but there was little reason to speak of the beginning of a new era of pessimism and distrust.

The main reason for this conclusion rests in the persistence of the belief in personal financial progress. As indicated by the continued large proportion of American people falling in what we have called the BB Group, high personal expectations and aspirations conflict with the prevailing social discontent. It is doubtful that the conflict must be resolved soon at all costs. For, contrary to some theoretical views, dissonance can often be tolerated over long periods. In 1973—the year of the most rapid inflation, of Watergate, and of the oil crisis—many observers thought that the resolution of the conflict in belief systems would inevitably take the form of pessimistic views winning out over optimistic ones. Yet the influence of one-time events in overcoming long-ingrained attitudes should not be overestimated. How people's attitudes will develop is difficult to predict. But, in the opinion of some experts, further growth of the economy has become impossible irrespective of people's wishes and desires because of the limitation of natural resources. We turn to this argument in the next chapter.

25
GROWTH AND PROGRESS

The first twenty-five years following the end of World War II witnessed an unprecedented growth of the American economy. Yet in the early 1970s it was argued that the "economics of more" neither would nor could any longer persist. There were those who thought they discerned a radical change in American life styles and concluded that the American people and especially younger people were no longer interested in acquiring more and more consumer goods or even in improving their financial situation. There were others who concluded that, even without a change in people's wishes and desires, the depletion of our natural resources together with the increasing pollution of air and water would make it necessary to limit growth.[1]

The argument that optimistic expectations about rising living standards have come to an end has, of course, been refuted in earlier chapters (see especially Chapter 12) where it has been shown that in the early 1970s the American people, and especially younger people,[2] did not say "No" to the consumer economy. Surveys produced no evidence of Americans having reduced their consumption aspirations. Having continued to be optimistic about the trend in their income and in their standard of living over the next several years, their wants for consumer goods and services remained substantial.

It may be argued, however, that changes in life styles reflecting an opposition to the consumer economy are in the

---

[1] See, for instance, Reich (1970) and Slater (1971) on radical changes in life styles; Meadows et al. (1972) on limits to growth.

[2] As noted in Chapter 12, the expression "younger people" applies to those in their twenties who are married and/or have entered the labor force. The Survey Research Center samples exclude other younger people (teenagers, students, drifters, etc.) so that no findings are available about them.

offing and will be visible only in future surveys. Therefore, it is relevant to note that substantial changes in life styles are nothing new. Several such changes have occurred or have begun in the last few decades and are still progressing. The most important of these, which we shall review forthwith, have strengthened rather than weakened the consumer economy.

Changes in Life Styles

Among recent changes in life styles, we may note first the trend toward smaller families and the change in sexual norms as well as in the role of women. The very substantial change in the labor participation of women in the United States is a case in point. As recently as 1940 in America, and in other highly developed countries still today, most women had jobs only before they married; the top labor participation of women was reached in their early twenties, at which age about half of all women were working, while in older age groups labor participation fell off sharply. But by 1970 in the United States the curve depicting the proportion of women with paid jobs in different age groups had two peaks—the second one in the age group 45 to 54. In 1970, both at that age and in their early twenties, 55 percent of all women had jobs. This development occurred in practically all income groups except among the very rich. In other words, shortly after marriage, when they have small children, many women leave their jobs but return to work when their children reach school age.[3]

Why did millions of women 40 years of age or older, many with husbands earning an above-average income, return to work? Survey data revealed a variety of pecuniary and nonpecuniary motives. Money, or more correctly, what money could buy[4] and the desire for higher living standards played a large role in the complex motivational patterns, as did interest

[3] See Katona et al. (1971, Chapter 10) for an extensive discussion of this development and its comparison with Western European trends. See also *Monthly Labor Review*, June, 1970. In 1971 the Survey Research Center found 37 percent of all married white women working full time or part time in outside jobs as against 24 percent in 1951.

[4] To quote the answers of just two women to the survey question of why they took jobs after not having worked for many years: "To make it possible for my children to go to college" and "Money is more important than whatever it is that comes next in importance."

390

in activities or desire for self-fulfillment and for participation and prestige. The surveys indicated that the life styles and the goals of families with two wage earners changed, with the desire for progress and advancement, both in careers and in living standards, becoming more rather than less important.

Galbraith speaks of the "servant-wife" and asserts that "The servant role of women is crucial for the expansion of consumption in the modern economy" (1973, p. 33). This assertion is hardly compatible with the fact that in the 1950s and 1960s the acquisition of a very great number of consumer goods coincided with a sharp increase in the number of women working outside the home.[5]

Among further changes in life styles that have had an effect on consumption has been the trend in recent decades toward more casual living. This trend has greatly influenced consumers' buying behavior and reduced the sales of the clothing industry all over the world. Related to this trend, and even more relevant in bringing about new life styles, is the increased importance attached to leisure-time pursuits that has emerged since World War II. Leisure, viewed as one of the good things of life, has come to be identified with activity and with doing a great variety of enjoyable things, rather than with rest or doing nothing.

Most activities we cherish after work, on weekends, and during vacations have one predominant characteristic: they are expensive. American families need a car, and often two cars, to go picnicking or to reach their boat or cabin at a lake or in the hills. Weekends and vacations are satisfactory only if one is on the move and eats out. The expected further growth of the recreation industry may bring about changes in the distribution of consumer expenditures but will hardly reduce them. Our present leisure-oriented society is not devoid of striving for progress and growth. In evaluating the economic impact of leisure-time activities, we must consider not only the large number of goods and services they call for but also the fact that people are stimulated to exert greater effort to acquire the income needed to partake in the desired activities.

Many of our leisure-time expenditures are for services rather than goods. Since the late 1940s there has been an increase in

[5] Galbraith is, of course, correct when he says that "Without women to administer it, the possibility of increasing consumption would be sharply circumscribed" (1973, p. 37).

391

the proportion of income spent on services and a decrease in the proportion spent on goods. The American society has even been called a service society. To some extent, to be sure, the growing proportion of expenditures on services is a statistical artifact resulting, first, from such developments as greater relative increases in the price of services, increased intererst payments due to the growth of consumer debt, and an increase in imputed rent due to the growth of home ownership. More important still is the fact that the largest increase in the number of people employed in service activities has occurred among government employees and primarily teachers. Although the latter perform a service rather than producing goods, they ought to be classified as members of knowledge industries rather than of service industries.

The hours of leisure occupied with television viewing and automobile riding as well as with spectator sports far exceed the hours spent by the average person on cultural activities. But it is worth mentioning that in the last few decades the latter have also increased greatly. The growth of groups performing serious music and theater, as well as of painting and sculpturing groups, in all regions of the country, including many middle-sized towns, has been well documented, as has the increase in book publishing, in which area the rising sales of serious paperback books are most impressive.

This expansion of people's horizons is probably related to the spread of formal education as well as to affluence, so that the greatly increasing education of American youth is relevant in our context. Willingness to postpone entry into the labor force and the earning of money to get a college education, and even postgraduate training, must be explained in terms of both material and spiritual values. The young men and women in college and in medical school, law school, or graduate school trust that they will enhance their earning power through additional training. In addition, it is safe to assume that, for many, nonmaterial benefits provide an effective motivating force toward seeking more schooling.

The increasing educational level of the population makes possible the "knowledge society," in which economic developments and innovations are a function of scientific progress. Research and development become those aspects of industrial development that make the difference between successful or unsuccessful business firms. An ever-growing part of GNP is devoted to the production and distribution of knowledge.[6]

The indirect effects of higher education as a breeding ground for a change in life styles may be more important than its monetary effects. "The more the better," a slogan frequently condemned with respect to material goods, remains a valid recipe for cultural values, education, knowledge, and the arts. Education opens the way for a broadening of wants. Instead of people being concerned exclusively with egocentric wants, there are numerous signs of a transformation of the "I" into a broader "We," consisting of an identification with one's neighbors, one's community, and one's environment. We are concerned not only with our own and our family's health, but in our own interest must also be concerned with the health of other people in our community and with progress in medical science. Interest in schools and in adult education does not stem solely from concern with our own family, but has a much broader base. What goes on in our neighborhood becomes our personal concern. Developments in our country and even in the entire world—prosperity or depression, war or peace—are felt to affect us personally. Wherever the principle of a common fate prevails, an expansion of the ego takes place. Identification with a broader whole and a feeling of belonging give a new dimension to personal striving and to what we consider growth and progress.

Consumer expenditures on services and for knowledge or cultural purposes contribute much less to pollution and to the exhaustion of natural resources than expenditures requiring the production of an increased quantity of consumer goods. This important advantage of recent trends toward a service and knowledge society leads us to a discussion of the problem of limiting the growth of the economy.

Limits to Growth

The studies of D.H. Meadows and associates (1972) are based on the extrapolation of past trends. They indicate, what should have hardly been new, that an exponential growth of

[6] As has been documented by Machlup (1962).

population and of industrial output must clash with the finite nature of agricultural and industrial resources and with the deterioration of the environment—pollution of air and water, overcrowding, problems of disposing of waste. Meadows concludes that a collapse is unavoidable—it is projected for the beginning of the twenty-first century—unless new policies are adopted to transform our society into a nongrowing state.[7]

The most common criticism of Meadows's position has been that he has not taken into account the possible balancing effects of the price system (shortages being overcome by higher prices reducing demand or producing alternative supplies). In many instances this criticism is justified; yet, as has become clear during the oil crisis, pricing out the poor is not an acceptable solution when the shortages concern essential goods. The solution to the problem must be sought not in the purely economic realm, but in the realm of the psychological—in what people's belief systems are and how they may change. It is the weakness of Meadows's thesis that being based on simple extrapolations it assumes that human behavior will remain unchanged at greatly different levels of resources, production, population, or pollution. No thought is given to the variability of behavior and the possibility of learning.

Before continuing with that line of thought, let us say first that with one aspect of the problem of growth one can hardly take exception. There would seem to be little question of the need for limiting population growth. Substantial progress toward "zero population growth" has been achieved in some countries, including the United States, but not in some other less-developed countries.

Let us note further that limitation of the growth of industrial output would hurt those countries and those people most who do not share the high American standard of living. The poor in the United States, including many belonging to racial

---

[7] Needless to say, the exhaustion of material resources, indicated by the computer for the twenty-first century according to current estimates of world reserves and projected needs, is not the same as the energy shortage of 1973–74. But deficiencies in the oil supply due to lack of foresight in previous years, insufficient refining capacity in the United States, and political developments in the Middle East have dramatized the problem of limits to growth. Yet W. D. Nordhaus (1973) in a study of the long-run energy prospects concluded that alternatives to present energy sources will become available at prices that will not be excessive.

394

minorities, and the people in Africa, Asia, and South America, can hardly be expected to renounce growth because of the excessive use of natural resources by the wealthy.

We shall neglect here the problems confronting the poor in the United States as well as abroad and consider the impact of a no-growth economy on the American people as a whole. Having shown that belief in progress and optimistic expectations have served as incentives for Americans to strive for higher income and improved living standards, we must ask: What would happen if these optimistic expectations were to be disappointed? It would be worthwhile asking this question even in the absence of environmental conditions that may retard further growth. The fulfillment of high expectations may become more difficult in the future than it has been in the past. When very many people expect or aspire to very much, the probability of disappointment increases. The observed impatience of Americans to accomplish what they desire within a short time, rather than being satisfied with slow and gradual improvement, also enhances the prospect of disappointment.

In a survey conducted in May, 1972, respondents were asked how they would feel if there were to be no improvement in their standard of living in the next five years. It should be noted that the question was asked at a time when the majority of Americans reported improvement in and satisfaction with their standard of living.[8] The question referred specifically to the actual standard of living with which the respondents had expressed satisfaction and asked them to say what their reaction would be if their situation were to remain unchanged.

As shown in Table 25-1, among all families the frequency of somewhat or highly favorable reactions to no change in the standard of living was 61 percent, and the frequency of somewhat or highly unfavorable reactions 38 percent. There was hardly any difference in this respect between upper- and lower-income families. In contrast to income level, however,

[8] In the same survey respondents were asked about satisfaction with their standard of living and were provided with a 7-point scale for their answers. In a representative sample of all individuals, rating 1 (delighted) was given by 7 percent, 2 by 34 percent, 3 by 40 percent, 4 (mixed) by 11 percent, 5 by 4 percent, 6 by 2 percent and 7 (terrible) by 1 percent. The 7 percent of respondents not satisfied with their standard of living are omitted from Table 25-1 because their response to absence of improvement is of little interest.

age made a great difference in how people evaluated the absence of improvement in their stanard of living. The frequency of the most negative answer, "Rather disturbing," was by far the highest among young people and fell continuously with advancing age. Taking both unfavorable responses ("Somewhat disappointing" and "Rather disturbing") together, their frequency was close to 60 percent among those under 35 years of age and 50 percent in the age group 35 to 45. In the age group 55 and over the frequency was under 20 percent.

Whether or not a family had already made some and anticipated making more progress was likewise of great importance in determining the response. Of the BB Group about one-half gave unfavorable responses, while among members of the NonBB Group only one-third said they would be disappointed or disturbed by the absense of further improvement. Expectations are powerful; if we expect an improvement and do not get it, we tend to be more disappointed or disturbed than if we had not expected it.

The effect of past and expected progress on the perceived importance of further progress is not identical with the effect of age, although the former is not independent of the latter. Only a bare majority of the BB Group was under 35 years of age, and among those under 35 years of age only slightly over 50 percent fell in the BB Group.

TABLE 25-1
Reactions to No Change in Standard of Living during Next 5 Years
(Among respondents satisfied with their standard of living, 1972, in percent)

No Change Would Be	All Families	BB Group*	NonBB Group
Very satisfactory	18	14	20
Quite all right	43	37	46
Somewhat disappointing	25	32	21
Rather disturbing	13	16	11
Don't know, not ascertained	1	1	2
Total	100	100	100
Number of cases	1196	435	761

*Better off than 5 years ago and expect to be better off 5 years hence.
The question was: "Suppose 5 years from now your (family's) standard of living was the same as now—you were managing to live on your income pretty much the same—would that be very satisfactory, quite all right, somewhat disappointing, or rather disturbing?"
Source: Survey Research Center and Katona 1974b.

It appears therefore that no change in their stanard of living over a period of five years would be disappointing or disturbing to very many young Americans as well as to very many who feel that they are making progress.

If, as Meadows proposes, limitations to growth were to be imposed, great psychological problems would arise. Our consumer economy with its substantial advances in living standards cannot survive without visions of betterment and progress. At present, as our surveys have revealed, progress is identified by most Americans with growth of income and of the quantity of goods and services possessed. What is essential is to retain the prospect of improvement, regardless of what it is that may be considered improvement. A redefinition of progress is needed so that people identify an improvement in their situation less with an increase in the quantity of material goods and more with other aspects of the quality of life. There has already been some movement in this direction as indicated by the growing share of income spent on services and knowledge discussed earlier in this chapter.

Let us repeat: The term progress, like the terms improvement and betterment, is used to represent subjective notions. Progress stands for what people themselves feel are improvements. It is the image people have that serves as an incentive.[9] What is required is the strengthening of wants and aspirations that use up fewer of our limited resources and contribute less to the deterioration of the environment than does the acquisition of increased quantities of consumer goods. The proven adaptability of human motives and wants to changing conditions offers the best hope for reconciling the incentives derived from the prospect of progress with the requirement of improving the environment and conserving natural resources. A redefinition of progress in this sense is far more desirable than a scaling down of present wants because aspirations toward progress represent the strongest motive for working hard. Should nothing be done but to restrain the present desires for progress, not a stable no-growth society would emerge, but one in which economic conditions would deteriorate.

---

[9] This use of the term image is in line with its usage by Boulding (1956) and with our operational definition of belief in progress as a feeling of being better off than several years earlier and, at the same time, expecting to be still better off several years hence.

397

Looking Ahead

In 1974, when this manuscript was being readied for publication, new and severe problems arose. Rapid inflation continued in that year even though a recession began in activities directly dependent on consumers, such as the automobile industry and residential construction. We reported in Chapter 8 that the recession was foreshadowed by a sharp decline in the Survey Research Center's *Index of Consumer Sentiment*. The *Index* fell in the summer of 1973 because rapid inflation, particularly in food prices, made consumers pessimistic and even despondent. Then came the Watergate revelations, eroding trust in the government and its ability to cope with inflation and unemployment. In the fall and winter of 1973 the oil crisis brought forth severe doubts about the prospects of the economy and triggered further inflationary price increases. In the first quarter of 1974, GNP, consumer incomes, and consumer expenditures, measured in constant prices, were all lower than a year earlier.

At the time of this writing it is not yet possible to evaluate the impact of the oil embargo fully. It may suffice to say that while shortages in oil products and the disruption of driving habits represented short-term effects, enduring damage was caused (1) by the substantial increase in the cost of all forms of energy and (2) by the realization on the part of the American people of being dependent on actions by a few oil-producing foreign nations.

Pessimism about economic prospects deepened in 1974 when the government initiated restrictive policies in order to fight inflation and permitted interest rates to advance to unprecedented high levels rather than taking any action against the steadily deepening recession.[10] It has not been realized that in two greatly differing situations different policies are needed. What may have been called for in Situation 1, characterized by prosperity, growing demand, full capacity operations, ample supplies and rapid inflation, may not be justified at a time

[10] The Survey Research Center's Index of Consumer Sentiment fell from 88.4 in the fourth quarter of 1972 to 75.7 in the fourth quarter of 1973 and 58.4 in the fourth quarter of 1974. By comparing this decline with the declines shown in Chart 6-2 of this book, we find that consumer confidence and willingness to buy declined in 1973-74 to a far larger extent than prior to the 1958 and 1970 recessions.

when Situation 2 prevailed and rapid inflation coincided with a recession, slow demand, unused capacity, and shortages. In most people's minds, the calamities of recession, rising interest rates and rapidly advancing prices were associated with each other. Thus in 1974 the government's restrictive policies and its pronouncements about reducing expenditures contributed to a decline in confidence, a decrease in consumer expenditures and a rise in unemployment, and at the same time failed to arrest the spread of inflationary psychology.

At that time leading economists in the government and private business as well as in academia were widely quoted as saying that the two principal goals of economic policy, full employment and stable prices, were impossible to attain—our knowledge and the means at our disposal being insufficient to realize both objectives at the same time. This is no doubt true—and acceptable. But does it follow that the two more modest aims, low unemployment and small price increases, are also impossible to achieve? Is it true that a further improvement in the standard of living of the masses can be accomplished only at the price of rapid inflation, which ultimately cancels the improvements in living standards? In fact, for a number of years in the 1950s and 1960s the standard of living of most Americans rose substantially at a time when there was little unemployment and creeping rather than rapid inflation. What new developments have occurred that would make impossible in the future what has been possible in the past?

What was new in 1973–74, in contrast to earlier years, was worldwide inflation. Large price increases occurred in all highly developed countries—United States, Canada, Western Europe, Japan—as well as in most lesser-developed countries. The prices of agricultural products, of natural resources and energy advanced rapidly all over the world. This observation led to the most popular explanation of inflation in 1974, which consisted of the argument that world resources were not sufficient to feed the growing world population and to provide it with raw materials. But experience during the past hundred years indicates that shortages, though they have occasionally arisen, have always been overcome rather quickly. Agricultural yields have risen enormously and new sources of energy have been discovered, multiplying the output and usually glutting the market a few years following the shortages. What is new and what may make past experience inapplicable today is the cause of the shortages, an unprecedented increase in appetites at the same time all over the world.

Shortly after World War II the consumer economy and the improvement in the standard of livng of the masses coupled with rising expectations were restricted to the United States. Later, these aspects of affluence spread to a few other highly developed countries. In the 1970s people all over the world, regardless of the level of their actual conditions, wished to partake of the American standard of living. They felt they were entitled to an improvement in their material well-being. The simultaneous rise of appetites throughout the world was a major factor in demand exceeding supply and a major explanation of worldwide inflation.

It is a topsy-turvy world in which increasing desires for improvement are seen as a catastrophe. Wanting more and striving for more should be viewed as an advantage stimulating economic activity as it has in the United States during the last twenty-five years. To be sure, too much of a good thing may be damaging. What we have to recognize is that the task of differentiating between the right amount of stimulation and too much stimulation cannot be one that is impossible to handle.

At a time when mistrust of the government is widespread and when prices continue to advance, people must learn to have faith in their money. This is difficult but likewise not impossible because, as we have shown at the end of Chapter 9, a climate of runaway inflation in which people abstain from putting money in banks, consumers buy in advance of their needs in order to beat inflation, and farmers and businessmen withhold supplies in anticipation of higher prices, has not developed (or developed to a small extent only). Moreover, it takes time for the productive capacity of the nation to catch up to the extent required as a partial remedy both for rapid inflation and large unemployment. We have argued that little credence should be given to the notion about the advent of a new era of pessimism, stagnation, or contraction. While many Americans have lost faith in the economy and in the government, few have lost faith in their own ability to advance. Sooner or later consumer aspirations will again stimulate the economy.

400

Psychological economics will have to play a role in accomplishing what is required. The progress of this new discipline as related in this book must be viewed as a beginning. Advances in theory and in their practical application must go hand in hand. It will remain true in the future as well that fluctuations in unemployment as well as in prices depend to a large extent on what consumers do. In this situation, the psychological analysis of consumer attitudes and of consumer behavior represents a major and important task.

APPENDIX

The Survey Method

Most of the data presented in this book have been collected through sample interview surveys. Interviews with representative samples of the population constitute the principal methodological tool of psychological economics. It is therefore necessary to describe the basic principles that govern data collection by means of such interviews. Surveys serve the purpose of accumulating knowledge in many areas not connected with economic processes. Although much of what will be said in this chapter is applicable to all kinds of surveys, our discussion will concentrate on the clarification of the purposes and methods of economic surveys.[1]

Economic research is either based on records or derived from personal contact with decision makers. Most *records* are prepared for practical or legal purposes. For these reasons, corporations, for instance, prepare balance sheets and profit and loss accounts, and firms as well as individuals file tax returns. Business firms, trade organizations, and governmental agencies also prepare collections and analyses of records in order to conduct their business rather than for the sake of obtaining scientific insights. Thus each life insurance company summarizes the data on its own business, and associations of life insurance firms provide assistance to individual companies by preparing statistics on the total amount of premiums paid in

---

[1] For early discussions of the methods of the surveys used in this book, see Chapter 15 of Katona (1951) and the article by Campbell and Katona (1953). In later years each volume of the *Survey of Consumer Finances* issued by the Survey Research Center contained a chapter on methods. On sampling see Kish (1965), and on interviewing see Kahn and Cannell (1957).

403

the country. Since imports are a major source of government revenue and information on imports is useful for trade, an agency of the federal government collects and analyzes data on foreign trade. Sometimes trade associations and government agencies organize their records according to theoretical principles and publish them in a form suitable to convey an understanding of developments. The most important example of a systematic organization of economic data is the work carried out in the Department of Commerce in estimating the size of Gross National Product, national income, and many other aggregate measures of economic activity. This work provides source material for scientific research, which is then carried forward by economists in government, private business, and universities, who analyze the relationships among the variables recorded so as to test hypotheses and theories about causes and effects.

Not everything that is relevant is recorded, however, and much information is not recorded in the way it is needed. In order to determine how prices have changed, for instance, it is not enough to have access to files and archives. Enumerators of the Bureau of Labor Statistics visit a sample of retail stores and determine there the prices of a sample of commodities in order to compute the retail price index. *Personal contact* with decision makers—government officials, businessmen, as well as consumers—represents the method of obtaining a variety of data not available from records. The decennial census provides some basic information through personal contact with all households in the country. But complete enumeration is an impractical and inefficient method in many instances. Today the Bureau of Census determines the number of employed and unemployed people through sample interview surveys, and other government agencies, private business firms, and independent research groups proceed in the same way both for practical purposes and for the sake of enriching economic knowledge.

Psychological economics, in contrast to most other fields of economics, is not in a position to rely on basic material collected for practical or legal purposes. Naturally, it can and must make use of a multitude of available statistics and refer to corporation reports and files for indications about the process of decision making. But as a rule empirical studies initiated and guided by the aims of behavioral scientists serve as

404

its principal source material. Studies of change in attitudes and expectations and their relation to behavior call for the collection of new data. This is done primarily by the survey method, which may yield data representative of the chosen universe (the entire population of a country or selected subgroups of the population). Field observations and experiments may supplement the survey method.

History of Surveys

Sample surveys as a source of scientific data are of fairly recent origin. The first economic survey, based on a very large number of households selected by unsatisfactory sampling methods, was the study of consumer purchases conducted in 1935–36 as part of the WPA program. Data on income and expenditures were collected in this study as well as in a second nationwide survey by the Bureau of Labor Statistics in 1941–42. During the same period, in the decade before Pearl Harbor, scientific progress was considerable in several related noneconomic fields. First, psychologists and sociologists turned to the problem of attitude measurement and devised methods for the quantification of attitudes and opinions. These methods were tested in many small surveys, conducted most commonly among college students. Second, sampling as part of mathematical statistics made rapid progress and opened the way for determining, within established margins of error, values representative of a population consisting of millions of units by collecting information from a few thousand or even a few hundred cases. Third, polling organizations were established and made sample surveys well known, popular, and widely trusted. Their success in the late thirties and early forties in predicting election results on the basis of small-sample interviews demonstrated to the public at large that people in all walks of life could be approached with what might seem rather personal questions and that answers obtained from a small sample could have significance far beyond the importance of the relatively few people actually interrogated. Market research made successful use of the same methods at the same time by determining people's brand preferences or listening and reading habits. Advertising agencies, newspapers and

405

periodicals, as well as the radio, became big users of the sample interview survey.

During World War II, several government agencies took up the task of measuring people's attitudes toward public issues connected with the war, among them many economic issues. Their purpose was to advise policy makers about the need for and the methods of disseminating information and, in some cases, also about the need for new regulations. The Army and Navy Departments had special staffs conducting surveys among soldiers and sailors concerning their motivation, attitudes, fears, and expectations. Methods of measuring the intensity of opinions, especially, were greatly improved by the work in the army. The Division of Program Surveys, an agency established in the Department of Agriculture under the direction of Rensis Likert, conducted a number of surveys on wartime issues and pioneered in devising psychological methods of interviewing. In 1942, that division began its program of psychological-economic surveys with a series of surveys conducted for the War Finance Division of the Treasury Department. Their major purpose was the measurement and improvement of the effectiveness of war bond drives. Then, in 1944, the Division of Program Surveys began its operations for the Board of Governors of the Federal Reserve System. The major original purpose of these surveys, directed by the author of this book, was to measure the distribution of liquid-asset holdings among the nation's consumers and the attitudes of consumers toward those holdings. The surveys soon developed, however, into projects encompassing practically all aspects of economic psychology in the consumer sector of the economy. Since 1946, these surveys of consumer finances have been conducted by the Survey Research Center of the University of Michigan, which was established in that year by the principal personnel of the Division of Program Surveys.

The Functions of Surveys

Surveys collect data not otherwise available in order to answer the questions, How many? Who? and Why? We may illustrate the functions of surveys, first, with a reference to an industry that is rightly proud of the extensive archives it keeps.

406

From its records the life insurance industry can determine the total amount of life insurance in force in the country and the total amount of life insurance premiums paid. But it cannot find out how many Americans carry life insurance. There are people with several policies—some have more than ten——contracted with different companies. Collating the records to avoid duplications is impracticable because in view of the very substantial residential mobility of the American population the same person may be recorded at several different addresses. Therefore, in the 1950s the Survey Research Center was commissioned to find out the proportion of insured people in the entire population as well as in significant subgroups—such as income and age groups—by interviewing a representative sample of the American people.

The answer to the question, How many? represents the starting point for more significant inquiries. For instance, it is important to clarify the relation between income and life insurance. This question again cannot be answered from records, because people do not communicate changes in their income to their insurance company. Needless to say, it is most important, especially in times of inflation, to find out whether the amounts of insurance carried are keeping pace with increases in income. Surveys yielded data about the proportion of income used for premium payments by different income, age, and occupational groups, as well as by urban and rural families. The question about what groups hold what assets and what attitudes was also answered according to religious preferences and political affiliations. By thus answering the question, Who?—which economic or demographic groups carry larger or smaller amounts of life insurance, for instance—we contribute to answering the question, Why? But this approach to finding reasons for economic behavior does not suffice because even in demographically and financially homogeneous groups there are great variations in ownership of life insurance (as well as of other assets). Sociopsychological variables must also be considered and can be studied through survey research. The same survey used to determine financial data (income, amount of life insurance owned and purchased, and so on) and demographic data (age, education, and others) may also serve to measure people's opinions, attitudes, and expectations. We mentioned earlier (Chapter 16) how differences in opinions about the purposes of life insurance served to explain differ-

407

ences in life insurance ownership and thus contributed to answering the question, Why?

In place of life insurance we could have taken any number of other examples to illustrate the functions of survey research. Let us look at just one further example from a fairly new industry. The commercial aviation carriers and the government supervisory agencies have, of course, data on plane tickets purchased, and records enable them to prepare tabulations about passenger miles flown, but not to answer any of the following questions: How many Americans fly frequently (more than ten or twenty times a year, for example), how many rarely, and how many have never flown in a plane? How greatly has the number of people traveling by plane increased during the past few years? What is the relation of business to nonbusiness travel by plane? How are air travelers distributed on the income and age scales? Data yielding information on these and many further questions were collected through sample interview surveys conducted by the Survey Research Center and have contributed to answering the question of why some people fly often, some rarely, and others never. Further information relevant to this question in the early years of the jet age was obtained by studying such psychological variables as anxiety about flying and desire for speed in relation to the frequency of air travel.[2]

Such illustrations of the functions of survey research in the area of specific industries may serve to supplement the explanation given in Chapter 4 about the use of surveys in the collection of basic economic data. In analyzing the relation of micro to macro data, we said that total personal income is determined for the national accounts from social security records and partly also from federal income tax records. Thus it is known what the income of all Americans was in a given year or a given quarter and by how much it changed from the previous year or quarter. But an increase in personal income by, say, 10 percent does not mean that the income of all families rose by 10 percent; some families will have much higher gains and some even losses in income. Only through surveys do we find out what proportion had large or small gains and what proportion unchanged or declining incomes. Survey data further reveal the distribution of income, that is, the proportion of families in

[2] See Lansing (1958).

408

various income brackets and the extent of concentration of income. The question, Who? is answered by collecting demographic data for groups in the various brackets and with different kinds of income changes. The behavior of these different groups may then be analyzed on the basis of further interview questions; thus it may be determined whether there was any correlation between the size of the family income, or income increases or losses and, for example, the number of cars purchased or the amounts of money saved.

Attitudinal data, collected in the same survey as income data, substantially increase the potential scope of the analysis. In this book, data on changes in income in the years preceding the interview have frequently been combined with data on income expectations. In addition, and most importantly because of inflation, attitudinal data on feeling better off or worse off have been substituted for data on actual income changes, and information on expecting to be better off or worse off has been used instead of income expectations. Correlations of these data with behavioral changes, as presented in Chapter 10, reflect the kind of economic analysis made possible by survey data.

Having thus described the functions of surveys, we may generalize as follows: The primary purposes of surveys are to obtain information on trends over time and on functional relationships among variables. This statement has, first, a negative implication: Determination of a position as it prevails at a given time is not the major purpose of surveys. To find out how many people are optimistic at a given time or how many expect prices to go up may be of journalistic value since it makes for interesting reading, but such findings do not constitute major goals of survey research and are subject to large errors. By formulating the questions about optimism or price expectations in different ways, it would be possible to obtain different absolute frequencies. But by using the same wording of a question in successive surveys, each time with a different representative sample, time series can be constructed which not only yield important insights into economic behavior but are also subject to much smaller errors. Although we shall come back to this point later, it may be mentioned here that reporting errors tend to be constant if well-trained interviewers ask the same question in successive surveys, and therefore do not greatly influence the comparison. Relations between variables—between income and liquid-asset holdings, to mention two financial variables, or between age and installment debt, or between optimism and purchases of durables, to mention demographic and psychological variables—are likewise subject to smaller reporting errors than absolute measurements and are of crucial significance for science. Absolute measurements represent but the starting point for studies in behavioral economics. This is true both of measurements that are quite reliable, as, for instance, of the number of automobile owners and purchasers in a given year, and of those that are subject to fairly large errors, as, for instance, the mean amount of liquid assets held per family at a given time.

Sampling Design

The aim of sampling is to make the sample as representative as possible, so that measurements based on the sample can be taken as equivalent to similar measurements based on the universe from which it was drawn. This ideal can be approximated but not fully achieved. The sampling error expresses the probable range of differences between measurements derived from a sample and measurements of the universe, or between measurements from one sample and measurements from many other samples drawn from the same universe.

In probability samples, every member of the universe—that is, of the population studied—has an equal or known chance of being selected. Interviewers' bias in selecting respondents is excluded, and sampling errors can be calculated. In some few instances probability samples may be drawn from lists. Suppose the universe in which we are interested and from which we want to draw a representative sample consists of all families who are permanent residents in a given town at a given time, or of all employees of an industrial corporation at a given time. Suppose, further, that lists containing the names of all members of the universe are available. (With respect to residents of towns, this is the case in many European countries but not the United States; with respect to industrial employees, it is more generally true.) Then a sample can be drawn by counting out, say, every tenth or hundredth name on the list. Similarly, if telephone owners with listed numbers are considered the universe and no distinction is made between business and residential telephones, it is easy to draw a probability

410

sample from telephone books. This method of selection permits no exercise of choice on the part of the investigator.

When no lists are available, as, for instance, for the total population of the United States, more complex procedures must be used. Area sampling permits the determination of the location of each respondent so that no latitude is left to the interviewer in selecting the respondents. In order to draw a representative sample of all families in the United States, the process of random selection must be repeated several times. First, as in many samples used by the Census Bureau as well as in the samples of the Survey Research Center, a random sample of counties is chosen. (A list of all counties in the United States is, of course, available.) Then a sample of towns and open country areas within the selected counties is drawn. Then, within a city, for instance, a sample of blocks is selected (by numbering all blocks in the city from maps). Then all dwelling units in the selected blocks are listed—enumerated through field trips—and a random sample of dwelling units is drawn. Finally, all respondents living in the selected dwelling units are listed, and either one of them is chosen at random or the family heads constitute the sample. This procedure determines precisely which individuals the interviewer must call on.[3]

The size of a sample, that is, the number of cases designated for interviewing, depends first of all upon the degree of accuracy desired—the sampling error being a function of the number of cases. The extent of the desired breakdown of the findings also plays a role in determining the sample size. Fewer cases are needed when only data derived from the entire sample are required than when, in addition, breakdowns by subgroups such as occupational, age, or income groups are desired.

The larger the sample, the smaller the sampling error, but after reaching a certain minimum size the increase in reliability resulting even from doubling the sample size—by making, perhaps, 6,000 rather than 3,000 interviews—is often of little

---

[3] The given description of the principles of sampling remains correct even though in actual practice the procedure is somewhat more complicated. In most surveys, for instance, stratified samples are used. (Stratification represents a method of systematic and, nevertheless, unbiased selection.) The details of sampling design and sampling statistics are outside the scope of this book.

relevance for the problem studied. On the other hand, the smaller the sample the easier it is to make sure that well-trained interviewers use identical methods and thus to reduce the reporting errors. (In addition, of course, the smaller the sample the smaller the cost of a survey.) Using the entire universe in any survey would represent an uncontrollable task and be subject to large errors if anything beyond simple factual information were collected.

The samples of the Survey Research Center represent cross sections of the population living in private households in the United States, excluding Alaska and Hawaii. Transients, residents of institutions, and persons living on military bases are not included. The method known as multistage area probability sampling is used to select a sample of dwelling units representative of the nation. First, 72 primary sampling units (each composed of a county or group of counties) are selected, 12 of the largest metropolitan areas are selected with certainty, and 60 other sampling units are selected by probability methods from among all remaining counties in the 48 states.

In each primary sampling unit three to six secondary selections of cities, towns, census tracts, or rural areas are made. In the third stage of sampling, urban blocks, or small portions of rural areas are chosen. Finally, for each survey a sample of dwelling units, in clusters of about four, is drawn from the block selections—always by a process of random choice.

The basic unit for sampling is the dwelling unit and, for interviewing, the family unit. A family unit is defined as all persons living in the same dwelling unit who are related to each other by blood, marriage, or adoption. A single person who is unrelated to the other occupants of the dwelling, or who lives alone, is a family unit by himself or herself. In some dwelling units there are two or even several family units. In 1970 about 2.4 percent of all family units were secondary units unrelated to the primary family occupying the dwelling unit.

Regarding the size of the sampling error, reference should be made to the detailed tables presented in the monographs, *Survey of Consumer Finances*. It may suffice to report here that the sampling error (one standard error) of survey findings is 1.6 percentage points provided 1,500 interviews are available and the reported percentage is approximately 50. If the reported percentage is around 20 or 80, the sampling error is 1.3 percentage points. The sampling error of the *Index of Con-*

412

sumer Sentiment is 1.2 points. Figures representing one standard error mean that the chances are 66 in 100 that the value estimated lies within a range equal to the reported percentage, plus or minus the sampling error. If the sampling errors cited above are doubled (two standard errors), the chances are 95 in 100.

The Interview

There are various forms of personal interviews. At the one extreme, the interviewer may use no questionnaire whatsoever and, at the other, he may use a detailed reporting form with spaces to be filled in with check marks or figures. Especially in sociological or business surveys and case studies, in which a small number of respondents are interviewed by those in charge of the survey, the first method has been used to advantage. In these cases, the interviewer may believe that he needs no standardized questionnaire. Like many personnel officers when they interview applicants for jobs, he knows what he wants to find out and formulates on the spur of the moment the questions to obtain the information he needs. This procedure is not without danger, because the interviewers, being fully aware of the purposes of the survey and the implications of their questions, are often led to ask questions that, by their phrasing, bias the results. Furthermore, the questions asked by different interviewers may vary. Therefore, interviewing without a questionnaire does not yield comparable data from different respondents. Because of the possible influence of the wording of a question on the replies received, survey measurements derived from a large number of respondents must be based on identical, and therefore predetermined, questions.

Having interviewers fill out reporting forms that contain not questions but column headings, such as occupation, age, number of workers, size of farm, and so on, is the traditional method of censuses and enumerative surveys. Except where applied to very simple, factual matters, the procedure is less than adequate. Careful studies have revealed that different interviewers formulate different questions for the same purpose and that these questions often yield differences in the answers. When the inquiry is directed toward such complex matters as income, assets, or attitudes, reporting forms cannot be depended on.

413

Between these two extreme forms of interviewing are those that make use of a questionnaire prepared in advance. There are different kinds of questionnaires. Some resemble the reporting forms, and others the conversational interview that makes use of no preformulated questions. A questionnaire in which the questions are so formulated that they allow only for "yes," "no," or "don't know" answers, to be indicated by the interviewer by means of check marks in the three boxes that appear after each question, is very similar to a reporting form. The task of the interviewer is simple—he need only read the questions and make check marks—and the quantification and tabulation of results become almost automatic. Closely resembling this method are multiple-choice questions: The respondent is given a set of alternatives and chooses the one that most closely agrees with his situation or opinion.

The fixed-question free-answer method of interviewing widely used by the Survey Research Center differs from the methods just described. It makes use of open-ended questions, which call for full answers in the respondents' own words. Although the questions are formulated in advance and are used in every instance without any change in sequence or wording, the interview becomes a conversation between interviewer and respondent instead of a cut-and-dried interrogation. The respondent is encouraged to express his opinion in his own words or to describe his situation in detail. The most important open-ended question is an inquiry about why the respondent said whatever he said. The form of what is called a nondirective probe may be simply, "Why do you say so?" or "What do you have in mind?" This approach, together with carefully prepared introductory statements about the purposes and the importance of the survey, is conducive to creating rapport between interviewers and respondents. Motivating the respondent to give complete and truthful answers, and to spend a comparatively long time with the interviewer, are primary conditions for the success of psychological-economic surveys and can best be achieved by making the interview an interesting experience for the respondent.

As examples, it may suffice to point to a question frequently cited in this book, namely, "Would you say that you and your family are better off or worse off financially than a year ago, or in the same situation?" Whatever the answer to this multiple-choice question is, the interviewer queries, "Why do you say

414

so?" In reply, important and quantifiable information may be obtained consisting of references to an increase in wage or salary or an increase in prices. In any case, the original answer is clarified, and it is made certain that respondent and interviewer have understood each other. Similarly, to the frequently cited question about whether it is a "good time" or a "bad time" to buy automobiles, for example, additional information is obtained by a subsequent probe. It makes a great difference whether the answer "Good time" is explained by indications of satisfaction with current prices or by the expectation of future price increases.

It is imperative that survey questions be formulated so as to be unequivocally understood even by respondents with limited formal education. Beyond this self-evident requirement of questionnaire construction, we must refer to two major problems in selecting the topics of inquiry. First, because human memory is fallible, questions about distant past events yield biased information. It is of little value and may be greatly misleading, for instance, to ask about income received or attitudes and expectations held several years earlier. Second, the level of information of people should not be overestimated. For example, multiple-choice questions about the extent of price increases during the preceding few months may evoke prompt answers, but many of them will be guesses or ad hoc answers made up on the spur of the moment relating to something about which the respondent knows very little. A funnel arrangement screening out uninformed people or permitting the analyst to differentiate among people with different degrees of information is useful and often necessary as, for example, when something as limited as the extent of information and concern about the stock market is studied.

Mail Questionnaires

A survey by means of a mail questionnaire is of course very much less expensive than a personal interview survey and therefore permits the use of much larger samples. Mail questionnaires also have the advantage of enabling respondents to give carefully considered answers, sometimes even based on looking up records they may have.

On the other hand, the response rate to mail surveys is often so low as to make their use inappropriate. A 30 or 40 percent response to a mail questionnaire is ordinarily considered a highly satisfactory result; usually the response rate is lower. Some people just do not want to be bothered, others are not interested in the questionnaire, and still others do not want to commit themselves in writing. Those who do not respond may have special reasons for not responding and may differ in income, assets, or opinions from those who do respond. Therefore, there is no assurance that information obtained by mail is derived from an unbiased selection of respondents.

A second disadvantage of mail questionnaires is that they must be short and simple or the chance of getting replies becomes even smaller. Lengthy and complex inquiries, therefore, cannot ordinarily be made through the mail (except in those instances in which members of a group are highly motivated to reply to a questionnaire sent by their organization).

Little attention has been given to a third basic fault of mail inquiries. There is no assurance that the respondents understand the written questions, and no assurance that the analysts understand the replies. Even carefully formulated and relatively simple questions may be misunderstood by the respondents, and simple answers misunderstood by the analysts—and there is no way of finding out the real meaning of the answers.

There are, nonetheless, many instances in which mail questionnaires are appropriate and an adequate response may be expected. This is true when the questionnaires are sent to a group interested in or concerned with the subject involved. For example, the interrogation of employees and workers of a single firm, or of students and faculty members of a college, on issues widely discussed by them may be conducted by mail. Furthermore, there are instances when the opinions of those who do not return a mail questionnaire can justifiably be disregarded because the survey is meant to ascertain the opinions of people interested in the particular subject.

Telephone Interviews

Surveys conducted by means of telephone interviews also cost very much less than personal interview surveys. Phone calls to people who are not at home cost practically nothing, while traveling from home to home for personal interviews takes much of the interviewers' time whether or not the people are at home.

The disadvantages of telephone interviews are also fairly obvious. Absence of rapport with respondents, the impossibility of proving to the respondent that it is a bona fide interview, difficulties in asking indiscreet questions or questions concerning matters that are thought to be private (for instance, income), the greater probability of misunderstanding a question or an answer may be mentioned in addition to some sampling problems—for example, huseholds without a telephone, unlisted numbers, business firms. In spite of these problems telephone interviews are often very successful and can sometimes be carried on as long as half an hour.

Most difficulties disappear when the telephone is used to reinterview respondents who have previously been interviewed in person. Rapport has already been established and personal questions have already been asked. The interviewer may refer to her earlier visit and explain, for example, that she just wants to find out whether the expectations the respondent had expressed earlier had been realized. Since reinterviews are most important just for this purpose, the Survey Research Center conducts telephone reinterviews, but no "cold" telephone interviews. It is fairly easy to adjust for the sampling problem that arises when part of a sample is newly drawn and part consists of telephone reinterviews (see Schmiedeskamp, 1962).

The Panel Method

Even one reinterview may be called an example of the panel method. Usually the expression is used when the same sample is interviewed several times in succession. The most important functions of the panel method are (a) to provide information extending over a long time span and not subject to errors or memory, (b) to enable the investigator to analyze the impact of an earlier event on later activity, and (c) to analyze the characteristics of people whose situation or behavior changes from one interview to the next.

Little needs to be said about the first function. It may suffice to recall the data on durable goods bought and credit incurred

417

by the same families over a time span of four years as cited in Chapter 12.[4]

As to the second function, we may recall that only through the panel method was it possible to study the impact of attitudes or financial situations reported in one interview on subsequent behavior reported in a later interview, as we did when we studied the impact of optimism on borrowing or of liquid asset holdings on saving.

Regarding the third function, it is important to keep in mind that for the sake of determining the kind of change that has taken place reinterviews with the same families are not only not necessary but may even distort the picture. Two successive independently drawn samples, conducted by the same methods and asking the same questions, are the best way to find out, for instance, how the *Index of Consumer Sentiment* has changed. However, to determine in a reliable manner what kinds of people have changed their opinions and attitudes or the amounts of their savings, the same families must be interviewed more than once. The study of the behavior of the changers often provides significant information about political as well as economic matters, for instance, about differences in behavior among those with differing opinions about the pace of inflation.

Panel bias and the dropping-out of panel respondents are the well-known drawbacks to the panel method. As to the latter, some respondents are not willing to be subjected to a lengthy interview several times. Panel losses are by far the largest between the first and the second interview and may become rather small after the third interview. Unfortunately, such losses introduce a bias because it is primarily busy people, with relatively high income and education, as well as poor and uneducated people, who refuse to submit to repeated interviews. Those in the middle income, age, and educational brackets are more easily accessible.

Panel bias often takes another form as well. The panel member knows about the kinds of things that are being studied and may therefore follow certain news and developments with greater interest than other people. For instance, questions about inflation and its effects may be unsuitable to study ex-

---

[4] There have been psychological studies in which a panel has been followed for several decades or where successive generations were interviewed, but such studies have not yet been extended to economic matters.

418

clusively from data obtained from a long-established panel. This form of bias usually results only from several interviews conducted with the same people in the course of a year rather than from annual reinterviews.

On the Reliability of Surveys

One of the major reasons why sample interview surveys provide indications of probable magnitudes rather than "true" values has already been discussed, namely, the absence of complete enumeration. Sampling errors are, however, measurable—provided probability sampling is used—and the probable limits or reliability may thus be estimated in advance. Some estimate of probable errors as the result of nonresponse can also be made at the conclusion of a survey. Obviously not every person falling in a sample can be interviewed; some are not found at home even on repeated visits and some refuse to be interviewed. A response of 90 percent or more of designated respondents is usually considered highly satisfactory; a response of 75 percent or less, unsatisfactory. Many steps are usually taken by those who conduct surveys to reduce nonresponse and to motivate respondents to participate as, for example, writing explanatory letters to respondents in advance and using only well-trained interviewers.

The quality of the interviewing staff and its ability to motivate respondents appear to be essential conditions for reducing reporting errors as well, which are not measurable and often detract substantially from the reliability of data collected. A carefully prepared questionnaire can do much to eliminate one aspect of reporting errors, namely those due to misunderstanding of questions or answers. The quality of the questionnaire can also play a significant role in avoiding memory errors, ad hoc answers, or answers determined by idiosyncratic considerations and temporary changes in mood. But the impact of either pride or modesty and of attempts to please or mislead the interviewer will still remain. One saving factor in this area, however, is that it is very difficult to give consistently incorrect answers to many questions. Therefore, inconsistencies in information received from the same respondent provide a warning signal to the analyst. Secondly, and most importantly, as mentioned earlier, it is highly probable that the proportion of

419

exaggerations due to pride or of understatements due to modesty as well as of various other reporting errors will remain fairly constant from one survey to the next when conducted under similar conditions a few months or even a full year apart. Therefore, determination of change—either in attitudes or in economic data—will be less subject to bias on account of reporting errors than information on either attitudes or financial matters at any one given time.

It may serve the discussion of reliability to provide illustrations of certain areas in which experience has shown that survey information tends to be relatively reliable and others in which it is relatively unreliable. In the latter category is information about the size of bank deposits, common stocks, and other assets. What kinds of assets or investments a person has, and how much he has, are often viewed as private matters so that respondents must be highly motivated to participate in such a study by being convinced of its scientific value and the anonymity of the data supplied by them. Moreover, some forms of assets or bank accounts are often forgotten, or not mentioned because they are jointly held with a relative and therefore not viewed as the respondent's asset. Sometimes pride but more commonly modesty—or a reluctance to admit to the size of one's assets—plays a large role in the answers given. Furthermore, the ownership of many assets and especially of common stocks is highly concentrated among a small proportion of people. In the usual samples, holders of very large assets-—valued at several hundred thousands of dollars or more—are infrequent and yet such holdings significantly influence the mean amounts. "Oversampling" of geographic areas in which wealthy or high-income people are known to live has been successfully used to overcome this problem. In two studies, the results of which were used in Chapter 16—Projector and Weiss (1966) for a Federal Reserve study and Barlow, Brazer, and Morgan (1966) for a Survey Research Center study—a more efficient method of sampling was used through access to tax information provided by the Internal Revenue Service under suitable guarantees of confidentiality.

The most efficient method of obtaining asset data probably consists of combining personal interviews with the perusal of records. As Robert Ferber (1959, 1966), who directed the Consumer Savings Project of the Inter-University Committee for Research on Consumer Behavior, has shown, it should be possible to supplement data derived from a random sample of bank accounts with information obtained in personal interviews about the income, age, and attitudes of the owners.

Survey research is most reliable if it is directed toward obtaining information on variables that are widely represented in the universe. For example, to study the impact of inflation on food purchases the entire sample is relevant. In contrast, in a study of the impact of inflation on the buying or selling of common stock, only a very small proportion of the population sample is in a position to give information that reflects their probable actions.

It is axiomatic that information respondents desire to communicate is the easiest to obtain. In this category falls such information as why, in their opinion, certain developments occurred—for instance, why incomes or prices went up—or why they hold certain attitudes—for instance, that a recession is more damaging than inflation. It appears, then, that the method used by the Survey Research Center, which combines the collection of attitudinal information that people like to provide with that of financial data, serves to enhance the interest and the motivation of respondents.

Business Surveys

Surveys of business firms and business managers often present problems not encountered in surveys of the general population. The most obvious are the problems of sampling and weighting. It goes without saying that the General Motors Corporation or the plans and attitudes expressed by a spokesman of General Motors cannot be treated in the same manner as a small firm or the plans and attitudes of its owner. In the quarterly surveys conducted by the SEC-Commerce Department on planned capital expenditures, the sampling problem was simply solved by interrogating all "large" firms and only a sample of "smaller" firms, and there was no need to weight the responses because the answers are expressed in dollars. Thus the reply of General Motors carries very much greater weight in the published aggregate anticipated expenditures than the reply of a small firm. In surveys collecting attitudinal data—for instance, on location decisions as reported in Chapter 20—it is, however, often necessary to publish the responses of large firms separately from those of small firms. This solution is, of course, also used in distinguishing responses of high-income families from those of low-income families.

As to problems in interviewing, it may be said that it is often more difficult to get information from individuals in high-income brackets about their private finances than comparable information about corporate finances from business executives. Considerations of secrecy or confidentiality sometimes make it difficult to get certain types of information from either of these groups, but considerations of public relations promote access to the latter. It was often found to be fairly easy to arrange for extended interviews with several executives of large corporations and to obtain from them not only verbal replies to the questions asked, but also access to company books and numerical data. As might be expected, business interest in public relations may have an unwelcome aspect as well. In some few instances business executives attempted to use the interview as an occasion to influence the interviewer and impress hm or her with the merits of the firm's policies. Such attempts at persuasion are, however, hardly difficult to resist.

The most suitable procedure, both in business surveys and in surveys with high-income individuals, is to collect attitudinal and financial data at the same time. This fact has, unfortunately, not been taken into account in the quarterly surveys of the SEC-Commerce Department, which consist of very brief forms mailed to business firms, requesting them to fill in the data on their planned investment outlays with no explanations whatsoever. This method is used despite the fact that, in a few studies in which firms were asked why, in reporting on plans, they had either overestimated or underestimated their actual outlays, valuable insights into investment decisions were obtained. There seems to be little realization that prediction is greatly facilitated if the size of investment plans is supplemented by an understanding of the reasons for them.

As an example of neglecting to collect financial data, we may refer to one of our own surveys discussed in Chapter 20. We found that a few business firms made substantial investment outlays at a time when their economic situation was judged to be unfavorable. That study would have been much more useful if it had also collected data on the size of investments made by firms that operated under either favorable or unfavorable conditions. In business surveys financial informa-

422

tion gives weight to attitudes, and attitudinal information serves to explain behavior.

Experimentation

In concluding, a few words must be said about research in psychological economics conducted by methods other than surveys with representative samples. Case studies with a single firm, or a small number of firms or individuals not representative of any universe, are valuable in the initial or exploratory stages of research because they represent an important source of hypotheses. In the later stages, case studies may be useful when unusual situations are observed, which call for an intensive study of decision formation. Such detailed individual studies might have been appropriate, for example, when certain firms were found to have made investment outlays under unfavorable circumstances, as cited above. The utilization of a major innovation may serve as an additional example for an occasion of case studies. Surveys with a small number of firms or individuals—10 or 100 cases, for instance—as well as laboratory experiments have a place in psychological economics for the purpose of describing behavior under specific circumstances.[5] For example, immediately following major unexpected developments it is seldom possible to conduct large surveys with representative samples, but small samples may well provide useful information on first reactions to the new developments.

Unlike laboratory experiments, surveys cannot manipulate independent variables. They are, however, in a position to make use of changes in variables as they happen to occur. Then "natural experiments" may be conducted, for instance, in the case of a change in legislation or major stock market movements. As a somewhat different example, the study of the saving process following the introduction of a large number of private pension plans (Chapter 15) may be recalled. In that instance it was possible to make use both of an experimental and a control group: to interview employees who recently have been enrolled in private pension plans as well as employees without such plans. Studies in which before-and-after at-

[5] See the arguments of Wärneryd and Olander (1972).

423

titudes and behavior were compared were also conducted at the time the war in Vietnam ended—regarding attitudes toward military expenditures, for instance—and when price controls were introduced in 1971. In these instances there was no manipulation of variables, nor could use be made of control groups.

Laboratory experiments in which these conditions are fulfilled can be helpful, for instance, in analyzing probable reactions to price changes as well as to clearance sales and other forms of promotion. There are many marketing problems as well to which economic psychologists may contribute greatly by conducting experiments. No doubt, under certain conditions the laboratory situation may be made rather realistic.

Large-scale field experiments are difficult, expensive, and likewise subject to question about whether they reflect realistic conditions. Manipulation of income is possible in the form of making extra payments to participants selected for an experiment. Such an experiment was conducted on a very large scale and with greatly encouraging results in the late 1960s and early 1970s by the Institute for Research on Poverty, funded by federal agencies, in order to study the change in economic incentives in response to the provision of a "guaranteed income" over several years. Findings on the relation of hours worked to total income appear highly realistic and generalizable to conditions beyond those of the experiment.

In spite of this success, it appears doubtful that such experiments involving the manipulation of many people will become common. The cost of such experimentation is very high and the establishment of realistic conditions is far from assured, particularly in advance of the experiment when the funds would have to be made available. Therefore, it is to be expected that the survey method will continue to remain the principal tool for testing and improving the insights of psychological economics.

BIBLIOGRAPHY

Adams, F. Gerard. "Consumer Attitudes, Buying Plans, and Purchases of Durable Goods: A Principal Components, Time Series Approach." *Review of Economics and Statistics* 46 (1964):347–355.

Arrow, K. J. "Mathematical Models in the Social Sciences," in D. Lerner and H. D. Lasswell, eds., *The Policy Sciences.* Stanford: Stanford University Press, 1951a.

Arrow, K. J. *Social Choice and Individual Values.* New York: Wiley, 1951b.

Barlow, Robin; Brazer, H. E.; and Morgan, J. N. *Economic Behavior of the Affluent.* Washington: Brookings Institution, 1966.

Bauer, R. A., and Bauer, A. H. "Mass Society and Mass Media," *Journal of Social Issues* 16 (1960):3–66.

Bauer, Raymond A., and Greyser, S. A. *Advertising in America: The Consumer View.* Boston: Harvard University Press, 1968.

Boulding, Kenneth E. *The Image.* Ann Arbor: University of Michigan Press, 1956.

Boulding, Kenneth E. "Human Betterment and the Quality of Life," in B. Strumpel, J. N. Morgan, and E. Zahn, eds., *Human Behavior in Economic Affairs.* Amsterdam: Elsevier, 1972.

Bowen, Howard R. *Social Responsibilities of the Businessman.* New York: Harper & Brothers, 1953.

Bowen, H. R. *The Business Enterprise as a Subject for Research.* New York: Social Science Research Council, 1955.

Bruner, J. S. *The Relevance of Education.* New York: W. W. Norton and Co., 1971.

Burns, Arthur F. *Economic Research and the Keynesian Thinking of Our Times.* New York: National Bureau of Economic Research, 1946.

Burns, Arthur F. "Keynesian Economics Once Again." *Review of Economics and Statistics* 29 (1947):261 pp.

Burns, Arthur F. *Prosperity without Inflation.* New York: Fordham University Press, 1957.

425

Buskirk, R. H., and Rothe, J. T. "Consumerism—An Interpretation." *Journal of Marketing* 34 (1970):62 pp.

Cagan, Phillip D. "The Effect of Pension Plans on Aggregate Saving." National Bureau of Economic Research, Occasional Paper 95. New York: Columbia University Press, 1965.

Cagan, Phillip D. "The Monetary Dynamics of Hyperinflations," in Milton Friedman, ed., *Studies in the Quantity Theory of Money*. Chicago: University of Chicago Press, 1956.

Campbell, Angus, and Katona, George. "The Sample Survey," in Leon Festinger and Daniel Katz, eds., *Research Methods in the Behavioral Sciences*. New York: Dryden Press, 1953.

Campbell, Angus, and Converse, P. E. eds. *The Human Meaning of Social Change*. New York: Russell Sage Foundation, 1972.

Committee on Price Determination. *Cost Behavior and Price Policy*. New York: National Bureau of Economic Research, 1943.

Curtin, Richard T. "Index Construction: An Appraisal of the Index of Consumer Sentiment," in L. Mandell, G. Katona, J. N. Morgan, and J. Schmiedeskamp, eds., *Surveys of Consumers 1971–72*. Ann Arbor, Mich.: Institute for Social Research, 1973.

Curtin, R. T., and Cowan, C. D. "Public Attitudes toward Fiscal Programs," in Burkhard Strumpel, C. D. Cowan, F. T. Juster, and J. W. Schmiedeskamp, eds., *Surveys of Consumers 1972–73*. Ann Arbor, Mich.: Institute for Social Research, 1975.

Dunkelberg, William C. "Forecasting Consumer Expenditures with Measures of Attitudes and Expectations." Unpublished dissertation. Ann Arbor: University of Michigan, 1969.

Dunkelberg, William C. "The Impact of Consumer Attitudes on Behavior: A Cross-Section Study," in B. Strumpel, J. N. Morgan, and E. Zahn, eds., *Human Behavior in Economic Affairs*. Amsterdam: Elsevier, 1972.

Eels, Richard. *The Meaning of Modern Business*. New York: Columbia University Press, 1960.

Fair, Ray C. *A Short-Run Forecasting Model of the United States Economy*. Lexington, Mass.: Heath Lexington Books, 1971.

Federal Reserve Bank of Boston. *Consumer Spending and Monetary Policy: The Linkages*. Boston: 1971.

Ferber, Robert. "Factors Influencing Durable Goods Purchases," in L. H. Clark, ed., *Consumer Behavior, Vol. II*. New York: New York University Press, 1955.

Ferber, Robert. *Collecting Financial Data by Consumer Panel Techniques: A Pilot Study*. Urbana: Bureau of Economic and Business Research, University of Illinois, 1959.

Ferber, Robert. *The Reliability of Consumer Reports of Financial Assets and Debts*. Urbana: Bureau of Economic and Business Research, University of Illinois, 1966.

Festinger, Leon. *A Theory of Cognitive Dissonance*. Stanford: Stan-

426

ford University Press, 1957.

Fisher, B. R., and Withey, S. W. *Big Business as the People See It.* Ann Arbor, Mich.: Survey Research Center, 1951.

Friedman, Milton. *The Theory of the Consumption Function.* National Bureau of Economic Research. Princeton, N.J.: Princeton University Press, 1957.

Fromm, Erich. *The Revolution of Hope.* New York: Harper and Row, 1968.

Galbraith, John K. *The New Industrial State.* Boston: Hough- 1958.

Galbraith, John K. *The New Industrial State.* Boston: Houghton Mifflin, 1967.

Galbraith, John K. *Economics and the Public Purpose.* Boston: Houghton Mifflin, 1973.

Gordon, R. A. *Business Leadership in the Large Corporation.* Washington: Brookings Institution, 1945.

Gordon, R. A. "Short-Period Price Determination in Theory and Practice." *American Economic Review* 38 (1948).

Griffin, C. E. *Enterprise in a Free Society.* Chicago: Irwin, 1949.

Gurr, Ted Robert. *Why Men Rebel.* Princeton, N. J.: Princeton University Press, 1970.

Harris, Louis. "Public Credibility of American Business." *Conference Board Record,* March, 1973.

Hendricks, Gary; Youmans, K. C.; and Keller, Janet. *Consumer Durables and Installment Debt: A Study of American Households.* Ann Arbor, Mich.: Institute for Social Research, 1973.

Hymans, S. H. "Consumer Durable Spending: Explanation and Prediction." *Brookings Papers on Economic Activity,* 1970.

Juster, F. Thomas. *Household Capital Formation and Financing.* New York: National Bureau of Economic Research, 1966.

Juster, F. Thomas. "On the Measurement of Economic and Social Performance," in *Economics—A Half Century of Research, 1920-1970.* 50th Annual Report of National Bureau of Economic Research, New York, 1970.

Juster, F. Thomas, and Wachtel, Paul. "Inflation and the Consumer." *Brookings Papers on Economic Activity,* 1972a, 71–114.

Juster, F. Thomas, and Wachtel, Paul. "Anticipatory and Objective Models of Durable Goods Demand." *American Economic Review* 62 (1972b): 564–79.

Kahn, R. L. "The Meaning of Work," in A. Campbell and P. E. Converse, eds., *The Human Meaning of Social Change.* New York: Russell Sage Foundation, 1972.

Kahn, R. L., and Cannell, C. F. *The Dynamics of Interviewing: Theory, Techniques, and Cases.* New York: John Wiley & Sons, 1957.

Kaplan, A. D. H.; Dirlam, Joel B.; and Lanzillotti, R. F. *Pricing in Big*

427

Business: A Case Approach. Washington, D.C.: Brookings Institution, 1958.

Katona, George. *Organizing and Memorizing.* New York: Columbia University Press, 1940. Republished in 1967 by Hafner Publishing Company, New York.

Katona, George. *War without Inflation.* New York: Columbia University Press, 1942.

Katona, George. *Price Control and Business.* Bloomington, Ind.: Cowles Commission and Principia Press, 1945.

Katona, George. "Effect of Income Changes." *Review of Economics and Statistics* 31 (1949a): 94–103.

Katona, George. "Analysis of Dissaving." *American Economic Review* 39 (1949):673–88.

Katona, George. *Psychological Analysis of Economic Behavior.* New York: McGraw-Hill, 1951.

Katona, George, and Morgan, James N. "The Quantitative Study of Factors Determining Business Decisions." *Quarterly Journal of Economics* 66 (1952): 67–90.

Katona, George. "Rational Behavior and Economic Behavior." *Psychological Review* 60 (1953):307–18.

Katona, George, and Mueller, Eva. "A Study of Purchase Decisions," in L. Clark, ed., *Consumer Behavior.* New York: New York University Press, 1954.

Katona, George. *Business Looks at Banks.* Ann Arbor, Mich.; University of Michigan Press, 1957.

Katona, George. "Business Expectations in the Framework of Psychological Economics," in M. J. Bowman, ed., *Expectations, Uncertainty, and Business Behavior.* New York: Social Science Research Council, 1958.

Katona, George. "Repetitiousness and Variability of Consumer Behavior." *Human Relations* 12 (1959):35–49.

Katona, George. *The Powerful Consumer.* New York: McGraw-Hill, 1960.

Katona, George. "On the So-Called Wealth Effect." *Review of Economics and Statistics,* 43 (1961):59–60.

Katona, George. *The Mass Consumption Society.* New York: McGraw-Hill, 1964a.

Katona, George, and Lansing, J. B. "The Wealth of the Wealthy." *Review of Economics and Statistics* 46 (1964b):1–13.

Katona, George. *Private Pensions and Individual Saving.* Ann Arbor, Mich.: Institute for Social Research, 1965.

Katona, George. "Anticipations Statistics and Consumer Behavior." *American Statistician,* April, 1967.

Katona, George. "Consumer Behavior: Theory and Findings on Expectations and Aspirations." *American Economic Review* 58 (1968):19–30.

428

Katona, George, and Mueller, Eva. *Consumer Response to Income Increases.* Washington, D.C.: Brookings Institution, 1968.

Katona, George; Strumpel, Burkhard; and Zahn, Ernest. *Aspirations and Affluence.* New York: McGraw-Hill, 1971a.

Katona, George. "Consumer Durable Spending: Explanation and Prediction," a communication, *Brookings Papers on Economic Activity* (1971b), 234–39.

Katona, George. "Theory of Expectations," in B. Strumpel, J. N. Morgan, and E. Zahn, eds., *Human Behavior in Economic Affairs.* Amsterdam: Elsevier, 1972a.

Katona, George. "The Human Factor in Economic Affairs," in Angus Campbell and P. E. Converse, eds., *The Human Meaning of Social Change.* New York: Russell Sage Foundation, 1972b.

Katona, George. "Cognitive Processes in Learning: Reactions to Inflation and Change in Taxes," in L. Mandell et al., *Surveys of Consumers 1971–72.* Ann Arbor, Mich.: Institute for Social Research, 1973.

Katona, George. "Psychology and Consumer Economics." *Journal of Consumer Research* 1 (1974).

Katona, George. "Persistence of Belief in Personal-Financial Progress," in Burkhard Strumpel, ed., *Human Needs and Economic Wants.* Ann Arbor, Mich.: Institute for Social Research, 1975.

Katz, Daniel, and Kahn, R. L. *The Social Psychology of Organizations.* New York: John Wiley & Sons, 1966.

Katz, Daniel. "Psychology and Economic Behavior," in B. Strumpel, J. N. Morgan, and E. Zahn, eds., *Human Behavior in Economic Affairs.* Amsterdam: Elsevier, 1972.

Katz, E., and Lazarsfeld, P. F. *Personal Influence.* New York: Free Press of Glencoe, 1955.

Keynes, J. M. *Treatise on Money.* London: Macmillan & Co., Ltd.,1930.

Keynes, John Maynard. *The General Theory of Employment, Interest and Money.* New York: Harcourt, Brace, 1936.

Keynes, John Maynard. "The General Theory of Employment." *Quarterly Journal of Economics* 51 (1937).

Kish, Leslie. *Survey Sampling.* New York: John Wiley & Sons, 1965.

Kosobud, Richard F., and Morgan, James N. eds., *Consumer Behavior of Individual Families over Two and Three Years.* Ann Arbor, Mich.: Institute for Social Research, 1964.

Kuznets, Simon. *Capital in the American Economy.* National Bureau of Economic Research, Princeton, N.J.: Princeton University Press, 1961.

Lansing, J. B. *The Travel Market.* Ann Arbor, Mich.: Survey Research Center, 1958.

Lansing, J. B., and Morgan, J. N. "Consumer Finances over the Life Cycle," in L. H. Clark, ed., *Consumer Behavior, Vol. II.* New

York: New York University Press, 1955.

Lewin, Kurt; Dembo, Tamara; Festinger, Leon; and Sears, P. S. "Level of Aspiration," in J. McV. Hunt, ed., *Personality and Behavior Disorders*. New York: Ronald Press Company, 1944.

Likert, Rensis. *New Patterns of Management*. New York: McGraw-Hill, 1961.

Likert, Rensis. *The Human Organization*. New York: McGraw-Hill, 1967.

Machlup, Fritz. "Marginal Analysis and Empirical Research." *American Economic Review* 36 (1946), 519–55.

Machlup, Fritz. *The Production and Distribution of Knowledge in the United States*. Princeton, N.J.: Princeton University Press, 1962.

Mandell, Lewis. "Consumer Perception of Incurred Interest Rates: An Empirical Test of the Efficacy of the Truth-in-Lending Law." *Journal of Finance* 26 (1971), 1143–53.

Mandell, Lewis. *Credit Card Use in the United States*. Ann Arbor, Mich.: Institute for Social Research, 1972a.

Mandell, Lewis. "Industrial Location Decisions in the Detroit Area: A Report to New Detroit Incorporated." Ann Arbor, Mich.: Institute for Social Research, 1972b. Mimeographed.

Mandell, Lewis. "Consumer Knowledge and Understanding of Consumer Credit." *Journal of Consumer Affairs* 7 (1973), 23–36.

March, J. G., and Simon, H. A. *Organizations*. New York: John Wiley & Sons, 1958.

Maslow, A. H. *Motivation and Personality*. New York: Harper & Brothers, 1954.

Maynes, E. Scott. "An Appraisal of Consumer Anticipations Approaches to Forecasting," *Proceedings of Business and Economic Statistics Section*, pp. 114–23. Washington, D.C.: American Statistical Association, 1967.

Maynes, E. Scott. "The Power of the Consumer," in B. Strumpel, J. N. Morgan, and E. Zahn, eds., *Human Behavior in Economic Affairs*. Amsterdam: Elsevier, 1972a.

Maynes, E. Scott. "Consumerism: Origin and Research Implications," in Eleanor Bernert Sheldon, ed., *Family Economic Behavior: Problems and Prospects*. Philadelphia: J. B. Lippincott Company, 1972b.

Meade, J. E. "Is the National Debt a Burden?" *Oxford Economic Papers* 10 (1958): 166ff.

Meadows, D. H.; Meadows, D. L.; Randers, J.; and Behrens, W. W. *The Limits to Growth*. New York: Universe Books, 1972.

Miller, Herman P. *Rich Man Poor Man*. New York: Thomas Y. Crowell Co., 1971.

Modigliani, Franco. "Monetary Policy and Consumption," in

Consumer Spending and Monetary Policy: The Linkages. Boston: Federal Reserve Bank of Boston, 1971.

Moore, W. E.,and Sheldon, E. B., eds. *Indicators of Social Change.* New York: Russell Sage Foundation, 1968.

Mueller, Eva; Wilken, Arnold; and Wood, Margaret. *Location Decisions and Industrial Mobility in Michigan, 1961.* Ann Arbor, Mich.: Institute for Social Research, 1962.

Mueller, Eva, and Morgan, James N. "Location Decisions of Manufacturers." *American Economic Review* 52 (1962), 204–17.

Mueller, Eva. "Ten Years of Consumer Attitude Surveys: Their Forecasting Record." *Journal of American Statistical Association* 58 (1963a):899–917.

Mueller, Eva. "Public Attitudes toward Fiscal Programs." *Quarterly Journal of Economics* 77 (1963b):210–35.

Mueller, Eva, and Lean, Jane. "The Savings Account as a Source for Financing Large Expenditures." *Journal of Finance* 22 (1967):375–93.

Nader, Ralph. *Unsafe at Any Speed.* New York: Bantam, 1965.

Newcomb, T. M. *Social Psychology.* New York: Dryden, 1950.

Newman, Joseph W., and Staelin, Richard. "Prepurchase Information Seeking for New Cars and Major Household Appliances." *Journal of Marketing Research* 9 (1972), 249–57.

Nordhaus, W. D. "The Allocation of Energy Resources." *Brookings Papers on Economic Activity,* 1973.

Nordhaus, W. D., and Tobin, James. *Economic Growth,* Vol. V of Fiftieth Anniversary Colloquia, National Bureau of Economic Research. New York: Columbia University Press, 1972.

Nourse, E. G. *Price Making in a Democracy.* Washington, D.C.: Brookings Institution, 1944.

Packard, Vance. *The Waste Makers.* New York: David McKay Co., 1960.

Paxton, E. T. *What People Want When They Buy a House* (based on a report of a study conducted by the Survey Research Center for the Housing and Home Finance Agency, U.S. Department of Commerce). Washington, D.C.: 1955.

Pratt, Robert W., Jr. "Marketing Applications of Behavioral Economics," in B. Strumpel, J. N. Morgan and E. Zahn, eds., *Human Behavior in Economic Affairs.* Amsterdam: Elsevier, 1972.

Projector, Dorothy S., and Weiss, Gertrude S. *Survey of Financial Characteristics of Consumers.* Washington, D.C.: Federal Reserve Board, 1966.

Reich, Charles A. *The Greening of America.* New York: Random House, 1970.

Reynaud, P. L. *La Psychologie Economique.* Paris: Librairie Marcel

Riviere et Cie., 1954.

Schmiedeskamp, J. W. "Reinterviews by Telephone." *Journal of Marketing* 26 (1962), 28–34.

Schmölders, Günter. *Psychologie des Geldes*. Hamburg: Rowohlt, 1966.

Schumpeter, Joseph A. "The Decade of the Twenties." *American Economic Review* 36, (1946).

Shapiro, H. T., and Angevine, G. E. "Consumer Attitudes, Buying Intentions and Expenditures: An Analysis of the Canadian Data." *Canadian Journal of Economics* 2, (1969), 230–49.

Shapiro, Harold T. "The Index of Consumer Sentiment and Economic Forecasting—A Reappraisal," in B. Strumpel, J. N. Morgan, and E. Zahn, eds., *Human Behavior in Economic Affairs*. Amsterdam: Elsevier, 1972.

Sheldon, Eleanor B., ed. *Family Economic Behavior: Problems and Prospects*. Philadelphia: J. B. Lippincott Co., 1972.

Shonfield, Andrew. *Modern Capitalism*. Oxford: Oxford University Press, 1965.

Simon, H. A. *Models of Man*. New York: John Wiley & Sons, 1957.

Simon, Herbert A., and Newell, A. "Human Problem Solving." *American Psychologist* 26 (1971), 145–59.

Slater, Philip. *The Pursuit of Loneliness*. Boston: Beacon Press, 1971.

Smith, James D., and Franklin, Stephen D. "The Concentration of Personal Wealth, 1922–1969." *American Economic Review* 64, (1974), 162–67.

Sprinkel, Beryl W. *Money and Markets, a Monetarist View*. Homewood, Ill.: Richard D. Irwin, Inc., 1971.

Strumpel, Burkhard; Novy, Klaus; and Schwartz, M. S. "Consumer Attitudes and Outlays in Germany and North America." *Jahrbuch fuer Sozialwissenschaft* 21 (1970), 1–48.

Strumpel, Burkhard. "Higher Education and Economic Behavior," in Stephen B. Withey, ed., *A Degree and What Else?*" New York: Carnegie Foundation for the Advancement of Teaching, McGraw-Hill, 1971.

Strumpel, Burkhard; Morgan, James N.; and Zahn, Ernest, eds. *Human Behavior in Economic Affairs, Essays in Honor of George Katona*. Amsterdam: Elsevier, 1972.

Strumpel, Burkhard. "Economic Behavior and Economic Welfare-—Models and Interdisciplinary Approaches," in B. Strumpel, J. N. Morgan, and E. Zahn, eds., *Human Behavior in Economic Affairs*. Amsterdam: Elsevier, 1972.

Strumpel, Burkhard; Schmiedeskamp, Jay; and Schwartz, M. Susan. "The Function of Consumer Attitude Data beyond Econometric Forecasts," in L. Mandell, G. Katona, J. N. Morgan, and J. Schmiedeskamp, eds., *Surveys of Consumers 1971–72*. Ann

Arbor, Mich.: Institute for Social Research, 1973a.

Strumpel, Burkhard. "Economic Life-Styles, Values, and Subjective Welfare—An Empirical Approach," in E. B. Sheldon, ed., *Family Economic Behavior: Problems and Prospects*. Philadelphia: J. B. Lippincott Company, 1973b.

Strumpel, Burkhard. "Economic Well-Being as an Object of Social Measurement," in B. Strumpel, ed., *Subjective Elements of Well-Being*. Paris: OECD (Office of Economic Cooperation and Development), 1974.

Strumpel, Burkhard. "Economic Well-Being and Social Change," in B. Strumpel, ed., *Human Needs and Economic Wants*. Ann Arbor, Mich.: Institute for Social Research, 1975.

Survey of Consumer Finances. Monographs annually published in the year following the survey from 1960 through 1970, by Survey Research Center staff. Ann Arbor, Mich.: Institute for Social Research. (Before 1960, the findings were published in various issues of the *Federal Reserve Bulletin*.)

Surveys of Consumers. Ann Arbor, Mich.: Institute for Social Research, *1971–72*: Lewis Mandell, George Katona, J. N. Morgan, and Jay Schmiedeskamp, eds., 1973; *1972–73*: Burkhard Strumpel, C. D. Cowan, F. T. Juster, and Jay Schmiedeskamp, eds., 1974.

Survey Research Center. *Industrial Mobility in Michigan*. Ann Arbor, Mich.: Institute for Social Research, University of Michigan, 1950.

Sutton, Francis X., Harris, Seymour E.; Kaysen, Carl; and Tobin, James. *The American Business Creed*. Cambridge, Mass.: Harvard University Press, 1956.

Toffler, Alvin. *Future Shock*. New York: Random House, 1970.

Toynbee, Arnold J. *America and the World Revolution*. London: Oxford University Press, 1962.

U.S. Department of Health, Education, and Welfare. *Toward a Social Report*. Washington, D.C.: U.S. Government Printing Office, 1968. Reprinted in the series Ann Arbor Paperbacks. Ann Arbor: University of Michigan Press, 1970.

Wärneryd, Karl-Erik, and Olander, Folke. "The Place for Laboratory Experiments and Small-Sample Surveys in Economic Psychology," in B. Strumpel, J. N. Morgan, and E. Zahn, eds., *Human Behavior in Economic Affairs*. Amsterdam: Elsevier, 1972.

Wertheimer, Max. *Productive Thinking*. 2nd ed. New York: Harper & Brothers, 1959.

Zahn, Ernest. *Soziologie der Prosperitat*. Köln, Germany: Kiepenheuer, 1960.

INDEX

436

437

Rothe, J. T., 386, 426

safety, 259, 262
sampling, 405, 410–413, 421
Samuelson, Paul, 379
satisfaction, 156–158, 221, 380–384, 386–387, 395
satisficing, 297
saturation, 14–15, 153, 155, 249
Saving, 36, 155, 229, 270
  and age, 237–238
  and income, 237–238, 240–242
  and inflation, 133–134, 144–146, 243 (see also Inflation)
  and interest rates, 244, 342
  and wealth, 247–251
  contractual, 230
  definition of, 230
  discretionary, 31, 231
  for retirement, 245–247
  in good and in bad times, 13–14, 239–241
  purposes of, 233–235, 240, 248
  residual, 232
  versus spending, 237–238
savings (reserve funds), 253, 256 (see also Assets)
  accounts, 232, 263–264
  Bonds, U. S. Government, 255–257 (see also War Bonds)
  composition of, 259–261
Schmiedeskamp, Jay W., ix, 417, 432
Schmölders, Günter, 7, 432
Schumpeter, Joseph A., 53, 432
Schwartz, M. Susan, 432
Sears, P. S., 430
Securities and Exchange Commission, 65, 324, 421–422
services, 28, 188, 392–393
Shapiro, H. T., 80, 432
Sheldon, E. B., 431, 432
Shonfield, Andrew, 61, 308, 361, 432
shortages, 394, 398–400
Simon, H. A., 215, 287, 297, 432
Sindlinger, Albert, 80
Slater, Philip, 389, 432
Smith, James D., 254, 432
social indicators, 16, 380
social learning (see learning)
social psychology, 49
social responsibility (of business), 308–313, 315–316
social security, 231, 245
Social Science Research Council, 287
societal discontent, 195, 352, 382–383
speculation, 267–268
Sprinkel, Beryl W., 344, 432
Staelin, Richard, 220, 431
standard of living, 184, 235–236, 376, 395–397, 399–400
stereotypes, 206–207
stock market, 100, 224, 266–269
stocks (see common stocks)
Stolper, Gustav, ix
Strumpel, Burkhard, ix, 80, 189, 381–383, 432–433
supply and demand, law of, 6
survey method, 21, 403–404, 421
survey questions, 75, 78–80, 413–415

surveys
  function of, 406–410
  history of, 405–406
  reliability of, 419, 421
Survey of Consumer Finances, 22, 103, 160, 179, 191, 244, 253, 256, 264, 274, 339, 354, 403, 412, 433
Survey Research Center (SRC, University of Michigan), ix, x, 22, 66, 67, 77–81, 103, 115, 156, 159, 162, 178, 194, 223, 234, 253, 257, 265, 268, 271, 275, 313, 315, 320, 327, 354, 382, 389, 390, 396, 406, 407, 408, 411, 412, 414, 420, 421, 433
Surveys of Consumers, 433
Sutton, Francis X., 307, 433

taxes, 172, 261–263, 338–341, 349, 354, 358–360
tax cut of 1964, 13, 112, 210–212, 339
tax increase of 1968, 116, 210–212, 340
telephone interviews, 416–417
theories, 214
time perspective, 45
Tobin, James, 379, 431, 433
Toffler, Alvin, 215, 433
Toynbee, Arnold J., 364, 366–368, 374, 376, 433

uncertainty, 202, 214
unemployment, 100, 104, 120, 123, 165, 173, 399
  and inflation, 171–172
unexpected developments, 86
U. S.
  Bureau of the Census, 22, 25, 100, 229, 404, 411
  Department of Commerce, 65, 324, 404, 421, 422
  Department of Health, Education, and Welfare, 380, 433
University of Michigan, ix

Vietnam war, 113–115, 120, 360

Wachtel, Paul 97, 134, 427
Wants (and needs), 153, 155, 157, 366, 393
War Bonds, 255–256, 260, 406
Wärneryd, Karl-Erik, 423, 433
Watergate, 148, 200, 241, 352, 398
wealth, 247–248, 253–254, 266, 344
wealthy people, 22, 261–263
Weiss, Gertrude S., 253, 255, 256, 420, 431
welfare expenditures, 356–357
Wertheimer, Max, ix, 215, 433
Western Europe, 190, 192, 282, 361
West Germany, 234, 282
Wilken, Arnold, 431
willingness to buy, 32, 74
wishes, 156–157
Withey, S. W., 313, 427
Women, working, 390
Wood, Margaret, 431
World War II, 88, 103–105, 162

Youmans, K. C., 427
Young people, 24, 26, 181, 185–186, 384, 389

Zahn, Ernest, x, 7, 432, 433

438